Also from Tisza Publishing

T.R.'s Summer White House, Oyster Bay

Private Good Luck

Pappus - The Saga of a Jewish Family

From the Ashes - The Documents of a Jewish Family

Copyright © 2025 by Sherwin Gluck
All rights reserved, including the right to reproduce this book or portions thereof.
Published in the United States.
Library of Congress Control Number: 2021920743

Gluck, Maria
As I remember... / Maria Gluck
p. cm.
ISBN 978-0-9672543-3-3 (perfect binding)
ISBN 978-0-9672543-4-0 (hardcover binding)

1. Gluck, Maria, 1916-2013.
2. World War, 1939-1945 - Personal narratives, American.
3. Jews - Czechoslovakia - History - 1918-1938.
4. Jews - Czechoslovakia - Biography.
5. Jews - Hungary - History - 1919-1944.
6. Holocaust, Jewish (1939-1945) - Hungary - Personal narratives.
7. Jews - United States - Biography.
8. Jews - United States - History - 20th century.
9. Jews - Israel - History - 1948-1952.

Printed and bound in the United States of America

First Edition
Edited and Book Design by Sherwin Gluck

As I remember...
by Maria Gluck
A story about Life in Europe.
2009 October 19

As I remember...

Maria Gluck

Tisza Publishing
New York

Table of Contents

Introduction i
Beginnings..1
My Mother's Family..3
Childhood on Our Farm 9
Life in Our Village..21
Our Escape to America..35
Welcome to Columbus: Starting Over in America...39
Army Induction and the War...53
Losing Uncle Julius and Finding Our Own Way...55
California Dreams and New York Realities...59
The Last Goodbye..67
Painful Burdens..69
My Father's Other Brothers and Sisters...77
Uncle Lajos - From Captivity to Catastrophe 81
The Last Ship Out: From Czechoslovakia to America...................................85
Searching for Survivors..91
About David...93
From Clay Avenue to Flushing: Sisters, Work, and the Move That Saved Me 105
About Hermine..113
About Herman...125
Polyán, Swept Away by the Storm 133
Encounters with Europeans in America..143
About doctors and healthcare..149
About home health aides...163
Rail Road Episode 177
On Politicians / Leadership… 181
On Jealousy..187
On Hatred..191
On Love 203
Last thoughts...205
My prayer...207
Appendix..215

Introduction

The original story "As I remember." by Maria Gluck

This is a statement about the story and the writer. How it came about. It is a story come to life. Unexpectedly, I started to fill in the missing spots. My youngest brother Irving could not remember his childhood life growing up. Therefore, he asked me if I could tell more about it. He would like to know our family history, whatever he missed out. He has no one to ask. It was a very difficult task. There was more involvement than just to fill in the empty spots. It was a very complicated era.

It is a life history about 110 years of our family's history and the Holocaust as the family went through heartaches, hard work struggling, trying to survive. We were a well established family, respected, and all of a sudden some surprises appeared from nowhere. Therefore, when I tried to tell the history it spread out much more than just the spot.

In a sense, we are very lucky to reach our senior years, as they call it the golden years. I am thankful to our Almighty that allowed me to have my memory and be able to write and remember. This book started to be simple, but it became more complicated.

My brother kept all the letters our family received during the war. He's the one who saved them. When I found out, he asked me what he should do with them.

When he asked me, I thought I would like to see them and maybe put them in an album to preserve them. When he brought them over, it was amazing what I found in those letters. They are priceless to us. I went through every one. It wasn't easy, but I decided to read and organize them. There are about 30 books. Many of those letters were written by our brother's children, their mother, and our father. That is all we have from them.

My brother translated at least 200 of them from Hungarian into English. One of his sons bought a computer and taught him how to use it. He became very good and typed them all into the computer to preserve them. That was at least two years before I came to live with my brother.

He started to work and typed my handwritten stories into the computer. He has many typed in already. His son also taught me how to use it and purchased me a microphone connected to the computer. I did not have to type, just read into it that's all I need to do. This way it made it much easier and less time to do it. This is the way I become a writer. I wasn't taught to be a writer, to me it come naturally.

That's how I came around to write and express myself as I did. The more that I have written, my dearest brother was very impressed. He would not let me give up. I wrote other articles and before I knew it, I became more involved and created our life history. It combined a family life history from A to Z.

My age it is the late 96 years. I wrote individually about our family. First I tried to sort out the most important one. Later on I try to remember

2/1/011 6. a.m Tuesday (8)

8) maibe it shoed. They lern from as
as poseble. This is the bigest problem w
young and even the grown up. Avery
raning! Wher to? Why kan we lern to se
I know I was ther to To. I have long wa
ther subway som times have to taik bus
wassent easy. I left in af time to be sho
in time. with to much hasel. manny
ther was dalays on subways. maybe n
tudays. Now I don't know I hop it is bette
than I remember trying Improuve th
hop it is better. I alwais have Long way to
Long walk both way, back, and forth. Som
lot hours. It bekom a long day. My Jo
was Imporltion. I never took it for Grante
I was self roporter. no one to depend on
it wasent to much manny eder. You have n
good meneger and lerne hau to love
men no mor dan you realy ned it and
at list what avesporeble. I was that for w
one panny aday. I try to leve by that. an
always rememberd dat. now as im retiere
back I wonder what kond of than to better n
maylie perchaps. We lerne ou past! Ther is al
to lerne never to loit. If we kep open mind
And you fined away avvithing is poseble
(6.30) in amerika. This is my advais to you a
em

Begain   5.30 a m.   (1)
nice   This is a new story.
from w/ 1) to write about a somting
                 Boy thoth douth to spare oly
next is   or ads to aur prablem. Just like
a new   it sems no one like to adment
subjekt   for one thing or the other,
#H   prablem wich dos hart up and the
to 10 the   to lerne how to kondukt dam selmself
in story   hat, Improove ther life in stad
2)   "my God what a bame" thay dek
if day just wood try it, hamach better
wood be. Furst ther are the Arabican Nation
eprens, the Iranian. If dos peopel just wood
for amit and lessen, Open ther yes, ears,
Breans. Ther is ther komon sare. I'm
day have some maligeble people hoo nos
is Fridam, and what is kontrol. and what
tiektiter sheps. That is what day have. I shor
ar people hoo wood agre with me, ther life
isted thay bekom a moon to the safering
do. Som of tham wood be hapyer if thay
lev in peace. Instad fiteng and roning
ther life. Thay leder hoo daznit have any
how to roun ther bontry or how to be a
I'm troying to point outh what is the
it problem al over the wold. And we are
in it. It afecks us the americatix diply.

separately the continuation of our life history. I feel that it is a very interesting story from the beginning to the end. I wrote everything by hand. Different stories in a short time. Many pages in a very short time in one sitting.

"*As I Remember...*" is the continuation of the European and the Holocaust era combined as a survivor of the Holocaust. We were able to get out in the last critical moment from a very troubled world and we left behind the rest of our family and lost them. Maria Gluck, 3/11/2013.

Maria, 96 with her brother Irving, 91. Photo taken November 14, 2012

Editor's Note

This volume includes the memoir Maria Gluck completed in 2009, *As I Remember…*, along with her later writings. Her typed files — created using ViaVoice — have been gently edited to preserve the nuance of her voice while avoiding unnecessary duplication.

The appendix contains the additional works Maria composed after she finished the memoir: short stories, reflections, social commentary, essays, and two fictional pieces — a brief dream story and a much longer narrative inspired partly by her own experiences at a Catskill Mountain resort. Most of these later writings were written after she gave up her apartment and moved to live with my father - her brother Irving. They often revisited stories already told in the memoir, sometimes with greater detail. In such cases, the details were preserved by moving them into the memoir itself, while the repeated passages were removed. Her essays also included many recurring sections on leadership, healthcare, jealousy, hatred, and love. To avoid further repetition, these themes were retained either as stand-alone chapters in the memoir or as single essays in the appendix.

This book fulfills Maria's wish: to share her life, her love of family, and her truth with future generations. May her words continue to inspire memory, reflection, and hope.

I would like to thank my family for their patience as I worked on this labor of love. I could not have done it without their support—especially my wife, Hanit, who carefully read and commented on an early draft filled with repetition; my daughter, Noa, for her thoughtful comments on the final draft; and my daughter Naomi for her suggestion on the cover photo.

I promised my Aunt that I would publish her writing. Most importantly, I have kept my promise, and I hope I have done so in a way that would have made her proud.

כִּי יִדֹּר נֶדֶר לַיהוָה אוֹ־הִשָּׁבַע שְׁבֻעָה לֶאְסֹר אִסָּר עַל־נַפְשׁוֹ
לֹא יַחֵל דְּבָרוֹ כְּכָל־הַיֹּצֵא מִפִּיו יַעֲשֶׂה

"If a man vows a vow unto the Lord, or swears an oath to bind his soul with a bond, he shall not break his word; he shall do according to all that proceeds out of his mouth." Bamidbar 30:2

- Editor

Chapter 1
Beginnings

I'm trying to write what I remember, because my brother Irving asked me, so many times, why I don't do it? I would like to tell about it here. I shall begin..............

I came from a very *balabuste*[1] family, well-known and respected. My grandfather, from my father's side, was well-to-do. He died before I was born. My grandmother on that side had passed away before I was born, too. I was named after her.[2] As I look back, they were not old by today's standards. They had a large family, and by the time I came along, all their children were already married.

We had a grocery store and also we sold liquor and other kinds of drinks in bottles. When I was older, I helped out selling or whatever I was able to do.

Besides that, we had the best land at that time. Now it's controlled by Slovakia and we are unable to get payment [compensation] for it. Some of the pieces of land were worth a lot of money. We were well known in the district and well to do. My grandfather owned some forests. The property was worth a lot of money. We were rich and famous. As it was, I remember my grandparents had five boys and three girls. The sisters, after they married, moved to different cities and weren't close to us anymore. Marriages were arranged - it wasn't voluntary, like falling in love. If you were still single by 20, they called you an "old maid." Later they had families of their own. I never had the chance to meet them. My father over the years used to go to visit his sisters, wherever they lived. They were in all different places, scattered around, and it was difficult to get together with them.

All the sisters passed away when they were young. At that time, people considered age 50 to be old. The last sister, Zsani, lived in a small place named Szürte; it wasn't very close to us. My father had to take a train to go there. He was told only after 30 days when she passed away, so he would not have to sit Shiva. When he got the news, as I remember, he was very upset. Naturally he went immediately to visit his sister's family, and to the cemetery. She was married to Izidor Klein. He had a flour mill. He was doing well and had a large family. We never met our cousins.

After they passed away he never missed going there every year before the holidays to visit their graves at the cemetery. It wasn't easy for him. He had to travel quite a long distance by railroad. Each one had their family, but I never remember seeing them or talking about them. But our father went to see them once a year.

---

[1] well cared for, religious, and close-knit family

[2] Her paternal grandparents were Emanuel Gluck, who died March 19, 1901 and Mari Lazarovitz, who died in 1915. Maria was born in 1916.

My father was the youngest child, and he and one other brother who was the oldest, stayed at home. They remained in the same village where we came from. This uncle was Lajzer bacsi.[3] He was the oldest in the family. He lived in the same village as we did only a few blocks away. He had four daughters. One came to America; her name was Bertha. The second was named Rezsike, and the third was Mariska. Another lived in Szatmar. Her name was Sarolta. She had two daughters. We used to see them sometimes. They came and visited their father, Lajzer bacsi. Unfortunately, he passed away sometime in June 1941, after we came to America.

My father had three brothers in America. They came here to America when they were very young. At that time [the late 1890's and early 1900's] you didn't need any visa or even money. It seemed like they just wanted a challenge - they left and tried to find their own destiny. And it seems they succeeded. They worked hard. Our family heard from only one of them, namely Uncle Julius. He wrote to us and corresponded with my father. He came quite often to our home in Europe. He was very nice. Whenever he visited Europe, he stopped and always visited us and stayed for a while. As we were growing up, I remember we were always ready to welcome him. We were very happy to see him, even as children. Only through him, my father used to hear about his other brothers. They never wrote to him, he did not expect it from them. My father was the youngest in the family. The other brothers were Julius, Henry, Lajzer, and Martin. Each one had their own family. We never heard from our cousins in America, except through my Uncle Julius. We used to hear from him about his son Arthur and his daughter Elsie. They also had their own family.

Whenever our Uncle Julius came to visit us, I asked him to tell me about America. He used to tell me how hard he worked. He always reminded me that in America you have to work very hard. "Money does not grow on the tree," he would say. Later I used to ask him and tell him that I would like to come to America. He always reminded me that I have family in Europe. You cannot leave there. It's a very hard life in America. You cannot go there. I kept on asking him. I told him that I will work. Somehow when I look back I always dreamt about being in America. I loved my family more than possible. I thought about how would I feel if I really would live my life? At that time I was certain that it would never happen. My Uncle always found some excuses and a reason not even to think about it, so the time passed without hope. I never believed it that it will ever happen, that I will ever be here. But I never gave up!

---

[3] **bácsi** – a Hungarian term of respect for an older man, roughly meaning "uncle" or "sir," often placed after the first name (e.g., "Lajzer bácsi")

Chapter 2
My Mother's Family

I will go back again to my childhood and continue with my mother's side of the family. My mother came from a very balabuste family, one of the best. She had two brothers. Every one in their family was well respected. My grandfather was Yoseph, also known in Hebrew as Joszef Shmaja. Our grandfather was educated in Hebrew. He went to yeshiva, had a very fine background, and was well respected - one of the best families, loved by everyone. I never knew if he had any brother, or where he came from.[4]

I only know more about my grandmother. I remember her name in Hebrew was Haia-le.[5] She came from Homonna,[6] but they decided to move to Lelesz, which was a larger village. They settled there and opened a small business. He owned a small grocery store in a family setting. They lived there and owned the house that it was in. They struggled and tried to manage the best they could. They always spoke Yiddish. I understood every word, but I couldn't speak it. I spoke Hungarian with them. My grandmother also had a very religious family background. They raised their three children and gave them all a Hebrew education. It was a close family.

My mother's side was modern in some ways, more outgoing, but were more religious - and they were students in the yeshiva. By the way, my father was also very kosher and religious, but not as much. From my father's side they were also kosher and followed everything, but they were more modern! They were also educated with the same beliefs, but not in yeshiva. Even then it wasn't enough for my grandparents.

We used to visit our grandmother quite often. We were always welcome there. My grandmother talked about this one sister she had. Hers was really a religious marriage in Munkacs,[7] the largest city. She married a yeshiva

---

[4] He was born September 4, 1851 in Palágy (Palágykomoróc), Hungary

[5] **-le** – a Hungarian diminutive or affectionate suffix, often added to a name to express closeness or endearment.

[6] Actually she was born in a town near Homonna called (Palócz) Pavlovce nad Uhom, Hungary on July 17, 1858.

[7] Munkatch (or Munkacs) Hasidism (חסידות מונקטש) is a Hasidic sect within Haredi Judaism of mostly Hungarian Hasidic Jews. It was founded and led by Polish - born Grand Rebbe Shlomo Spira, who was the rabbi of the town of Strzyżów (1858-1882) and Munkacs (1882-1893). Members of the congregation are mainly referred to as Munkacs Hasidim, or Munkatcher Hasidim. It is named after the Hungarian town in which it was established, Munkatsh (in Yiddish; or in Hungarian: Munkács; today: Mukachevo, in Ukraine).

bucher[8] from one of the best yeshivas - well known. He wore a shtreimel.[9] Later he became one of the Munkacsi Rabbis. He was a very well known person. We had a Rebbe[10] in Munkács. He was known all over as one of the highest class - well respected. He was very knowledgeable. People came to him from all over for any advice. He was one of the best. Later, this sister and her husband became one of the closest friends of this Rebbe and his family. We did not visit my grandmother's sister. We did not have an opportunity. They lived far from us. Our grandmother was not able to travel. This sister used to come and visit our grandparents when she was able to. She was extra kosher - the highest. Very strict. She brought her own dishes and cooked and prepared her own meals. They would not eat anywhere - not even in their own sister's home - even though they also kept strictly kosher the same way.

When the High Holidays came - Rosh Hashanah and Yom Kippur - our grandparents were active in the synagogue. They believed wholeheartedly. They conducted their daily prayers and raised their children to believe in G-d - our G-d. They taught us never to forget there is a G-d.

Even at the last moment, just before we left our home to begin our journey, our grandfather and uncles said, "Never forget where you are coming from and who you are. Do not forget to pray every day." Even in their letters they wrote: "You must remember our G-d. Never forget how to pray every day." Every morning, whether you had time or not, the first thing was prayer - the morning prayer before breakfast, and another prayer after eating - every day. Then came working hours to take care of all the other business.

On the High Holidays, our grandfather was asked to conduct the prayers. He was very knowledgeable - from A to Z. When Yom Kippur came, he conducted the prayers.

The night of Yom Kippur, when he chanted *Kol Nidre*, the synagogue was all filled. Even Christians came to the temple to listen. There wasn't enough room for them - they stood outside, listening to our grandfather conduct the ceremony. His voice was so beautiful, and the way he conducted the prayers - he was talking to our G-d wholeheartedly. The people listening

---

[8] A student at a yeshiva. A naive, shy, scholarly person.

[9] A shtreimel (Yiddish: שטרײַמל shtrayml, plural: שטרײַמלעך shtraymlekh or שטרײַמלען shtraymlen) is a fur hat worn by some Ashkenazi Jewish men, mainly members of Hasidic Judaism, on Shabbat and Jewish holidays and other festive occasions.

[10] **Rebbe vs. Rabbi** - A rabbi is generally a teacher, spiritual guide, or community leader with formal rabbinic ordination (semikhah), often responsible for interpreting Jewish law (halacha) and leading services in a synagogue. A rebbe (especially in Hasidic tradition) is more than a rabbi — he is regarded as a spiritual master, mentor, and intercessor whose guidance extends to every aspect of a follower's life, both religious and personal. The Rebbe during Maria's lifetime was Rabbi Chaim Elazar Spira (Shapira). He passed away in 1937, and his son-in-law, Rabbi Baruch Yehoshua Yerachmiel Rabinowicz, succeeded him.

to him were convinced there is a G-d, and some had tears in their eyes. I remember it very well.

And whenever there was a special occasion - and every New Year - he was asked to conduct the ceremony, and he did. His two sons followed in his footsteps. They were also well educated, talented, with beautiful voices. They believed in our religion and never forgot who they were.

As I grew up, I used to walk to see them - my grandparents - on Saturday, or on Sunday with our parents when we were allowed to drive, which was much easier. On Saturday we could not drive. We also kept our Jewish faith, though not as strictly as they did. We kept kosher, kept all the rules, and prayed every day. Our father was busy, but every day before he left the house, he prayed first. He would never eat before he washed his hands and said the prayers before and after eating.

Our mother's side was different than our father's side, but both sides were among the nicest families and well respected. I am very proud of my background and heritage as one of the nicest families.

Our grandparents had three children. The eldest was our mother, and two sons. As we were growing up, I remember them. By then they were married.

Their first child was my mother and her name in Hungarian was Lena and in Yiddish, Liba. My mother married very young and did not have a chance to socialize. She used to tell us that when she was almost seventeen years old she was married and by nineteen had their first child. That time they married very young. That was the custom at that time. The young people did not even know each other. The parents chose the wife or husband. They made the arrangement for marriage. Whatever the parents chose, that was it! She always used to say, that she wouldn't want her daughters to marry very young. They should enjoy life before they get married and start raising a family. As I see it today I believe that she was right. I agree with that philosophy.

My mother used to talk about how she met my father. My father's parents were rich, just the opposite of my mother's side. They were in a small business. When the two sets of parents met, my father's parents offered a good life and bought expensive jewelry. It would be a very promising future for the young woman. Therefore, my grandparents agreed to the wedding. My mother's parents were very young and they couldn't afford to have any better arrangement for marriage. Therefore the parents agreed that for both sides it was a good catch.

My grandparents first son, born after my mother, was named Lajos and in Yiddish, Labele. He was married and lived close to my grandmother and grandfather. He married a girl from Homonna, where my grandparents came from originally. His wife's name was Etelka.[11] They had no children. Lajos bacsi was also in business. He had a yard goods store. He made a moderate living.

---

[11] **-ka / -ke** – Hungarian diminutive suffixes expressing affection or familiarity, often added to personal names or nicknames, comparable to "little" or "dear" in English.

The youngest son was named Márton. He married a girl from Lelesz. Her name was also Etelka and her family was from Helmec. Her father had a clothing business. I don't know what else they were selling, but it was an established business. Also it was a respected family. They had a good business. Both sons were also very well respected, were educated in Hebrew, and both were leaders in the community.

Our Uncle Márton, lived nearby in a city named Helmec. It was a larger city. At that time, he made a nice living. He used to be in business selling shoes. He was helping his parents, but they could not stay with him. By then he had four children of his own. I only remember that one daughter's name was Magda. She had brothers, but I don't remember all their names. They were very young and we used to see them, but not often. I know they had more children. I know one was Hercu. The youngest that I remember was Emil.

Magda, the oldest child, was very beautiful, but later on she became ill. She wasn't able to walk. My uncle tried to take care of her. He tried to find a doctor who was able to help, but this time they couldn't find anyone who could tell what the problem was. They never gave up and were still looking for help. He had the other boys too, so he was very busy all around. There was no telephone at that time, and transportation was very complicated. My grandmother used to see them all the time and stayed over there place.

Our grandmother wasn't well. She had problems of her own. Our family used to help them however we could. Since we had the farm, we gave them whatever we had - flour, potatoes, vegetables - every time. Sometimes, when our grandmother wasn't feeling well, our father used to bring her over. This way, it would be easier to help her, and on the weekend our grandfather used to come to stay with us. We had enough room for them both, but he had the business - he had to take care of it.

Then our mother became ill. She could not get around, and our father was one of the best. He continued helping his in-laws, in addition to taking care of his own family. We needed help with our mother because she was sick and not able to do what we needed. We were very young and going to school, and we were not able to do too much.

We had one doctor who was in charge around the village. He was also our own family doctor. I should say he was the only doctor around. At that time, we did not have any insurance - I do not know why. So wherever we went, we had to pay cash. We had the property, but not enough cash. Later on, we had to sell some of the farmland. We had nothing to fall back on. I'm trying to make it easier to understand and explain it briefly.

So many years of trying to raise the children and take care of the family - it became very complicated. Meantime, my sister and I tried to learn whatever we were able to. When our mother passed away, it became very difficult for all of us. We had to step in and take over the chores - taking care of the family, cooking, preparing all our meals. We didn't have any choice. We got some help at home. Our oldest brother, Lajos, also helped us with the cooking.

Our grandparents went through so much - losing a daughter so young and seeing her suffer, and not being able to help her. After that, I used to go there to help them whenever they needed.

It seems I was the only one who was able to help them. I loved them very dearly. I was very happy to go and help whenever they needed me. It wasn't easy. To get a doctor was more complicated, and it was very difficult to reach one. My uncle spoke to the doctor there, and he sent out the medication, and I had to make sure my grandmother was okay. If there was any problem, when they needed something, I would go to see their son in Helmec and get more medication if she needed it. It was a very long walk, and it took a long time to get there. This was their life - the way it was - there was no other way.

Meantime, our sister Hermina was very busy. She didn't have much help. We were all alone, but we tried to manage. She was very good too; all the responsibility was on her, and she became very good at it. Our oldest brother Lajos - he was very good. He was married by then, and his wife was trying to help us. Together, we managed the best we could.

Meantime, our grandfather and his eldest son Lajos made an arrangement. When the time came, he wanted to build a building that would be enough for both of them - his parents would stay with them. Where they were living then wasn't big enough for both families. He thought this would be much better. His parents would have more comfort and someone taking care of them. They were about 80 years of age. They were not very strong people. They had problems. We also, by then, tried to make arrangements. We had decided we wanted to come to America. We didn't have any chances to better our life. This became more complicated. We decided that later on, when we would settle in America then the rest of our family would follow us.

We would never believe or think what was about to happen. That it would never happen. Otherwise, I don't know if we would have been able to leave them. Our heart cannot even think about them now - every thought - those heartaches are torture. I cannot accept or believe what happened. What reason? It is unforgettable, unbelievable, even as of now. Even though I try to put the words together the best I could, it makes it a little difficult. I can't even imagine.

Chapter 3
Childhood on Our Farm

I'm going back to continue my childhood growing up in a small village. Originally, I came from Czechoslovakia. I was born there in 1916 - it was quite some time ago. As they used to say, "a lot of water went down into the ocean." As we were growing up, our mother was very busy raising her children - and all the other work kept her very busy. With small children, sometimes she was getting help. We also had farmland. We had a steady man that lived with us for a room and board, who was helping out, taking care of the animals, and worked all around - whatever was needed.

My parents had nine children. The first, a boy, died around 10 years old. Then Lajos was born. After that, another boy died very young in an epidemic along with a girl that died after childbirth. It was a terrible hardship to endure - you can imagine, losing three children. My mother was never able to forget them.[12] My mother told us about them, but I don't remember their names. So I remember growing up with six of us. We all had dreams. My oldest living brother was Lajos, (Hajem Labele in Hebrew). After the tragedy, another son was born, whose name was Dezső (Duvid). Next was my sister Hermine (Hencse). Then I was born, my name is Maria (Marjem Hendle in Hebrew). I was the seventh child. Two years later my brother Herman was born (Hersmandle). Finally, my youngest brother, Ignác (Jichuk in Hebrew). He changed his name in America to Irving.

> ***Editor's note:*** *According to the birth registry from Polyán, the following children were born in our family:*
>
> - *Emanuel Glück, born 13.07.1902, died 1911*
> - *Lajos Glück, born 13.09.1904*
> - *Ferenc Glück, born 13.04.1907, died 29.12.1910*
> - *Sarolta Glück, born 04.01.1910, died 15.01.1910*
> - *Dezső Glück, born 11.01.1912*
> - *Hermine Glück, born 06.04.1914*
> - *Mária Glück, born 16.08.1916*
> - *Herman Glück, born 16.11.1918*
> - *Ignác Glück, born 14.11.1921*

---

[12] The birth registry shows that Emanuel Gluck was born first on 13.07.1902, and died in 1911, Lajos Gluck was born on 13.09.1904, then Ferenc Glück was born 13.04.1907, and died 29.12.1910 (age 3 ½) while Sarolta Glück was born 04.01.1910, and died 15.01.1910 (age 11 days - just two weeks after Ferenc), then Dezső (David) was born on 11.01.1912.

I remember when Irving was born. I was five years old. At that time people could not go to the hospital to have children. The doctor would come to the house only if you needed one and if you paid for it. Mostly there was a woman that brought babies into this world. She took care of the birth. Whatever was needed, she helped to do. She was there. She did not need credentials. She was very good and was an older person. When my brother was born, I was near my mother, waiting for the baby to be born. I didn't know whether it's a boy or a girl, but I was waiting for the good news. Finally the woman that was taking care of my mother called out that it is a little boy. I was the nearest one and was the first one to see the baby. I was so happy that we had a little brother. It seemed like my mother was okay, but she stayed in bed. At that time we used to have a lady to work for us, helping my mother with the housework and around the children. I always offered my help, but my mother refused it because she felt that I have time to work and worry. "You'll have plenty of time when you will have your own family."

My brother Lajos was already a big help for all of us. As he was growing up, there wasn't any requirement to send children to school - he was helping our father and went with him wherever he went. To work on the farm, we had a few places that needed extra hands. We had different fields, and it kept my father busy - all summer and fall - to plant the seeds and to prepare whatever was needed.

As my brother was growing up, he took an interest in the farm. As he was the eldest, he did everything what was needed. He worked very hard. He helped make sure the people followed the instructions and the work was done right. Meantime, he learned - he became an expert - and he was still very young. He was able to take over. He learned from our mother also and was able to help - and he became a good helper to our mother.

Usually Friday our brother Lajos went fishing to make sure we have something for us to eat for Saturday - he was helping to clean it and prepare it. Later on he learned how to cook the other dishes. He was very good help to our mother. He worked whenever she needed - all around - he never complained. He just did it.

When it came to Friday, we used to prepare our meals for Saturday. We were Jewish - we kept kosher and kept our religion. Our mother worked very hard raising the family. She did the cooking, baking bread for our family. She used to bake seven or eight large bread, challah, cheese danishes, cakes. We prepared everything from scratch. It was more work than assumed - it took time. We could not go out and buy it ready-made.

My father was very busy and always had people working for us. We lived on a farm and we had a business in the house where we lived. We had a large property. We had at that time a house in the village. The other villagers had houses that were like ours, but we had a very large property in the front and the back yard. We used to raise horses and cows. We also had a backyard, a very large one, where we grew vegetables: potatoes, onions, celery, parsley, cucumbers, and other vegetables we needed.

Maria, ~15, standing amongst the flowers in the front garden. ~1931

We also had fruit trees - plums, apples, peaches, prunes, grapes and nuts. Some of them, different scented, we planted in the front yard. During the fall, I also remember that we used prunes to make "Lekvar." We had a large bowl, made from copper, and prepared fire underneath it and put prunes in it and stirred it for hours and hours until it became jelly. We also had cabbage during the fall and our father prepared it and made sauerkraut. In between the sauerkraut we had apples and believe it or not it tasted excellent. We were self-sufficient. In general, things didn't exist in our village like in a large city, where you could buy most of these very easily.

In the front we had a very large, beautiful garden. We had all kinds of flowers. We took care of them ourselves. My mother loved them! She used to work in the garden for pleasure, she loved flowers. After the winter, we cleaned it. She had special roses that bloomed before Passover, and then oleanders, etc. And in winter, we had a large room where she kept the oleanders to prevent them from freezing.

As I remember, when I was growing up I used to take care of that garden. My sister and I used to take care of it for many years after my mother passed away. It was a difficult time in which we had to grow up to be responsible for each other. We always tried to help each other - we learned that from our mother. She loved us all. But when she was alive she would not let us do anything in the house. We never worked on the farm. My father was very busy in the home and all around the house, in the business, and on the farm. We had one man steadily. He worked wherever my father needed him and he helped with whatever was needed. He was with us for many years. I remember we had someone to help our mother.

We used to raise tobacco and wheat during the summer. We also raised geese, ducks, turkeys, chickens, and a few cows and horses. We had the poultry so that we would have eggs for cooking and our own meat, and I helped to feed them. The cows were milked in the morning and evening and we prepared the milk into butter, cheese and yogurt, like sour cream. We also sold them for meat. We raised horses to help plow, to pull our sleigh and wagon, and even for the army. My brother Lajos trained them.

We built a large building for tobacco. We had to have many helpers to plant, harvest, and sort the tobacco. It was hard work. It took a lot of time. We used to help in that building to put up strings, making sure to make every line separately. The government would not pay unless it was first class tobacco. They took all the tobacco, but they paid pennies. My brother Lajos wanted to do that and he helped my father. They were working very hard. It cost us a lot of money, but sometimes it was not worth it. The tobacco belonged to the government. Whatever they decided, they did. Mostly they assessed us and took it for taxes. This was what the Czechoslovakian government did at the time. The taxes - they decided. Otherwise, you were 'free' to do whatever you wished - under their law. They would take your last dollar for taxes, and if you didn't have any money, they took whatever you had.[13] They didn't care.

All year we worked very hard! In the Springtime, we prepared the plantation; in the Summer we cultivated and gathered the tobacco together, and hung it up to dry; then in the Winter we had to sort, smooth and grade the leaves - according to a guide - and then tie them together. My father paid

---

[13] This is known as "tax-in-kind" - any taxation that is paid with goods or services rather than money.

workers to do all that and he hoped to get back at least the cost. This was also a dream. Tobacco was controlled by the government from start to finish. We had to deliver the tobacco at a certain time, and when that time came and everything was finished, our father and brother delivered it exactly following the order, and to our surprise the government took it all for the taxes. We were not allowed to keep any of it, not to use or smoke. They even came to investigate if you hid any leaves for yourself! Everything had to be submitted. The finance department sent out surveyors to check if they could find anything to penalize you. What they said you owed, that was it - and we owed them more taxes than ever. They didn't care how hard we worked on it or how much it cost. Or how much the taxes really were. We got nothing, not even enough to pay for the tax! They paid us whatever they felt like. This was the biggest disappointment. We couldn't do anything about it.

I look back at what a shame it was! Why did we work so hard to raise tobacco? What did we get in the end? The same disappointment. We worked so hard - for what? In the end, they took it all. We could have raised other crops - vegetables, potatoes, or corn. It wouldn't have been as big, and it would have been less expensive - the government wouldn't control it. Even though we would still have to pay taxes, it would have been less since the taxes were higher for tobacco than for other crops.

We worked so hard - and in the end, we needed money for our personal needs, for our family. Luckily, we grew our own food - but what about clothing? And what about everything else that was needed? How could you take care of your family? Educate them? Give them a better life? What about doctors?

As we were growing up our mother wasn't feeling well; she had a serious problem. We were all young and missed her moving around us. We knew only that she wasn't feeling well. We did not have a doctor around at that time. We had to travel quite a distance to see one. We had to travel that time on horseback or a carriage. In the winter, we could not go with the carriage, but only with horses pulling a sleigh; it was the only way to get around. I don't know how our father was able to manage it. We had one doctor, appointed as the district doctor. He went around to check if everyone was okay. This doctor came out to the village to check on all the people for all kinds of problems. He was struggling all around visiting who ever needed his help to prevent some kind or another epidemic. He was something like the Red Cross.

I remember when Irving got sick - he was still about 6 or 7 years of age - we had a serious outbreak of measles. At that time they had to close down all the homes that had infected people in them and to be separated from the rest of the family. They placed signs on homes and people couldn't go out. Other people were put to sit in front of their homes. This way they followed the rules. It was serious. We had a separate building then and had no problem.

At that time, our mother was still alive, but by then was losing her health. She remained with the other family and the children. Our father remained with Irving, and later so did I. The meals were prepared by our mother. We were separated completely from her. She brought the food and placed it on the ground and left it there. Then our father picked it up and brought it in for the three of us. That's the way we had our meals until this epidemic got better. When the doctor came to visit all those people who were affected, he saw me - I was still with my mother in the beginning - and I wasn't feeling well. I had a sore throat. I was ordered to go and stay with Irving. Therefore, I also had to be separated from the rest of the family.

The three of us stayed together and I helped my father. We took care of Irving together. We had no contact with the rest of the family and no one else. Luckily I got better quickly, it must have been a cold only. When the dear doctor found out, I still had to remain there until the epidemic was over. But my brother Irving - he did have it - and our father had to bathe him every day and follow instructions. The doctor came every day. Finally, it cleared up. Before we were able to go home, they came out with a large truck. The doctor ordered and said to make sure that everything is sterilized, the beddings and everything, not just ours but everyone who had this problem. Only then were we able to go back to the rest of the family.

It took two months to clear the situation up. No one died at this time. This happened in other villages, not just in ours, and there was a big scare. Thank goodness our brother got well.

Afterwards, he came around but not as often. He was in charge of many villages. He lived in a small city. He had his office in his home and lived there. There weren't many doctors available and there wasn't much of a selection. There was another doctor and a gynecologist. I don't know if he did other things, like general practice. When a woman had problems with the childbirth, they went for him to come over to their home. He helped with whatever they needed.

I will go back to our mother. Later she was very sick. We could have any other doctor or a specialist if you needed one, but we would need to go further to a bigger city, like Ungvar or Ujhel, to find one. We lived in Czechoslovakia. For a better specialist we would have to go over to Budapest, Hungary. At that time Ujhel was also in Hungary. We had to have a passport and visa in order to get there. Our father used to take our mother there and stayed over for weeks, because she needed more help. She suffered a lot with pain, therefore they didn't have any choice. My father rented a place to stay, and took care of our mother. Each time it happened it was very expensive. We didn't have any insurance, as I remember, no one had. If you didn't have any cash, there was no way to get help. We had to sell some farmland or borrow money. We had no choice.

The doctors in Budapest told our father that if she does not have surgery, she will not make it. There was no other way, but our father thought maybe he can wait. Maybe someone else can help without surgery. He was told he cannot delay. If he waits, it will be too late. He decided against surgery at that time. He was afraid that something would go wrong. They came home to think about it. Meanwhile, they gave her medication - but it did not get better.

It was very difficult and we children were at home with the helpers. There was a hired hand who was looking out for the farm. Also, we had a woman coming in to help us - trying to do whatever was possible. She helped milk the cow and she pulled the weeds before they set their roots. They were nice people. Our family made them a better life, and they helped us. They had jobs and we could not do it all alone. Our older brother Lajos grew up very fast. He also took care of us to make sure that we had food, as we were growing up. My sister Hermina and I were getting older, but still not old enough to take care of our responsibilities. But time passed by.

I remember, our sister Hermina was very young, but had already started cooking and baking. At that time in Europe if we wanted to eat we had to cook from scratch, such as bread. We had a wooden dish like a tub with four legs on it. My sister Hermina could not reach it to work in it, but somehow she managed. We had a stool and we used to stand on it! We used this stool also to sit on it to milk the cows. She also helped prepare the challah for shabbas. She must have been about 10 or 12 years old when she was doing that. Little by little she started to cook all the meals. She was a responsible person.

Our mother continued going down, and was very sick. Our father decided to bring her back to Budapest where the doctors wanted to operate, but by then there was no hope. My father took her back to the doctor in Ujhely, a city which was also in Hungary but closer to us, hoping he could do something, anything, to help her. He took a room and stayed with our mother together. All she could do was to take painkillers. We children were left alone again. After so many years watching and seeing the suffering, we were unable to help. We were not able to visit our mother - the city was still nearly five hours away, and it was too expensive to go there. There was no telephone - and not much mail, either. Not much hope. At home, we tried to do whatever we could.

If she passed away in Hungary, it would be more complicated to bring her back to us in Czechoslovakia. When someone dies there, they cannot bring them home across the border - it doesn't matter what. Our father wanted her to be back with her family before she died. He made arrangements for an ambulance and a doctor to come out from Hungary, because he didn't want any trouble at the Hungarian border. She was still alive.

It was a slow, difficult journey with the ambulance. On the way home, by then, it was too late. She left us. When they crossed the border the doctor said that she's resting and asleep. With that he was able to bring her home back to us. Therefore, we didn't have a chance to see her alive.

My brother Ignác was 10½ years old and I turned sixteen two weeks after she died. After the funeral we also tried to adjust our life to do the best we can to help each other. My sister took over her role.

By then, our brother Lajos had already got married and had a little boy whose name was Emil. Our mother was still alive when he was born, I remember very well. We were all very happy. Our mother helped with her

Emil Gluck, with my mother sometime in 1931

first grandchild. Our brother and his wife used to live with us. We had plenty of room. We were getting along well. We all helped each other.

When my nephew was born - I was always around. And I liked to watch how the mother took care of the baby. Whenever she was feeding him or changing the diapers, I was already ready to help her. I knew they were very busy. I knew the baby was still a baby, and the mother was very careful so the baby would not get hurt.

At that time, they used to like a pillow, and they would put the baby in it after cleaning him up. Very carefully, she placed the baby in the pillow - the diaper was already on the baby. Then she put the bottom side of the pillow over the baby, then folded in both sides, and used a ribbon over the baby and tied it - and now she was able to pick up the baby safely, without getting hurt.

Usually I like to volunteer if I can help. Naturally I was rejected because I wasn't old enough to take care of a tiny baby. But one day she was very busy, so she allowed me to help her. And I asked her to watch me - I will be very, very careful. And when I finished she was very happy. She saw I was able to do what she needed to do. From then on, I was around to help. But to carry the baby it was much easier with the pillow. The baby was safe. That was the way they did it in my time. They are doing this until about seven months - until the baby got stronger and was able to sit up by himself or herself. When not in danger, they moved the baby from the pillow - when it was strong enough to be able to handle without fear. After a year my brother's wife Etelka, gave birth to a little girl. She was named Libele after my mother (Lenke in Hungarian). This was the second child.

I remember when my brother got married. He was only 20 years old. His wife was the same age. She came from Lelesz, the same town where our grandparents lived, from a large family. It was not too far from us. There were more Jewish families in Lelesz than in our small village - we had only a few Jewish families and their daughters were older. There were other girls, but only non-Jewish ones. As I said, our grandparents lived there, and one of our uncles from my mother's side.. Our family was well known there. People respected them - and respected us. Her father made a living buying and selling horses. They were dealing with people. That was a good business. Their background was entirely different from ours - not much in Hebrew or anything else. They were not religious people, but they did keep kosher.

I also remember the bargaining before our brother Lajos was married. Since we did not have any opportunity to meet anyone special, if you wanted to meet someone, it was usually by introduction - that was the style. We called it a shidduch.

One day, one of my grandparents' friends came over and wanted to know more about my brother. It happened that the girl, her name was Etelka, was their granddaughter. The girl's grandmother kept getting together with my parents, trying to work out the matchmaking. It took time to work it out. It was conducted just like a business. The young couple never talked to each other before they were married. That was the custom. In those days, a girl needed a dowry. The boy's family would ask how much the girl's family could give as a dowry before the wedding. All of that had to be worked out in advance. That was the way boys and girls met in those days. The young couple met only just before the wedding. Whether they liked each other or not didn't matter - it was already done. The families wanted them to get married. They were able to give her whatever she needed. Finally, after they agreed on the money, but before the wedding, they deposited or paid out the money. The wedding wasn't a catered affair - it was all prepared at home.

It happened that my sister-in-law was more experienced in traveling around. She was more outgoing and was the oldest in her family. I think there were three more girls for a total of four and three brothers. Their mother was more outspoken. She was different from her mother - she was very well-mannered and a very nice person. After the wedding Etelka moved in with us. We girls were very happy! She was like a girlfriend. We didn't have in our village Jewish girls our age, only Christians. We accepted her like she would be our eldest sister. We had no problem with her. Etelka was very smart. I was always asking questions whenever I had an opportunity. Otherwise as a young girl I was very shy. Our mother was with us at that time. Whatever she could, Etelka was helping us. She did not have too much experience about housework. She learned and was able to do more. We loved her. And their children - I must say those children they were beautiful and very smart - all of them. And such young children.

We were going to a Catholic school and I became very friendly in school with people. Our village didn't have any Jewish girls. They were older women. We had two families that had about five girls and one boy, Ignác's age. Hermina was very outspoken even as a young person. I was very shy, but good-natured, and with my sister-in-law being with us it was better for me in growing up. I used to read a lot.

People were coming from the mountains, they were carrying goods on their backs to sell products to make a living. Usually they stopped by in our home and we gave them food and shelter. My mother used to buy the best selling books from them. They were selling books in the Yiddish language and story books of all kinds. She used to tell us stories and taught us how to read. My mother always said to be sure that we read a lot. Whenever my mother had time she was reading these books. To us it was like today, when you watch a good movie. The books gave us a feeling that were interesting and we had something to think about it. To us this was entertainment. That time, there were no movies, no television - not even a radio. There wasn't even any fashion magazines to see how people were dressed - you cannot even imagine what life was.

Sometimes during the week my sister went to the library to get some books and on Saturday I went to the garden, sat on the grass, and enjoyed reading them. There wasn't too much of anything else to do. I was a very fast reader and tried to educate myself. I learned a lot. I loved reading all kinds of books, especially in Yiddish. I knew how and I understood it. Some were in Hebrew and interpreted into Yiddish. We had a teacher who taught us to read Hebrew and interpret it into Yiddish. I could speak Yiddish well and understood what was translated in Yiddish from Hebrew. I used to love to read them and I started very young. We had lots of books about our history and about the first World War. I read them all. By the way, our parents went through the first World War. We were also interested to know about life - about our body and how it functions - since in the elementary school they did not teach us that.

My brother David was full of life. He loved dancing, but we didn't have any socials in our village, only Christians did, and sometimes young Jewish boys and girls used to go together. We didn't have any other Jews. It was tough. We didn't have the opportunity to socialize. We tried our best under the circumstances. When I was a little older I loved dancing, but I did not know how, so my sister-in-law was teaching me, but it wasn't easy. Then I found someone who was a dance teacher, but the family would not approve of it. But one Saturday, David surprised me, he brought the teacher to our home to teach me how to dance. The teacher was very good. In Europe we used to have Gypsy musicians, some were very famous. The dance teacher was too, this particular one was one of the best, well-known. My brother David asked him to teach me a few lessons. I was very happy. I was good. My new problem was that there wasn't any place to go dancing.

One day my brother heard that there will be a dance in the next town. He asked me if I wanted to go there, but how can I go? If our family finds out it could be a problem, but David liked to dance, and he was a great dancer. When the time came he asked me to go with him on the bicycle. I agreed without telling where we are going and I went with him. We had a good time just dancing. He knew some people there. He was more outgoing.

As David was growing up, he had his own ideas. He was different from all of us. Our eldest brother Lajos had no choice - he had to stay on the farm. He felt our parents needed him more there. He believed David should learn and help out on the farm, too. It would have been easier for all of us. All the young people we knew became farmers and we grew up among them.

But he had already made up his mind, he did not want to be a farmer, and he would not give up. You could not reason with him. He was trying to get into his own business and become a salesperson. He started in business - funding it all by himself from our home. Before you knew it, he got his wish.

We began getting back letters and samples - mainly pictures - from different companies. He had made some connections, but no money. He started traveling around and whatever he wanted to sell he sold from the bicycle. It was enough to get started.

Still, our brother needed a place to stay in the city. He had an idea - he would open a small business in Helmec, the city where one of our uncles lived.

David began a business there. Our brother was very ambitious. He was never lazy. He located and found a small place - just what he wanted. By then, he had a month's down payment for the rent. He also had the merchandise - he got it on consignment.

Okay, now he had the business. He never worried where the next bread was coming from. He always said, "It will be whatever it will be."

He decided to do the best with that store. His display was set up behind the window. As young as he was, he tried everything by himself.

When our mother passed away she was 48 years old. She worked very hard all her life. Raising children, there were times when we didn't have any help. Also I remember that on Saturday when we were going to visit our grandparents in the next town, the place where they lived, their village was much larger than ours and more Jewish people lived there. It took us an hour of walking to get there - it was 2 km. We usually walked on Sabbath. On the way, as we were going, people stopped us to talk to my mother. They were giving compliments and remarks about how we are growing up, getting to be nice young ladies, and she will get help - and that I look like she does. She was very proud of us. She was very happy I remember during the good times when she was well.

She used to bake for the holidays. She made all kinds of Danish, cakes, and rolls with cinnamon and poppy seeds together around. It was delicious! In Europe at that time if you wanted something you had to know how to make it because you couldn't buy it. At that time most people were very good. They exchanged recipes. Sometimes on a holiday people would stop by and we always had something to serve them. On Fridays we used to be very busy. It was a busy day, cooking, baking, and of course, cleaning. This was a routine event. When Friday came we knew our job. After our mother passed away, we had to do whatever we needed to do. We always knew our jobs and sometimes we got some help. My sister did all the baking and cooking. She took care of all that. My sister was very good. I did all the cleaning, scrubbing the floor.

Even before the measles epidemic, we had built a nice new home. It was built from bricks and we had a wooden floor. It was very nice. Before that, every Friday I was scrubbing the dirt floor spotless. This was in the old building where we used to live and were raised. Even our grandparents used to live there. At that time we all lived there. I used to even paint the outside walls. I liked to do it. It was a very old building. It was a ranch house with large rooms. The roof was covered with straw. There was an all purpose room. All of us slept in that room. We had long tables there. We had another room in the back where later my brother Lajos and his wife moved.

Later when we built the new building on the other side, we moved in there. In the front was the grocery business. Before that, there was an old building, a couple of blocks away where we had our business, namely the grocery business. With the new building it was more convenient and better. We had in the new place, very nice living rooms and the business. The one bedroom was not very big, but it was modern. By the way, we used to burn wood in the stove. We used it for heating and cooking and baking. Only for baking we used the old building's brick oven, it was big enough for seven large round bread and we could bake in it, like csolent[14] with beans and meat. We learned how to make it and it was very good and tasty. Usually it was an overnight baking and cooking. It always came out well baked. We did not see that in America.

In the old building we were cooking and baking. We used wood and that's what we had to have for winter. We had to chop the wood ready to be used. When my brother went out to cut some wood, he was preparing it for the winter heating. The stove had on the top a small oven that was big enough to cook a few things and on the back part of the oven there was room for light baking, such as potatoes or bécsitük.[15]

We used to raise potatoes and pumpkins in our garden and it was delicious. We did not have a refrigerator. We stored potatoes in the basement. The basement had an even temperature all through the year. In the winter it did not freeze so there was proper protection. It was built in such a way that it maintained an even temperature.

In the new building we had a modern stove, but it also burned wood. We also had a forest where my father had some people to cut down trees as we needed. Most people had to buy it.

---

[14] Cholent (Yiddish: טשאָלנט, romanized: tsholnt) is a traditional slow-
simmering Sabbath stew in Jewish cuisine that was developed by Ashkenazi Jews first in France and later Germany. It is related to and is thought to have been derived from hamin, a similar Sabbath stew that emerged in Spain among Sephardic Jews and made its way to France by way of Provence.

[15] bécsitük is Hungarian for squash/pumpkin

Chapter 4
Life in Our Village

As I was growing up remembering our parents, our father was small built, and so was our mother. None of our family was overweight. All of us were very slim. We were very active girls. Our hobby was hand embroidery. In our village in the winter the people used to make towels from linen. They had the equipment for weaving manually. You would not believe how hard they were working. Even the threading was made beautifully. I used to watch them how they were making it. They made beautiful tablecloths with all kinds of designs, each more different than the other. As I look back everything was made by hand from scratch. Although the people in our village were farmers, they were very talented. Most of the people went to school until sixth grade. They were required to go up to the age of 16 years.[16] After that, if they wanted to continue their education, they would have to go to another city to study. At that time life was quite different. Some of the people were well-to-do. They were leaders in our village. They did not have any special education, but learned from their parents. We had a shoemaker in our village and he did very well. He made very beautiful boots and shoes. You could never tell that they were homemade. It was expensive, but we did not have any manufacturers in our village, only in the large cities.

The better class of people learned from each other, from their parents or grandparents, because after all, they were from the farm and were self-sufficient. Some of them were very talented and one could learn from them also. As a little girl I used to watch them, and I admired how beautifully they made the things they were making, and it was very interesting. Our parents used to buy from them all the linens, tablecloths, towels. They used to make towels and tablecloths without design also. I learned from them how to embroider. My sister and I learned fast. We used to buy the instruction papers and we learned how to embroider. Here in America, I haven't seen anything made like that. They were very beautiful and well made. Made in our village.

When you make the embroidering, you have to count every thread and the different stitches. It was not very easy to do but we learned. I learned how to make beautiful designs also on tablecloth. It came out very nicely. I also did it on hand towels. We were able to do whatever we wanted. We brought some to America and gave it to our relations.

My sister and I we were able to make beautiful figurines with all types of patterns, everything from scratch. For this type of work you had to count the thread without any prints. We copied it from the papers and followed the instructions and that was it. It was hard work, but I liked it. I became very good at it. Whenever I had a chance I was working on it. I liked to do it in our school because there was someone who gave us some information. We

---

[16] ***Editor's Note:*** *although in rural areas like theirs, many children only completed up to age 12 despite formal requirements.*

learned how to follow instructions. I learned how to crochet later. It took a long time to finish whatever we were making. We weren't doing anything else, but we helped lighten things for our mother. She was still with us. Sometimes we had steady helpers in our home. They were there whenever my mother needed help. I was about eight years old when I began to crochet or perhaps earlier. I had more time than my sister. She was busier. She was two years older. The lady that came to help our mother was very nice and very helpful. Her name was Istvanne Toth. She used to come to us for a long time and I knew her very well. Whenever she was with us I was anxiously interested in everything. She wasn't an educated person. She was interested in earning money. She had a large family and needed help herself. They were poor people.

We also raised horses and cows. We kept Saturday as a holiday. It was our day of rest. We didn't work and our store was closed. The cows had to be milked every day and that included holidays and this lady was doing it, she helped with everything. We lit the candles on Friday evening and she was there to maintain the stove so that we can be warm during the winter. We kept a kosher home and we maintained it as such.

Our father used to go to temple every Saturday and holidays. We did not have a regular temple in our village, but we rented a room and we went there to pray. It requires to have 10 people for a quorum and sometimes we did not have the 10 people, so we hired a man from the neighboring town to come to have 10 people and be able to maintain a complete service as required. This person came from Lelesz where our grandparents lived. It was 2 km from our village. We had only five Jewish families in our village. My brothers were young and therefore they did not qualify to be counted. To qualify one had to be 13 years of age to be counted as a man. There were times that we needed more people to maintain the 10th person as required. Because we did not have enough men so my father went to Lelesz to the temple. The only time he didn't go was when there was a good reason. We maintained our prayers at home, as I mentioned before, we were kosher, but we were not overly religious.

Once a week a person came to slaughter chickens, geese, or ducks for the weekend so we would have food for Saturday. We did not kill the animals that we raised. The person that came to do that, usually on Thursday mornings, was a very religious individual called a Shohet.[17] This individual studied to do this type of work. This was his profession. He was paid for his services to prepare our chicken or whatever we had. According to our religion it is the only way to have meat. We had a butcher, but not all the time - only sometimes. If we wanted some beef, then our father went to the city. about 8 km away from our village. There, they did have a steady butcher. Our father used to buy it there. That's the only way we had beef or whatever meat you want. We did not have a wholesaler like we have in America. Here in

---

[17] a "shohet" (שוחט) is a person officially licensed by rabbinic authority to slaughter animals and poultry, known as "shechita", for food according to Jewish law (kashrut).

America you go to the butcher shop and buy what you want. In our village everything was from scratch. We raised the chickens, and even calves. In the city, they could not raise any chickens or animals, but there was a marketplace. There you could buy anything - whatever you needed. During the summer, farmers took produce in from the farm to the large city market if they had something to sell, such as eggs, chickens, cows, horses and calves. We also sold to the butcher in the city.

Non-Jewish people in our village slaughtered their own animals: pigs, calves, rabbits and so forth. They used the animal blood for cooking purposes. We, the Jewish people, are not allowed to do that. We also need to make the meat kosher by applying salt upon it and after half an hour to wash the salt out and then we soak for an hour to clear the blood out from the meat. After all this has been done, then it is ready to prepare and cook whatever you wish to make.

As I look back, preparing for Shabbos - what it was like? All week, all of us kept very busy, each one of us with our responsibility. Everything should be prepared on time on Fridays, to make sure we have food for Shabbos. We kept our rituals - we believed wholeheartedly and followed. We made sure we had challahs, breads - even pastry. Not fancy - but it was delicious. Danish, all kinds. That took a long time to prepare. We got up very early, and every day, to make sure we had food for breakfast. We did not have any cereals to open up. We had to prepare. We had our milk and bread - potatoes, vegetables - what we grew in our garden. And naturally, the wheat for flour was from our farm.

Usually we had meat every Friday and Saturday. It was prepared before the holiday. We had a large brick oven that we used to bake bread in, as well as bakery goods. We prepared all the food in special dishes. We made cholent, adding beans to meat, vegetables, and other things included. This was prepared, baked overnight, and it was ready for Saturday's dinner. After the wood burned out, the ashes were pushed aside and then bread, food, or whatever was prepared for cooking or baking was put into the oven. Some of our Jewish neighbors used to come over and brought their food to cook there because they didn't have a place like this oven. We always helped anyone that needed help. Our family always reached out and was ready to help.

Sometimes individuals came into the village carrying things on their back selling their wares. Whomever wanted to buy bought clothing and other items from him. Many times if he came to us, as a fellow Jew, we bought from him and he stayed with us overnight. My father never turned away any poor individuals that came to our door. He helped them the best he could. These individuals were in their middle-age. Every so often they came around to sell their merchandise and we always managed to buy from them. Since they stayed overnight we gave them food. We did not know them and we didn't see them before because there were always different people coming to our village. They were complete strangers, yet they were very friendly. To us it didn't matter that he needed help. After they ate dinner we gathered around him and he was telling us the story of his life and travels.

We had a Hebrew teacher. He came from Poland. We also had teachers from Helmec. In this city there was a yeshiva where our father was able to select young men that wanted to come to our village and teach us in Hebrew and Yiddish. We got together as children of the same ages with the families and it was easier for all of us and then we were able to get a good Jewish education. There was no other place to go except the next town and in Lelesz.

Our grandfather and grandmother, from our mother's side, lived in Lelesz. My brother Irving was sent to study there. We did not have other children of his age and therefore we did not hire a private Jewish teacher. Our father wanted him to continue his education. As a youngster he had more opportunity to learn in Lelesz. He stayed with our grandparents. From our father's side our grandparents were all gone. Irving used to come home for the weekends. Each time when he was going back to our grandparents he took whatever they needed from our farm for them. We loved them both.

Our parents used to go there and we girls went with them. They were the only family we had. The other relatives we hardly saw. It seemed like every one was busy making a living. Uncle Márton lived in Helmec. He was my mother's brother. The transportation in those days was by horse and buggy. To walk there from our village would take half a day. As we got older we were able to go more often with a carriage. We passed by many farms. It was a beautiful sight. My father used to go to the wholesale house for grocery shopping for our store. Many times my father went to the city especially during the summer. He would walk. The horses were needed on the farm to prepare the land for seed and to cultivate it.

In the city there were cars or taxis and sometimes they were pulled by horses because of gas shortages. We did not have any farm machinery, such as tractors to do the farm work so mostly everything was done with horses or other farm animals. The ground had to be prepared and all that took time. It was hard work. We helped at home. We had a big backyard and that had to be planted also with corn, potatoes, and other vegetables. We did not as girls do farm work. Every summer it was the same repetition. Plowing the land, planting the land, preparing it for seeding - and the tobacco had to be planted individually. We were busy all year around. And the springtime usually had floods in our village.[18] That created a tremendous stress for everyone. Some of the farms were higher and they were protected by being higher than the flood level. Many times in our village we had to use boats to get around. People were trying to stop the flood, but they could not. Our home was on higher ground so we were safe. However some of the homes were flooded. Eventually the floods receded and then the village became somewhat normal. All this took several weeks. After the farm was dry then again it had to be planted in many areas. It was a difficult life for everyone. The government, at that time was Czechoslovakia, did not give any help even though there were a lot of losses. Everyone had to be on their own. The losses were lost forever. There were no such a thing that you can deduct it from your taxes. The

---

[18] The Latorica River flowed behind the house at the far end of the backyard.

government decided how much you owed and that was it. That was our life in our village.

I'm returning to our father. He wasn't a strong man. He was very nearsighted and wore glasses. He was able to manage himself with a cane. Without glasses, he was not able to see - almost blind. Believe me I never knew how he was able to get around by himself. As I go back, I cannot even imagine how he was doing all those businesses, yet he did. When I was older I knew when he was coming home from the city. It was a very long walk, all over farmland - no buses, no cars. The only thing was horses and buggies - nothing more, until later on. Many times, I used to go to meet him - especially in the evening I was very concerned about him - I knew the route that he usually came home. It was difficult to see too far and you had to be almost in the front of the person to see them. I could not see him in the darkness, and in the dark, he wasn't able to see at all. He just used a cane - that was his sight. It was very easy to get lost - especially at night. My concern was that we would not see one another, even with good eyesight. There were not many people walking in the area. It looked like a desert, but of course it was all farmland. My father was always happy to see me, and I was the happiest person - thank goodness he was safe. And from then on, we walked together. I felt relieved. He was tired but he never complained.

I'm going to go back to my school life - all of us were going to a Catholic school. Unfortunately no one realized at that time that I was nearsighted. I needed eyeglasses. I kept it to myself. As I mentioned before my father wore eyeglasses because he was nearsighted and he used to go to Ungvar, a city, for his eye exam. The teacher knew that. The teacher asked me after he wrote something on the blackboard what it was that he had written, and I was able to answer because I was sitting close by. That was helpful. Later on, I was moved further back from the blackboard, and I had difficulty to see what was written. One of my friends sitting next to me knew that I could not see well, especially from a distance. And she was a very big help to me. She used to whisper what I needed to say to the teacher and because of that the teacher never knew about my nearsightedness.

My teacher and my family discovered it when I graduated from school. My teacher should have known that I had an eyesight problem. Why didn't he? It took a long time, many years before they discovered it during my graduation. I was then 16 years old. Earlier we had an elderly teacher for a couple years while I was in school and he retired. After that a young teacher came and took over the school activities of teaching. If I would have gotten my eyes examined and had proper glasses I would have done much better. I did not have any glasses until I came to America. Here I got eyeglasses, not right away, but after I was going to night-school to learn English. The teacher was an optometrist. He asked me to read from the blackboard as he was teaching us English. I could not see. He asked how did I get this far in school? My brother David went to this school to learn English before, and the teacher knew him, so he told my brother what happened in the classroom. My uncle heard about this and he recommended an eye doctor, a friend of theirs. I did a lot of close work as a child, like sewing, and all this time, I did not wear glasses. In America, I got my eyesight back.

How could I be so nearsighted and my family did not notice it? The family was busy as I was growing up and there were too many things going around, especially my mother's sickness. We were busy all around. Otherwise, I was all okay. To do needlepoint as I did it was very close work. I was working in the evenings by oil lamp. We did not have electric. No one had in our village.

In our village on Sundays the people dressed up in their best clothing or dresses and went to church. We used to watch them. It was very nice to see them. They were religious people. After a couple of hours they were returning from church and in the afternoon we used to sit outside on the benches in front of the homes and we were meeting people there. We were just relaxing or sitting or we used to go for a walk and meet our non-Jewish friends. We spent a couple of hours with them. We enjoyed ourselves. Our business was closed on Saturday and Sunday. All the work stopped except feeding the animals. This was a real holiday. Sometimes we used to visit our grandparents in our carriage. From our village to the next was a long walk, approximately 2 km. My father's oldest brother lived a few blocks away from us and we used to visit him too and his son-in-law and children. He, our uncle, had grandchildren, a boy [Tibor, Tibi] and a girl [Clara]. He also had a grocery store in the front of their home and a small farm.

We never had any problem with anyone until the Hungarian government took over our part of the country - then the situation changed.

Uncle Márton, my mother's brother, had a shoe store in Helmec. His family lived there, next to the shoe store, in an apartment house. My father used to stop by every time he went to this city. Later as my brother Irving became older he used to take our father on a bicycle to and from the town. This way my father was able to get around more easily.

I mentioned it before that he was small built. He looked older than he was because he had a beard and mustache. My older brother Lajos worked on our farm and helped my father. Lajos was tall, well-built, and good looking and a very hard worker. Whatever was needed he was always there. To have a brother as he was is hard to find. He was a very unusual person. We also had a man working for us steadily.

David was a different person. He did not want to do anything with the farm. Lajos thought - maybe David would be able to help - at least in the business. He tried to convince him. We had just built another building near our home to transfer our grocery store, so it would be easier. The other store was a little farther away, and it was difficult for us to go there. This way, it was much easier to take turns and do the job in the business and at home - because by that time, the rest of us we were going to school. It was required by then. But David had another plan and dream. He wanted to have a different life. He was more outgoing and very smart. He did whatever he wanted. When he was growing up, going to school was not required. He was a self-educated individual. He started corresponding with different companies and wanted to go into business.

Once he made contact with the company, it was very easy for him to get merchandise and only when he sold it then he paid for it. I remember at one time he ordered beautiful window curtains, some tablecloths, or whatever he felt that he would be able to sell. He tried it. Finally, he decided to sell and travel on the bicycle from one village to the other. He succeeded and was able to make a few Kronan [Czechoslovakian currency]. This way he was a happier person! He felt great that he tried it. He never gave up. He would not know anything about farming, but he always helped out my father with his earnings.

Later he rented a place in Helmec. I must say, he didn't have any money, but he was ambitious and courageous and he knew where to start. My youngest brother Irving was very close to David. Irving was the youngest. He was going to Hebrew school first in Lelesz and later our father sent him to the yeshiva to continue to study in Kiralyhelmec. If he wanted to come home he could have, but he was very close to his brother David and usually stayed with him. He finished his high school in Lelesz and then he registered for the Polgári[19] for further education in Helmec.

Irving was always with David, they were very close to each other and got along very well. When David opened his business in this city, Irving was there after school to help him. They lived together sometimes in an apartment and sometimes when it was difficult to pay the rent then they stayed in the back part of the store. It had enough space to have a bed and they stayed there until business improved and David rented again. Whenever David needed something, Irving was there to help him. Irving was his right hand.

Irving did not have a place to stay overnight because it was expensive as I mentioned before, so he and David stayed together.

In those days, the custom was if a child wanted a Jewish education, they would have it - the congregation would help them. For example when being in the yeshiva, individual families would give food on different days for the students. Every day, another family would host the student - this made the cost less. This way they were able to continue their yeshiva education. This was organized by the Jewish congregation to help students pursue their Jewish education. Everyone invited students and it went around like a circle. Sometimes, if they could get a room, it would cost less - and the child would be able to get his Hebrew education and also learn in yeshiva. This was very important to a Jewish family. Other children might come from nearby villages as well. This way, they had a better chance.

---

[19] *Polgári* refers to middle school or civic education. In Hungarian usage, a *polgári iskola* was normally a four-year middle school (grades 5–8), offering general education. For most girls, including Maria, the *polgári iskola* marked the end of formal secular schooling. The *Polgári* in Királyhelmec likely offered Irving an extended track that kept him there through his late teens, alongside his yeshiva studies.

As I mentioned before, the back of David's store was just big enough that both of them could sleep there. I don't think they had a bed - they just slept on the floor. They had a sink. This way Irving had a place to sleep - and at least it wasn't a strange place. They became very close. After school, when Irving came back, he was also a big help for David. They built something together, and David depended on Irving. As young as he was, he taught Irving his business and relied on him more than he should have. If David needed something, it was easier to send his little brother to exchange whatever he needed.

At this time one of our cousins was married and decided to come to Helmec to open a store for himself. Later they had a little girl and also there was another cousin from our village, Rezsike, our Uncle Lajzer bacsi's daughter, that lived in Helmec with her husband. He was not in business. I do not remember what he did. My uncle suggested to me to try to go to Helmec because there was no other way to do anything in our home except to learn how to sew. I liked the idea of going to Helmec. Maybe I would be able to learn how to make new patterns. My father looked into it and found a good place. The family used to sell yard goods. They were well-adjusted and were well known.

One of the daughters opened a dressmaker shop of her own. I was told she would take me in and teach me, but I have to do whatever she needs. To teach a beginner she can charge while a person learns. I agreed and I went there, but I didn't have any place to stay and eat. Our cousin Rezsike and my father agreed that he will give them whatever we can. So we gave them potatoes or flour for bread in exchange so that I will be able to stay with them. This arrangement was a short one, about six months. I also helped her in her home, this way we were able to work it out. With the sewing arrangement, I did not do too much. I had some idea of my own and I learned by myself. She told me to go to do finishing jobs, namely hemming, only on the least expensive dresses. She hired a young lady who was already a dressmaker, and she paid for her work. She was a helper, but she was very good. I was watching them while they were working, but it's not like if you are doing it yourself, and because of that I didn't feel like continuing any further.

The other cousin from Szürte, as I mentioned before, was in Helmec and they were the ones who had a baby and she needed help for a while, so I just helped out taking care of the baby. She went back to work with her husband. She wanted someone that she could trust with their baby and she asked me if I would help her out. I didn't have to do anything else and I could stay there with them free. I agreed for a short time until the baby got older so that she would take her to the business. At this time they couldn't hire a babysitter. I personally believe that they could not afford it. I cooked once in a while but the food for the child was already prepared. I just dressed her and kept her clean and fed her. The child got to know me, and I loved her. Sometimes I cleaned the kitchen. The baby started to crawl all over and when I tried to do something, she came to me.

On Saturday, the store was closed. My cousin was well dressed, beautiful, and she gave me clothing, whatever looked well on me. She let me wear it and we went after dinner for a promenade. In this city after dinner, young people, singles and couples used to go for a walk. The streets were spotless. It was like window shopping, looking at different windows as they were well decorated with their products. I took their baby, dressed her up nicely and went with the baby carriage. I received a lot of compliments. They told me that I am grown up and I look like a young lady. This was enough to make me happy. At this time I never believed that we would be able to come to America, or that the world would go mad. It was very peaceful at this time. The people at this time in the town were very friendly. They were respectful all over. We had all types of religious denominations, but never knew that we were different. We're the same flesh and blood.

I continued to learn sewing on my own by sewing. That was what I was hoping for. I used to try to learn on old dresses. My Uncle Julius used to send us packages with old clothing and I used to fit them for my sister or myself. I used to open them up and examine the dresses to see how it was made. I took measurements because I did not have a pattern, and even if we would have had patterns, even then, I would have to learn the different sizes for different people. Later I was making clothing and dresses for my sister and myself. The problem was that we had to try them on to see how it looks and how it fits. Is that short or is it long? It had to be just right. So I needed to make a small adjustment, I tried everything until it came out the way I thought it should be. My sister was a perfectionist and everything had to be just perfect, but she didn't feel like standing too long. Sometimes I had to do it without her trying it and when I finished she was much happier. I never sewed for other people even though I would have liked to. I wasn't ready yet. I needed more training. As I was growing up, we children liked to have dolls, so I decided to make them from rags. We learned from each other as children. We used to get together in the backyard with plenty of room and we used to sit under the trees for shade as little girls and we made dolls. We had plenty of rags and the dolls came out nicely. But we always tried to do it better and better and this was the way we learned to make them. Some of the children learned how to make these from their mother. We went to the same school and we knew each other and we never had any problem at this time with religion. As I mentioned earlier I was going to a Catholic school. That was the way and we were happy.

The old building where we lived was our father's parent's home. First they lived there. Now we lived there. This was our grandparent's first home. When they moved there they bought properties and farm land and established themselves also in business. In this old house, the floor was just plain dirt smoothed with water. This had to be done every Friday to make it clean and neat. I was doing the cleaning up daily with just a broom to sweep it. The floor was spotless. We did not have any mattresses, so we used straw and covered it with linens. My sister and I used to sleep together in one bed since it was large enough for both of us. It was very comfortable. We hung the dishes up after they were washed to dry. It was like a display in the kitchen. We had cabinets for small dishes, but for the pots and pans, it was a different story. We had separate dishes for meat and dairy. The front of the kitchen was decorated with designs, it was beautiful. You had to see it to believe it. The people were very smart because they used to clean the dishes with ashes or earth to make the silver shine and be clean after it was washed.

Mother used to light candles for Friday night, twelve of them, and said her prayers. The candlestick holders were made from brass. Every so often we had to clean it because it became tarnished. After we used them then we cleaned them for the following week because the brass has to be maintained often to keep it clean. They looked like new after we cleaned it.

Many years later, when we built a new house, it was different. It was a brick building with wooden floors. The roof was covered with square, asbestos plates. It was a tall building with high ceilings. Inside, the walls were all white. By this time, David was able to get beautiful curtains, and small dressers. We covered them with handmade embroidery. In the other room we had closets and were able to hang up our dresses. This house was somewhat smaller than the one we lived in. In the smaller room there were beds and whenever our grandparents came over they were able to stay there. Later, David and Irving used to sleep in that room.

The property was very large. We separated the properties from our neighbor's and in the front facing the street we had two gates that opened up to let the carriage, horses, and animals get in and out, otherwise it was a completely private, enclosed property.

When it was hay time, they piled hay up on the wagon very high and the person sat on top directing the horses and bringing the hay home from the farm. Farming was not easy! It was a year-round job beginning in the springtime and lasting all through the summer and then of course going out many times in the winter to feed the horses and to bring lumber from the forest and again in the springtime plowing, seeding, preparing everything that was needed. That was the way everybody did their own farming completely.

Before the wheat could be brought home they had to assemble it on the farm in such a way that the wheat would dry completely during July and August and then it was brought home for storage and for machine separation. It was interesting to watch how smooth this activity took place, and they knew how to do it. There was a man from a different town that came around to thresh the wheat for everyone. He used to bring in a tractor (before that they used animals) to pull the threshing machine. There were two types of machines: one they used to separate the wheat from the straw into bags and the other machine was like a tractor. The threshing usually took a couple of days, depending upon how much threshing had to be done. The people on the top of the machine that separated the straw from the wheat were helped by other people transferring from the machine to the storage area. This was where the wheat and straw were stored from the rain after it was gathered from the farm. During the threshing the bags were brought up to the storage room and then the threshing people got a share of the threshed wheat for their services. After threshing, the straw was brought to the back of the storage building and the people working there were piling it up carefully so that it could be used all through the year. After the threshing, the wheat was gathered and stored in our building, then every so often, we had to go to the mill to have flour made for our consumption. Of course the wheat was used for flour and the straw for the animals to lie on it or whatever it was needed for. We used to sell wheat also, but most of it we kept for ourselves so that we would have flour whenever we needed it. Our father and our brother Lajos used to take several bags of wheat with the wagon into the next village to the mill, where they paid to grind it into flour. There the machine separated it into light and dark flour. I never saw how it was made into the flour. All this was a routine event for us, and we paid for all these services.

Going back a little in history, before all this happened, people from the northern part of Czechoslovakia, men and women, dressed up beautifully with embroidered shirts and dresses. This was their homestyle clothing. Up north, the region had mountains and they did not have any good land for farming, so these people used to come down to the south, where we lived, to earn some money. In this way they were able to maintain their lives up north. When they came down we hired them to work for us during the threshing season. This was long before machinery was available in our village for threshing. They had a type of wooden club and we gave them a canvas stretched out and the straw was placed on it. With the club they hit the canvas and that was the way they were able to separate the wheat from the straw.

These people stayed with us for a couple weeks. They slept in the same place where they were threshing and used the straw for their beds. They all slept there together. This was common and these people were used to it. They were hard workers and they required a good meal, three times a day. There were three or four couples that came and we had to cook for them and it wasn't easy. We had to feed them on time. They ate big meals from one large pot. They were nice people, I don't remember what language they were speaking. This situation was going on all the years I can remember.

We had a neighbor across the street that was a machinist and he used to work with machinery. This man was an unusual person. He was very smart and he knew almost everything. If someone had a problem, he was there to help with money. He had a family and children. I remember that there was a rumor that he was a communist[20] or perhaps he may have been a Russian. He was a professional person and may have been educated in Russia. During those periods some people were taken prisoner without reason. This may have happened during the first world war and the countries were being established, like Czechoslovakia. He was able to live in this village without any trouble. Perhaps he may have changed his name when he settled down. He wasn't a criminal, one could see it, and no one bothered him and he never bothered anyone. He was a good citizen and a very hard worker. We were friends with him. The family lived quietly, and the children were very young.

---

[20] "communist" was a dangerous accusation at that time.

He had a little girl, perhaps six years old, and she was outside playing by herself. All of a sudden we heard someone singing with a beautiful voice. As we were listening, we finally realized it was his child with such a beautiful voice. This happened before the second world war came upon us. This man's name was Gecse.

When my oldest brother's wife was delivering their first baby, we needed a doctor because there were some difficulties. The lady that was helping the delivery of the baby thought that they should call a doctor to help out because it took a long time to make the delivery. This man that I spoke of before, Gecse, went on a bicycle to the city and asked the doctor to come out, and he did. The doctor stayed there with my brother's wife for a long time, and finally the child was born. It was a baby boy. He was named Emil. The doctor charged 1000 Kronin for his services. That was a lot of money at that time, and this man Gecse thought that the doctor wanted to make more money and that's why there was even more of a delay.

My brother Irving didn't like Gecse because he shot at Irving's dog. The pellets from the shot went into the dog's legs and sides and he could not walk. Irving took her into the tobacco building. He placed straw on the floor so the dog would be comfortable. He took food and water to the dog daily and finally after many weeks, the dog became well and was able to walk again. Gecse claimed that the dog was barking at him while he was on the bicycle passing by in front of our house and he took his rifle and tried to scare the dog. Yet he shot at the poor dog and it must have suffered a lot. Legally nothing could have been done. We did not know anything about Gecse's personal life, however, later when the trouble began and the Hungarian government took over our area, all of a sudden, overnight, he and his family disappeared. No one knew what happened to them. The rumors were always that he was ready to go anytime.

These were our neighbors. Next to Gecse was Gerenyi and his family. In the next building lived Török and his family. They had a large yard, wide and long. They were also well established and their children were married and had two buildings. Their building was newer and built very well.

In the Török family was a grandmother who used to prepare medicine from weeds. Some of those preparations or directions how to use the weeds were better than what the doctors would have prescribed in those days. Her medicine helped. My brother David is an example. He was taken into the Army. He was going on the train to the Army and the window was open. He rested his arm on the window and the train traveled fast. David was young at that time, he didn't realize what happened, but he got a draft and he could not use his right arm. He was discharged because of that and the government didn't do anything to help him. When he arrived home he went to private doctors. They tried everything possible, even injections, and nothing helped. This grandmother, Török neni,[21] told my brother what to do and he followed

---

[21] **néni** – Hungarian for "aunt" or "Ms.," used as a respectful or affectionate term for an older woman, not necessarily a relative.

her advice. She gave him some weeds and told him to soak his arm and hand in warm water with them. It helped and eventually it cured his right arm and hand.

On another occasion, as a young girl I was doing something and all of a sudden my finger was hurting me. I started to help myself. We had our own knowledge what to do. There was a drugstore in Helmec and if we needed something we were able to get it there. Our mother was not alive, but my father used to go there and he got anything we needed in this pharmacy. It was like a second doctor. It was natural to go there first, and there they recommended what to do and gave us medication over-the-counter. The pharmacist gave some sort of a solution or ointment since we couldn't run to a doctor with everything. Usually it helped, but this time nothing helped. My finger was so bad I could hardly stand the pain. I was crying. My father took me over to Török neni and she went into the other room and made some mixture in a pot and she gave it to us. She told us how often to change the dressing. I tried this mixture that our neighbor gave me and it helped me and my finger was getting better. She told me that I could have lost my finger because it was very inflamed. I must have had an infection. I should have gotten a real doctor before I went to the pharmacy. This lady across the street did not have any medical background, but she must have learned from her grandparents about home remedies. We knew her very well. Anyway she helped us and did not charge anything for it. She did it from her heart and also as a friend. She did not need the money because she was well-to-do.

A couple of years later my sister-in-law, Etelka, my brother's wife, had a little girl and she was named after my mother. Her name was Lenke. We tried to help out the best we could. We all got along well. We all loved their children.

Our roads were not paved. In the summer, it was dusty all around. The sidewalks were not paved either. When it rained we walked in the mud up to our ankles and sometimes more. Our shoes were made so they will go up high enough so that we could walk in this type of situation. We did not have electricity, and we used oil for lighting.

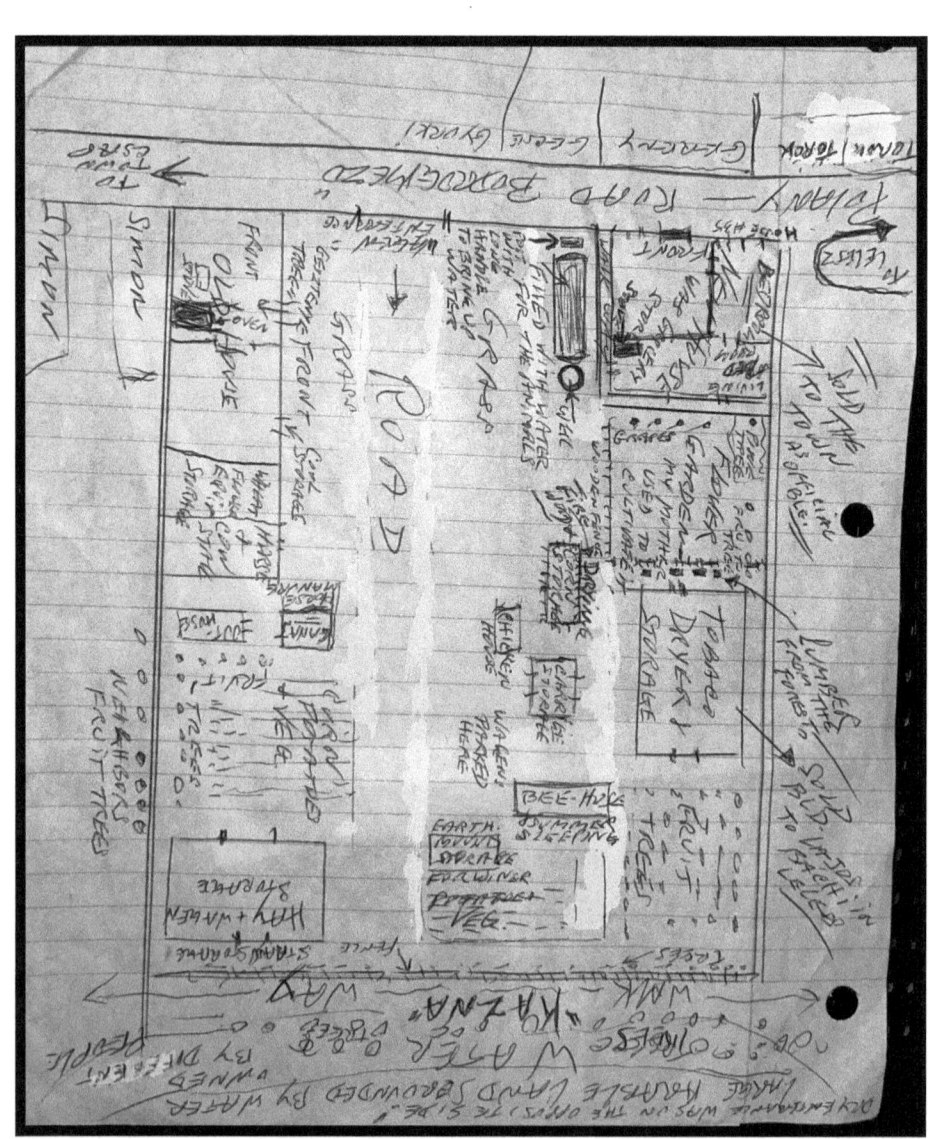

Hand-drawn map of the property in Polyán - by Irving ~2010

Chapter 5
Our Escape to America

The last time our Uncle Julius came to visit us from America, my brother Dezső tried to get to know him. He wanted to come to America. He was older. At this time life was as usual, we didn't have any problems. It was still peaceful and there were no rumors going around. My brother tried to convince my uncle to help him to come to America. We would pay all the expenses for anything he had to do. Dezső asked my uncle to give an affidavit. It was necessary as a guarantee that he will not depend upon the government for support.

At that time we lived in Czechoslovakia and from there it was no problem. It was much easier to come to America and there was no waiting. It took both sides time to get all the papers together that were needed, the visa, the money, and also the papers from America. My uncle was not willing, but somehow someway his son Arthur would do it. He was in the manufacturing business making scales, conveyors, and industrial equipment. Finally he did it. He sent the necessary papers.

After that, rumors were going around which we did not know, but our uncle in America heard that some sort of a problem was going on in Europe. They never realized what would happen. Because of that, his son sent the papers very quickly to get my brother out and in 1938 my brother succeeded and was on his way to America. We were also considering to come to America, namely the two girls and the two boys at this time and therefore, we had to try to sell our new building. The question was who will buy it. We needed to do it in a hurry and there was no time to waste. Finally, the town leaders in our town decided that it would be useful as an official building for the town. They did not have one, and our building was new and was very good for that purpose. Finally our father succeeded and sold the building. Shortly thereafter, Dezső, now David, arrived in America and went directly to Columbus, Ohio where my uncle lived with his son and family and we too were preparing our papers to get ready to go. This was in 1938.

After David arrived he started working, but he couldn't speak the language. It was difficult to get a job without knowing the language. He couldn't get a job that he really wanted to do, therefore, he had no choice in the beginning - he had to do whatever he was able to do to get work or else. Later he tried to help us to get the papers, that is, the affidavit. By then the rumors became stronger. Bertha, our cousin who was also in America, wrote to our uncle and our cousin in Ohio. They knew very well that we were hard workers, he had seen this many times when he came to Europe to our house, and we were good people. I and my sister Hermina finally convinced our uncle to help us because here in Europe where we lived there was no future for us.

Our cousin Arthur sent us the affidavits for four of us: for my sister Hermine and me, and Herman and Ignác. He's the one we owe our lives to.

He's the one who saved our lives. He is the one we all should remember - for what he did. We began to prepare our papers and put everything together. The war was about to begin and we did not have time to waste. This was in 1938 and the rumors were very strong. My brother Irving, the youngest was supposed to go to college. At this point, everything stopped. Both he and my other brother Herman had to do homeguard training, and Herman even began hard labor. All in preparation for war. We used to hear people coming around and telling us about what's going on in Germany - it was unbelievable. This story was a well-kept secret but the situation was very bad. Little by little we heard more stories and saw more people running away. No one would ever imagine the stories to be real, but in America there was more of the real story. Finally all our travel papers were ready. We received a telegram from Prague that permitted us to go there and get the papers, and from there to go to America.

At the same time that we received the telegram from Prague with everything ready, the war in Czechoslovakia broke out and it was invaded by Germany. At that point after the invasion it was very difficult or dangerous to go to Prague. Our father decided to wait until perhaps they'll stop fighting - it was better to wait at home. We were just hoping, but instead of getting better the situation became worse. The war spread and the fighting did not stop. Our father got information that the Czechoslovakian passport will not be good and we will not be able to use it. There was no chance to use the papers from Czechoslovakia. We were in a hurry to make new papers to get out through Budapest, Hungary.

Now we needed new papers and had to start all over again creating more expense and requiring more money - which was also running out. We needed it for the trip. The situation was getting from bad to worse. We were hoping to get the papers faster. Father was very busy. People from everywhere were trying to get out by then and they were getting worried also. Finally, we got the papers before it was too late. My sister Hermine and Herman went to Budapest because she thought she would be able to finalize the necessary documents faster. We were able to get the permission because we had all the arrangements before from Czechoslovakia, therefore, we were going to go to America. By then my sister had gotten all the papers we needed and we had the permission to leave the country.

As my sister was making arrangements with the shipping companies to get four tickets, she was told that they would give it to us only if we pay with American dollars. They were not accepting Pengös, the Hungarian money.

My G-d! Now the second time we were ready, how could this happen to us? My sister Hermine sent a telegram to our Uncle Julius and told him what has happened. We have the money, but we weren't able to convert it into dollars. Also, the ship was leaving soon and this was our last chance to go with this ship. Leaving in just a couple of days, it was the last one to leave Europe from the Cunard Companies lines. I don't remember for sure, but we had all our passports. The two boys received their passports in Budapest. The ship company okayed two tickets only, but we needed four. We were waiting restlessly. When all of a sudden a telegram came from Helmec telling us that only two tickets arrived and that our sister sent a telegram to America, and she cannot get the dollars in time. This was our the last hope. Ignác and I were waiting and hoping that maybe we'll hear good news. Meantime our sister was frantically checking to see if the answer came from America. No answer. She was very upset at the Embassy and started to cry loudly. She wanted all of us to go out together after all that she went through and all the money spent. We have the money but no dollars. All of a sudden someone there yelled out, here we just got the telegram and the money in dollars! Now all four tickets were ready, but we missed the ship! It sailed from Trieste, Italy and Ignác and I were still back at home. My sister sent a telegram to come at once without delay because we got the tickets. We have to go to Naples to get the ship! We must come tomorrow... this is the last chance!

It was dangerous everywhere, but at that time we had a very heavy winter with heavy snow like a mountain high. We didn't have any way of getting the telegram so my sister sent it to our uncle Márton in Helmec. He had to get a man on a horse to make a special delivery to us to make it in time. We had no time to waste, leave your home in a hurry! Our father helped us to pack and our brother Lajos got ready a sleigh and horses in a hurry. We went to Helmec and then, to Perbenik to get the train to go to Budapest. There Hermine and Herman were waiting for us and we were all together, the four of us. We were young so there was someone who was helping us with whatever we had to do. Finally we went through Yugoslavia overnight and then checked our papers at the border and we stopped in Naples. We were there for a short while waiting for the ship to arrive. The journey was long and dangerous because of the war.

Before my brother David left home, he gave me a beautiful necklace - it was made in Czechoslovakia. It wasn't a custom-made. It was a crystal that was set in platinum - it was very unusual, in a cluster setting. I never had seen one like it anywhere. I was very happy to have it - that I would keep it forever. I did not have a chance to wear it. I was very seasick on the ship. It lasted until we arrived to America - my sister Hermine wasn't so sick.

There was a young man who was in charge with us in the ship who helped us. I wanted to give him a gift. He deserved it. I wanted to show him I appreciated whatever he did. Under the circumstances, we did not have any money. And as I was searching, I could not find anything else - only my necklace. I was trying to make a decision. I came to the conclusion and decided to give it to this man. He was such an extraordinary person, I just could not walk away without giving him something. And that's what I did. When I came to America, I was looking all over to get one like that. There was none.

Many years later I was looking back - I was thinking. I hoped he returned to his family safely - this happened to be the last ship. We were very lucky to be here in America - safe - after what we went through, I was happy with what I did. I always cared for people - I never was selfish. I wasn't rich - worked very hard trying to make a living. If anyone tried to help me, I was always grateful. I still feel the same way. I did not have any idea how much that necklace was worth - I wasn't concerned about that.

He was an Italian man, but it did not matter who he was - in my mind, he was one of the nicest people, and I was grateful. And because Czechoslovakia is not in existence anymore, we cannot have a duplicate - never will be. I'm sure the price went up. But it does not matter now. We lost much more than that. We lost our property and our family - what was priceless - all in the Holocaust era. And that is much more than anything in the world - cannot be replaced.

When we arrived to New York I felt fine. We arrived February 21, 1940. Our cousin Bertha was the only one who came to bail us out from the ship. She made all the arrangements. They checked all our bags and papers and finally she took us to her home. She lived in the Bronx. They had a very small apartment - no children. We had dinner there and that night we had to go to Aunt Jenny - she had more room. It wasn't too close to her house. We went to Manhattan by car. We met the family for the first time, and stayed there only one night.

We didn't have any money left for the train to go to Columbus, where our Uncle Julius lived and David. I think it was $50 to get to Columbus. Bertha sent a letter to my brother David for money so we could go there.

When we arrived to our aunt's house it was quite late. We took our first bath there. She wanted to be sure that we are clean and everything spotless. And finally she gave my sister a pocketbook as a gift. I'm sorry even to say it, it was a very cheap one it may have cost her a dollar. My sister used to say that it was nice. Why couldn't they buy another one for me also? I did not get anything from them, not even a cheap bag. When we arrived, we went through cross examination. They did not speak our language well, and we did not speak English. Bertha translated. We tried to learn a few words here and there. You can imagine how difficult it was. By the time we cleaned up, after a shower, all of us were exhausted. We went to sleep very, very late because my aunt kept on talking and talking. We got up and we were told that someone will take us to the train to go to Columbus. This was our final destination. That day was President Washington's birthday. It was a holiday.[22]

---

[22] February 22, was a national holiday in the United States at the time.

Chapter 6
Welcome to Columbus: Starting Over in America

The next day at noon we finally arrived in Columbus. Then we had a better welcome. Especially our brother - our brother David waited for us there. It was a very happy reunion. He took us home. Our Uncle Julius set up a small furnished apartment for us, which was very nice of him to do that. We had 3 beds, a small kitchen, and small dinette with one sofa bed and some chairs and another small living room. It looked very nice.

This apartment was on the top of the Kruger grocery store - our uncle owned the building. It wasn't a bad section and we were very happy there. By this time everything caught up with me. I started to have headaches. We arrived during the week and by the weekend on Sunday, we already had people visiting us. Our uncle was arranging jobs for us. It's not what we would want or take. Even though we couldn't speak English, we started to learn real fast. We learned in Europe some. We had gotten a Hungarian-English dictionary, and we were good students and learned important words. We understood more, but we spoke only a little. In Europe, I was a dressmaker and it was different there. In Europe, dressmaking was very expensive and I tried to learn to do the best I can. When we came to America, I needed some clothing. I used to make it for ourselves. I made Spring coats by hand. It was very nice. It took me a while to make it.

I will go back to Uncle Julius. When we arrived to Columbus, OH, the next day we settled down. Our uncle had already arranged to have a job for all of us - it did not matter what we were able to do - just a job. He did not care what kind of job. He would not waste - not a minute! We could have had a better job, but he did not know us. He knew what he wanted - we must have a job - and he did it. We did not have a chance even to look around - I was 23 years old.

My sister was first. One day, a woman came with my Uncle to interview my sister. She was very nice. She needed someone to help her. She went to work and she had children. She wasn't sure if my sister could handle it because Hermine was very young. She was only 25 years of age - and beautiful. Also, she was a very good cook and baker. She was able to do anything and everything. My uncle assured the woman that my sister did it at home. She spoke Yiddish and so did the woman. She hired her immediately - five days Monday to Friday, sleep - in, and she will come home on the weekend. They were husband, wife, and four children going to school. They were businesspeople, but didn't pay much. She could have done much better with another job and more money. She went there as a housekeeper. This included cooking, taking care of the children, cleaning the house, and whatever they needed her to do. We promised that we will do anything we need to do. There was no choice. But for that work she should have gotten more money. As young as she was, she was one of the best cooks and bakers - and she was a very hard worker. It is a shame Uncle Julius did not take time to give her a chance to get an easier job. She was very smart - was able to do other things. But it seems he did not care.

Now as I look back - when he used to come to visit us in Europe, we treated him very nice - especially my sister. Every morning she made breakfast - special for him. After that, he made sure to walk in the garden - our uncle loved flowers, and we had beautiful ones - all kinds of flowers - roses. Our sister knew that. Therefore, she made sure to put different flowers every morning in his coat lapel. He used to stay with us for a couple of weeks, and my sister never forgot to do that. Our uncle was very happy and loved our sister especially. When our mother was with us, she did the same. We never asked him for any money or payment.

With me, Uncle Julius had someone too, also for a housekeeping job, but I wasn't feeling well. He decided that I will not be able to work as a housekeeper. He looked around and a couple of days later he found me a job at a dry cleaning store where they needed someone to do alterations. After cleaning, if they had any damage or buttons missing, I was to repair them as it was before. It was easy. The owner was very nice. My uncle spoke with him. He looked me over. He looked happy to see me. My uncle was proud of me, and the man liked me immediately. He hired me. This was my first job. They had many people working there and my sister could have done the same. It would have been much easier for all of us.

The forelady, who was in charge there was very nice and befriended me. From then on, we became friends. and she admired my boots. They were different because in Europe when we came it was very cold winter and heavy snow. These were the best boots that I ever had.

I don't remember how much she paid, but I'm sure it was not the top price. I worked five days a week for about nine hours a day. I travelled by bus and had to be there by 8 AM. The lady was in charge and she was very nice to me. She talked to me in English. She was happy with what I did because I had the knowledge how to do it. That is, I knew how to sew. I was able to do it without being able to speak the language, but little by little I learned and I wanted to learn more. The traveling wasn't easy. It was time consuming.

Every Sunday I had to prepare complete dinner because my Uncle Julius and his wife came over for dinner. I was by myself doing the shopping and preparing for the dinner and cleaning our apartment. I washed all the beddings and all the clothing for the boys and myself. It was just like in Europe the only difference was that it was in a bath tub. We did not have knowledge and money to use a washing machine. I don't even know if there was any at the time.

On the weekend my sister came home. So with my other brothers and David, he also moved in with us, it was a family. When Uncle Julius came we had to give him some money to save for us. Every Sunday, he used to come to collect the money - even if it was one dollar. He opened a bank account for each of us to deposit it into the bank. He said that if you don't have enough money, you still must learn to save. Even if it's fifty cents each time, even that will help to accumulate and before you know it, it will grow. Each time you have a chance you have to add to it, even a penny. You will learn how you can manage your money. Because when you need it, no one will give it to you. We learned that very fast. Once a month he charged rent for the apartment we lived in. It was automatic. I worked very hard all week, long hours and the traveling back and forth - and did the shopping. And hand washing all those linens for the bedding - sheets took close to an hour! By Sunday, our home was spotless.

Herman was only 21 years old. He also wanted to work. He worked for our cousin Arthur in the machine shop, helping to make conveyors and crushers. He was an inventory person.

Ignác was just 18 years old and he went to study English, first in high school, and then in the University. He worked as a night watchman in a paint factory and he maintained the boilers with coal during the night. During the day he went to school. Our uncle did a good job. All of us worked and were happy, but unhappy too. This didn't matter to anyone.

After a couple months working in the dry cleaning store, I asked the forelady if she could help my sister and give her a job. She answered yes. And then I felt that my sister didn't have to work as hard as she did. The lady said that she will talk to my sister whenever Hermine wanted. I told my sister she could leave her job. And she should come to the place where I work and it will be much easier.

A couple days later she left her job and came to the place where I worked. Our supervisor liked us both. We became very friendly. She took us out to a nightclub. We told her we do not eat outside, but she insisted that we can find something to eat. We had no choice, so we did. Other times we invited her to our home to have dinner with us. We remained friends with our forelady from that place for a long time.

My sister learned the language faster than I and she began to look for another job. She found one in a very large department store, namely the Lazarus department store. She was a saleslady. Her first job was to sell gloves. She was very ambitious. She was a very good saleslady. They liked her very much and she was doing very well. She also had to do minor bookkeeping.

After that she decided to go to work in an office. She was looking for a place where they would hire her and train her for the job. She went to be interviewed and got the job. It was in a movie theater's office; this was an accounting office. At that time they used a comptometer. It was like an adding machine, but much more complicated. She was very happy and it was good for her because she wanted to improve her life and receive more money. Finally she was on her way up.

As you remember, I talked about it how she managed and fought for everything, step by step, to get what she needed. She was very smart. She was very responsible for all four of us including David. She knew a little Yiddish and understood some German. And when they were talking to her she was able to adjust herself accordingly. For a girl her age and coming from a small village, she educated herself very well. She was reading and even corresponding in English. She was very brave. She was liked by whomever she met. She wasn't shy and once she made up her mind she was able to whatever she wanted to do. I was just the opposite. I was also very persistent, and did it in the long run. I studied in Europe and I was very good in math. My sister used to ask me why I don't get a job in an office? She wanted me to learn the machine that she was working on and to do what she did.

But I always liked to sew. As I was growing up, I tried to create a doll from a dress and make their clothes. I always was very careful which way it looked the best. I used to make beautiful dresses - they looked very pretty. And later on, I made my own clothes - my own ideas - something different. I didn't want to see myself in the same dress walking on the street. It was a small village - it wouldn't be a good idea for me. I tried to create different ideas, different clothes. I also must mention all my sewing came from used clothes.

Later on, as I was growing up, walking or going somewhere, I was stopped to ask - where did I get that dress? When I told them, they admired it because I looked different. I had a very nice figure - like a model - looked different. I haven't seen someone else walking around like me, like a twin sister.

When we came to America, I wore those dresses that I created from those old clothes that Uncle Julius sent to us in Europe. They were beautiful, so I used them to make our own clothes - they looked beautiful. You could never tell. Our cousin Bertha's husband was a designer for one of the high fashion companies. When he saw me, that was in New York the day we arrived here - we had dinner there - it happened I wore one of my skirts and a blouse. It looked beautiful, I must say. When he saw me - the first look - he asked me where did you get this blouse? I was surprised - why did he ask me that question?

It was very simple, but the blouse had a different style - and the print was also perfect with the style. It looked beautiful, and unusual. When I told him I made it, he asked me, "Where did you learn how to sew?" He was amazed when I told him. He examined it very carefully, inside and outside. Believe me or not, he got some ideas from that one.

I could have continued in that line of work. This was one of the occasions. There was another opportunity. It was a clothing designer's job.

I tried to get a better job for more money. Whenever I saw an ad in the newspaper - or I'd just walk in to ask if they had any openings for any job - I could feel I was not afraid. I had the courage - maybe I will try and see - nothing to lose and something to gain.

I knew as I was getting around, they would usually show you what your job was, and from then on I learned how to get around and was able to see what I wanted to do. I was very observant and was willing to do whatever I needed. I could not see any problems. Comparing Columbus to New York City - there weren't too many opportunities to choose jobs, and there were no subways around - only buses. The transportation wasn't good. We had to change buses a few times - it depended on where you were going.

Besides all these ads, I learned and managed to get interviews - sometimes it wasn't the job I would like to have. Sometimes you do not know unless you go and see for yourself - and then you decide if it is what you are looking for. It was never easy. Sometimes I became frustrated. Sometimes it took a little longer to find a better job. Sometimes they did not like that I did not speak the language - or it was just an excuse - although I myself did not like that person. The first look was important.

Each time I changed a job, the next one I tried to get a better job with more money. That's the only way to improve yourself in the job field - get more money with it. On the way, I learned how to succeed, and on every job I learned something different - all gave education to better my life.

I want to go back to the designer's job. I was still in Columbus. I was looking for different jobs and answered a newspaper advertisement - sewing or cashier - anywhere. I knew I can do it.

I looked up manufacturing, where they do all kinds of sewing. I did need a job - I must find one. Next day, I tried and went in. I was still wearing clothes I made. By then, I started to sew more clothes for both of us - my sister and myself - also I designed them. I never used ready-made patterns. It was different. People gave compliments. I must say, they looked very nice and did not look homemade. I made it better.

When I went to look for a job, it was at a company manufacturing men's suits. It did not matter what kind of sewing - men's or women's or anything else - I hoped I would be able to do the job.

The man came out and greeted me. He looked to be a nice person. He asked me questions. He could see I just came to America, just by looking at me. He was very nice. I told him I am looking for a job - I do some sewing - my own clothes - and I designed them also. I am not a dressmaker by trade, but I am able to sew and design my own clothes, and I am wearing one of them.

Then he looked at me and said, "We do not have the job that you are looking for." He asked me if I knew how to make a culotte.[23] At first, I didn't understand the name - what he asked. Then he explained it to me, so I understood what he would like to have.

At that time, women did not wear slacks - which is what he really wanted. It was something new. There weren't too many around then. They were making better men's clothing, and now he would like to have a woman's suit.

One skirt on the outside - inside would be shorts. They couldn't tell it wasn't a skirt. As they walked, the skirt in the front would open up - and then

---

[23] A culotte is a garment that resembles a skirt but is actually split like pants - essentially wide-legged shorts or trousers that give the appearance of a skirt. At the time, it was a new and bold fashion choice for women, who typically did not wear pants in public.

it showed the shorts. This was the latest fashion just coming out. Therefore, if I could make it, it would cost him much less than a professional designer who was already doing that. I told him I understood what he wanted. I would need someone as a model so I could take measurements and see how it fits. I never did that before, but if he gave me the opportunity, I would try to create one - so he could see how he likes it.

I felt I am able to do that. He asked me, "When can you start?" "Okay, you could come in and I'll give you a chance." I took the job temporarily to see what I can do. The next week, I went in. They took me in. There was a large room with a large table, and it looked like a designer's room - everything. I just had to start. Then a young lady came in. She was a nice young lady. I took her measurements - whatever I needed. I was given plenty of material to make - whatever I needed - to create that skirt with the short inside.

I was told, "You can use as much as you want to - whatever you need." I saw enough material to try my best - and as many as I wanted to create - and then I did. I remember it came very naturally. I had all the confidence. I would be able to make one for them. I knew exactly what he wanted me to make - so I did. Then he also asked me if I could make a short jacket to go with the skirt. A men's festoon. At first, I wondered - why did he ask me to make that short jacket? He wants me to make the jacket while they're making men's fashion - okay - it looks different.

He was a very nice man - he never bothered me. He came in to see me, to ask how I was doing. He gave me whatever I needed. I created both of them - the skirt and the jacket - and they looked very nice. But I wasn't a designer. I did not have any training to do that. He wasn't looking for that - he knew exactly what he wanted and had faith in me. I was there for a couple of months and kept on trying to do more than one, to see which came out better.

A couple of months later, he came in and asked me if I could make a ladies' short coat - in a men's tailoring style. He wanted a woman's jacket made just like a man's. I knew exactly what he meant - a complete suit. I told him, "I know exactly what you want. If you want me to, I'll try it."

Oh yes - he wanted me to, so I did. I was able to. I had done it for myself - why not for him?

I designed and fitted the young lady. I told him - because he was an expert in men's clothing - before I started the jacket, "I'll do it men's style, but you're the expert - I'm not. So I don't want you to be disappointed if I don't do it exactly the way you want.

I gave him whatever he wanted. Then I finished it. He came to me very nicely and explained, 'As I see it, you are able to create one - or a few - but here, since we spoke about it, I need a designer because I need to have quantity in wholesale.'

And I thanked him for giving me the opportunity to show him my ability - what I can do and create.

Yes, he liked it. He knew I did whatever he wanted - and with that, I left. That was the end.

Later I found out - I looked by myself - he used me. I made him a sample, gave him the idea, and it was very cheap. For a designer, he would have to pay much more! Therefore, he took a chance with me. He believed in me. Why not? He had nothing to lose. In a nice way, he got all the ideas - and since he already had a designer for men's clothing, now the same designer can do the ladies' too.

They can make copies without any problem - with his own designer. Why not? He was a very smart man. He got exactly what he wanted - and let's say, almost for nothing. He had the latest fashion. He would make enough money - a very smart man. A good businessman, I would say. He was the first one with this latest fashion - he came out with a good business. Especially something new like that.

This was just one occasion - there was another place. This one was a place where they made fur coats - one of them was mink - very expensive. They were looking for someone who knows how to sew in the lining in the mink coats. I answered that ad. I went for an interview - it was a very small place. They had a store downstairs in the same building. When I went in, they told me exactly what they wanted me to do. I would be one person to do the job.

I know how to, so why not? I took the job and went home. I was told to come in on Monday. I did. And when I came in, the man showed me exactly what he wanted me to do. When I looked at the work - for me, it was easy. I had my idea and was able to do it. I started to work - they gave me the coat and the lining - I should put the lining in. I did it without any problem. When I finished, they were happy. Also, I knew exactly what they wanted. I did not get the amount of money that they would have to pay someone else - but at that time, I did not care.

I was happy to have a job - whatever I could get - I had to support myself. I needed that money. I always tried to work - whatever I could. Later on, I tried to improve my jobs, but my English wasn't the best, and it took me a while to learn. I used to go to see a movie. They had the best ones. I could not understand everything. It was a silent movie. That was my best teacher. I tried to learn whatever I was able to. It helped me with my English. I was able to speak and get around, but I continued to go to a night school twice a week to learn English, and how to be a citizen. The most important thing was the language. I wanted to be able to speak because it would help me to get a better job and a better life, and get ready for my citizenship papers. This I took very seriously. I wanted to become an American citizen without any delay - it takes five years to be here to get it. I was the happiest person when I did.

And with better English, I was able to improve my life. I never gave up. I was always ready and willing to do whatever I had to. It was difficult to find the right job. I went through hardship, just like anyone else. It wasn't easy sometimes. I wiped my tears off my face and went home disappointed.

In Columbus, I was working a second job that David got me with better pay, but longer traveling time. It was a balloon factory. They taught me how to use their paint on the balloon when there was an order for it. I'm talking about a large balloon they used to use in the war. Everyone did a different job. I had to go in a hot oven where they made the plastic for the balloon. I had to clean it with alcohol most of the time. I was there for a while, then I decided to look for something else.

Barrage Balloon training in Camp Tyson, Tennessee.
Library of Congress, LC-USE6-D-008677

As I mentioned before, I was very good in math even though I didn't speak well, so I could become a cashier. I tried at the place where my sister was working, at Lazarus' department store. I mentioned that I was looking for a job as a cashier, but I was rejected.

My next job was at a very well-known nightclub - one of the biggest. It was very busy. It was something different. They were looking for one person for a cashier job. I went for an interview - it seems I was able to do the job even though I never did this type of work. I had to work at night and I was the only cashier sitting in a small cubicle and a tiny little window facing me, where the waitresses paid the customers' bills.

They showed it to me - what I needed to do. I had to add up their bill, get the total, without an adding machine, and had to charge two kinds of tax: a sales tax, and a nightclub tax. I was told how much to charge. I had to do it very fast - you have no time to lose - not even a minute. I must say, you had to be one of the best who knows how to add or deduct and figure out at the same time how much tax I should charge - both were different percentages. I was surprised myself, as I go back - how did I do that? Where did I get that brain? I don't know, but I did it. I did not feel nervous or worried about it - and did not hesitate. I always have confidence in myself. I know I can do the job, and I always did. I was never let go because I did not do the job right.

The boss told me that he will give me a try that night. If I was able to make it and everything was okay, then I was hired.

The hall was very large and they served food and liquor. To my surprise, there was also dancing. They were very busy. The waitresses brought the money from the customers. The tip was included in the bill and I had to add them up very fast. And I made sure that I was doing it correctly. I was responsible for every penny. If it was not correct then I had to pay the difference.

The next day, my supervisor came in and he told me I did a good job. If I want to have a job, they were very happy with my work - I did everything very well. They liked me. Every penny was there. It was not short. In my experience, I was never short. The taxes and everything was perfect. I liked it. I took the job. Going home at late hours, I had to take a bus. The food there was not kosher, this wasn't a Jewish place. The food was vegetable or a sandwich, but when time came to eat, at dinnertime, it was very busy and I didn't have a chance to eat. There was no time for it. I was very hungry, and a couple of weeks later I went into the kitchen and asked the cook for mashed potatoes, because I was very hungry. That was my pay. I was told that I can have whatever I wanted. I told them that I cannot eat meat. The hostess who was in charge - she was very happy with me. Usually she would serve me, but once she screamed at me, "Don't bother me, I'm too busy." I got very upset and went home.

The next day I called the manager and told him what happened and that I was very upset and I do not want to go back to work. He asked me to come back and said that he will straighten out the situation. He said that I should have asked the hostess because she would have helped me, but I did not go back to work. Instead I decided to go back to pick up my pay. The hostess said I should have come back when they asked me. She spoke to my boss and was told because I did not come back when he asked me, now he doesn't want me. I didn't want to go back anyway. It was a very hard job and for that type of work I wasn't getting enough money for what I was doing. To get sick over it wasn't worth it.

I needed the job, but I began to look for another one. It took awhile to get a job. I was looking full-time to get a job. This time I got a job in a well known hotel. The food was very expensive. It was a very nice place. It was a one-person office. Lunchtime was very busy. There was no music at any time. I worked as a breakfast and lunch cashier. At least I liked it. I was there for a while. Where I was working it was very cold and there was too much draft. I dressed properly. I started to have lots of pain in my back and my side. At first, I didn't think anything of it.

Meantime even though I was going to night school to learn English, I learned on the job whatever I had to do. If at any time I couldn't remember something, I looked it up in my notes. It was much easier.

Two ladies used to come in and it happened to be the hotel manager who was afraid to hire me because she thought that I wasn't good enough. The other lady, her friend, said you did not like her and this is a big place and she's very good. She was very nice to me. Wherever I went I was doing a good job. I was good at it, but I had to leave this job because of my health.

I always took my job very seriously. I was, and still am, a perfectionist - even though no one is perfect in this world. We all make mistakes. I did also - just not on the job. Private life - that is a different story.

Just before I left Columbus, the last job was in a grocery store in a very rich neighborhood, not too far from my home. There I received more money, because I was paid only cash and wages, not food. I worked there very hard. I had to go there by bus in the early hours - luckily it wasn't too far from me. My job was as a cashier at the checkout counter. I also had to mark the prices on the items and place them up wherever they were supposed to be. My supervisor there told me he was happy with my work. When my sister asked me to come to New York, I gave them notice. I was told, "If you ever need a job, or come back to Ohio, you always have a job here." As I look back, I remember all my jobs. I was happy with every one of them.

I worked there until I left for New York. Our cousin Bertha wanted us to come to New York because in Columbus there wasn't too much of a chance to meet people. She felt that in New York we have a better chance.

Hermine decided to stay in New York. She decided to rent a room only. We thought that later, when Herman and Irving will come to live in New York, we will make different plans but sometimes plans don't work out. It was a very difficult decision to make. I felt that Irving had just come home from the Army. He was in hell. I wanted to be with him when he needed me most. I had a terrible time to make up my mind. Hermine needed me also. She came to New York for a better life. Without me it would be more difficult for her to get adjusted. And I was also told that I will get a better job there. Finally, I left Columbus.

After the Army, Irving decided that he wanted to go to the Ohio State University, one of the best colleges. My cousin Arthur graduated from there and was a respected and active alumnus, and now his son was going there also. Irving did not have to pay because he was a veteran on the G.I. Bill of Rights. Therefore, he remained in Columbus.

Let me go back to before I went to New York. As I mentioned before, Herman was working for our cousin in the manufacturing business. After a while he left and worked in a drug store and then again cousin Arthur asked him to return to work for him. He was able to speak English much better. He was a very bright young man who was able to learn to use various machinery and different tools. They were quite complicated machines. After he left my cousin's business the second time, he worked in another machine shop. At this place, it was piece work - they paid according to the amount he produced. This was for the war production. He was happy making more money.

I also mentioned before that when we came to America, Irving worked in a paint manufacturing company, and was going to school.

Then, in March 1943 Irving was called into the Army. My G-d, we were all falling apart. Heartaches again, one after another. Soon after, he went to Camp Wolters, Texas. First he didn't know where he was going, but as he arrived he called us and told us he was in the infantry training. He wanted to go to Europe. He felt maybe he would be able to see and help our family, maybe to save them from the Germans and the Hungarian brownshirts.[24] This was his idea. He didn't think otherwise. We could not change it anyway. When he went into the army, he wasn't a citizen yet, but it didn't matter, he became a citizen later in North Africa. He actually volunteered for the infantry. All this came through within the drafting system.

When we learned what was going on there, we lived in fear by day and night and were praying, worrying. Was it not enough that we left our family in Europe? We were hoping maybe by chance Irving will get in contact with our family, but this was just a dream, we knew that it was almost impossible. How could he? But inside we were hoping and were afraid. I don't know which one was the worst. There was nothing we could do to help. We tried to write to our family, but there was no communication from either side. It was also difficult to write to Irving to find out where he was because there was no address and it was only a military address referring to New York. It took a long time before finally he wrote to us.

Going back to 1940, that year, we heard from our family. Our oldest brother, Lajos, was taken to the Hungarian army. We only had a few letters from them and after that the letters we sent came back. There was no communication with Europe.

Germany was moving into Hungary and the whole situation there was horrible. We lived in a nightmare not knowing what was happening to our family - to the children, to our father, and to our brother Lajos. When Irving and I left our home in Polyáni, we did not have a chance to think it over that we were leaving our family behind. My father who went through so much, and now once again they were crying. I see my brother's face when we left. He was crying and calling out, "Don't work hard and take care of yourselves!" Father cried out, "We will not forget you. You are a family, take care of each other, help each other!" We planned to write once we will be in America. We hoped that in a short time we would be settled and we would be able to bring the whole family to America.

My father planned to sell everything. Then they would have enough money to come here, but this plan disappeared. The Germans changed all

---

[24] **Hungarian brownshirts** – Members of the fascist Arrow Cross Party, allies of Nazi Germany who carried out mass killings and deportations of Jews in 1944–45.

this. From Hungary it was impossible even in good times. The system[25] there would have taken years for a person to get out from there. But from Czechoslovakia there would have been no problem during 1938, however our uncle did not help us, what a mistake. They were afraid that they would be stuck with us. And to come to America later was impossible.

Other cousins wanted to come to America also but they were also given up by my uncle and cousin. On the other hand, they were scared from us and worried, they wanted to stop us from coming here, they wanted to cancel all of us at the last moment because other cousins wanted to come also. The only thing that saved us at the last minute was that our father and uncle Lazar bacsi, who lived in our village, wrote to Lazar's daughter Bertha. She lived in New York. They wrote asking her and telling her to intervene because that would be a big mistake to cancel our journey to America.

They could have come if they wanted to. They would have had to pay their expenses also. They had families. The four cousins were older than we were. Also, when our uncle Julius came to Europe he stayed with us, we took care of him. Sometimes we did not have enough money to entertain him. We had to borrow some. To make it short, he was very happy with us. We really liked him. My father always corresponded with him. Why did he come to visit us if he did not like us? We never charged him any money for what we did. So, therefore I felt he could do us this favor.

My father wasn't able to see well without eyeglasses. Without glasses he couldn't see anything. I must say, he did have a very hard life. He was able to find anything anywhere and he was able to speak to anyone. He could write and approach people with their proper title in the business and these people respected him in the community.

Europe's life was different. It was a small country, not like in America where everyone is Mr. or Mrs. There in Hungary or Czechoslovakia you've got to give them the proper title. That meant a lot to those people. If you used the proper title they were more inclined to be helpful. You had to be very careful how to address these officials. All this was before the war. My father was very well respected in the community as well as in the government offices. My father himself worked very hard just before the war.

Our mother's sickness was very expensive and took a lot of money. Therefore with all that hard work no one would ever believe it that we didn't have enough money. We did not know what will be the next day.

We could have sold some property. I don't know why we didn't, it was very good land. It was not the right time or there wasn't the right person, a buyer, who would pay the right price for it. Therefore, we struggled and did what we could. From the outside they thought that we were rich, but inside it was a different story. My sister-in-law Etelka wrote to us in her last letter that when you left us, you all will forget about us. But should you care what happens to us she wrote that they didn't have much food to eat, they had a

---

[25] The U.S. quota system, established by the Immigration Act of 1924, greatly limited the number of immigrants from Eastern and Southern Europe.

flood in the village, and at the same time our brother Lajos, was taken into the Hungarian army. There was no one to help after the water receded. They had no food, and no horses, everything was gone. In our backyard we used to raise vegetables, potatoes. But now my sister-in-law was all alone and had five children, one was born after we came to America, his name was Zolika.[26] She was telling us how tired she was. She was working in the yard by herself so that they would have some food planted. She wrote that our father was crying a lot. He was happy to know that at least we are safe. He did not know that Ignác was in the army, since by then there was no communication and the war was on.

Etelka wrote that she had to get ready to go to bed because it was too late and she was very tired. At the same time my brother Lajos came home for one day and he too wanted to write, but his hands were shaking so much that he asked her to write to us. This was the last letter we had from them.

In this same letter our little nephew wrote to us saying that he wished he could be with us and wrote to uncle David. "We do not have too much, but you know everything. I cannot tell you. When will we see you, we hope soon." We still have that letter - my brother saved it all those years.

He asked me, what we will do with all these letters? I took a look to see what he had there. To my surprise he found in a box of letters from our father, grandfather, our uncle Márton. Letters from Irving, during the war years. All these letters are very interesting - it is a treasure for us. I decided to put them all in a book. And that's what I did. I put all those letters into about 30 albums. I tried to put them according to the dates written or received. It is very impressive. Now you can take a look one at a time and pick up any book and read those letters. At the present time, Irving decided to translate them into English. This way his children will be able to read it and may write our history.[27] Therefore, I'm writing this my way. I am trying to remember everything that I can, the original way, and I hope that I will be able to finish it.

---

[26] Another daughter was born to them, Kornélia, on August 17, 1942.

[27] *Private Good Luck*. Tisza Publishing. 2019 and *Pappus, The Saga of a Jewish Family*. Tisza Publishing. 2021

Chapter 7
Army Induction and the War

I will go back to write about my brother Herman. He was also called into the Army. He was drafted. He had to report for exams.[28] After Irving had to report for the exam he had to go to a training camp in Texas. Herman remained in Columbus. The five of us still lived in Columbus at that time. They assigned him for k.p. duties.[29]

He was young and he did not understand English. He wasn't a strong person. We took care of him at home. He was very smart and he was a very good child, just like all of us. We all have a tender loving feeling. He was a special child and was a very good person. When he was going to school he was a good student. He received good grades at all times. I think because of the language difficulties they put him on k.p. duty. He worked in the kitchen most of the time. He was doing the dishes. He worked very hard and was there working long hours, more than at home. He became sick from doing all those assignments and working on the dirty dishes. It was enough to get sick from it. We treated him like a baby at home. After he was sick they transferred him into the hospital. He felt better. With another job assignment similar to that he would become sick again. He was reclassified.[30] After that he was discharged from the Army. He was very lucky that he was able to come home. I think after that time our cousin took him back to work in his business. He manufactured scales and crushers for the industry. There he did whatever was assigned to him, but during that same time he was going to night school, as we all did.

The Jewish community had a special set up for foreigners, like we were, they were teaching us English. We were graded. After, he took the test to learn the citizenship requirements and to understand how to take the citizenship test. We learned how to read and write English. And also we learned the American history. It was free, they did not charge for their services. We learned fast. We wanted to be able to speak English like the natives. Irving, during the day after working at night, he went to school to learn and he picked up the language rapidly, since he also went to the University for specialized education at the Ohio State University. He learned there the proper sounds and pronunciations with specialists that were experienced in teaching the English language to foreigners.

I believe that because he was able to speak so well and was very knowledgeable, that he was taken to the army rapidly. He was a good

---

[28] Military entrance exams determined fitness for service and classification. Language skills sometimes influenced assignments.

[29] Kitchen Patrol.

[30] Military reclassification could lead to reassignment or discharge if a soldier was deemed unfit for duty.

candidate. He was in the Army close to three years. From Texas to North Africa, and from there to Italy, France and Germany as a combat infantryman and a military policeman. He has four 'bronze stars.[31]' We missed him then a lot. Thank goodness that he came home ok.

As I mentioned before, Herman was working making small tools for the war effort at a local roller bearing factory. It was a national company [Timken Roller Bearing] and they were producing bearings for the war effort. He was very happy to be helpful and of course they paid more there. He was a very fast learner. He was happy to make more money. He had his citizen papers already at the time when he worked for the war effort. They showed him how to make the parts. He was working piecework. They were very busy. They needed these parts for the army. As the war ended, the manufacturing plant let most of the people go and they had to find jobs elsewhere. Herman did the same and went to work into a different field altogether.

---

[31] **Bronze Service Star** – A small bronze device worn on a U.S. military campaign medal or service ribbon to denote participation in a specific campaign or battle.

Chapter 8
Losing Uncle Julius and Finding Our Own Way

When we came to America, our uncle set up an apartment for all of us. We lived there and we paid rent. Every weekend we saw each other. Our Uncle also came to check up on us. He wanted to be sure that we saved enough money. Our uncle lost his first wife a long time before in 1922. He travelled a lot and he visited us in Europe. He spent time in a famous resort, maybe called Carlsbad.[32] Americans used to go there for vacation. It happened that he met someone there before, and then he returned again and married this particular lady. He brought his new wife back with him to America. We did not know at that time how and why it happened. Her name was Helen.

When we came to America we met her. She was a very nice person and well-adjusted and educated. She was younger than he was. It seemed like they were very happy together. Even before she got married she spoke English very well. To us she was very nice. She invited us for dinner sometimes. We saw them often.

Our uncle was teaching us and telling us stories and how to get around. I think he was very happy and enjoyed our company. He wasn't a young man, perhaps about eighty years old. He had a heart condition. But he never told us too much, especially about his health. One day his son called that our uncle passed away. It was a terrible news! We were sorry to hear about it and we were very upset. At this time he was the only one who was close to us. While he was alive everything was okay with his son and his family, but later we found out that the situation had changed.

Our cousin Arthur decided that we had to pay more rent. By the way, our uncle owned the properties. We thought that he was doing well. He was well-established. We did not know how many apartments or buildings he had. We saw that he had a nice home. He owned it. It was not in the richest neighborhood, but it was nicely furnished. The main thing was that they were happy. I don't know if Arthur was happy with his step-mother or even if he accepted her. I don't think that he ever accepted her. When his father, that is, Uncle Julius passed away, he decided to change everything around. Finally he told her to leave, so she did. He wanted to rent the place. We thought it was a terrible thing. She wasn't young herself. She was not able to work or to look for a job. Finally, she had no place to go. In the back of the house they had a garage where our Uncle kept his car. Because she had no place to move, they decided to move her in there.

You can imagine that after so many years, she was taking care of his father and he had the nerve to do it! I felt very badly, but there was nothing she, or we could do.

---

[32] Carlsbad is a spa town (now Karlovy Vary, Czech Republic)

As far as with us, he told us to pay more rent. We decided that we better move elsewhere, if we have to pay more than what we did. We got an apartment on Linwood Avenue about 5 miles away from where we lived. Irving rode around the neighborhood with his bicycle and found this apartment. Our cousin Arthur did not allow us to take any furniture with us. We bought beds, sofas and whatever was necessary. At this time, only three of us moved to the new apartment.

This apartment was in a better place, and it was a building with many apartments. There was upstairs and downstairs. Upstairs there were two bedrooms and downstairs was a living room, dinette, and a kitchen. Also, we had a basement. We had to buy coal for the boiler and needed to take care of it, too.

Our next door neighbors were also from Europe. They were a young couple. They were also Jewish and had come from Germany. Next to us was a private home. This neighbor had a shoe store in downtown Columbus.

We had a synagogue not far from our house and our cousin belonged there. A very nice family, named Roth, lived around the corner from us. They also were originally, that is, the parents came from Europe about 50 years before. They were well-established also. They had a large family. We used to go there to visit them from time to time. They were very nice people. They owned the home. When we came to America, the parents were alive. They lived together with their daughters. Since they came from Hungary, and spoke Hungarian, we were able to talk with them.

My cousin Arthur married one of their daughters. Her name was Flora. She was very nice and she liked us. She spoke English. She was a teacher and well educated. As I remember, there were three girls. The oldest daughter never married. She had the responsibility of helping the parents. I believe, if I remember correctly, that the other two girls married. They had very good jobs and they were good-looking. They had everything, so that any man would have been happy to have them. The oldest one remained at home helping the family. I believe that maybe that was the problem - she had difficulty finding a young man. They were very choosy, and I don't blame them for it.

The youngest of the Roth girls worked for our cousin Arthur. She was in charge of the manufacturing plant and she managed the office. She was the youngest person in the family. She was quite a capable young lady. She was working there for many years and she liked my brother David. He used to see her. David was young and good-looking. The girls liked him. He was lovable. He used to know very nice educated girls. I met some of them. He wasn't interested at that time to marry. He just liked to have fun. He loved to dance. He was very outgoing. This was his character and you couldn't change him. He was that way all his life. He always did what he wanted. He was a very good brother and we all loved him. He loved us all very much.

When Arthur passed away in 1973, his son Samuel, who was married and living in New York, decided to sell the business and that was the end of this episode.

We were still in Europe when our brother David started to work in America. Our uncle found him a job. He worked for a doctor who raised dogs. He hired David to take care of them. He couldn't speak English at all. And according to what I heard later I learned, that our uncle looked for any jobs as long as they would hire him, just like with Herman, myself, Hermine, and Irving.

David was working for this doctor for a while. I'm sure that the food was included in the wages. One day a fire broke out in his place where he lived and some of the family photographs burned.[33] We had letters from him at that time and were still in Europe. The fire was fierce and he was only able to save a few things. He practically lost everything, his clothing and whatever he had. His place was burned down completely. He was lucky he saved himself. This is what he was telling us in his letters. He felt very badly and was very angry about it. He left that job.

He managed to get another job, but the income wasn't enough. He liked to go out and that was expensive. Meantime our uncle and his son got very upset with his behavior. He should have saved money.

The story goes that we were planning to come to America, but our uncle was not too happy with David because he didn't have any money even though he worked, so they were afraid that if we come out here, we will do the same thing as he did, so they were afraid. But he was able to support himself and no one helped him. He did not ask them for anything.

The biggest problem that followed, was that they wanted to stop the paperwork, and wanted to change their minds about us, because they felt that they had enough with David and thought that we would do the same thing. They were ready to stop, as I mentioned the paperwork, to prevent us from coming to America. Meantime we're getting ready with our papers - the passports, etc. We were very surprised to receive a letter stating to our father that because my brother David misbehaved and doesn't listen to them therefore they were going to stop us from coming to America. They did not want us anymore. Even though our uncle knew that we were different, we would listen, but he was very angry at that time and ready to stop everything. The rumors at home were worse every day. We were very upset. My uncle, Lajzer bacsi from our village, wrote to his daughter Bertha to try and help, and our father wrote to Uncle Julius and to David, to not stop our papers because it would be a terrible mistake. They pleaded with David to please our uncle and his son. And that David should behave to prevent this situation from getting worse.

At this time other cousins wrote to our uncle asking him to help them to come to America. It also added to our problems. We were hanging on in a very thin thread. It was like a fire ready to blow up. We had to plead with him. Finally, we succeeded to cool the situation down. I mentioned this before that we went through more than enough heartaches.

---

[33] The singe marks can be seen easily on the photograph of his Grandmother Haia Schwartz.

When I think back it seems like a dream, but it was very real. We suffered all around. With all the bumps, things worked out and finally we arrived to America. We knew whatever is going to wait for us, good or bad, we will pass it. We did what we had to do, without complaining.

Haia Moskovics Schwartz, ~73 years old, in ~1931

Chapter 9
California Dreams and New York Realities

I would like to write more about our brother David. He was a good person, a hard worker, and he tried anything and everything. He wanted to be on his own. I don't know how, but he managed to find a way. Soon after Irving went to the Army, David wanted to go to California. He did not like the cold weather. He tried to remain in Columbus, but decided to go at this time to see California since he had heard a lot about it. He did not take too much time. His mind was made up and he acted accordingly. All of a sudden he was ready, he had an old car. I don't know how he managed it, but it was good enough for him. He left to California. He did not have anyone there and didn't have enough money in reserve, but that did not bother him. After he arrived there we did not hear from him for a long while. He became a bad letter writer. In the past, he was diligent trying to write to our family back home before the war. Now he liked to receive mail but he was very slow in answering. Finally we heard from him. He was working, but he didn't tell us what he was doing or what kind of a job he had. Actually it didn't matter to us as long as he was okay.

After the war, he told us that he met a very nice girl and they decided to get married. This came to us as a big surprise. We were happy for him! Finally, he will settle down. Originally Dorothy came from Chicago. She lived in California now. Both of them lived alone. She had many friends and also had a job there. She was an American-born girl. She was very nice and smart. I met her later and she was very good for David. I thought that she will be happy with him. She liked the same things as David did. They will make it. So far they were happy and we hoped for the best.

David wrote to us that he had established his own business, a furniture store. He always liked to begin big! Here was a large store where he did upholstering and furniture coverings. There was money in it. He did not do it by himself, but he had hired someone to do it. Before he went into this business he sold lamps, and he tried other jobs, too.

About 10 years after he left us in Columbus, they had their first child. His name was Freddy. They were very happy because before Freddy was born she lost a baby right before birth. They were happy that finally they succeeded. They wanted to buy a home in Long Beach.

He wanted me to visit them. He thought I might like it and remain with them in California. The baby was one year old at this time. I had a dilemma, though. When he asked, I had just moved to New York, following my sister who had moved there first. I wrote to them that I will go there for my vacation, and I told them that I will consider whether I will stay there or not.

In New York, I was looking for a job quite some time. I found a job - it wasn't very exciting, but I didn't want to be a beggar. It was a small store, and I was a cashier. I stayed there for a while. I was able to do the job very well. I was very alert and was able to understand more English - it wasn't perfect, but the work I did was. The store was in the Empire State Building - on 34th Street and Fifth Avenue.

In the meantime, I was looking for something better. I wanted more income. I was trying to better myself, but also some of the managers were very rude. I wasn't used to that type of people.

I was a refined person, with good manners, even though I was very young. I was always respected. I was always clean, properly dressed - as a matter of fact, well - dressed. I was also attractive and capable.

I had this job in New York, but New York was not to my liking. In the beginning it was very difficult. I had to spend my reserve to live there and the money was going faster than I was making it. Like anything else, the beginning is very difficult. Later, I was hired as a cashier in a famous dairy restaurant called Ratner's. They had a very good bakery for the restaurant and also for retail sales. The baked goods were excellent. They baked Jewish bread, Danishes, all kinds of cookies and desserts. People came from all over town. It was a famous, well-established restaurant. It was not cheap.

I liked my job. It was like home. I was happy. I loved it - I met many interesting people. They had a better class of people and families and others coming in there, but most of the people that came into a restaurant were businessmen of all ages. They respected my businesslike approach. I looked clean and tried to dress well - strictly business, but I was most pleasant to everyone without exception.

We had people like actresses, very famous people, to the restaurant while they were rehearsing. A gay man after that - and they bought coffee, as was every morning. I got to know them quite well. And businessmen were coming in daily also to buy coffee or whatever they wanted. But I also believed not to mix business with pleasure. Although the customers were very nice, you didn't really know who they were. In the end, I enjoyed everything there. It was hard work - really didn't matter to me. Did not matter how busy they were, I was happy. I liked my work. I was much happier when I was busy. The wages should have been better, they didn't pay much, but they paid weekly and that included two meals a day. The problem was that I was always busy to stop to eat, because I did not have anyone to relieve me. I was doing the cashier's job so I could not leave it to someone to take over. I was responsible for the money - if anything was missing, I had to pay the difference. There were no breaks to stop and eat. I didn't even have time to go to the ladies' room. I was having problems with my stomach. Eventually, I was in charge of the cashiers. I was there for 16 years.

This was a kosher restaurant. There were three shifts and three cashiers. We were selling cigars and cigarettes, and I was responsible. I had to keep inventory of cigars and cigarettes to be sure that they had enough, and I had to clean the cigarette display. It was attractive with a glass counter. I had to keep the books, records, and everything that went along with it. The place was open 24 hours, seven days a week. I was very proud to work there for so many years. I was trusted. My boss gave me all types of amounts to count and make deposits in the bank. No one ever complained that I shortchanged them.

It was a family business. It was run by sisters and brothers. Originally their parents came from Poland. They settled on the East Side. and started the business by themselves. The mother was the cook and when the father was alive he was working there, too. Little by little they became famous. They were strictly dairy, no meat was served. When I went to work there their father had already passed away, but the mother was alive. They worked hard for 50 years..

The two sons and the daughters were involved in business. As they grew up, they got married, each one had children except the youngest brother. He took over and was in charge of the restaurant. He was my boss. Their oldest son was in charge of the bakery. The girls were coming later, mostly in the afternoon or evening. They acted like hostesses. When they were very busy, especially in the evenings, holidays, and weekends, the older sister was working as a second cashier. They also had three managers - they were very well liked. When I came to work there, I was told that the place existed at that time about five years. I was respected and liked by all of them.

It was not an hourly wage; it was a weekly wage, and that's talking about six days - and sometimes Sunday evening from 4 PM until 2 AM. I went home by subway. It was not too far from my home - I had to walk from the subway on a dangerous road by myself. It was very scary. They never paid anything extra. I was waiting for an increase - but it never came. They gave me a day off - Saturday - the only time I would go in was if one of the family members were sick - otherwise I would not.

On Sundays, whole families came, and I had to work harder. I never even had a chance to have my dinner. I worked constantly without stopping. Sometimes the sisters would come in earlier, but not often. I would never believe it, that people eat out on weekends. They were always busy - lunchtime and dinnertime usually.

They grew rapidly and decided to expand the restaurant to next door, which was a very large place. They rented it just like the original place. This was very modern and much cleaner. The kitchen was all new and so were all the dishes. It was up-to-date. It looked very nice. The food was in demand - it was excellent. They were lucky that they had good cooks that stayed with them for many years. The cooks also came from Europe. They were with the family from the day they arrived to America. They were trained by their mother. They were honest, hard workers and the family was lucky to have good helpers. I got to know them. The waiters were there for many years, and they stayed with them, too.

My boss was an attorney; however, he never practiced. He was a wise man, but he was unwell. All of a sudden he passed away young. He was a very nice person. The other brother, who one was active in the bakery business, was able to continue for a while, but it was very difficult to manage. And my boss's wife - she did not care. She had no idea how to run a business. The children did not take an interest - they had their own jobs. All of them were working, made a living. I do not know what they did with their money. They never came to help out in the business. None of them - but they were able to take out food without paying for it. They came in without asking, just helped themselves. They were freeloaders - even the bookkeeper, who had been there for a long time. She worked five days a week, got good wages, and free lunch, but when it came to Saturday, she demanded a taxi to come for her - and she would never pay for it. They were all interested only in the money and the food.

It was a miracle that he was able to stay in business. Sometimes he knew - my boss - what was happening. There was no profit. He said it out loud and clear. He worked very hard so he didn't know what was happening, except he knew that the business was not producing enough money.

After he died, the family all disappeared. The business closed down. They did not even try to sell it. The children should have tried to learn the business - or tried to sell it. They weren't interested.

It seems it happens in most families. Money - money - give me money. Who cares what happens to you? If you are a good person and allow them to use you, before you know it, it becomes automatic for them. No questions asked.

After work I went home. I had to prepare food for every day and to have it ready, because I was tired when I came home since I didn't eat all day. It was very difficult and very hard for me. I should have changed jobs, but I was happy there and I ignored it.

Maria at work in Ratner's.

My family had been after me for a long time, so I decided to look for another type of work - in an office. I thought it would be much easier. I would have to work less hours, and I would get more money - and also have time for myself to socialize to meet someone that I liked.

This is important - I became wiser and chose things to improve in my life. Sometimes on the way, one forgets what is important for ourselves. We are too busy even to stop to think what's happening around us. Time passes by, and one does not even notice it. We cannot think of the future, only lightly, without serious thinking. By the time we wake up, it is too late to catch up what we missed.

As I see it, we should try to better ourselves. If we're able to find a way to do for oneself - to better your life - then we should. I was told as a young child that everything has been written already - what the future would be for that person, good or bad. G-d arranged our destiny. We have nothing to say about it. Sometimes some miracle happens, and we are lucky enough to be able to change our destiny. But don't wait for it. We do not know what will be our destiny. I think it's better this way. We just take one day at a time, and enjoy what we have, and don't let it get away. The biggest problem is to wait for something that will never come. It will create more disappointments, one after the other. Just do something - whatever you have to do - until you find what you really want to do, and be happy with it.

The feeling of being lucky often comes when something turns out even better than we expected. Just pay attention. If you have a family, sometimes we'll get disappointed - it happens in life - but try not to let it get you down. Try again, just go on and be happy whether you can or not.

When David asked me to go to California, I had already worked at this restaurant about 10 years. I did not take a vacation. When they let me work during my vacation they paid me for it. This was the only way I was able to save some money. Eventually, I decided to go to visit David. I did not see him for a long time. Instead of going somewhere else I decided to take my vacation there in California. I told my employer only that I was going to visit my brother, this way I would still have my job when I returned.

Finally I visited my brother and his family. They were very happy to see me. The baby, Freddy, was celebrating his first year. David had his furniture store. They had a lady to take care of the baby. David tried to persuade me to look for a job and stay there. I could not and did not see any good reason to stay there - if traveling around was only a little easier there, then maybe. If I would have a car, and if I knew how to drive maybe then it would have been easier for me to stay there. Looking for a job, I wasn't convinced that it will be a better opportunity for anything else. I liked my freedom in New York. I had the subway and I could come and go anytime without waiting for someone to bring me and take me around.

David and his family were very busy, too. They did not have much time for anything and not too much money either. The outlook was not desirable for me. In New York if I wanted to socialize on the weekend it was easier and I had a better chance to meet people. The trouble was that I worked six days.

When Sunday came I was also busy at home - cleaning, washing, and cooking. People usually went out on Saturday night, but for me, I was tired after working. I was just happy to be at home and I went to sleep.

On Sunday afternoons when I had a date, if I didn't care for the person, I let them go home and I did not have to stay out late. To me this was a way of saving time.

When there was someone who was introduced to me, it wasn't what I wanted. At that time it was difficult to meet young men and women. When I did go out, I went to the neighborhood in the Bronx (during that time the Bronx was a very nice place to live and go around) to dance. The difficulty was that I was not the going out type. I was more of a shy type and a serious person. The job was for me like going out socially.

I liked the people coming into the restaurant and I received many compliments. I always dressed nicely. I had, and have, good taste in clothing. My sister Hermina knew wholesale houses where she was able to buy our clothing cheaper. She knew my size. There you could not return it or exchange it. She purchased things that looked nice on me. On my job at the restaurant I tried to change clothing, a different one, everyday. I always looked neat and clean. So for me working was going out. This was very good for me. I didn't have to go out just to be busy because I was busy enough.

When I came back from California, I still did have my job. And also the lady where I lived said that when I come back I will have my room in the apartment with her. She was Jewish, a very nice, old lady. I felt safe living there. Her children used to come to visit her with her grandchildren. She had a very small apartment, but she shared it with me.

When we first came to New York it was impossible to find any rooms that would be desirable. My cousin Bertha was running around, I remember that, to help us to find a good apartment in a good location. The war just ended and that made it more difficult to find one. Finally we found this where I lived. She took us, but it was a very small apartment for the three of us: myself and my sister and the Lady. The Lady got for us a folding bed. We opened it when we needed it. She arranged everything so that by the evening, we were able to sleep. We had our bedding that we brought over from Columbus. My sister Hermine stayed with her for a couple weeks.

When I came back from California again she was happy to see me and we stayed with her for a while.

My sister Hermine was busy every weekend. She was working only five days. She had more time for herself. She met guys easier. Sometimes someone liked her and introduced her to someone else. Sometimes she went on dates on weekends. She also went on vacations. She wanted to meet a husband. She wanted to get married and she had a better chance because she was very smart, more outgoing, and it was natural for her to talk to anyone.

I was just the opposite. I wanted to get married, but somehow I didn't want to waste time. If I met someone either I knew right away it was not for me or it's not what I wanted because he was very stingy to begin with. They asked me if I have any money, they were not ashamed to ask me. They thought that being in America longer than they were, I must have money. I did not want to work with them or with anyone that just came to America. They went through a lot. Some of them were better than others. It may have been my fault. When I thought that a person may not be bad, it turned out that maybe I wasn't his type or maybe I wasn't what he was looking for. He just looked for a good time. He must have seen from the minute he came in that he cannot have a good time. It had to be my way therefore it was impossible to meet the right person. It was difficult to get rid of or get away from those that I did not like.

I didn't like someone that did not have a job. I met someone very nice and I used to play tennis with him. He lived with his parents. He was Hungarian and a friendly person. He was an accountant and was working for one. He never took me out - not even to dinner or a show. When I had a date with him and I was dressed very well, he wasn't dressed up properly. He didn't even offer to take me out for a cup of coffee. I did not care because I worked in a restaurant. Therefore I felt I wasn't really important to him. I was tired of wasting time with him. I gave him up, he did not want to see my way.

He watched for me. He knew what time I came home from work and used to stop me on the way and invited me out but he didn't want to listen. When I said 'no' that meant it. Usually, I thought it over carefully before I made up my mind one way or the other. In my mind I knew exactly what I wanted. I was not looking for money, but I was looking for someone who believed in the things the way I do. It was difficult to find one, sometimes I didn't know why. I really didn't have much time to think about it. Time passed by, minute by minute and I just gave up. Whatever joy as I had was good enough.

Chapter 10
The Last Goodbye

In 1939, after the Hungarians took over Czechoslovakia, the people in our village began hating us. The people that our father helped out they turned against us. This school and our teacher and middle schools marched and stopped in front of our house and where other Jewish families were and they were singing anti-Semitic songs. Hatred was there in the community. It was unbelievable. This was only the beginning. It was a Catholic school we went to. There are two schools in town. The second school was a Calvinist's [Reformatus] school. We never had any trouble with anyone, and we were well respected, as I mentioned in the beginning of this my writing.

When our teacher needed help on their farm we helped him with our horses. We always helped him with whatever he needed. We were good friends with his father and the son that followed as a teacher in his father's footsteps.

We knew most of the people in town. Rumors began overnight and more rumors were all around that when people were sleeping people disappeared. From prior information we knew what was the reason. You would never think about that what was in their minds. It was then a nightmare. What we heard - it was bad. We did not believe it that it can happen in our village or that our country will disappear as it did.

During this time they began setting up hard labor. My brother Herman and Irving were already called in, luckily they were not taken away. They were working at our place. My brother Lajos was home. Our part Hungary took over. The people in our area were originally Hungarians, that is, before World War One. We spoke Hungarian. In 1918 the Czechoslovakian government was established and the area became part of Czechoslovakia. Now the people wanted back the Hungarian government. They did not know what will be after that. And later as time went on they suffered also I'm sure. Their fate changed. Even then the Communist party existed, but in Hungary it was not allowed openly. They too felt all these changes and had to protect themselves. If they followed the orders then they would get better treatment.

Our uncles found out in Kiralyhelmec that they were picking up people and they disappeared. No one was able to find any trace of them.

The Jewish community began to live in fear and no one knew who was next. Minute by minute it began - the nightmare. After this episode we were very lucky. We received the telegram that we must leave at once.

Hermine and Herman were in Budapest as I mentioned it before in the beginning of my book. Irving and I were left at home. Without being noticed by anyone we left for good for Budapest and from there to America.

With G-d's help, it was a miracle all the way and ever since. I will never forget that as I looked back, I did not know or believed it, that I will never see them again. That is, our father and my brother Lajos and his family. Just when I parted, I remember seeing their faces, their tears all over. They were crying and telling me, "*Maria don't work too hard. Take care of yourself. Make sure, all of you, that you don't forget that you are one family, sisters and brothers. Don't forget to write to us."*

I never forgot those words.

Our brother Lajos was very good to us and helped us. He was a very wonderful brother and a son. By this time he had his own family. At this point I felt like I was frozen. I did not want to leave my father either on one hand, but I also wanted to live. What can a person do? that thought went through my mind. We would try to bring them out to America when it's possible - that was the original plan. Then we will be again all together as a family. That was our plan.

Our cousin Arthur, on the other hand, was afraid and he reneged in his thinking. We were very busy with all the problems that we had to take care of.

This was the last ship leaving Europe and we must make it without delay. We never knew what could happen. As we passed through different countries, we were stopped to have our passports examined. The war was on, will our ship be safe? I hope it will be, is what came into my mind. I did not say anything to my sister because she was busy enough to speak to those people we went to meet as they questioned us. Finally, a man was assigned to us - it was a big help. He took us around in Naples because we already caught up with the ship there. We made it to the ship and arrived safely into New York Harbor. We landed there. After that, we went to Columbus, Ohio as I mentioned before.

Chapter 11
Painful Burdens

When we lived in our uncle's place in Columbus, we were able to correspond with our father and family. However, by then my brother Lajos was serving in the Hungarian army. My father was struggling alone. We had the property, but no one was there to take care of it. My brother Lajos wasn't there. By then it was very bad. The children were without food. We did not hear from them. Finally, we received a letter from our Uncle Márton, my mother's youngest brother, telling us what was happening with our family and the children. They didn't have even a pair of shoes to put on their feet. They were walking with rags wrapped around them. Their feet were very cold and the weather was very bad. This was between 1940 and 1941, but I'm not sure of the dates.

David, our oldest brother here in America, went to the bank to borrow money to send to our family immediately. He hoped that maybe through the bank we would be able to get it to them safely. This way we would have at least some guarantee they will get it. We weren't sure if a letter would go through, but this way we thought that through the bank we'll know if they ever see it, or at least we'll know if they're still at home. After a couple of weeks we heard from our family that they did receive the money and they were thanking us for not forgetting them. That we would never do. We love them dearly. How could we forget them? We were here in America only for a short while and we didn't have a chance to do too much. We did not have money. David was here longer and had more knowledge than we had how to go about it and was able to do more, however, after that we did not hear from them.

We tried to get information from different channels. Finally, the war was over and my sister Hermine received letters from old friends we used to know back home in Czechoslovakia. In their letters they told us that they were taken away during the war and that many did not return. Also, they told about my brother Lajos, his family and our father.

In Lelesz, our grandparents and both of their sons and family didn't come home.

We did not know of what they went through when they were tortured, but later we learned from my Uncle Márton's son, also named Emil, what happened to our people. They were taken to Auschwitz, one of the German-built gas chambers. That is where they perished. I cannot understand why someone did not save at least one of them, namely, our little nephew Emil, my brother's son, he was then 11 years old. The youngest was about two years old. I just hoped at least one child could have been saved. I looked everywhere.

One of my nephews, my brother's son Sherwin, tried on the computer to find some information about our family. We learned about my brother Lajos from the German archives that he was working in a labor camp and died.

Before my sister got married we lived together in an elderly lady's apartment, as I mentioned. I remained there for a while but moved to a different place because this lady became sick and passed away. When my sister decided to get married, her fiancé Eugene wanted to have a wedding. He had some relations, but since we were only a few, he made all the arrangements for the wedding and paid the expenses. He also wanted my sister to stop working because he wanted to have a family. Eugene was in business and wanted to have a real home. He wanted to have a loving wife waiting for him when he comes home from work. Our sister agreed - she also wanted to have a family of her own. For the wedding, my sister wanted to have both boys come in from Columbus, Ohio. She also wanted them to come to New York to live. She felt that she would have liked us to be together, then we would have a better chance to improve our life. My brother Irving came to New York for Hermine's wedding. He stayed for a short while then he returned to Columbus. After he graduated, we wanted both of our brothers to come to New York. We thought it would be better for both of them.

After Irving finished school, at the Ohio State University where he studied economics, it was somewhat difficult to find a job in Columbus, but he eventually found one in Portsmouth, Ohio. Even so, we encouraged him to go to New York. He promised to think about it. We all missed each other. We did not have anyone else. With the job in Portsmouth he gained experience, but it wasn't what he wanted. After a long discussion, he and Herman agreed to give up the apartment in Columbus and come to New York. When they arrived, at first they did not have a place to stay. It was very difficult to find a decent apartment. It was very expensive, and of course we couldn't afford it. I gave the elderly woman I was staying with extra money so that I could have them over for dinner. She agreed - but later, she changed her mind.

They found a room, and later an apartment. After they were settled they went to look for jobs. Irving had been happy in Columbus. He knew more people in Columbus, especially from the University. In New York, he had to start all over again.

He met girls. I also told him to take his time. Do not jump into it. Take your time and be sure that it is what you wanted.

He was tall, handsome, and went through enough to know life and appreciate it. He was always an unusual person. He was the youngest and the smartest, and he got a good education. What do you need more to have the best of life? He really deserved the best. He told me he met a lot of nice people, but he wasn't sure about marrying them. I told him try to look back and you will have a chance to find the right person.

During this time, Irving worked very hard. He went through so much in life. Eventually, in 1960 he met someone and was happier because they got along well. He met her through an ex-girlfriend and she introduced him to her. Barbara grew up in Laurelton, Queens and was a teacher in one a school in Nassau County on Long Island. She was teaching little children that had special problems. She was the youngest teacher there. She was only 23 years old with a Master's degree. She was very nice and smart and both were happy. She lived with her parents, had two other sisters. They were younger. Within three months they were engaged and married. The parents were very nice people. I did not meet her in person until they were engaged. The only thing I knew about her was when she sent me a card.

I told him to wait because that wasn't enough time to know a person. I told him to wait to go out more, really got to know each other better, and then you have time to decide if that's what you want. He had seen her more often, as I noted above, they made the decision to get married. No one can tell whom one should marry. Especially how to choose your life. You have to live life.

We didn't believe in any divorce, usually you marry for better or worse. Sometimes, that is not the best because one can make a mistake and maybe it was a bad choice. That does not mean that you have to live a lifetime, if they have some kind of a health problem and you find out after the wedding. To live with that is not a good idea.

This episode happened after they became engaged. I had just moved into a new studio apartment and they came over to my place. The apartment was very nicely furnished. I was happy to see them and meet them. She was very nice, the mother and sisters were young and pleasant. To me they looked a little bit chubby. I was looking for any problem, I did not criticize them, but tried to make them feel at home. I didn't have to look too far - her ankle was bandaged and she wasn't able to walk straight. I asked her what was wrong? She told me that *she went horseback riding and fell off from the horse*. That can happen to anyone. She asked me about our family and whether we have had any divorces. I told her that we did not. I was puzzled why she asked that question. Then from nowhere was telling me that *if you have any problem, sometimes we have to ignore it.*

Next day, she told my brother that they were very pleased and happy to see me and my apartment. They liked me as well as my apartment.

After the meeting, I wasn't sure. When I asked the question what's going on with the bandage, I knew she wasn't telling me the truth. I mentioned that to my brother, that he should wait with this obsession to get married until he was sure everything is okay. He should try to find out more about her condition. It was too soon, but she didn't want to wait and neither did he. I didn't want to involve my suspicion, but if I would have been sure I would have tried to stop the wedding.

The parents invited my sister and me for dinner with her family. They kept a kosher home. We also keep a kosher home. Otherwise my sister and her husband would not have eaten there. They were a middle-class family.

After they were married, they came to visit me quite often. I got to see her more and more. My brother seemed very happy and that was the most important thing. He was independently working for himself in vending and he was able to buy a home on Long Island. Veterans got a lower interest rates, and that helped. They seemed to be very happy. She was a teacher and was working for a while.   After a couple of years, my brother wanted her to stay home - she agreed. They established themselves soon and had their first child, a little boy. We all were very happy - so was the young couple. They came visiting us regularly, and they were always welcome to my home. It was easier for them to visit me than for me to visit them. They were driving - they were able to get around, but I was not. I did not have a car, and I did not drive.

You would never expect anything to come up, especially in such a short time. You can never see or predict what comes next. this could be the happiest couple - ordinarily, they would be. Instead they found themselves in a position - unexpectedly - a new, worse position. Their future changed unexpectedly. His wife became very ill. She lost her vision for a few days and was hospitalized. She began to walk with difficulty - like dragging her leg. We did not know what was wrong. She never told us about any problem, but I knew she had a problem before marriage - this I am sure of. She knew her life history and kept it secret. I can see now why she asked me so many questions about divorce and family and many other questions. I was wondering why she asked me so many questions. I can see it, but now it was too late. My brother could have done something before their children were born, but after that, he was the type of person who takes the oath for better or worse. Therefore he did not. He could have annulled their marriage.

After the birth of their second child this situation became more problematic - The first doctor diagnosed her some kind of neurological problem - multiple sclerosis. Oh my! I never thought of that. She refused to accept it. My brother tried everything possible to get help. He researched for help from various parts of the United States: Manhattan, North Carolina, Idaho - even Canada, France, and Israel seeking doctors who were familiar with the case. At that time, it was difficult to diagnose multiple sclerosis. He did not know how big of a problem he was facing, but it would become the worst nightmare. Many doctors, knowing she didn't accept the original diagnosis, tried all sorts of treatments for other real or imagined illnesses. They were unable to give the exact name of the diagnosis or help her. After a while, when NMR scanning came out, and even though some doctors had difficulty interpreting the images, finally, the answer was given - the original diagnosis was confirmed and there was no medication. The illness moved very slowly but after the second child the problem was more definite.

He tried to raise his children and to give them a better life so they would not have to work so hard.

He tried to make a happier atmosphere for all of them. He had two jobs plus was at home taking care of his sick wife - and their two children were very young - the youngest just a baby. All this took years of struggle and research. There was not much hope left. He was a very good, honest soldier the second time around. He struggled but never gave up. He just kept on going - on and on.

He sacrificed his own life, went through so much heartache, and raised the children - he had no life. He wouldn't even listen to the suggestion to place her in a nursing home. And her family wasn't the best - they created more problems.

The mother wasn't able to walk. They tried to get help - the right help - it became more complicated. It looked like a very happy couple - it should have been. She had very good education - both of them - it looked like a perfect match. She was able to teach special children and all this went down hill. Stopped. Now where do you begin? Their children needed a mother the most. Every child needs a healthy mother and a good atmosphere to be raised properly. Children cannot understand what's going on with illness around - it affects the child's life. And their father had to make a living.

He tried to get someone to help his wife at home, so he could take care of their children to make sure no one gets hurt, and feed them, do all the chores, and take care of his wife. By then she wasn't able to walk, take care of herself, or the children. Under this condition, my brother made it sure everything was done - running back and forth between home and the business. He was busy 24 hours a day. He loved his family. He wanted and tried to keep them together at home under any condition. It is a miracle how he was able to do what he did. Eventually his wife needed 24 hour help - everything changed so tremendously - he found himself in a worse condition than you would ever imagine.

Unfortunately, one does not know what life has to offer, but if one would have known the situation then perhaps one could have avoided the problems that followed.

I felt that if the family would have known their background and would have spoken about it, then I would have been able to take it more readily.

Why was all this happening to my brother? He did not have a chance to have the happiness he deserved. As it was, he went through so much. He deserved a better life. I wish I could have talked him out of this marriage.

You can imagine what life was after that. I loved her, my sister did also. We tried to help her whatever we could do. But there was no medication that would cure this illness. There is a lot of research that is going on and I hope that soon they can discover the right medicine to help those that are afflicted with this illness.

During that time my brother established another business. It kept him very busy. He was able to pay his bills.

As I'm looking back, at her family side, they had more than enough problems. She had two sisters and one of them got married very young. She had her family, three sons, and then she also had MS. Later on both she and her husband were not able to take care of themselves. Their children were all grown up by then and they placed both their parents in a nursing home - it was not the happiest life. And the other sister, she's well, but suffered too. She has her own family - her daughter, and one grandchild. She had a son, but he died very young, maybe at 22. She was a nurse - and thank goodness she was well.

On September 17, 2004 my brother's wife passed away after 44 years of marriage. She's buried in a military cemetery. You know, since then he has been living by himself - getting along fine and enjoying his grandchildren.

Both boys are very good and beautiful sons. They are engineers. He gave them a very good education in two of the best universities and now they are trying to make a living - working very hard, both of them. I hope they will have the happiest family and enjoy life - they well deserve it.

They are both married and each has their own family. That makes me very happy. And I'm very happy for my brother - thank goodness at least now he has some of the happiness he so well deserved. His grandchildren make my brother very happy, and he is very proud of them. The youngest son has three girls and one boy. They're growing up beautifully and very smart. They speak two languages now and are studying another language. The first two they read and write perfectly, and the third one is coming along nicely. Thank goodness they are very happy children.

One of his sons - he is very close - they come in to visit him more often. He was the one who got my brother a computer and set him up - tried to teach him how to use it. And he succeeded! My brother is getting very good on it. He typed so many letters - what he saved from our family - oh, very valuable pieces for us. And also he types my writing - my life history - our background. I wrote all that - and many more articles - at his request. And now my nephew taught me how to use the computer, so I would not have to write by hand. Oh, it is much easier! It is unbelievable - if you want to do something, the age has nothing to do with it. Let's say - if you're lucky enough.

The older son has two children - one boy and a little young lady. My brother doesn't see them frequently. This son does not have much time to visit - only on the telephone. They talk to each other every day. This son's children are growing up, but are too busy to visit their grandfather. I think they will miss out a lot - not to know him better. He loves them dearly. He tries to help whenever he can - even now. His love never disappeared for them, but they're too busy.

Their father, my brother is a good father! He takes care of his little family. He is there whenever they need him, or vice versa. Both sons live close. If they need their grandfather to babysit, he's always available. He loves the children and grandchildren. He worked all his life. Nothing was too much - and he never complained.

Now I'm looking back - my brother still wants me to write more. I don't know how I did it. My brother was able to read it. I'm trying to finish as soon as I can. My writing is getting worse - my hand cannot follow me. I'm writing too fast - my hand cannot keep up. I would not be able to do it without my brother's help. I cannot type. At this time, I still cannot use the computer well enough. Therefore, I am writing by hand. I do not have any secretary - as of now, my brother is doing the editing. I am being tested - to see if my hand is able to follow.

As of now I've come to a closing point. I hope whoever will try to read it can understand why I am doing it. Life is very short - it goes by very fast. Therefore, we have to try to enjoy it while we have the opportunity. And we hope they're able to make it. We try to build a strong relationship with our children, and we hope that in time, they too will settle down and make their own life. That they will be able to make their own decisions - and the right ones. Try to give them, teach them, to have the right choices - in business and in personal life. Try to be the best under certain conditions. Sometimes it makes it very difficult. Try to give them all the education - whatever is possible. Sometimes we are facing all kinds of problems unexpectedly, and that sometimes makes it very difficult to get around. Take all this and try to understand why all this is happening.

My conclusion - I try to make people understand. They should never forget the destiny - it is not just for us - there must be a good reason our G-d helps to have a healthy mind.

I am writing about this situation so others can learn how to manage and make choices *before* it's too late. After this, maybe you could prevent other problems.

I am wishing you all the best happiness, best of health and hoping we all learn our lesson and live in peace together.

Chapter 12
My Father's Other Brothers and Sisters

I cannot speak much about our uncles from our father's side. When our grandfather settled in our village, it was a nice size of a family. They were young children. As far as I know, maybe there were three sisters. By the time I was old enough to understand what was going on, our father's sisters were all gone. Each one of his sisters was married - they had their own families. We never met them. I am not even sure how many sisters our father had. Just before we came to America, we had met some of their children - our cousins - and one of their husbands once. It happened at the last minute - they all wanted to come to America. It seems it did not work out. I'm sorry to say, they did not make it. Everything came so fast.

I assume the boys were not happy to live there. They were bored. They did not want to work on a farm. They did not want to be a farmer. There wasn't any social life - nothing - all closed in. The girls managed to get married - two boys remained and accepted whatever their responsibility was. The oldest son, our Uncle Lazar and the youngest - our father. The middle three boys decided to try their luck elsewhere. One of them was our Uncle Julius. He was a little different.

He remembered his birthplace - and his family. He kept in touch even after his parents passed away. He was the one who came back and forth quite often. He used to spend time with us whenever he came in from America - he came to visit his family, but spent the most time with us. We treated him very well.

When we arrived in America, my uncle Julius and his new wife - by then they were married a long time, over fifteen years - welcomed us. She was also educated and spoke several languages. They lived together until my uncle passed away. His wife was very nice to us. She invited us for dinner. We visited them often. Especially on Sundays. I would prepare a full course dinner for them. We loved them - all of us. He passed away very suddenly. We were very upset and very sad. It was too soon.

He had two children from his previous marriage. His wife, Aunt Helen, the step-mother, gave his daughter [Elsie] all the education, and made sure she could go out and do whatever she wanted. She could speak, but not hear. She lived in another city - not Columbus, but still in Ohio.

There was also a son [Arthur]. He had two children - a son and a daughter. He was married and well educated, studied at the best universities. He was very active at Ohio State University, and was the one who sponsored the papers for all four of us.

Arthur was in manufacturing - he worked with very large scales, some of which could weigh tons. We used to visit them, too and by then we were trying to learn English. He could not speak our language, so we weren't able to have full conversations with him. His wife Flora understood some of our language, so we were able to understand each other somewhat. She was quiet, introverted.

In the meantime, their children got married. His wife also went through some major surgery. Later on, she felt better. All of a sudden, he became withdrawn. He had to give up his business because of illness - he wasn't able to function physically and could no longer walk. He needed full time help. His son Sam had gotten separated - the wedding was annulled.

After that, Sam decided to come to New York. He met someone here at one of the universities. He had a PhD. His wife had one too - she was teaching art. They had three boys. It seemed they were very happy. Two of the boys were twins. The eldest grew up and moved to California. He went into filmmaking - animation, creating animated films. I think that's what you call it.

One of the other brothers - the third one - was repairing organs. They are still using those organs in churches. He is very good at it - today, not so many people can do that job. *[Editor's Note: Maria mentions two of the three sons. The other became an audio engineer.]* We used to see Sam from time to time. Sam's wife [Phyllis] wasn't as friendly, but she was nice whenever we got together. My second cousin [Sam] became very ill, and soon after that, he passed away - also very young. We were at the funeral. It was very sad. We never heard from them afterwards. That was the end of that part of the family.

Sometimes I used to hear from them. They used to live in Columbus, Ohio. My cousin's wife [Flora] also became very ill, and their son Sam was going back and forth to help - to care for her. His sister [Elsie] was married and had one son [Morton]. He was young, and all of a sudden he passed away. I heard this from his grandmother [Flora]. I do not know what happened to her [Elsie].

The only thing I heard was that ever since she got married, they stopped seeing each other. Sam expected that whatever remained from the business, he would receive from his mother. But she decided to give it to his sister [Elsie] instead. He was very disappointed, and that was the end of the family.

I just wanted to mention that money - even though they had their own life problems - it does not matter how educated they are. Still, there's always someone who, whatever the evidence, expects everything. Between sisters and brothers, it does not matter. They will compete with each other. It seems it happens all the time.

It seems it happens even in the best of families - even among the well-educated. Each one making a living, and still, that wasn't enough. It seems it's a worldwide problem - families falling apart, holding grudges and anger for a lifetime, even taking it with them after their passing. After that, we never heard from them again.

Later, we heard from someone that one of the sons [Barry Zeidman] got married. That was the end of what I heard about the family.

By the way, when my uncle passed away, his wife - my aunt [Helen] - had to move out from the home where she used to live with him. My cousin, her stepson, asked her to move out because his father owned the building. He owned a few buildings, and when he passed away, his son became the owner.

And just before my cousin [Arthur] became ill, he decided to send her back to the family she came from - the same family my uncle had brought her from when they got married and brought her to America. She happened to be a very nice person. She was always kind to us. I remember once she prepared dinner for all four of us. We found out later that she had disappeared. After so many years of marriage, my cousin made arrangements and sent her back to her family overseas.

I could not believe it. On one hand, Arthur did so many good things. My question is... why this? We never knew the reason. We felt very badly. Sometimes people do such unexpected things without thinking. They lived as very nice people. It was unbelievable. Everything ended so sadly.

Our father's two other brothers - when we were in Europe, we never ever heard from them. They never sent a note - not even to their own parents or anyone else. They disappeared from the earth. This is very difficult to believe. If not for our Uncle Julius, we would never know if they were alive or dead - speaking in plain English. Today it happens - quite often. At that time, it was unheard of. Their father left them an inheritance. In my opinion, they were not entitled to their shares - none of them.

I was quite young when I heard *about* them. When we came to America, we had the opportunity to meet our Uncle Henry's widow and children. Our other uncle, Martin, was also gone by then, and his children lived in Pennsylvania - we asked about them - they did not want anything to do with us. We never met them. They were very strange people - they didn't even want to meet us. Like complete strangers. Hard to believe, but it is true. No family ties at all. We did not want anything from them.

Thank goodness - we managed very well without them.

We did not have a big family, but we respected each other and cared for each other - and we were there if we needed help. As you can see - take a look - I and my dearest brother, we show a good example. You can learn if you really want to.

It does not take too much time or money to have a good relationship and a loving family. Maybe one day they will be able to see - if it will not be too late. People are too busy. Perhaps the climate is not the right one, but the time passes by so fast.

Chapter 13
Uncle Lajos - From Captivity to Catastrophe

I'm going to go back to writing about my Uncle Lajos bacsi in Lelesz. I wrote about him previously. The eldest son, also a yeshiva boy, he was better educated and more modern. His wife came from Homonna. They used to live there before they moved to Lelesz and settled there. He had a yard goods business. He was living in the same building where his business was. After they married, they wanted to have a family, but they didn't have any children.

He would have loved to have a family, and they tried to do whatever they could, but without luck. The medical system there at that time was not up to date as it is today in America. His wife Etel had family in another city and asked one of her nieces[34] to come to live with them. They took her in and treated her as if she was their own. When we came to America, she made a living in Lelesz by learning how to make corsets, under garments for women. At that time, we made our own clothes. We could not buy ready-made at that time - maybe in the largest cities you would be able to find it - but we had to make from scratch all our clothing. Some of the items were difficult to get ready made, so she went into that business. She made bras to order. She stayed with them for a few years. There was also a very nice family in the neighborhood. They became very friendly, and the girls from that family used to come and visit our uncle and aunt like one family. The girls came from a large family that also needed help. Our uncle was helping them however he could.

My uncle used to tell us his plans to build a larger and a newer building at the same place. He hoped to have a larger building and more room and he planned to get his father and mother to move in with them. He wanted to take care of his parents. They were not rich, but their love was there. This is what he was planning all the time.

I wanted to go back in history to his younger life. When he was married the first world war broke out. My mother used to tell us about it when we were little. Her two brothers, Lajos and Márton were taken into the Army. At that time, Russia was involved, and Lajos was captured by the Russian soldiers - back then, they were called the Cossacks.[35] He was taken as a prisoner. They were very brutal. They treated him inhumanely. He was kept there for many years. Finally, he escaped, and by then I was very young. I remember the time when he walked into our home unexpectedly - our mother and the family were surprised and happy, it was a big excitement. I could not

---

[34] Bella Moskovics

[35] The Cossacks (Hungarian: Kozaksz) were Slavic military communities known for their fierce independence, horseback fighting skills, and brutality. In Jewish memory, they are especially feared for the 1648-49 massacres led by Bogdan Khmelnytsky, during which nearly 100,000 Jews were murdered - the worst atrocity against Jews since the Roman destruction of the Second Temple in 70 C.E..

imagine what was going on. Our mother was the happiest person, and it was the biggest surprise, because they had never heard from him after he was captured for so many years. They had no idea what happened to him - dead or alive. You can imagine, when he went back to his wife and his parents, what it was like to live with the pain of all that time.

Later on, I found out from my mother. She told us. What a story - how he got away and how he walked all the way from Russia to our home without any food. He just kept on walking. He was quite a way inside of Russia and to get home was difficult and far. After a number of weeks finally he made it. By the time he arrived home, Lajos was very sick and almost blind. It was a miracle that he was able to make it. He recovered, but not completely. He tried to manage their life as best he could. Still, he was never the same. He had a problem with his stomach all through his life. It left a mark on him. He was never a laborer. He studied the Talmud [Jewish writings] and he was a very fun person. What he went through was enough for a lifetime. But he came home to his wife and she was the happiest person.

She was reading always and hoping every day that he will come back. She did not hear from him for a long time. Nobody knew what happened to him. All this time she was waiting for him. Her family lived quite far away. She was just hoping from day to day. In the meantime, at home she lived alone, she was young and far away from her family. She was waiting for the good news about her husband. She was trying to adjust herself the best way she could.

One night she was telling what happened to her as she was sleeping, being all alone, being young and her husband was somewhere but she didn't know where, only thing she knew that he was in the Army. That night she heard a noise, someone coming in unexpectedly, and she knew they were dangerous people. She heard them talking to each other. She recognized their voices. She knew right away who they were - her neighbors. It happened late at night. She was frightened, but there was no way to escape. She knew if they found her there, they would have killed her. She was very scared and feared for her life. They came in to the room, but she covered herself so they would not see her, made believe that she's asleep, tried not to move, and was very quiet. She heard them walking around and gathering whatever they could find. After all that, I don't know if they knew that she was there or not. She did not care about whatever they took, but she was happy that she was alive and this is what she was telling the family. The next day, she tried to forget what happened. She never reported them. She knew if she did, she would be in danger. What she went through that night was enough for a lifetime, she could not forget it. She was very lucky and grateful they overlooked her.

As time passed by, everyone was trying to make a living. When the second world war broke out our father also tried to follow-up as to what to do. Are we going to go to America and would we have to start all over again? The situation was bad and money was very tight. Then, as I wrote before, we had to change papers from Prague to transfer the papers to Budapest. We weren't sure whether we would be successful or not. Finally, we succeeded, we arrived in America. We settled down and tried to get a job and learn English so that we can better ourselves. We were trying to correspond with our family back home. For the time being we were able and it was okay.

In one of the letters our Uncle Lajos bacsi mentioned that he was going to build a new house and could not get any lumber. Our father wrote to us that we have a wooden building where we dried the tobacco and he offered to Lajos that he would take it apart, which they did, and Lajos had enough lumber to build a home. At this time we stopped growing tobacco and we didn't need the building. My uncle bought everything he needed, paid for the job - to the builder, and applied for the building permit, but was rejected by the local officials.

During the same period my grandfather closed their business and sold his house hoping to move in with his son soon. Now their plan fell apart. Therefore our grandparents had no place to move to. They thought it may be temporary. They thought they would be able to stay in the synagogue, but unfortunately, the synagogue's wall fell apart and there was no money to fix it. The congregation did not have enough money, and there were too many people around. They were forced to find another place. Unfortunately, the winter was coming and our grandparents had no place to go. They did find one, but they had no money to pay. Luckily, nearby there was a relative, second cousins, old neighbors, that had a home and gave the place for our grandparents. After all, the families were trying to help each other. They moved in and settled down. Meantime, there was a very bad winter snow, and unfortunately, one of the walls collapsed there too. There was no way to fix it - only three walls remained. And my grandparents, they were freezing, with no heat, nothing much left. Can you imagine that, the winter came and it was very cold in the house and they didn't have any money or anything else? They were in the middle of 80 years and had to live like that. My grandmother was a sick lady. One of the nicest people you could have and we loved her. Can you imagine watching them live like that under such conditions?

As I heard later on, our grandfather passed away. In a way, he was lucky. The other Jewish people - along with our grandmother and the rest of our family - our father, our brother, our nieces and nephews, and their mother - all those people who were still at home were picked up - and the rest, you know. This happened toward the end. The hatred by then was in full bloom. There was no way to stop it. By then, there was nothing left - only a nightmare, and whatever they left behind.

After the war, some of our neighbors wrote to us, and some of the people that survived also wrote to us, and told what happened. Some needed help, others took over our property and did with it whatever they wanted. We did not go back. We didn't have anyone there to see.

Chapter 14
The Last Ship Out: From Czechoslovakia to America

These neighbors we once trusted were our friends. Later, when the situation changed, in the beginning our relationship with them changed slowly, and there was no problem with them. We tried to look forward and were always hoping that our dream will come true, that all of us will be together again in America. I would never think about it any other way. We would never have believed what was coming next. This was unthinkable at that time and our hope was that we will be able to get out somehow. After two years of preparing new papers and transferring them to Hungary we succeeded.

Before we could succeed however, our father had to search and find out how can we get help that would make it easier to get out from Europe. There were other people who tried the same thing. There were many people that were trying to get out, and for many it was hopeless. Under the Czechoslovakian government, we already were called in to the American Embassy, the visa was waiting for us, our papers were ready. We could not believe that overnight there will be a change of government. It happened just at the time that we were called in and were ready to go. We thought that it cannot be true that this would happen! We lived in Czechoslovakia, yet the area in which we lived was Hungarian territory that was taken over 20 years earlier by the Czechoslovakian government under Masaryk and Benes in 1918. Masaryk was involved in establishing the Czechoslovakian government with the help of the American government. He saw the opportunity and succeeded in establishing the Czechoslovakian government. With the new border, the situation changed and people had more freedoms that they didn't have before. Historically, in 1918 there was a Russian Revolution in our area and when Czechoslovakia came into existence things became better and the situation was peaceful.

I must go back to the time before the foundation of the Czechoslovakian government. Originally this area was Hungarian under the Austrian Hungarian government, but Russian Kozaksz [cossacks] used to come in since the border was very close. These soldiers that came into our area were very bad. I don't remember a lot about them, but they were hurting people. They treated the people very badly. The Kozaksz were torturing people and stealing from them. They misbehaved as soldiers.

World War I ended and the fighting stopped. Many families suffered and some lost their whole family. Then, when the Czechoslovakian army moved in, we were very happy to see them and they took control and things became better. There was freedom of movement. At this time everyone tried to get back their normal life, whatever was left of it, and deal with it. This government existed only 20 years. It wasn't easy to live there. The people maintained the Hungarian language as before because this was Hungarian territory originally. As a matter of fact, that was the reason why they joined with Germany. The payment was that they would get back this part of territory from Slovakia. When the Czechoslovakian government was re-established after the second world war, our part became again Czechoslovakia.

Inasmuch as this region of Slovakia belonged to Hungary, the people at that time were fighting to get back to Hungary. By the time they realized what was going to happen it was too late because Germany already integrated Hungary and controlled them.

In Czechoslovakia, we had freedom alright, but the taxes were very high. Whether you had money or not you had to pay your taxes. As long as you followed their rules you were alright. You did not need to use titles when you spoke to an official like you needed in Hungary.

When we heard the bad news that President Masaryk of Czechoslovakia passed away we felt very badly. What would be now? We did not know what would be our future. We didn't know what will be waiting for us. Right after that, without delay, people began to fight in Prague, Czechoslovakia. That was the day that we were supposed to be there to pick up our visa and then we would be on our way to America. You could not predict anything in advance. How could you? The horror followed one after the other. Czechoslovakia lost Sudetenland and then it continued as you know the history. At that time, no one believed that there will be war. People felt that war never worked anything out, but only caused suffering. The people should try always to work things out, but the people were not in control. Unfortunately, others would like to have what you have, they want things the easy way. Why should they work when they don't have to?

No one knows in advance what war will bring, but leaders can promise you an arm and a leg. That does not mean that the war will succeed. Usually it does not. All the promises they make disappear. Even if you remain alive you lose - maybe your family, or your loved one. Promises! They make promises wherever you are. Now you're here. Now you're trying to get back, but there is no sight of a better life. Where should you turn? To whom should you turn? All your friends are gone, family too! What do you have from all these promises? Only promises. The only thing left are your horrors, nightmare. Questions. I was not happy.

When I think of what I have had and that they are all gone, I cannot even wipe my tears off my face. My heart is beating, I hear it telling me, was it worth it for so much suffering around me and dying? And you, why did you do such horror, nightmares, many sufferings, was it worth it? Now you want help for yourself? You think you deserve it? I wanted to give it to you - you deserve the worst punishment! I cannot even do it. I'm not a killer. I cannot even if I wanted to. I cannot commit the horror you did to innocent people, to children! The more they cried the more you ignored it, and now you want me to help you! Do you still want to have a war? Why don't you try it and go fight by yourself! See how long it will last! Take your children with you and have a test. If you like it, how long will you last? You might find out if you want something for nothing. War means that! If you have money, why don't you try the other way? Send your children to learn and don't forget to teach them love, common sense, learning, respect, work...hard work is healthier. Laziness is dangerous. It is your responsibility to raise them, teach them, and love them. A child when born is innocent, they are here because you wanted them. Love is never too much. Show them the road where they will cross. There are some bumps, but you can learn if you're careful and then you can make it. It needs all your strength without any hesitation. You yourself may be happier and healthier. Therefore try to teach yourself and set an example. If you follow the rules you cannot miss.

I just speak from my heart and my experience. Sometimes what we know alone that is not enough, knowledge is very helpful, but you must have sometimes some experience and common sense so you can learn wrong or right. All this is as important as life itself, it's not easy. We have to learn how to manage it. It is all important, it does not come by itself. It is hard work. Every day you must see something that you are interested in. You may want to see if there is any possibility for improvement. If you can, that is good. If not, nothing is lost. At least get interested, this way you might learn something. We can always learn, but we never know when! If we close our mind and don't want to see or hear anything, life gets boring.

Everyone was trying to escape when they heard more trouble was coming and going around. Then we knew that it is time to get busy especially the young men and women. The question was where could you go? There wasn't enough time to get visas or permission. The country was closed down, you needed permission to go anywhere in the country, even in the neighborhood. Some individuals succeeded in getting out, but others failed. They were saying that if some individuals were involved in helping to escape, their life would be in danger if they were caught.

Where could people run, especially the Jewish people? At that time the Jewish people heard more about Israel even though it didn't exist yet. Only if you know the Jewish history, the Bible, and then you will understand me what I'm talking about. In Czechoslovakia we heard that the Jewish land needed people like farmers to rebuild. As you know, that land belonged to the Jewish people. It was difficult to get out, even to go there at this time. The Jewish people never gave up. Our people in our prayers, we always hoped that one day the Jewish state will be re-established. Young men and women were ready to do whatever they needed to re-establish the Jewish state. They needed help. They lived in kibbutzim. They wanted to improve the land there and they were ready to do anything necessary to cultivate the land and plant vegetables, fruit trees etc. The land wasn't developed yet and these young people wanted to develop it and build homes. Some successfully arrived to Israel, but there were obstacles. The biggest problem was that England was controlling this place called Israel before the state was established. At that time they called it Palestine.[36] But because of the White Paper, England controlled how many people could get in. They wanted to maintain their relationship with the Arabs and that's why the entrance to the land was difficult and nearly impossible.

When the second World War ended, those Jewish people that survived the horrors that were caused by the Germans, wanted to enter the Jewish land of Palestine. It was very difficult because Britain was not allowing them to go. It was a sad situation after going through all this hell in Europe.

After Europe was liberated there were a lot of sick people that survived to return again to hospitals in other countries. Typhus was around and some survived and suffered by this sickness, and others did not make it. One of our cousins from Helmec, Emil, Uncle Márton's youngest son, came back alive. He's the only one who survived from our closest family. He was about 16 years old and survived the horrors. The reason he went back to Helmec was that he was hoping that other members of the family would come back alive. He found two of his cousins from his mother's side there. A few other people came back here and there, but they weren't in the best of health. Our cousin Emil decided to move to Israel. He didn't have anyone there, but he met other people who were also saved. There, he started a new life, settled down and got married.

My cousin Emil (Uncle Márton's son) got married to Lili. Thank goodness, he built himself up and was able to educate his children. One became a lawyer - now he's a judge in Israel. The other son became a dentist. He's practicing in Israel. Both of the boys have families, which I'm very happy to hear. He can never forget the past, but he tries to live and enjoy his family. My brother Irving was there in 1968 and visited them with his wife and son Jerritt. From time to time they call us, or my nephew talks to them on the computer. I did not have a chance to see him again. I remember him only as a child. I am very proud of him, thank goodness. It wasn't as simple to accomplish everything he did.

As Israel was established it was much easier to live there, but they still had to fight the Arabs. It appears that this fight will never end. They worked hard and wanted to protect the country that was their lifesaver. Israel became a home for anyone at that time who wanted to come there and live there. The new generation created the country and now we are not going to lose it.

Emil wrote to us from Europe before he went to Palestine after the war how much they suffered and how his father passed away. These German guards kept him with his father and were torturing them. He wrote at that time that his father passed away in his arms. It is a miracle that he was able to

---

[36] At the time, the territory was formally known as the British Mandate of Palestine. This designation came from the League of Nations mandate granted to Britain after World War I, authorizing it to administer the lands that today comprise Israel and Jordan. British policy, especially the 1939 White Paper, severely restricted Jewish immigration.

survive. I don't have any more details of how he was able to get away.[37] I'm glad and thankful that he is in Israel. At one time my brother asked him if he wants to come to America? No way! He wanted to stay in Israel.

They are hopeful that one day they'll be able to live in peace with their neighbors. In my opinion, everyone would benefit by having peace. It takes a lot of work and if the Arabs are willing, they could and would benefit and improve the lives for all concerned.

My nephew Sherwin, married an Israeli girl. They visit Israel as often as they can.

When I was young growing up, I knew we had relations in America and we often talked about it. I did not know too much about America at that time. I asked questions from the people that had been in America and had come back to our village. My best friend's mother [Mariska Deák was her friend] was born in America and was an American citizen. I asked her why did you come back? Didn't you like it there in America? I asked all kinds of questions. My friend didn't know why her parents came back. She said that she will go back when she grows up. She had relations in America. She told me about food and how it comes in cans. You just have to open it! Dresses could be bought already made. I was amazed! I could listen to her talking to me, telling the real stories about America. This one was our next door neighbor.[38] When the world war broke out, they were worried, and people were restless. I heard my family talking that hopefully the American government will come and help. Most people believe that Americans are friends of freedom, they are hard workers, and goodhearted. Also England is closer to us, and they too will come and save our people. The people were hoping that this will come forth, but the suffering continued faster than they expected.

As I mentioned before, we were lucky with all the odds and ends that we were on our way to America. As I look back it was really a miracle! This was a lifetime dream coming true. Especially for people without experience, from a small village, we were able to get out even though we had bumps all the way and the road was never smooth for us. Someone asked how did you manage it to get out in that time? Since there was no way of getting out from one place to the other, each country was swallowed up by Germany and there was no place to go. We were lucky with the timing and being able to get onto the last ship leaving Naples to America.

---

[37] Emil Schwartz, Presentation by Emil Schwartz, Oral History, United States Holocaust Memorial Museum Collection, gift of Sherwin Gluck, Accession Number 2021.49.1, RG-90.181.0001, recorded April 8, 2021, Israel. Part of the Jeff and Toby Herr Oral History Archive.

[38] See *Pappus - The Saga of a Jewish Family* for letters from Mariska and her mother. Tragically, Mariska and her sister Anus remained in Europe with their mother, and they both died from illness - 9 days apart (1945/12/19 Mrs. Deak, neighbor in Polyán, to us)

If you remember the people from Germany came to Cuba and were trying to get permission to land, asking for asylum? They were trying the same thing, asking America to allow them to come in, but they were refused [the *SS St. Louis,* May 1939]. They were denied permission to come here to America. They knew that if they return to Germany, which eventually they were forced to, they would be eliminated by the Germans. Who would ever believe that this would happen? Some people tried everything possible without success.

Comparing what we went through to how things are today - we have in America all types of people that come in from anywhere without difficulty, without having their background checked, medical and otherwise. Before we were able to leave the country and come to America, we had to prove our health and have the medical papers, as well as our background checked. But the problem was that the Jewish people suffered all along and they were not wanted because of their religion. It was a sad situation for all concerned. Heartless individuals were running the country. The governments of the world have changed since the Second World War, hopefully for the better.

Especially if I remember stories from many years before - even before my time - the Jewish people were never a favored nation. We, as a Jewish people, always seemed to have trouble, without any good reason. I try to understand, even as of today, what is the difference between us or any other religion? We pray to our Almighty just like any other religion, except in a different language. As of now, we still have that trouble.

We, the Jewish people were - and are - hard workers. We do not wait for a handout. We try to do whatever is possible to make a living - and I must say there were many smart people. Even today, like it or not, there are many Jewish educators in all kinds of education, even science. If we take a good look, you will find there were always many smart people around, there always were, especially in this country, where we are lucky to have our freedom.

Isn't it time to grow up and accept us? Because we will never go away. We are here to stay, you like it or not, we are a nation just like any other nation, and no one has the right to come and destroy us.

Instead, try to learn from us.

Chapter 15
Searching for Survivors

When our sister Hermina was alive she never stood still. She was not just waiting - she was always actively looking for information about our family. She was corresponding with organizations to find someone from our family still alive, maybe our niece or nephew. It was hopeless. We received information, but it wasn't what we wanted to hear. This was also a disappointment. We only have a few letters from our brother Lajos after we arrived to America. He was taken into the Hungarian army. We have no pictures of him. It is in our heart and we are trying to visualize his face, whatever we can to remember him. All this happened in the 1940s. We received letters after the war from survivors who told us that in April 1944, at the end of Passover, our entire family was taken away. Most of the people from our villages around us were taken and also from the city of Helmec.

My grandmother was also taken, along with her sons - even though they had served in the First World War and had been imprisoned in Russia. You would think that would have been enough. Instead, again they were taken to the Army and later released from it to be taken to the Auschwitz camp, and then were destroyed by the Germans and their gangsters.

We never heard from them again.

Even now we are still hoping and waiting, but there isn't any trace of our people, our families, they disappeared from the face of this earth.

Can you imagine that we only had a few letters from our families that my brother Irving saved, correspondence with each of us? These letters are now over 60 years old. We are lucky to have them. That's all that we have from our family. This reminds us of our background when we read it and where we came from.

My sister wrote to our neighbors after the war ended, asking them if they have any information about our family. Across the street from us lived the Gerenyi family. They wrote to us telling us that they were helping our family and they were taking them to the destination, namely Ujhely.[39] This was the center point from where they were taken to the concentration camp. She wrote that they were getting ready to go and the children didn't have any clothing even to go there. She was making clothing from a linen for all five of them. When they were dressed up, they looked beautiful. They are in my heart and in my memory I cannot forget them. She also said in her letter that they went the next day, that is this neighbor, went the next day looking for them to take them some bread. But she was unable to find them. This was the last thing of information from them.

We learned later that they were taken to the concentration camp. My father gave his gold watch to this neighbor and told them to give it to our

---

[39] **Sátoraljaújhely** – A town in northeastern Hungary where, in April 1944, Jews from surrounding villages were concentrated in a ghetto before deportation to Auschwitz.

brother David or to us after the war. They asked us in a letter to help them, yet they were well established before the war. They were Christians, to them it didn't even matter, neither to us, what religion they were or we were. They were very nice people. We do not know whether her husband or the other neighbors came back from the war. I wish I could say happier news. But that was it.

Chapter 16
About David...

Editor's Note:

This chapter captures Maria's perspective on her brother David's final years and the painful distance that grew between him and his only child, Freddy. Her account is filled with love, frustration, and a deep sense of loss. But as with many family stories, it reflects only one side of a much more complicated reality.

This is what happened as she saw it. As she lived it. It is not the full story, but it is her truth. I include it for that reason - and for the honesty and love with which it was written. It closes the loop on his story - not with tidy resolution, but with lived complexity: pain, disappointment, love. The cost of survival.

David was always under financial stress, he had a temper - intensified by the weight of unspoken trauma, business losses, liquor - and strained communication at home. His trauma was the kind that leaves no visible scars but casts a long shadow: the trauma of survival. He was the first sibling to come to America, and the oldest to do so - just before the war tore Europe apart. Haunted by the pleas for help from the family he left behind - most of whom would perish - he must have carried the weight of that responsibility every day. The guilt of not being able to save them, an impossible burden he rarely spoke of, likely shaped every part of his life, including his relationship with his son.

David was far more comfortable in Hungarian than in English, which must have made emotional connections even more difficult for a child trying to understand his father. He also hoped Freddy would join him in running the family vending business. Freddy, however - despite pressure to meet expectations - chose a different path and became an extraordinarily beloved teacher.

None of this excuses the hurtful moments, but it does offer meaningful context. Families carry many truths at once, and memory usually reflects the emotional terrain of the one who is remembering. Maria's reflections are honest and heartfelt - shaped by memory, by pain, and by love. In reading, it's worth holding space for the experiences and struggles of everyone involved.

- Editor

David lived in California. When Irving got married, David wasn't feeling well. We siblings asked him to move to New York with his family. By that time he was in the restaurant business. He was a very good cook. He was the kind of person who wasn't afraid to try anything. He was a hard worker. We never knew how, but he always managed to find a way to bounce back. He never was on welfare! It did not matter what. They decided that it is okay that they will move to New York. When they arrived it was just before Irving's wedding. We didn't know first what it is all about. We didn't have any place for them to move in.

My sister was married and had two children herself. They had to move into my sister's new home. It wasn't big enough for all of them, but it was good enough temporarily. We all wanted to help them. My sister and her husband let them move in their belongings. They didn't have any furniture, only what they were able to pack in the suitcase, like clothing and small items. They had one son, Freddy. He was 10 years old. When they unloaded their stuff, my sister made room for them. They stayed with them. It was difficult. Eugene, her husband, was in the grocery business and he worked very hard. He was going first to the fruit market to buy fruit before he went to open his own store, so he had to get up a very early. There was not enough room - it was a small home big enough for only one family. I told him they can come stay with me. I will try to help them. I prepared for them dinner and bedding as well as I could. I had a studio apartment in the Bronx. It was nice for me, it was comfortable and that is what I wanted.

In my apartment I had a double sofa bed that opened up and was enough for three people in an emergency like this. The neighborhood was getting bad, but I felt at least I had an apartment of my own. They stayed with me for a while. At that time I was working in the restaurant from the morning to late evening. When I came home from work, I made my bed on the floor for myself and tried to manage things the best way we could.

Irving's wedding was getting closer. My sister and I we were busy getting ready and finally it was over. It was a very nice affair. Like any affair there were certain problems, but thank goodness it was over.

Now we had to do something else to help our brother David and his family. When they came here to New York we found out soon enough that he was broke. He had nothing left over from his business. I had to figure out with my sister what we should begin to do for them.

As I mentioned before, he wasn't feeling well and we had to get some help for him. He wasn't old enough to qualify for Medicare and he couldn't have Medicaid, we had a big problem on our hand. We did not know where to begin.

David's wife, Dorothy, was working in an office as a secretary before she got married. She was an American girl, mature and likable. She could easily get a job as a secretary. In New York they needed good secretaries everywhere and she could find a job very easily. She was afraid at first because she hadn't worked as a secretary after she married. I tried to convince her not to worry and I knew that if she didn't succeed in one place she could always get into another.

In the meantime, I said do the best and be happy with what you have. If you try to do more than what you can, you might lose what you have. I myself believe this and accepted it and worked for whatever I had. I tried and I was very careful. I was always careful and never spent money just to spend it. On the other hand, I tried always to do and to have what I needed. I try to help others whenever and wherever with what I could.

All these problems worked out after a couple of years. In the meantime David was able to manage to buy a home on Long Island. It wasn't in the best of neighborhoods, but it was satisfactory.

First, he tried to go into the vending business. He hoped that he could make it and settle down. The money was going quite well, but the neighborhood was going downtrend and he was robbed. Luckily he wasn't hurt. He eventually gave up the vending business. By then, their son Freddy was married. He and his wife had their own home and he became a teacher. He was very good, but after he got married he changed. He did not have too much time to spend with his parents. And could not help them either.

Finally, David went into the clothing business. He always wanted to be on his own and he could not work for other people. He started selling ladies wear such as underwear, pajamas, socks, and brassieres.

After all that, David was getting sick. He had good insurance and his wife was working with him in the business. She gave up her work in the office because that company moved. Their own business so far was doing well, it was okay and they were able to save a dollar.

David found out that he had problem with his heart and needed surgery. At that time they did not have implants as they do today. He told us that he must have bypass surgery as soon as possible and he cannot wait too long. He decided to have the surgery. He needed four bypasses. He went through a lot and at this time he was in his 60s, that may have helped. He had more than enough, with the pain and all. After this operation, he recovered - that prevented him from having a heart attack.

During this time, Dorothy, his wife managed the business. When David was ready to go home and was able to go to back to work, their son had their first child, a little boy. The grandparents were happy, but it wasn't a good relationship. Freddy didn't pay too much attention to them, he was busy himself and his wife wasn't very friendly.

Dorothy was a person who would get along with anyone. David was different - he could be more difficult. With him, it was often either his way or no way. Therefore they did not mingle too much. While Dorothy was alive, it was much easier. As it turned out, Dorothy got sick and needed help, and was seeing doctors. They had to purchase expensive medications. This was getting to be a problem. He did not have Medicare, only private insurance. It was good, but not enough to cover all the medications for both of them as they needed it. David was doing okay, but Dorothy was not. In a short time she passed away on September 27, 1987.

David had more problems. This was about five years after he had his surgery. His son was too busy to help him - before Dorothy passed away they had their second son.

Also, just before Dorothy passed away, a young lady walked into their store looking for a job. She was from Guyana and had no place to go. She was also looking for a place to live. My brother and Dorothy agreed to give her a job and a place to live with the idea that "you work for us and we will give you a place to live." My brother David gave this young lady the name 'Bibby.' I did not know her real name. She was experienced in business. They needed help and she was a very nice person. They all agreed to try it hoping that it will work out. Meantime, Dorothy was getting sicker. And unfortunately soon after that she passed away. This did not help David.

Luckily, he had this young lady now. She was a lifesaver for David. She a very unusual person who was interested in helping an older man without becoming romantically involved. He was very happy that somebody was around. With her help he was able to manage himself through this difficult time. They were getting along. David became also very sick and had more problems. At the same time, Irving had enough problems at home and it was a miracle that he was able to help our brother David. He loved his brother, so he tried to help him. David was in need of financial help by now. He was not happy with his son. Freddy didn't get involved with his father after his mother passed away. It became more of a problem when the mother-in-law of his son tried to butt in. That created more difficulties for him. David used to come over to stay with me in my apartment, both of them, David and the young lady. She was a very good helper and he trusted her. He treated her as if she would have been his daughter. He didn't have a daughter, but she made him happy.

In the meantime, again he got chest pain. He was seen by a doctor - he needed another surgery. I never thought that he would go through it again, but he was a very brave man. He used to tell me that he would not do it again. But now he had to. At this time, I also had a problem myself and I was not able to be there after the surgery. His son Freddy never visited him at home or in the hospital. David was very hurt. This did not do any good for him.

Bibby was with David for hours in the hospital after surgery. She called me after David had the surgery. We were hoping that he will get better.

A day before the surgery, my niece Linda took me to see David. I was very grateful. I was able to see him before the surgery. I would not be able to get there by myself. To take a taxi, a roundtrip, would cost too much. He was in the Long Island Jewish Hospital, the first and the second time that he had heart surgery. He managed and he got better, but not as good as it should have been, something was wrong. A problem developed, he had chest pain and needed a pacemaker. At that time we did not know that the pacemaker was defective. It did not work well and because of that he had a problem with it. He went in and out of the hospital.

When David came home from the hospital, Bibby was around. She was in the store with David, and helped him at home, but she did not do any cooking. David used to cook, but now he needed some help to do it.

The day he came home, that evening, again they robbed him. It was the second time and he was in bed. It was winter, and it was very cold. During the robbery, Bibby grabbed my brother David and ran outside calling for help and they were running together, with my brother in night clothing, barefoot.

The robbers ran away, the police came, but did not find them. That night Bibby saved him. If she wouldn't have done what she did it would have been very bad because they had guns and my brother didn't have any money.

My brother's health failed soon after. He was getting by, when suddenly he had lots of pain. He went to the hospital. The pacemaker wasn't functioning properly, and he was back in the emergency room. He was improving there. Then they had a room upstairs - and they took him up. There, the nurse - I was told - adjusted the pacemaker control in the wrong direction, and that killed him. Unfortunately, we were not there when all this happened, but Bibby was. One minute he was all right, the next minute he was gone. When they came down, she would not believe it when the doctor came to tell her. However, a nurse told us about what happened. That is the only thing we knew - what this nurse told us. He was much younger then than I am now.

On February 21, 1991 he passed away. This was the day when we arrived in America, although the year was different. His son was not told about his death. David told us that because Freddy was not around when he was alive and needed him, that when he's gone he did not want him to be at his funeral. He made us promise him we would not tell his son. David was heartbroken. Despite everything, he loved his son and his grandchildren, but Freddy and his wife deprived him of seeing his grandchildren. It wasn't the money.

The day after the funeral, I called his son Freddy and told him what happened. I felt very badly. He was very upset - he broke down and cried. He was telling me how much he loved his father. I told him, "Why didn't you tell him that before? Now you are telling me - it's too late. He cannot hear you." He blamed us, why we didn't tell him? We should have called him before. I told him that you are his son, you should have called me to tell me what happened. David told us many times - his son is a good son. But he also said his wife was the one causing some of the problems. I told him: "If you want to do something, you find a way. It does not matter how busy you are." I felt this was just a cop - out. Freddy should have paid attention.

Sometimes, the problems start when the mother-in-law and father-in-law interfere. That causes more problems than you can imagine. I saw this firsthand with Freddy's in-laws.

At the time of Freddy's mother's death (Dorothy):
I visited them only once - when his mother passed away. It was a social call.

His father was still alive. Her parents were telling us - advising his father, my brother - he should let them manage his business, that he should retire. They thought he had money - they demanded their share of it, claiming it was the mother's share. They thought he was a millionaire. They demanded their money back. They should have paid attention to how his business was doing - then they would have known he was broke. He was very ill. His money - what was left - was barely enough to live on. He lived alone. It wasn't enough. His expenses were growing by the day. When we went to see his mother last - her son was nowhere. He was outside playing with his sons.

Later, after Dorothy's death, at my sister Hermine's house:
And yes - his father *is* his father. In the meantime, the mother's family tried to decide what to do with his father and his fate. My sister and her good husband, my niece and I - we were all there. All day. My nephew was nowhere to be seen - yet he said later how much he loved his father. A man who truly loves his father should be there to say what he wants to say, not leave everything to others. What were they trying to do with his father? It is his father. He had nothing to say - yet these people thought they had the right to decide his father's fate. Even to talk about him. Who appointed them to be his spokesperson? How could that be? My sister invited them for lunch. She didn't have to. They did come - for lunch.

Years later, after my sister Hermine's death:
Later, my niece called her cousin to let them know her mother - my sister - had passed away. He never called back. Never returned the call. That shows what kind of people they are. All their connection ended there. It was a one-way street.

Bibby remained at the house after the funeral. After I called Freddy, he came over to his father's house and he hired someone to board up the windows so that no one would be able to go in. Instead of checking things out with Bibby, and straightening things out, she was kicked out from the house. She could have helped him with whatever he needed to do.

Before he died, my brother told us that he gave the business to Bibby. He did not have anything in writing. What he told all of us verbally, this is what he wanted to do. Therefore, whatever she did, we let her do it.

When my nephew called and asked what happened to the business, we didn't know because Bibby did whatever David told her to do. Would you know all the details of the arrangement with the owner of the store? What were David's intentions? Therefore, it became more difficult to transfer the business. I also did not mention that Bibby had a friend and she used to visit them and also used to stay with David and helped him in business. He liked her a lot also. Sometimes Bibby's sister and brother came to visit them and stayed over. It was like a family. Now I look back, David was happy. This way he wasn't alone. He had company. They treated him well, and respected him. Meantime he cooked for them whenever they were over. But they also took advantage of his goodness. He was hurt that his own family didn't care about him. He spent the money for whatever he needed.

My brother Irving could not be there as he would like to, neither could I. He was always welcome. He visited him whenever he could.

Soon after, his son Freddy found out that his father David borrowed on his house for whatever he could, to live and to keep the store, and for rent and the merchandise. He did not have a penny on his name, only debt.

Freddy, his mother-in-law and father-in-law, and his wife, thought that he's a rich man and that the business was a gold mine.

My brother Irving told Freddy to sell the house because the longer he kept it the more it would cost him. The interest rate at that time by the lender was 16%. The price of the house was going down and it was more difficult to sell it. Freddy did not respond to Irving, yet he asked me to help him because he was too busy in school teaching. The attorney asked him to sign the papers so that Irving would be authorized to act on his behalf. He promised he would, but it took him a year to do it. In the meantime, he could have saved the interest and so the interest ate up the house. By the time he responded, it was too late. The sale was only able to solve the problems with the bank and the attorneys.

To sell the house, the roof needed to be fixed because it was raining in one corner. The inside also needed to be cleaned up. That was the legal requirement so that the purchaser could secure monies from the bank to buy the house. So Irving complied with that and sold the house.

Irving paid out from his pocket whatever was needed. He also paid the funeral expenses and put up the monument. He paid all this from his own money, even though it is in a letter that Freddy said he would take care of the monument for his parents. Unfortunately he did not.

Sometimes people don't know a thing, they're only happy if they get money. They do not want to take responsibility for their behavior. They always try to find and blame others. Here is an example, we were good and we tried to do whatever we could. Sometimes a stranger comes into the best of families, and that's what happens to them. The in-laws try to dictate and try to run someone else's life. They have no common sense. They cannot understand and learn and respect the other person's feelings and try to appreciate whatever they have.

Don't forget your family because it is most important to have a good relationship with them. That way, you can work out any problem that comes along. It could have been done in this situation, therefore I cannot feel guilty. It is not my fault, one should think ahead. Freddy lost out, including his father's love.

Sometimes people are too busy, they don't realize that time flies fast. It passes by faster than you think. All this anger could have been love, happiness, and enjoyment on both sides and it was just wasted.

I remember when David came to New York, he gave his son everything. He loved him more than he knew. But a stranger came inside of the family and took over, and Freddy didn't have the courage to stand up and be a man.

Life twisted him around. A woman can do a good job - turn the best sons - into puppets. That an only son can be so irresponsible - an educated man - shows that education does not mean you have any judgment. Without common sense, education means nothing.

When my nephew became to be Bar Mitzvah, David wanted his son to have a party like every child has and every parent would like to give. David could not make a big party. He was not rich, but he did whatever he could. He took a Temple and arranged for the family to come to the party. We were all happy about this. We saw our brother enjoy it. After all, he only had one son. He made sure that he got a good education so that he shouldn't work as hard as David did. He should have a better life. All this came about. Freddy was smart and became a high school teacher. He married very young.

After graduation from the university, Freddy went to Israel and then from there to a Greek island. During that trip he met his wife. When he came home his parents weren't very happy and they said to him that you're very young and have plenty of time to get married.

Anyway, he moved in with her in her parent's home. Shortly after that, they got married. She had a brother who was in California and her father worked in a college in New York. The mother was a decorator. She was in business with another woman.

They were, in my opinion, middle-class people. We met them at the engagement party. It was a large party with other people. All her relations were there.

It was not my type of people. They did not keep a kosher home like we did. The date was set for the wedding. It was a catered affair and it was not kosher either. We were invited, my sister, her family, and I were there for the wedding.

They ordered kosher food separately for us. It was a fish dinner. And that was kosher. It was all right with us as long as it was kosher.

We were told to wear a long gown, but it was difficult for us to find a suitable one. First of all, it was short notice. We would have liked to have it when they asked us, but we did the best. When we arrived, we saw there was only one person wearing a long gown, everyone else wore whatever they wanted. We heard later that they were disappointed because they expected that we would pay for the special treatment, mainly for the food that they had to purchase separately because of us.

We all gave a gift at that time for their wedding. I gave a check for $100. My sister and I spent more for our clothing in order that we should look nice. Realistically speaking, we did not need to buy anything because we had different dresses, but we wouldn't say anything to them about it. I think that they were different type of people as I said previously. They were nice, but different. We did not care and we went on our way home.

With my brother David, it was a different story from the very beginning. At a later date, when Freddy's son had the Bar Mitzvah, we received an invitation to the party and it was to be at their home. They owned their home and it was in a good neighborhood.

After we received the invitation, we found out that they skipped the invitation to Freddy's father. His mother was not alive at that time. She passed away before. They did not have the decency to invite him to his grandson's happy occasion. We found out that they were afraid that his father may embarrass them with his behavior. The only behavior he had was that he liked to enjoy himself and to have a good time. I did not see anything wrong with that. That wasn't a good reason for not inviting him. His father was very hurt because of that. The party was at the *Tavern on the Green*. Here too it wasn't a kosher affair. All of us decided not to attend the affair, even though it may have been very elegant.

We have not heard from them thereafter and we did not know what has taken place with their second son, the youngest one.

To raise a child it's not easy. Obviously Freddy was ashamed of his father because he felt his actions would embarrass him - that was more important for Freddy than his own father. Everyone has feelings. Why can't people think it out and try to learn how to communicate? Maybe everything would just be better for all concerned.

In the past, I always sent Freddy and his sons a generous birthday gift and holiday gifts. The year after his father passed away, I decided to try to open up our communications with them. It was Hanukkah time, and these are the times I liked to send a gift for the children. Actually, I sent a check and this way they can buy for themselves whatever they needed. I also was sending my other nieces and nephews a gift at that time. I decided to write a letter and enclose a gift for both boys. I enclosed a hundred dollar check for the two boys, that included $50 for each. I thought that it was very nice and hoped that they will respond to me, at least that's what I expected. I wasn't guilty of the past episodes anyway. In my letter I asked, "Maybe your children would like to know about their grandfather's background?"

I received a letter back from Freddy, with my check inside, thanking me for my gift, but explaining they do not need my money. He said that one of his sons is an attorney and has a good job and is working with a very good firm. The other son is getting ready to finish college and does not need my money either. He was saying it as if now too much water ran down on the river. Therefore he does not need the family. He wrote that they are not interested to hear about the background."No, don't even think about it. They don't want to! They're not interested. Yes, you used to be our favorite Auntie." He even called my brother Irving his ex-uncle. This is what he wrote back to me.

I always liked to know our background and I've learned a lot as I remember and stated thus far, but he would like to have all that disappear from the face of the earth. Can you believe that? Due to his anger he did not want his children to hear about it.

I have no more relation with them at all. My brother wants nothing to do with him either even though he loved David so much. They were very close all their life, up to the last minute, he just cannot forget him. I don't even feel like writing about them anymore. I'm wasting my energy. It was so many years ago. Sometimes my brother speaks about them - he cannot forget his brother.

My best guess, it's been 20 years and we never heard from them. Hoping they are okay, living their life happy. And - wishing them all the best.

My brother Irving found a small book with Freddy's graduation papers, and he told me about it and I suggested that he should send it to him. We had the correct address, but a couple days later the post office returned it stating that there is no such address. Obviously he wasn't interested, not even in his own background. He did not want to know what was even in it.

After all that, Freddy's wife called and requested that if anything, even if 25 cents, was left over she wanted it. This was recorded on the tape recorder by Irving.

They thought we took all the monies that David had. Irving suggested that they can check it from the court all the activities that took place. One of Freddy's sons is an attorney. He could find out anything they wanted. Perhaps they did because there was no additional contact with them. They have decided that we are no longer his family. They do not want anything to do with us.

After all that, we checked into the address whether it was correct or not. It was his address and it was correct.

I like to look around and ask questions and try to educate myself. How could he be so shortsighted? He cannot accept what he cannot deal with and face anything. He does not feel that he ever did anything wrong. I remember the day at the beginning that we were very nice to him. After all, we all went through a lot in Europe.

In Europe our family disappeared and I would give anything if I could save one child's life.

It is very difficult, to even think about it, that a child could destroy a family because of the influence of a stranger. How could this be true? I can't believe it and accept it. It is very difficult. There isn't a day now that I don't think about this since we are only two of us here in America left from our family. The others are gone. Time flies very fast. There's not much time left.

Irving and I speak to each other more than once a day. I am very happy every time to know that he is well. I'm concerned about how he feels. I told him that we are both alike. Our feelings are the same. He comes to visit me whenever he can. If the weather is bad, I try to discourage him from coming to see me. And we feel the same way. We cannot change a person and I don't even try it. We cannot look inside of anyone. We have to accept whatever we see. I hope that he will take care of himself. He wants to help others, but not himself.

He has very nice children that give him comfort and peace. He did not have any life before because of the war years, that is the second world war. We have heart conditions, it is a miracle that we made it. No one knows the real truth. We do not talk about it. We only talk to each other namely, only Irving and I. Even then I try to keep back certain things and I do not want to mention to Irving to get him upset.

Now he's trying to accumulate some information that are in the letters to write a book. Perhaps it would have been better to destroy them, because whatever he did not remember was for the best.

Today it's an easier way of getting more information and he is working on it now. These papers and letters are very important. It represents our life. Not many people have a chance to have such letters which deals with similar history as ours in the original letters. I think it's very valuable for anyone to learn what life is. There is more to it than a person can imagine. People have no idea and can't imagine how much a person can endure. The suffering and pain. There is no one to hear our cry and wipe our tears from our face.

Why all this? Are you so busy to see how many people are crying for help? You can hear those cries. And now your own flesh and blood has the nerve to talk like this? Why? I have dozens of questions, but I cannot find the answer. Therefore I'm asking you, begging you, do something! You are our Almighty, we are looking up to you, and praying for you. On the way our prayers got lost somewhere in the cracks. Instead of getting better, it is getting all out of control. More you try, worse it becomes. Is there anything at all that we can do? I tried and am still trying. Some people are not happy with my idea and I cannot give up, not yet.

I have to figure out what else can help without hurting someone else. Right now I'm very busy trying to finish my life history. It is for my brother Irving. I told him about this writing and he told me he is very happy that finally I have decided to do it. He was after me to do it. But I wasn't sure if I will be able to do it.

At my age it is more to it than just to write. I had to remember the true story and it's not easy. But thank goodness it is much easier and faster than I thought. It is difficult to write as fast as I think. My hand is bothering me. But I cannot stop, I have a job to finish. Sherwin, I am hoping that you will understand and will be able to read it. It looks like I'm giving you another job, even before you have a chance to finish the other. You can wait with this, but it is easier to write it now. I just want to finish it. Sooner the better.

My handwriting became worse because I'm writing faster without stopping. Anything you do not understand in my writing, just skip it! You will type it better than I wrote in my writing.[40]

---

[40] Editor's note (2025): In 2021, Fred's son Josh reached out to me on *Facebook Messenger* with a beautiful note after reading "*Private Good Luck*" and recognizing that it was about his family. We have rebuilt what was so close to being lost - the family ties that bind us together.

Chapter 17
From Clay Avenue to Flushing: Sisters, Work, and the Move That Saved Me

I'm coming back to my sister Hermina. She and her family. She had two girls. The oldest was Linda and the youngest was Diana. They were beautiful children as all children are.

In the beginning, when Hermine got married it was very difficult for them to find an apartment. They lived with an elderly lady in the Bronx because it was so difficult to locate one.

Her husband's business was on Long Island, and it was very difficult because my sister worked in Manhattan. It would have been much easier for her to travel from the Bronx, but her husband was quite different and was quite strong-willed.

I had a long walk to the subway, and it was 'packed like sardines' as we used to say. The neighborhood was very nice. I lived there for quite some time, until I was able to get my studio apartment. It was on Clay Avenue in the Bronx, near the Grand Concourse. This section was still very nice, but little by little became worse.

I lived near one of my girlfriends, Sarah. She was married. They had only an apartment until they were able to get a home. Her husband was also from Europe. After the war, one of his brothers got married and my friend's husband opened a business in the Bronx.

I used to see and visit them. It wasn't too far from where I was living. In the meantime they had two children: a boy and a girl. When she got married she wasn't very young. It was very difficult for her to find someone she liked. It seems that all of us had similar problems. She was also my sister's friend. We met her while both of us lived with an elderly lady, Mrs.Kugler. She was about my sister's age. She was an American girl and she was very nice to both of us and we used to go out with her before she got married.

Sarah lived also in a studio apartment before she got married, and afterwards she and her husband moved into a house.

I did not know that my sister and her husband were looking to move out of the Bronx. Later Sarah told me that there was an apartment and urged me to come to see it. It was a very nice apartment and reasonable. I went to see the apartment and I liked it and I took it. After I moved, little by little I was furnishing it, very beautifully. This was my first apartment in New York. I was very happy about it - and with that, I was able to have my brothers come over at any time. They could have their meals and food with me, and I could help them settle down. It was easier for all of us.

After I was all settled in, my sister told me the 'good' news. What is it? They found a studio apartment similar to what I had in the Bronx, but her new apartment was in Flushing. It was a very nice building, and it was connected to the railroads and buses - everything was right there. I wasn't happy about it because if I would have known, I would not have taken the apartment. It would not matter how much it was or how much they wanted for it. I had no one there and it wasn't the best section. My new apartment was on the east side of the Bronx and I had lived on the west side which was closer to the subway. I could travel by bus to the subway in 10 minutes. I had to walk much further now and it was more dangerous. And now it took me two hours each way by subway and bus to visit my sister. Sometimes her husband drove me to the bus stop. Sometimes I stayed over. It bothered me, but there was no way out, so I remained there the best way I could.

I lived there for 20 years and I kept on working in the same restaurant, namely Ratner's, on Second Avenue.

Finally I decided to look for another type of job. My sister was after me to try to work in an office. That would be something that I would like. Maybe I could learn the work privately and it would not cost too much and I'll be in a better job and will earn more money.

Finally, I did it! I listened to my sister. She advised me to learn how to use the "Comptometer" office machine. What I didn't know was that this machine would soon be replaced by the computer. At this time, the first computer was a very large machine and the comptometer was a small machine like any office machine, except it was more complicated. Although I barely have been in school, I went to a school where they were specialized in teaching this. I had to pay for it in advance even though I had no money coming in and I had to pay the rent, and everything else. I worked very hard and did study as fast as I could to learn. It took me a couple months and I took the test. I passed it. I was all ready to go to work. In the school the teacher never told me not to take this type of work because they won't use them anymore, or that I should take something else. They guaranteed me that they'll find me a job. It was all false. After that, they did send me out for an interview, but there was no job there.

On my own I found a job, but it was very short-lived. The only thing it did was that it helped me to get courage to work and try cashiering. This too was replaced, little by little, everything was computerized. I was not trained for it. The only thing, I was lucky to get a job with an accounting firm. This became more complicated day by day. This accounting firm had customers out of town. I had to travel to different places, such as New Jersey or Mount Vernon. I didn't have a car and I had to take the railroad and I had to carry the machine with me and it was heavy. I was there for a while and then I decided to do something else.

The experience was a very helpful tool for another job with more money. Now I had some office experience. In the winter it was more difficult to travel, therefore I left this job also.

I found another job in the Bronx, where I still lived at that time. I thought it would be better to get a job there. The company decided to move their office into the Bronx, in a new section that was built recently. It was very nice and it was all co-ops. They did not have private homes there.

At that time companies were moving into the West Bronx because the rent was reasonable, and it was easy access there. My company also moved the store and office there. For me, it was easy to go there. I had to wait for a bus and transfer twice. It took more time to travel there. Before they moved the office, the old place was a terrible set up. The place was very old and the floor was all over like a railroad track. I don't know whether I told you that before. It was very dangerous and the place smelled like a chimney. There was no air and it was choking me from the smoke. There wasn't any restroom. All the people on the job were smoking. At my desk there were three girls. One was a very young girl who just got the job. The desks were put together. And the people were smoking all over. I never saw such a disorganized office. I was choking from the smoke and they knew it. I coughed and because of that they blew more smoke towards me in my face. It was very bad. It wasn't a healthy place to work. I was just working on the comptometer and the other people were in charge of the accounts payable. They had stores all around and this was their office. I worked on the deli department accounts. I was also checking the price of the items. Shortages existed in this department before and it was my job to see that every item that they paid for was correct.

The comptometers improved and they became more modern and smaller. I prepared the payment for the bills, someone checked it, and paid with a computer. I had no trouble finding some errors. Merchandise was missing but I paid. They had problems with this department. I showed them the problem on the bills.

With the girls, as I mentioned, they gave me all kind of problems. I was a good worker, maybe I was getting more money, but I was doing a responsible job. They were playing around and I don't know why they kept them. They must have had some reason. They produced practically nothing. I needed a telephone at my work to verify certain things that did not have a price on the bill since they changed it every day. I had to call the company to check out the price and see whether it's correct. I needed a telephone, but the other girls used the same phone. It was impossible to do the job. The other girls followed me to the ladies' room and I was told to leave my job. If I don't go, they will carry me out.

Finally, I went to my supervisor and told him what is going on. You talk to them. I don't know if he did or not. It was going on constantly. They were friends and the office manager was very friendly with them. It was one clique. Then I had to go to the boss. He was there in a separate room, and I told him if this doesn't stop I have to leave because what goes on is not healthy and dangerous for me. He promised me that he would change and take care of it. I know he liked my work and wanted me to stay.

The next day I had a Jewish holiday. I did not work on that day, I was off. After the holiday, when I came back I wanted to use the phone and I couldn't get to it. The tables were put together and I was unable to move it to get to the telephone to make a telephone call. I tried without success. I was trying to move the desk, I saw the legs were put into the track, the front legs, it was impossible to do anything. I was bending down looking at it, trying, when I felt something in my back snap and I was unable to move. I did not realize that I got hurt. How badly I had no idea! One of the managers asked me to get him a report from a file which I didn't have. I had so much pain in my back and it was getting worse. I couldn't walk and I couldn't sit. Even though he saw it, he only asked me what happened. That was all.

After I finished that day, I was trying to get a doctor, that is after work, but I couldn't. I wasn't able to go to work. I called the office manager and I told him what happened. When I can, I said, I will call them. I didn't think of calling an ambulance and no one suggested it. From home I did not call either. I thought privately it's better. Finally I did go to a doctor. I was told that I am very lucky and I should thank my lucky stars and Guardian Angels. I was hurt, my whole back was collapsed. They could not operate. The only thing I could do was to rest and wear a corset to support my back.

Someone suggested to me this is a compensation case and that I should pursue it. Before the accident, my doctor told me when he saw me that I have a weak back. That added to the problem. After that, I was unable to work. I was seeing doctors and was seeking compensation and had a hearing. I didn't have a lawyer and I didn't realize what would be and how bad it was. I liked my boss. He was very nice to me. I wasn't looking to make money or cause trouble for anyone.

After that, the company moved to the co-op. It was a month later that I returned to work because I needed the money. In the meantime, they closed the case and they said that the only thing I can get is occasional treatment and nothing else. I returned to work and I ran into problems. I was unable to sit or walk or work at the job for only a couple of days. Then I had no choice but to stay at home. Struggling, living alone, I was willing to do anything. I told my sister, but not the whole truth. I did not want her to worry. I kept on trying to get help. Everywhere I went I was told 'I can't help you.' At that time they didn't have what you have today. Today probably I could get some help right after it happened but then, so many years ago, there was nothing they could do. It was a fracture.

I was trying to reopen my case with the compensation board and this time I had a lawyer, but it seemed that it was not the right person. The second time I lost the case because I had trouble before with weak bones and the doctor was called in and testified to it. But no one mentioned that I did not have a fracture before and I was working all the time in the same company where I worked. They knew it too, but that wasn't enough proof. They did not want to analyze it. It was because of the uneven flooring that the company had to move their offices. The insurance company talked to me and saw it was very bad at that place because other people got hurt there, too.

I called the company to tell them that I will not return anymore because I'm not able. I lost my compensation case, and I tried to get disability. I did not know if I would get it. After seeing the employment office to register for Social Security, I could not work, and for how long I did not know.

I registered, I filled out the papers, and wanted to get help by myself as much as I could. I found a doctor who was trying to help me with heat packs and with whatever he could.

I was using up my reserve and no money was coming in for over a year. When I called Social Security, I was told that they thought I died or passed away. I told them, no, I'm here and need the money. I went to the office and I checked everything out and finally received all the cash that I was entitled to. In the meantime I needed medicine and they charged me for it because I was only 50 years old. I was a long way from retirement.

I was looking for another job after that and I was lucky I was able to find one on my own in one day. It was a much better job than before and with more money. I was supposed to start the next day. Unfortunately I couldn't even get up from the bed. I was very sick. I called the company who hired me, because I was supposed to start working there. I confessed that, I'm sorry, I'm unable to come to work and I told him why. He told me they will wait for me when I feel better. I could come in anytime. The job was in Manhattan. It was much easier to travel there. But it was hopeless. There was no sign that I will be able to work.

At that time, workers had no real protection. If you were laid off from your job, even for a good reason, you could not collect an unemployment check right away. You had to wait weeks to qualify. Even then you might not get it. Also, you had to prove it - give a proof you were looking for a job - and you must have at least names to prove it. It wasn't as easy.

And looking for a job I had to go through so much trouble. That time the bosses did not care how good you were. You could be the best worker - still, they would find excuses not to take you. Yes, they have the right. But now - take a good look - the revolution already started. The clock is turning back. Finally, they've gotten into the same position. They were let go - whatever was the reason. Let's say because of age - discrimination. Now the fired workers are fighting back. At that time you never heard about that. We did not have any protection. Now - you want something? Just go to court. Before you know it, you build an audience on your side - right or wrong - if you have money.

Looking back at my jobs - I was in a new world - without any experience, getting along with whatever arises. I never was afraid to take on a job. And I did well without any experience. I had no idea what we would be required to do on any job - and did well without knowing the language, hardly understanding what was spoken to me. I must say - I was very brave and I had confidence in myself. I learned how to sell my abilities. On a job - especially when you cannot speak or understand the language - in a new country, just trying to make a living, I became the best of managers. I proved it to them, wherever I went - all on my own.

My neighborhood was changing and became very bad. Hermina and Eugene were after me to move and to come to Long Island. They said it was better there. The drug problem was here, which I didn't know about. I lived in the back, facing the neighbors in the backyard. Recently, I noticed that there were lots of people always there. I did not know who they were, but later I found out that the senior home was sold for a drug rehabilitation center.

I began to be worried about the dangers of living there. When I first moved to the Bronx it was better because it was a residential section. At that time, it was a co-op housing unit and people were moving to that section. I wasn't afraid to live there. It was a Jewish section and one of the best places to live. It was like Brooklyn, but overnight everything changed. I could not even think of moving anywhere because I didn't have a job. I was living from the social security disability income - which was not much. Any place I would have moved, I would have had to pay much more rent.

One night, the apartment next door, an empty one, had been broken into. The super's wife came up. She had called the police. She was beaten up, too. She had come to me before and had asked me for money. She had two children, but she never had any money. She always came and borrowed a couple of dollars from me. I felt sorry for her and I always gave her some.

To my surprise, I found out it was her husband, the super, who had broken in there with his girlfriend in that apartment which was empty. No one lived there. The super's wife too, I found out, was also a drug addict. When her husband found out that she called the police on him, he beat her up. It was terrible. By the time the police came, her husband had disappeared with his girlfriend. No sign of them, no one was there. The police checked it out.

The husband, the super, was involved with a middle-aged man who was selling drugs. When you saw him he looked well. You would never believe it that he was a drug dealer. Sometime before, I met this man when I went down to pick up my mail. He was there with my super, and he started to talk to me. He was telling me he was painting the apartment - the door was open. He asked me if I want to see it, but by then I had a feeling to be careful and watch out. I had the inner feeling because I worked with people, and I got to know them well. I was always able to recognize that something was not the way it should be and at this time I had the same feeling. I was afraid to go in with them. But if I did or did not, it was a chance I will have to take, hoping I will make it okay.

He opened the door more. I didn't walk in - just stood near the entrance, hoping for the best. He was asking me about the wall painting, if I like it, what is my opinion. All I said was 'It's very nice, it's beautiful. Oh, yes you did a good job.' And with that I turned around and started walking, slowly but sure. After that, I went back to my apartment and then I realized what was going on. Things were getting worse. Then my mailbox was broken in, my check and my mail was missing. At that time I was on the social security disability and I was getting my check. I had trouble to get a replacement. I was really getting scared and really worried.

One day, my sister called me and said that her husband Eugene found an apartment for me, a beautiful one and I went there to see it. It was reasonable. This was the building where they used to live before they bought their house in Bayside. This apartment was not too far from them. It had easy access to the Long Island Railroad and also there were buses.

Hermine's husband Eugene came and picked me up and told me not to hesitate and not to worry. We'll manage it. And my sister said you know how to sew...you will work from home. She did not want to hear me say 'no.' I had no choice. I agreed to see it. Eugene came and I went with him to the apartment. It was larger than mine, had a nice size living room like I had in the Bronx, a larger dining room and the kitchen was beautiful - large with room for a dinette table. How can I get this apartment? Shall I let it go? No way! I took it without any delay. They would paint the new apartment the following week and I was supposed to move in at the end of the month.

That night I stayed over at my sister's house on Long Island. I planned to move into the new apartment in a week, on February 1st. I was very excited about moving. During dinner we received a call from one of my neighbors in the Bronx. I did not know her very well. She had just moved in. I also had a new super and I did not know him or his wife well either. The neighborhood was very bad all around. My neighbors were an elderly couple, very nice, and they were also Jewish. They should have moved from there a long time before. The whole building was undesirable. Danger was all around us. It was terrible to live there.

Anyway, that night the neighbor called because when they came home, they were beaten and robbed. My apartment was broken into also. My neighbor found my telephone number in my apartment, so he was able to call me. This was in the evening, and winter, and it was cold. Eugene and my sister drove me home to the Bronx. The police were there, waiting, looking around, checking. Everything was upside down. People said they saw two boys running from my place. They had adults helping them. The day before, young boys were waiting in front of my neighbor's apartment door when I left my apartment. I was sure they were the same boys that had been sitting in front of my building on the steps. They were always sitting there. They were not more than 10 years old, but you could see that they were not regular children. They were the type that were looking for something. I knew they were watching the older couple - and me too.

When I got the call that evening, I knew that my sister was right, I had no choice but to move. I was lucky all this time and this was a life saver. My sister knew more. She loved me and worried. We moved out everything we could that night - dishes, clothing, linens. Only the furniture was left. The next day, my brother-in-law brought a truck, and we moved everything to the new apartment - where I've now lived for 35 years.

Chapter 18
About Hermine...

We were a close family, all of us. My sister was truly special - smart, beautiful inside and out. She was working at home and was busy. She did not go to business herself. She was a good wife and mother and she loved her family. They had a small home and it was spotless. A small backyard and also in the front there is a small yard. She had beautiful roses in the front and also in the back. She planted flowers every year. It was a very good neighborhood. One of the best in Bayside. They moved there after they had their children. Before they moved there, they lived in the building where I have my apartment presently.

As time went on, Eugene later changed his business and went into another one, namely vending. He was successful in the business and he was very careful what he did and how he spent his money. He did not run around or go out on a special occasion. My sister kept a kosher home and her husband did not eat out. My sister was a very good cook. She always had healthy food for her family. She made it sure that her children ate healthy food and her husband also.

He worked very hard all his life, therefore he expected the best food. He would never put up with just any type of food. When he came home, everything was and had to be on the table, ready to eat. The children were waiting and they ate all together like a family. He loved his children. They were his life. Anything they wanted he purchased for them. On the weekend they stayed home. On Saturday he observed shabbos and did not do any business.

In a way he was tired and worked hard, it got easier with the vending machine business. At least at this time, he didn't have to get up and go to the market. He had more time to spend with the family. It was better all-around. It was closer for me also to see them after I moved to my new apartment. I was able to walk to see them on Saturday. It was a long walk, about 30 minutes, but the neighborhood was nice. The trees hung over the street and there were flowers as I walked. It was pleasant. I loved my walk. It reminded me of our home in Europe.

Whenever I came to my sister's home, she always had the best food - pastry, cookies, sponge cake, coffee cake and the best cheese danish. Everything tasted just like back home in Europe. I wasn't as good of a cook or a baker. She was a wonderful cook, and I learned from her. We shared recipes, baked together, made pogácsa. My sister always prepared special food for Saturday. She invited me for dinner regularly, and when I came I never came empty-handed. She'd tell me, *"You spend too much - you need it for yourself."* It was a full course dinner. And she never missed my birthday. Every year, her family brought cake and candles.

Her children were growing up and that kept her busy, They were going to school. It was enough work for her to do, but she visited me often, and I helped her whenever I could. She never missed a day calling me. She didn't take time out for herself.

They were very busy people and they were trying to save so that they could go to Florida and retire there. This was my brother-in-law's idea. He used to live there and had a business there some time ago. He was planning to go back as soon as he retired.

Linda is their oldest daughter. She studied and received a Masters degree in social work. I remember that she got a job in a nursing home in Queens. She was happy there. She worked there for a while and everyone liked her, but she decided to take a job with the state of New York. She specialized in psychiatric work.

Diana was their youngest. She was very bright and beautiful and she had her own mind. It wasn't easy to change her. She always wanted to be in the theater for acting. She went to the Bronx High School of Science. It's one of the best. As soon as she was old enough to register there she did, and she was accepted. Her father took her there every day. She was happy about it, because it was very difficult to get in.

Later she went to a beautician school to learn makeup. She was anxious to follow anything that took her closer to what she really wanted. She learned hairstyling in school. She got a job at Macy's department store in Manhattan, and that was a big step. She was liked by the people because she did a very good job. Here she was getting a good experience in the field, but too many people wanted to do the same thing. There was more competition in this field. She stayed at Macy's for a couple of years.

Finally she wanted to change jobs, but still doing the same type of work somewhere else. She found someone that recommended that she go to register in another department store. She was accepted at Sax Fifth Avenue. She was excited about it. She started to work there. She met different people and she liked her job. It was difficult because you really had to know your job very well to do whatever was necessary. She did not have any problem with that. She worked there for a while. She met all kinds of people, different ones, they were friendly and through them she was getting closer what she was looking for. Meantime she moved out from our parents home and moved in with a friend. She was very young, and her parents weren't ready for that. She was too young to move out. At this time, people were thinking differently and it was difficult to accept it by her parents. They wanted her to finish college and she had time to do whatever her dream was. They were not able to change her mind, you can take it or you can leave it. She continued whatever came her way. She never stopped thinking until she succeeded.

Finally, Diana met more people who were doing make-up in a theater. Being new, she had to join first the union. It was almost impossible. You really have to be lucky! One of her friends knew someone who belonged to the union and was able to help her. She had to take a test or possibly more courses because you really have to be very good before you can get into the theater business for makeup. It took quite some time but she did not give up. Finally, after all this hard work she went all over to find someone that would help her. She followed her heart, and her friend 's advice, and finally she succeeded to get closer and closer. She was getting one job and little by little she managed to get into the union.

This field was overcrowded. There were more people for the jobs and there weren't too many jobs for this type of work. She was very good and she was getting more experience and she knew what they wanted. She happened to be there just at the right time when they needed someone. This was at the union where she was looking for a job. She became and was a member of the union and they asked her to go to the theater. She was very happy and took a job. She wasn't lazy and was always ready to work and never stopped. She was getting into more theaters. She was doing quite well. She was getting more calls and she was always ready to go. Sometimes, they called her privately for a wedding to do the make up for the bride or newspapers called to make up different people for photographs and in different fields. Now she was able to do whatever she wanted. Some of them were large companies that called her in different theaters to do make up. Actors and actresses, businesspeople, and in advertisement. Whatever was needed she was able to do it. As of now she became one of the best makeup experts. She does whatever she likes and she's happy.

She lives in Manhattan and sometimes she comes to visit me. She is busy even now. Her parents would be very proud of her. Her sister Linda became closer and they are both happy. When her parents were alive they lived in Bayside. Linda was working as a social worker for a state hospital. She was happy there and she liked the work. She was socializing, but it took her awhile to settle down. My sister and her husband decided to move to Florida because he retired as they planned. They bought a home in the resort area. They kept the home in New York. Linda remained in New York and she lives there presently. When her parents moved out, she took over the home and takes care of it. Her parents were happy in Florida. Even from Florida, my sister called me four times a week. Since she had more time, she decided to do the things she always wanted and to keep herself busy.

My sister never painted before, except when she was going to school, and that was a long time ago. She never thought how much she would enjoy painting. She remembered that she was very good at it then. So she decided to try to do some painting and she liked it and it became a hobby. There were competitions between seniors that were doing the same thing. There was an instructor who helped them to start and some of the people there were experts, they were very good. Others were beginners like my sister. In the meantime, her husband, Eugene, took up golfing. He learned very fast and that kept him busy. He too met some people there. They were both very happy. The climate was excellent and better than in New York. They were there during the winter and during the summer they returned to New York for a while. Eugene didn't like the cold weather. They came back to New York because in the summer in Florida was very hot. This accommodation was good because they were able to come back to New York for the summer climate and had a place to come to. They had a place to stay wherever they wanted to. This way they did not have to look for a place to stay if he wanted to return home for the summer.

Linda was still single and there was enough room for all. They came back every summer to spend time with the family. I was invited many times to visit them in Florida, but I declined. I would have had to fly to go there because that would have been the best way to go. Whenever they were coming back to New York or going to Florida they were driving. I didn't have a car to go by car and I didn't drive. However, when they returned to New York we were able to get together and to see them. Whenever my sister came back she always took over the house chores just like before - cleaning and cooking. As soon as she was settled, she invited the whole family for a full-course dinner - homemade, prepared by her alone, for twelve people. No shortcuts. She never wanted help - *"If I do it, I know it's done right,"* she'd say.

She baked the very best of goodies! This way the whole family was together and we were able to talk and see each other. Otherwise it would have been impossible. My older brother David and Dorothy and their family lived in New York also and he was able to visit them. Dorothy was very close to us and was always very nice. My sister was always looking for a chance to see them. Their son was already married at this time. We were invited to Freddy's home only once to visit them and have dinner there. And that was it.

My brother Herman was single and he used to come over anytime he wanted - he was always welcome - since he lived not far from me. He mostly stayed on weekends. He rented one room from an older family in a private house. He had cooking privileges even though he didn't do too much cooking. He liked to live there and he stayed there for a long time. After the husband, who was also a Hungarian passed away, Herman remained and lived there. The wife was a head nurse in a local hospital and she was a very nice person. She treated Herman as a friend, and he got to know her well, even though he wasn't an outgoing person.

Irving used to live in the same house as Herman with the same people before he got married. After he got married he moved to Syosset. Herman was able to travel by bus to my house anytime he wanted and he stayed there overnight sometimes, even before my sister moved to Florida. When my sister left and went to Florida, my brother Herman missed them a lot. When they returned from Florida during the summer, my brother visited them more often. It was just like before, my sister prepared dinners and we were all invited. Irving was married by then and he, his wife, and his two sons were invited also.

Later, as time went on, Barbara, his wife was unable to walk and she was confined in a wheelchair. It was very difficult for her to go into the house. My sister used to set up tables and chairs in the basement. They had a finished basement for entertainment and it was clean. We had dinner downstairs with the door open and had fresh air and it was very nice. We used to be very happy about it. She was the only one who always went out of her way to bring us together.

I remember when my older brother David got sick the last time, my sister in Florida also got sick and she needed major surgery, she went through with it and she was better, but my brother David passed away. She was not able to fly at that time and therefore she couldn't come to the funeral. She felt badly about it. She wanted to be there because we were a very close family. We were at the funeral, but as I mentioned it before, David's son was not there. A couple years before my brother's wife Dorothy passed away and then the whole family was there, but not now for his father's funeral, it was a different situation. My brother Irving took care of everything.

Later my sister still came back to New York and did everything as routinely as before. She always continued and she never complained. Always with her kind heart. With her personality or attitude she was ready and willing to do whatever was right and she enjoyed it. The last time she came back, she did complain about not feeling well. She mentioned that it was difficult driving - not like before. With all that she again invited everyone in the family for dinner. Every year she used to do that - invited my brother and his family, the children. She worked very hard. She prepared everything by herself. She made a big dinner - cooked and baked the best cakes. It was about 12 people. We all enjoyed it.

By the way she was beautiful. Even now she looked nice. She was young in age and look. She never looked her age. She was slim, medium height, she was well-liked by whomever she met. She had no trouble getting along with people or any one of us in the family. Sometimes it happens that in any family there may be disagreements, but not between us. We solved any problem that came about the best we could.

My older brother David sometimes forgot and he liked to tell other people what to do and that sometimes created friction, but two minutes later he apologized and everything was all over. He couldn't be angry either. I'm happy to say that my family was different. We did what we could and were willing to do the best that was possible. Many people are different, we had enough to share. We tried to be careful to make our own needs satisfied. We learned to manage with whatever we have, no more and no less. All of us worked very hard.

This time, when my sister came home she was doing wonderfully, walking. She did not have any sign of a heart condition, but she complained of stomach problems - whatever she was eating affected her. In the local hospital they saw that she had ulcers. She was treated for the stomach - otherwise, she was okay. No one told her or mentioned that it could come from her heart. This came to us as a surprise. Just before they were getting ready to go back to Florida, she didn't feel well. All this happened on the weekend. She went to the doctor in the neighborhood and told him about her stomach. She had trouble again and it was bothering her more that night and the doctor told her to take a Tylenol. She did that, but she still was not feeling any better. Her family was at home at that time. They did not know that she was getting worse. All of a sudden, she had pain, and they rushed her to the hospital emergency room. It was in the evening by then and her family took her to Long Island Jewish Hospital to the emergency room. They took her and immediately we found out that she had a slight heart attack. The doctor told them that they could have prevented it if they would have come in a little bit earlier.

Oh my gosh, they never expected what happened. How could this happen? She never complained. Then we learned that it was more difficult for a woman to be diagnosed than today. They didn't study women at that time as they do today. Therefore if it was her stomach it was a sign, but they never knew it. We all learned about it. It was very difficult to understand why and how this would happen to her. She was young - in her late 70s. The doctors never noticed it in the past even when she had the surgery. She was checked out thoroughly and there was no sign of anything. It wasn't a long time before that she had the surgery. We were told later it does happen sometimes you don't even know or have a sign of it.

She remained in the hospital and she was getting better. We hoped for the best for her and that she would get well. She was there for a while and then she came home from the hospital and was ready to go back to Florida. The doctors advised her that she would be better in Florida because of the warm climate than to remain in New York in the cold climate.

Incidentally, I just had major surgery in the Presbyterian hospital in New York while my sister was in Long Island Jewish Hospital recovering from the heart attack. She came out from there before I did and wanted to visit me in the Presbyterian Hospital. Her family brought her there to visit me. She could barely walk, but she insisted on seeing me. We were both happy to see each other. That was her love.

As time came they decided she would go back by airplane. She wasn't in a position to drive back as they used to. And the doctor advised her also not to drive. So they left for Florida after the high holidays as they always did. She flew, and my nephew Sherwin drove with Eugene to bring the car back to Florida. There she felt better and was getting better for a while. Her husband Eugene was a good helper. He was very handy and was able to do almost anything. He could repair anything as needed. He learned how to cook. When you have to learn you do, that is if you want to, and Eugene was able to do it.

On Friday in December she prepared dinner for Sabbath because she does not cook on Sabbath. She did not complain to Eugene, but the next day she called her daughter Linda and wanted to know how she was, but she couldn't get her. I think it was one of the holidays because she was not working, maybe New Years, she wasn't home at that time. My sister called me because Linda usually tells me where she was going in case her parents call looking for her, wanting to know where she is, this way they will know and will not worry about her. This is what happened at this time. My sister was looking for her and I told her where she was. She stayed over at her girlfriend's house and my sister knew her girlfriend and where she was.

After that my sister became very sick all of a sudden and her husband Eugene rushed her to the hospital. They tried to help her, but they told her that she would be better off in New York. She was advised to have heart surgery, bypass surgery. She remembered what my brother went through and because of that she didn't want to go through all the suffering. At that time bypass surgery was the only thing they could do, not like today, where they can place a stent into the artery and that corrects the situation. She decided not to do the surgery. There was nothing else there that could save her life. She chose that whatever will be, will be. She would use only medicine. However, that did not help. Because of that, when she came out of the hospital, even though she felt a little better we lost her very fast. Eugene called Linda his daughter, asking her to come to Florida because her mother got worse and she was in a coma and didn't have much time. The doctors told him it will be anytime and that she will not make it.

Linda at once was on her way to Florida, but by the time she arrived and met her father at the hospital, her mother passed away. She wasn't able to see her alive. Later she called me from Florida telling me what has happened. She was very upset, heartbroken that she was not able to see her mother alive. We never expected that this would happen so soon. You would never expect such shocking news. You are never ready to accept and face it. It is unbelievable. The shock - you cannot believe what you hear. We have no choice - just face it - try to do the best we can.

We never know - our life is a mystery. There is no guarantee what will be next - we cannot plan that it will be the way you want it. Life can become more complicated, minute by minute. Our life - is like a puzzle - trying to find some answers why all this is happening.

In Florida, Eugene and Linda were getting ready and planning to bring her back to New York to bury her here. They made arrangements for the funeral from there. She passed away January 3, 1993.

When they came back, the funeral was held here in New York. Otherwise, it would have been difficult for us. It was unbelievable that she was gone in such a short time. We couldn't believe that it was happening to us. We were brokenhearted to learn about it. My sister deserved the best. As young as she was - only 78 - she was the best sister anyone could want to have - I am very proud to say we all loved her dearly. We missed her - all of us - very much. I just cannot believe she left so soon. Even now, so many years later, when my telephone rings I feel like it is she calling me because when she lived in New York and whenever she came to visit, she used to call me everyday, it did not matter how tired or busy she was. We were very close to each other. It was a close family.

After Hermine died, her daughter - my niece Linda - took over calling me every day, just like her mother. I used to see her whenever I visited her parents. Since I moved to Flushing, I have seen her more often. She was busy with work and life, but she never forgot me. That love was passed down. She was going out dating with her friends. Her mother was hoping that soon she will decide to settle down. She was busy. She wasn't in a hurry and she was having a good time meeting nice people. She was and is very attractive, well-dressed, and she always looks well. She had a good job and she liked it. She used to eat out. She didn't bother to cook. When her parents were here in New York, they took over everything. She was happy having them here.

My niece was very happy and she was seeing someone at that time before her parents left for Florida. She liked him and was considering him as a potential husband. They hoped that she would consider him more seriously. This was before Hermine had her heart attack a couple months before. Linda wanted to have the family meet this young man. They dated casually, nothing more. Her parents met him a few times before and after Hermine became ill. However, things slowed down. Linda had more than she could handle after the funeral.

Passover was just a couple of months after my sister passed away. In the past Linda went to Florida to spend Passover with her parents. It was easier for her as well as for them because the climate was better there. This year was the first Passover in New York.

I tried to have my family over to my place in the past for Passover. I used to make the Passover in my home. I made kosher for Passover and prepared everything. We missed our sister very much. Everyone was doing whatever was necessary. Linda and Laszlo, both were invited and everything turned out well.

Just before the holiday dinner my niece Linda announced that she got engaged and she showed her engagement ring. We were very happy for them. They did not want to delay their wedding, so they decided to make a small one. The happiest moment that my sister was waiting for so long - finally, it came true - the dream she was waiting for. It would have been her happiest day, except I'm sure my sister would have made a bigger affair. I thought that it was the right person. He came from Europe a short time before and spoke Hungarian. Eugene remained here in New York for Passover and to help her with the arrangements. Her father agreed that she could do anything that she wants.

In the meantime, I was busy cooking getting ready to make the Passover dinner. They asked me to go with her to look for a wedding dress. I did. It was the evening before Passover. This was the first time that Laszlo was coming over and I wanted to be sure everything was just right. I had to watch the stove. Eugene suggested that he will watch it until I'll come back with Linda. Also my youngest nephew Sherwin learned how to cook and offered to help me to watch. I always made sure to do whatever I could to help him. He learned by necessity. This way he was able to eat whatever he wanted to make. At the university he had to cook for himself. This helped me and I was able to go with Linda. We went looking around, but it was not easy to find one that she liked. We came home and it happened to be that the dinner was very good. I prepared a turkey. I roasted it. I made a full course with whatever we needed for Passover. I was preparing it all week to be ready in time for Passover. I had 11 people over.

I felt badly this time that Barbara was in a wheelchair and I have a very small apartment and it would have been difficult to come into my apartment. Before all this, she was able to walk and stand and I always welcomed her. I felt very badly at this time because she couldn't come. I sent her some food so that she would have a share from our dinner. My brother couldn't prepare for Passover so he bought ready-made and the family had food at home during the week.

The table was very nicely set and we had the best dessert. It was impressive, and we did the seder properly. The next day, every one came back for the second seder. Eugene went through so much during the months before that when time came to sit down for dinner he just collapsed. We did not know what was wrong. We called the ambulance and it took him to the nearest hospital. Linda and Laszlo went with him and he remained in the hospital. We wanted to know what was the problem. He was kept at the hospital for a day and then they discharged him. He felt better after he came out from the hospital. He did not pay attention to himself. He did not eat properly. That evening Linda and Laszlo came back to the house for dinner, but as I mentioned Eugene remained in the hospital. After he was discharged and came home, he came back to eat with us.

Laszlo lived alone in Brooklyn. It was quite a way to travel every night. After a couple days he didn't come back, but said that after he gets married he will be closer and then he will come more often.

After Passover, Linda found a wedding dress. It had to have a small alterations that would take a little time, but it would be ready for her wedding. She had to go to the store for a few fittings to be sure that it's right. The time came that the dress was finished, but Linda had other things that she had to attend to. She was busy and didn't even take time to eat properly. I was concerned about her. I made sure that we stop off to eat something. I couldn't do what she had to do.

Finally the time came, and they had the wedding. The dress was very nice and so was wedding. The whole family was there and her friends also. It turned out to be, in a way, a very happy occasion. But did it have to be without her mother? We missed our sister Hermine. And it happened to be a very nice young man - she would be very proud of him. It paid off. When she met him for the first time, she did not know the young man would marry her daughter. She saw him only once, but she knew it was the right person. She was telling me - "It seems it will work out." She approved of him. My niece waited a long time, but at least succeeded.

The day after the wedding, the couple went for a honeymoon. Her father Eugene remained in New York and stayed at his home. After the Jewish holidays, he left to Florida as usual. After she got married, Linda still called me. She even took me to the emergency room when needed. I always tried to manage on my own. I didn't want to be a burden. But she never made me feel like one. That's love.

Linda took over and made arrangements with her father whatever was necessary. Later her father continued to come to New York and stayed with them. In the house everything remained the same way as it was before: the furniture etc. Linda didn't have to buy anything to furnish the house.

Later, as time went on, Linda had a little girl, Jessica, a beautiful, smart, loving child. All of us were delighted watching her growing up. I used to babysit for her as she grew up. I told her stories and she liked them. I enjoyed my babysitting job, although it wasn't really a job because I adored her. She waited by the door for me, danced when I arrived, and whispered little secrets in my ear. She doesn't visit as often now - she's busy with school and activities. But the love is still there. I'm proud of her and her parents. She gave more love than I could ever give. Eugene used to come in from Florida every year and he loved Jessica and she loved her grandpa.

In December 2006, Eugene was not feeling so well, so Linda went to Florida to see him. I would have liked him to come to New York because it would have been easier for both of them. He felt it was her home now and he did not want to come because he felt better in Florida. He became sicker and Linda couldn't go there with her family. Her husband had a job here in New York. He couldn't just pick up and go. However, he decided to go there for a short while for a visit. Later, Linda went there with Jessica. Finally she was able to get someone to help her father who stayed with him and thereby was able to help him and remain at home. The doctor was good, but did not help much. The visiting nurse was coming in every day.

The family from New York went there to be with him. Eugene helped Linda and told her what to do because he felt that he's not getting any better and therefore he will not be here much longer. After he passed away, Linda brought her father to New York and he was buried next to my sister Hermina. It was March 1, 2007.

Jessica became 13 years old and had her birthday party in the temple where she became Bat Micva.[41] Her parents gave her a very nice party - something to remember. The family was there and everyone enjoyed it. It was a great event.

Jessica is very good in school. She is a great student. She will enter high school pretty soon.

When Linda's parents moved into Florida, Linda called me almost every day. Today she carries on the same way. She does not miss one day without calling me. When something special comes up she calls me. If I ever need something she is there to help me. I don't want to keep her busy because she's busy enough. Thank goodness, I manage very well. I appreciate her help immensely. I try not to depend upon her. Her own family keeps her busy enough.

One story I'll never forget... When we came to America my sister was working with her first job ever and seeing the first paycheck. She came home only on the weekends. She was staying and working five days as a housekeeper. She earned very little because she was getting room and board. She was worth more money, but it was the first job and first paycheck. She

---

[41] **Bat Mitzvah** – Jewish coming-of-age ceremony for a girl, usually at age 12, marking her religious maturity and responsibility for observing the commandments. Her Hungarian phonetic spelling is preserved here.

came home to us telling me what was her intention. She wanted to send some money home. She put one dollar in the envelope to our grandfather. Our grandparents needed help, especially at that time. She mailed it without delay. A couple of months later the last letter we received from them and they said they did receive a letter with one dollar. They said how happy they were and they needed it badly. They were thanking her and they'll never forget it and she'll be well remembered by them. How grateful they were. We still have that letter in the writings. My sister is not with us, but from memory she never will be forgotten. All her life, she was also the best person, I miss her very much.

My niece Linda, her daughter, calls me now almost every day. Whenever my phone rings, I always think it is my sister. It's like hearing my sister again. We were always very close family. I don't know how someone in a family is unable to work out any of the problems, so they could enjoy life together. A good family relations in my opinion is very important in life. Money is secondary, health is the most important. If you have your health you can do whatever you want, and you're rich. This way you have a better chance to succeed in life.

Chapter 19
About Herman...

During Christmas seasons, we had Gypsies who played music. They were very good musicians. They also made special ornaments that looked like real life. They used to carry them by hand and they were going from house to house celebrating the Christmas. And they were singing their Christmas carols and other songs carrying the "Bethlehem" - I'm not sure if that is what they call it. With Mary in it looking like a live story. It looked beautiful - every year the same thing. Before one of these holiday celebrations, without notice, unexpectedly we heard music. The Gypsies were playing music in front of our window. Usually, they do it so they can collect some money. It was at night, so it was very quiet all around. The music started so unexpectedly and my brother Herman was there.

All of a sudden when this music started, he got very scared and started to run to hide, but there was no place to hide. He was running all around, scared, trying to hide under the sofa. He wasn't able to - there was no room there. By the time we noticed, it was only a minute even, that was enough for the child. They tried to calm him down.

Next minute only thing we knew and saw, was that he wasn't able to speak because of the scare. Next day our brother David took him to the doctor in Helmec. He did not find what was the reason, but our brother still wasn't able to speak. He told him that my brother needs a specialist and that he would have to take him to another place where there would be a doctor that would help him. After that our brother David took him to a large city called Ungvar[42] to see a specialist - maybe he could help. He was checked out by the doctor and they were told that this comes on unexpected. Children and sometimes grown-ups may be affected, however he gave some medications and told David to watch him and make it sure that he does not go through this type of episode again. He will get better in time and if not then we should take him back to him. He could not see any other problems.

We know the cause - he was scared from the unexpected music. It was enough to scare everyone, even grown-ups, for all of us - even if it was just for a minute. By the time we stopped them, it was too late. You never know what a truth it is - your whole life can turn around in a second. Luckily, after a short time, he got better. We tried everything to help. As I remember, my brother was about 5 or 6 years old. How can you predict what will be one minute to the next.

In a couple weeks later he was able to speak. Happily, it got better. We were all happy. One never knows, however sometimes, it can happen.

Herman was very clean and spotless as a child and he was very neat. He was about five or six years old, and every evening, when he went to bed, time after time he had a hanger. As he undressed, he must have that hanger to

---

[42] Ungvar is now Uzhhorod, in present-day Ukraine.

change his clothes for the nightclothes. The first thing was to hang up his clothes. He removed them and hung them up on that hanger and made sure that not even a little crease or wrinkle was on it. It was in the usual place every night - as a routine, all by himself. This was going on for a long time. He always hung up his clothing on a hanger, like the grown-ups. He did this nightly. Next day again. He was a very adorable child.

Our mother kept all of us clean, spotless. We learned from her. I don't know why, when I was about 10 years old she sat down sometimes, she was speaking to someone. She did not notice me. I was standing real close to her, I could feel her body next to mine. I was always around even when she wasn't feeling well. I was trying to help her with whatever I could. I loved her so much that I always wanted to hug her as a child. I could not have a chance since she was always busy. When I wanted to help her, I was told that I am too young. Wait when you grow up.

As of now I started to continue my writing, I remember and cannot forget what happened to our family. If only we could predict the future then perhaps we could have changed our destiny, but as it was no one could believe or expected what has happened.

Before this horror our village was a nice place. It was peaceful. There wasn't much to do for young people, especially if you're Jewish. We were younger than the other girls, however, even then we used to visit them. They were older, but they had the same problems also. In a small place like this everyone was busy.

Now as I'm writing, I'm trying to remember whatever I can, to put together some information. I find myself remembering so closely that, just like as it would be now, my mind takes me back without straining myself. It comes naturally. It's flowing in so fast that I hardly can catch up with it.

As I look back, they were gangsters, animals, killers, not humans. How can this be? Very low class, the worst of what humans that ever was put in this world. They were not humans. So many people were guilty for not lifting a finger to stop it! This cruelty should have been stopped right at the beginning. It's been said that the fear is worse than any sickness. In the beginning they could have been able to stop all this. They are part of the human race that did not bother to help them. I'm so deeply involved going on deeper with my story, my feeling gets out of control and it is very difficult to stop. It affects me very deeply. I wake up my inner feelings, just pouring out what I remember and what I forgot. I can't ever forget!

I ran out of paper, and ink, my hand cannot keep up with my brain's dictation. I am faster than my hand can write it. It feels like in business, the boss dictates to the secretary, she's very good but cannot follow because the boss goes too fast. This is the reason even my pen is running out of ink. As of now, I used up five pens in less than two weeks. I'm only writing part-time. I knew I had a good reason to write. I didn't start before, but now I do it because my brother Irving asked me so many times so I decided to do it. I'm surprised myself how easy it comes back without any problem in a very short time. As I am very lucky and happy that I've decided to write. My brother is very happy that I did. He didn't and couldn't have any knowledge because as a child we had many problems not knowing what was going around. I am in a sense happy that I'm able to and blessed at my age and so many things we almost throw out, when I had the idea to look over all the papers that my brother accumulated. I've suggested to save those papers and put all of them in the book. My brother has about 30 books. They are all from our family writings.

I am going back to our brother Herman. He was younger, and he was able to get a better job after struggling with English - tube bender - a chance for a better job. He wanted to make more money to be able to better his life. He was still a young man. He and our youngest brother Irving - they were very close to each other.

Later on, Herman was able to get a better job with the Defense Department - they were making small tools, all sizes, whatever they needed. He worked there for a while. He made more money. He liked the money - and the wages were more than he ever made.

When Herman moved to New York, he was working one evening, and his boss asked him to help do something before he left. All of a sudden, a shelf in the warehouse came loose and fell on him. He got hurt and had a fractured ankle. He was taken to the hospital. That was the end of the job and after that, he was not able to work. This was a compensation case, but somehow, if you don't have a lawyer to fight for you, you get nothing more but suffering. Yes, you have to be a fighter to get justice - otherwise, as I mentioned, you get nothing, even though it wasn't his fault. Unfortunately, the guilty one has attorneys, and they win for them. Where is justice? The innocent loses the case. This is what happened to my brother.

He had to stop working. While he was recovering, he was called in for jury duty. He met someone who used to play in the stock market. He told him how to work in it. He liked it. When he came to New York, he decided to go in deeper - more money invested - and it seems he became very good at it. Almost an expert. He made money in it, and sometimes he lost. But he did not care when he lost. Finally, he made money. It kept him busy, and this became his life - day and night.

It was like he was addicted to the stock market. He was so busy with it that he forgot even to eat. We were concerned about him and his health. He had ups and downs - just like the market. Our sister and her husband Eugene - they had ideas about stocks and investments. He also was a businessman. He was in business for many years. But Eugene was able to control himself. He did only whatever he wanted, and was very careful how he spends his dollar. Money wasn't coming easily. He also worked very hard all his life, and now he and my sister were close to retirement. He was planning for it and he did not want to jeopardize it.

Our brother Herman was single. After Irving married, Herman moved into the room where Irving used to live. It was better for all of us. Now both of my brothers and the rest of the family would be able to visit me anytime. I had the opportunity to make them welcome - any time. I was able to prepare food or dinner whenever they wanted. Also, Herman was able to visit our sister and stay over from time to time - even in my own apartment whenever he wanted to. I had only a studio apartment. It was very nice. I had enough room for him when he stayed over.

All along Herman worked overtime. He was always too busy and did not take out time to eat. Plus losses in the stock market from the Cuba sugar crisis,[43] before we knew it, he became very ill. I myself and my sister could not take care of him. He needed more help. By then he was very deep in the stock business. He forgot to eat and that added more to the problem. Whether we liked it or not we had to place him in a sanitarium to stabilize him.

Sometimes I thought, "what if one of my family members needed help?" If I got married to the wrong person, then this family member would have a problem, and I would not be there to help him.

Here I was, with my brother. He was struggling, I was trying to remember my father and my oldest brother - when I said goodbye to them, they were crying, and their last words were: "don't forget sisters and brothers and family. You should help each other no matter what." These were the last words, and when I looked at their faces, they were full of tears, heartbroken. I was hit by this. At that time, I would never believe it - this is the last time that I will see them.

My brother Herman went through a lot. He worked very hard, he didn't spend the money on himself. When he came to America, he worked whatever he could get, to try to save even a penny. I felt he was not well; he needed someone to look after him. We all felt this way.

We have the right to live, we have the right to happiness. I agree on that. Maybe if I had a chance to meet the right person, then I probably would have looked into it in a different way. As it was, it changed the situation.

I was very concerned about him. He became involved in a situation - it was so dark, he could not even have a chance to think about it himself. He was going through this crisis and he really needed help. I tried, with what responsibility I could. My sister tried. We could not do much because I cannot drive and going around was a hardship, but my home was open for him. Whenever he needed me, I was there and tried to help him whenever and whatever I could - financially and emotionally.

Many years later, he was hospitalized. He went through surgery, and with that another ordeal and suffering. He was also a veteran honorably discharged. He served in the American Army only a few months. He was in and out of the VA hospital, and finally in his old age, an assisted living facility.

In a couple of years the money he saved so hard - every penny that he deprived himself of, everything even the proper food that he ignored, everything he kept from himself - was gone. It cost lots of money and we could not tell him that it was being used up. He would be very upset and would walk out if he knew. He would not stay there. We had no choice.

---

[43] a stock collapse that wiped out many small investors

Irving could not take care of him - he had his own problem. Even that was too much.

Our brother Herman wanted us to take care of his business. He was not able to take care on the stocks. By then everything was changing. The computer came in the stock exchange. You turned around, and suddenly it was more difficult to manage - especially when your life wasn't set up for business and I could not take care of it. For me it was getting more difficult to travel around by bus and subway. I wasn't able to.

Our brother Irving, he lived close to the assisted living where Herman stayed. He was visiting often. They were very close to each other. He tried to help him more. I tried to manage his affairs as much as I was able to. It was impossible.

I made sure he's not losing his hard-earned money. I paid all his bills and tried to manage whatever I could. He thought that since I'm alone, I have more time to take care of it. The rest of the family were too busy with their own.

I was concerned with what will be - he was running out of money faster than it was coming in. It was disappearing. The stock prices went down. When he found out, he wanted to buy more. Here he talked as though he still had all the money. He had no idea how much it cost for the place he was in - it wasn't worth the high price.

We did not tell him his money was shrinking - that there's not enough left. Or rather, that while we still had enough, the problem was we were concerned that when, or if, he finds out how much money went into the home that he is living in - and the stock is going down, some of them even out of business - he would be shocked. I had a health insurance for him and was paying for it. The medication at that time - we had to pay for it and they were very expensive - he needed more.

Unfortunately, the help in the assisted living wasn't too great. They charged a lot of money for the help they gave. We did not have any choice because they charged everywhere the same rate and some places even more. We paid for the services, but he was not getting it. They hired people that could not even speak the language and made it more difficult for him. The owner was interested only in money and was not paying attention to get proper help for 24 hour services that were paid for. Most of the people in this place were older people and needed help. This was a private place. It didn't help him that there they gave more of a certain medication he was supposed to take and of course they sent him to the hospital to stabilize him. All in all, the services that were paid for was neglected because they were not paying attention to the people in the home.

Again, he didn't feel well and from the assisted living they brought him to a hospital, but they did not treat him well. He wasn't able to eat by himself and they did not bother feeding him or calling us to say what is the problem. They brought in the food and left it there until someone would come to help him to eat. Nobody did.

He called us, and my brother went there and talked to them - without any result. My brother told them he is going to take him home. They were killing him. By then, the assisted living where he was would not take him back. We were told he cannot go back there. He must be hospitalized. As it was, he was in a terrible condition by then.

He wasn't able to walk. My brother took a wheelchair and took him home to his house. The hospital they threatened him for going against their advice. Irving ignored all that.

Irving's wife passed away in September. He brought Herman out from the hospital on December 16, Herman's birthday. The people that were helping Irving's wife came back to help my brother Herman and to care for him. They had worked with his wife taking care of her for many years, and now Irving asked them to come back and help our brother. When they came back, in a couple of days, we saw improvement. He was able to eat and walk. And he was happier. He was getting better in my brother's home. We paid all the expenses from his money - whatever it was, we did not care anymore. The most important thing was to help Herman.

In January he didn't feel so well. Irving took him to the doctor and the lungs were clear and the girls were trying to help to feed him properly and he was happy and felt better but still he didn't have enough strength.

Then a visiting nurse came to see our brother - to check him out. All of a sudden she told my brother Irving that Herman must be hospitalized at once - he has very high blood pressure. Irving believed her. He took Herman to another hospital, where they kept him a couple of days. They wanted to put in a feeding tube - we do not know the real reason. It must have been one of the student doctors who had no idea what he was doing. Instead of putting the tube into his stomach, it went into his lung. The doctor ran to get an x-ray machine to see if he did the right thing. By the time the doctor returned, he passed away. One of the ladies who was helping him was there when this happened.

She told us what happened. She did not know what was happening there. He was better when they took him upstairs - and a minute later, he was dead. Why all of this should happen? Negligence - carelessness - no one cares.

Unfortunately, the lady should have spoken up and say that she would feed him! He ate before without a feeding tube, why couldn't he eat now?

This lady was working with my brother helping his wife for ten years or more and he feels that she should have known better - maybe Herman would be still here with the living. You can imagine how my brother felt all along and still does. He took him out from one hospital and these ladies were very good and were able to help him so that in a couple of days he was able to eat. After that he went to the second hospital. In a couple of days he was gone. We had questions but no answers......

We missed our brother, and now something changed - our destiny. We deserved it - even sometimes we deserve much more and never get it. The situation came without expectation - very surprising, all of this.

Now we are not the best to be enjoying it fully, but I try to do whatever I can, little by little, and I am happy about it. I always try to be happy. I never blamed anyone for my past, whatever it was. I was happy and thankful for it. It made me happy when my family was happy - that was important. If I seemed displeased, it was only if they weren't happy.

Now also, I never expected anything from my family and never once expected them to reach out for me. I was an independent person. Also, I would like to mention about myself. All my life I felt I am different. I am a creating person. I always try to look neat and present the best of myself. I never copied others. I always knew what I wanted. I kept myself busy and didn't have much time for anything else. I tried to be clean inside and out. At my job I was polite and happy even though there was responsibility. At home, I was always very handy, and was able to do whatever I needed. I never spent more than I could afford. I was always respected and never was rich, but it never bothered me. I never had a charge card.[44] I knew my limit. I was a very good manager. I thought before I spent my money. I tried to live modestly. I tried to get along with my family. We were always close to each other and always helped each other and never criticized each other - accepted each other as we are. If I could help, I was willing - to the best of my ability. I think I did that with Herman.

Life was always a struggle - nothing comes easy. This is what I experience now. Whatever it is, it's never too late. You do not have to be married to enjoy life. That does not mean to run around to live a happier life. That does not mean you have partners. You can have a good time just getting together, seeing friends, and enjoying each other's company over a dinner conversation. I can have a wonderful time. It means something to get a little compliment, which is honest and sincere, not just empty words. I don't go for that - never did. I never looked for something for nothing.

---

[44] "Charge card" here refers to a credit card.

Chapter 20
Polyán, Swept Away by the Storm

This is about our family life in the village of Polyán, Czechoslovakia where we lived. The Hungarian name for it was Bodrogmező. Our parents were regular people. Our father was in business and has been doing farming. He was well known and respected - people liked him. Our mother was also a hard worker and respected. They got married very young. Their parents on both sides were very well respected and were business people. They settled down in this small village. Most of the people were farmers, hard workers - they were respected and everyone got along quite well.

The villagers were some Catholics, some Protestants, and a few Jewish families. The people in this village lived peacefully without any problems. They worked together peacefully. The children were playing together. There were two schools in town. The people in this village were farmers. The Jewish people were farmers and business people.

Whenever there was a need for help, the villagers were hired and were given a job. Some of these people were middle-class and able to take care of themselves. Some of these people who could not make a living were hiring themselves out for farming as helpers. They were hired whenever they were needed. They were happy and willing to come to work. Otherwise they would have difficulty in making a living. They have had families of their own. Everyone tried to improve their life.

The village had two schools, two churches, two teachers, and one priest - and in the Protestant church, the teacher acted as a minister. As for the Jewish people, there were not enough of us to build a temple, so we rented a room in a house. In between, we would go to another town for services, because locally we did not have ten adults to make a quorum. In the next town, Lelesz, where we went for services, there were more Jewish people. There were businesses and they had a temple. That town had a mixed population with different religions. In this country, there was freedom of religion and freedom of movement - you just had to follow the law. The taxation was very strict, and the government decided to collect tax directly by district.

In our village, the children got along - there were no differences between them. As for the Jewish children, a Hebrew teacher was hired to teach them at home. It was important that the children have knowledge of their religion. It was too far to travel daily or weekly to the next village for Jewish education. In
that town there were more opportunities. In our village, after regular school, they came home and studied Hebrew with a private teacher. The people in our village lived in harmony.

When the weekend came - on Sunday, early in the morning - the first thing was to clean the front of their building, out toward the middle of the street. There was no such thing as a street cleaner - therefore, everyone did it for themselves. They cleaned their own backyards, and everything looked nice and clean - spotless. You would never know that this was the same village before and after the cleaning.

The church bells would ring, and families went to church dressed nicely. As they came home from church, you could see them, beautifully dressed, walking together, parents and children. They made their own dresses. There was no such thing as ready-made, like in the U.S., where you could buy what you liked - if you had the money. Everything was made from scratch. The average dressmakers made dresses, but it was expensive. They didn't have canned food. You had to bake your own bread. For cooking - everything was made from scratch, too. You were lucky if you had something to cook.

Life was never easy! As the children were growing up, it became more difficult to find ways to educate your children - that is to say, to go to a higher educational school. It was almost impossible. There weren't any higher educational schools nearby, and in the larger cities where schools of that nature existed, it was very expensive. Room and board - and the school - were expensive. Therefore, the children followed their parents' footsteps.

These people were naturally smart. They were unbelievable. They made their own linen. They were excellent. They were excellent cooks. They prepared their own food for their weddings. Their friends got together and helped each other. Everything was set up like it would be a catered wedding. Everything was arranged in the backyard, with all the decorations and music.

Gypsies who lived in the village were hired to play their violins and other instruments. They danced and drank and had plenty of food. They were happy people - and hard workers.

We were also happy people - we did whatever we had to. On Sunday, after they came home from church and had dinner, they came out in front of their buildings. There were benches, and we were watching people walking by - some stopped for a conversation. This was routine in the village. The young people got together and went for a walk. They all knew each other. There was nothing else to do.

Sometimes, they made some arrangement in school for shows with the students. These shows were almost like professionally arranged and done. Sometimes the population got together and they also made some sort of a show and entertainment. They sold tickets for it. They were not professionals, but it was successful. Most arrangements were in school.

There were places, like bars, with large rooms for dances for young people. Those that wanted to attend purchased tickets to the dance. Most of the music was played by gypsies, and it was Hungarian - such as "Csárdás." These musicians were very good. Some of these gypsies played beautifully and were famous. Our local gypsies were doing it just to make a living. Not too many people hired them - they were afraid to do business with them. They were very poor people, and realistically speaking, they were not treated properly by the community. These people tried to help themselves, but they were not trusted by the locals.

In our village, we had gypsies who would visit. One older gypsy woman was known to be very good at telling fortunes. People said what she saw came true. I remember hesitating to see her. I was afraid of what she might say - afraid she'd say I would never make it to America. I wasn't ready to hear anything bad. At that time, before Germany's rise, everything still seemed okay. We didn't have the paperwork or affidavits we would need to leave our home in Polány.

Whenever our uncle came to visit from America, he always reminded us: "In America, you have to work very hard. Money does not grow on trees!" That was his message - over and over.

But the gypsy woman said something different. She told me, "I see a big trip coming. Very soon, you will travel. You will be packing your suitcases. But there will be problems."

She said I would arrive in America after a long trip. I would be surrounded by people who were not as good as I had hoped. There would be difficulties. But, she said, eventually things would turn out better. Still, she never told me I would be happy. That part I remember clearly. She also said we would experience great heartache. And looking back now, I can't believe it - what this person was telling me came true..

I must tell you that I myself never believed in fortunetellers. First, I would not plan anything - whatever they would advise me. As of now, I don't know whether it's yes or no. I know one thing - that I tried with another lady later, in America, since I heard that she's very good. She was supposed to be the best there was in fortune-telling.

I used to see her all the time coming into the business where I worked. She was working, doing odds and ends. She was very young. I found out who she was, and I asked her why she gave up fortune-telling. I found out that she had been suffering with headaches and she couldn't handle it anymore. The pressure that came with fortune-telling - she couldn't bear it anymore. It was the doctor's advice that she had to stop, and she felt better.

I asked her if she would do it only once for me, and I would appreciate it. I was willing to pay whatever she wanted. This was the second person in whom I ever believed when it came to fortune-telling - and she proved it. She felt sorry for me, she told me later. She agreed to come for dinner with me. I asked my brother to come with me, and we went out for dinner.

She told me not to ask any questions. She would just have the dinner and enjoy it. If there was anything important, then she would tell us. We should not question her. We would have to be satisfied with whatever she had to say - and nothing more. I agreed with her.

We finished our dinner like nothing had happened. Both sides were happy and we parted. It wasn't like a business meeting - it was like a family dinner. She didn't give any information at this time. She understood what I wanted to know. I must say that she was very good. Whatever she told us later - it happened. I also knew that she was holding back something. It was better, according to her, that I not know.

Soon, we found out - whatever she said, it was true. After that meeting, we did not see each other. We parted as best friends. I never went back or looked for another fortuneteller. Just like with everything else - there was good and bad - take it or leave it. But you cannot build your life on it. Sometimes it could be a very dangerous road to follow. Therefore, you have to learn how to manage your life on your own.

You have to follow your better judgment. Learn how to communicate. Take your time if you do business or personal that is more involved. Your personal life is like a marriage - you must be extra careful. It is much easier to be careful than to be sorry.

I will try to continue the story about my village where I came from. Up to 1938 everything was all well until then. We never had any problems before this point. My father was always there - he helped the others whenever help was needed.

A new teacher was chosen to come to teach in our village - prior to this time the teacher we had retired. He had been there many years - he settled in our village. He established himself there and his family. This teacher was a young man that came into our village. He was energetic and had a beautiful voice. He was a Roman Catholic.

Before the Czechoslovakian government was established in 1918, it was Austria-Hungary and the town was called Bodrogmező in Hungarian. After 1918, they could continue to teach, from 1918-1938, the Hungarian language. The population was Hungarian. Both languages - Czechoslovakian and Hungarian - were allowed to be taught in the schools, but the Czech language was emphasized, to be studied a certain number of hours per week. That was part of the study program.

Czechoslovakia existed 20 years, then unfortunately everything changed. Thereafter, the people in the northern Sudetenland - there were some uprisings. They hoped to go back as part of Germany, and the Hungarians thought they would be able to be reunited with Hungary - each back to their own country, as it was before 1918. The Germans promised that they would get their land back. Each country would be united with their motherland - therefore they went along with Germany. They never dreamt that Germany would double-cross them - which they did. They learned the hard way, but it was too late. The match was lit, and the fire was on, and no one imagined what would be coming next.

Everything happened so fast that the people were not prepared for this tragic situation! It was a horrible nightmare. Unfortunately, people didn't have a chance to get out, and they did not have any knowledge of what would follow. The Jewish people suffered most - approximately 6,000,000 were murdered by the Germans. If they would have had a chance to get out, they would have gone to a safe place. However, unfortunately, Israel was not yet established and was controlled by the British. They had the so-called "White Paper" that limited migration to the future Israel. The British had control of the land - in cahoots with the Arabs - due to the oil that was needed by them.

The people in this world have really no good reason to hate one race or the other. It's not a good reason to be hateful. The older generations were not educated enough about the previous civilization.

At the present, Israel has improved life for everyone - even for the Arabs that come to the hospitals, and the doctors take care of them. Unfortunately, the Arabs have not gone into the 20th century with their philosophy - and they do not accept progress. They themselves would have a better life by working together and educating their children without hatred - teach them brotherhood. Unfortunately, again, they will not accept changes in their education for the 21st century. They all could improve their lives by helping to create peaceful coexistence with Israel. This is where the problem exists throughout the world - not accepting progress.

Selfishness, stupidity, ignorance, hatred of the fellowmen - without knowing why. Their philosophies have been twisted to their favor. If the leaders of these people would want to live together in harmony, all of them would benefit by it. They presently live backwards, going back 2,000 years without advancing. I'm trying to sort out these problems and to see what would have been - if anything - to prevent the situation that we went through, if it could have been prevented.

As I look back, I had knowledge about something that was to happen, because some people were running away from Germany in 1937. Some of the people stopped by our business. I was young - I heard my father and a man talking, and the man was telling him stories about what was happening there in Germany. He knew only that they were picking up Jewish people - that was the beginning - and those people disappeared, and they never heard from them again. He had no idea what happened to them. He was running away so fast, he did not have a chance to see his family. He left without money, no food, and no clothing - he was running ever since.

Thinking back, I asked myself - how far would he be able to run? Sooner or later, they would catch up with him. He was running in the wrong direction - the Germans were coming in the same direction. I hoped that he had a chance to go to a safe haven. Who knew what happened to his family?

At this period of time, very few people knew what was going on in our country. We only had one radio in our village, so that people were able to hear what was going on. If we could have known at that time, our family could have escaped and saved all of us. We lived at the Czechoslovakian and the Hungarian border. We did not have any war yet. It was a peaceful country.

At this time, the people were not informed enough to know what to do. The world has changed during the past 70 years quite a bit. No one had any radios, television, and newscasters as it is today. It was a completely different world at that time. The communications and the world were quite different.

With the population, the government was smart. They gave the hope that Germany will help them to get parts of Hungary that were lost during the first war - the people innocently went along with them. The people in the area of Czechoslovakia always wanted to go back to the old Hungary. Their cooperation with the Germans cost them their own lives and their families' lives. These people hoped that it would be better for them to be part of the mother country. Thus, they helped the Germans to succeed - but in the end, they paid for it dearly - a high price.

Finally, they allowed it to happen - the genocide of millions of Jewish people that were destroyed! Who will help them now and give them a good living, help them to get a job? If they were sick, the Jewish doctor would help them, and if they needed medication, they were able to get it. But now, what do they have? What did they gain? Whom are they going to blame now? No more Jewish people left in their city and country. What religion are they going to go after now? How far will they go? It appears to me that this will never stop. This can go on forever, and they will never learn! If the present wasn't enough - how much more will they need? It is unbelievable how the world turns against one religion - who helped them in every way.

Innocent people - children - what happened to them? Including my family - my father, my brother, his wife, and their children - all perished. Never heard from them. After we left home, we did not see them or have not received any letters after 1941.

The population over the world may wake up from this nightmare - or maybe they're celebrating their success, whichever! I hope that they wake up! It is a good lesson for them - this tragic situation. In general, the people of the world knew what was going on there - they were just watching, listening, and they did not lift their finger to help them or to stop them. Some apologized because they knew that they have sacrificed lives of so many innocent people - and those that did help were very brave people. Some people were lucky - they
were able to get out. Some of the countries were trying to help them - to give them asylum. Some of the biggest countries allowed only a handful of people to come in, and many were forced to go back and die. My question is: how do these people feel now, after what happened, all that took place?

Those countries that refused entry are guilty, as they helped to pull the switch. They ignored everything they have heard or have seen - to them it was unimportant. To them, there are only rumors. But to me, it is very important - because if there is just a little wind, before you know it, it becomes a hurricane.

You never know. However, there must be a sign that can be predictable. Therefore, one should never let it go until it is investigated - and pay attention to it.

After the war, we received letters from all kinds of people - some of the survivors. They called themselves all friends. In our village, they have had a lot of losses. This was the Second World War.

They were not tortured as our people - namely, the Jewish people. And if these people would have wanted to rebel - referring to the true Christian people - they could have done something. Everyone was waiting for a miracle to happen.

There's a price for everything. Sometimes you might pay - and it will cost you your life and your families! Was it worth it? There are all kinds of people in this world, and they are willing to do anything - even killing innocent human beings. Life is sacred - and no one has the right to take it.

In the beginning, all those countries that were involved with Germany - they trusted them. Were they blind? The leaders never learned the truth. They themselves were in trouble. Later it was too late! Some that survived - they became wealthy. They stole everything from the Jewish people. They destroyed their lives and their own country.

The situation was very bad. The neighbors wrote that they suffered so much, and they didn't have anything to eat or clothing. They asked us to help them to come to America. They had no one to turn to for help. They wanted to go to school, but they couldn't afford it.

They tried to convince us and tell us how much they have helped our family - how they were hoping that our brother's children would be coming home. I remember, before they took them away - my father and my brother and their children - how much they suffered and how much he went through. No food, no clothing, only suffering. They did not have any money to buy things, and no one was there to help them. Now they have the nerve to ask us? Telling us how good they were to my family? They were watching our families taken away. They themselves are telling us how our belongings were taken away. They took everything that was possible as soon as our families were taken away. They were telling me how they were taken away - also how they were taking our belongings.

We had our business, a large building with a large farm, animals, horses - and even the government was helping themselves from the products of the land. This happened to be Slovakia.

In order to claim it, we have to hire an attorney or go back in person. Thus, Slovakia controlled the area where we lived after the war, and they took over all our property and any of the income that it generated. They were also in cahoots with the German government and helped them to take our people away. You can't imagine how much our people suffered - and we here in America suffered by knowing how much pain they went through. Even today, I cannot forget those beautiful children. They were very smart - we have some letters from them. They wrote to us after we arrived to America in 1940.

Unfortunately, the trouble began long before - after the Hungarians took over in 1938, and then in 1940, the men were taken away for labor by the Army, and there were no people to do the farming. Unfortunately again, the people were in trouble in their own home, because there wasn't any food for their children or for adults. What would you do if you were in their position?

After the labor camp, the people returned and began to work on the farm again, but in many cases it was too late to do anything on a farm. And the political situation changed - the followers of Germany created more problems - the Jewish people were assembled and taken away. Besides that, the brownshirts, followers of Germany, were doing their dirty work.

Later, in Slovakia, the government took over, and the people reported - according to the letters we received - that they had to learn the Slovak language, and they had a lot of problems.

Those Jewish people that survived and came back from the concentration camp wrote to us and told us that the people in the villages and towns were not willing to help or return the things that they had taken from the survivors' families.

I will try to go back and make it so that you can understand this era. To put it in proportion to what went on - 6 million people, yes, they were Jewish - what did they do to these people and their countries that they had to be destroyed? How come that no one stood up and spoke up for them at the very beginning and defended their fellow human beings? What did they do to anyone, besides being Jewish and following their own religion? Can you answer me that one question? I may have millions of questions. If you can find one reason why they deserved it - killing innocent people and innocent children! There was no one from the beginning to speak up for these people! The whole world was looking, but no one stood up willingly to stop this massacre - this genocide.

A small group of men decided to destroy another group of people - and their followers were worse because they did not speak up and did not act against the destruction of humanity! They were gullible! And they believed that everything would be just fine once they destroyed the Jews! Why was it that so many people lost their mind?

This wasn't enough - one man with military power was able to create genocide, not only in his country, but in all the countries in Europe! There were different religions in every country, yet they did not speak up. I must tell you that even though they claimed to be innocent - they weren't interested in committing the crime - but they are part of the group that did. In my opinion, they are all guilty. Some did not live long enough to see the punishment that they deserved. Some escaped, and some poisoned themselves to avoid a just punishment.

Seventy years later, I am lucky enough to be here, in my right mind, and be able to write what I remember. I have a good memory. I consider myself lucky - especially at my age. It seems that the whole world went crazy! They lost their senses. On the other hand, I can't blame the world - but the countries, and their leaders, and their followers.

But let's say - if they wanted help at the first uprising, when it began - those people must have known what was happening around them. Okay! One man, ten men, a thousand men. One country was bigger than that. How could they overlook what was going on around them? What did they think? Were they so sure that they would succeed? This, I really cannot understand. And it's very difficult to understand that those people did not hear them! What did they do to them? What was that anger, that madness, that created all this for so many helpless people?

Just answer one question - as I have been reading some of the letters that we saved from people who came back from the Holocaust - where could they go back to? Obviously, they were there because there was no other place to go. Also, these people were hoping that the rest of their family may come back - however, they never did. Unfortunately, only a handful returned - and they were still living in fear.

My brother Irving likes to save papers - and we have many of the letters that came not only before the war, but after the war from neighbors that lived in Polyán. Letters from different people who went through so much. I'm trying to translate these letters into English from Hungarian. I tried to read every one of them - nothing but heartaches. I have much more to do. I hope I do have time and will be able to translate them all. It is unusual to have so many letters, which I should thank my dearest brother - he saved them all. I didn't know he has them until recently. I tried to sort them out, and I had the biggest surprise at what I found. Those letters are at least 70 years old - for me, it is priceless.

It makes it very difficult to go through - one after another - but I went through them. It makes it very difficult and heart aching how my loving family disappeared in such a horrible way - I cannot accept it, and it is very difficult to deal with. Oh my, I do not wish anyone such a heartache. No one ever should go through that.

We try to be strong, but pain is pain. Sometimes it hurts so much, I can hardly bear it. My brother and I - we both feel the horrible weight we carry day in and day out. Each one of us, silently. Only once in a while do we try to express our feelings. We both try to cover up on the outside what we feel on the inside.

Oh my G-d, what happened?
I would never, ever have believed
this horror - this nightmare - could have happened.
My beautiful family... children...
And no one stopped them.
I can never forget that - or forgive.
I will repeat and repeat again,
Hoping maybe somewhere, someone will listen -
And try to do something about it.
It should never, ever happen again.
My heart is aching so much.
Nothing - and no one - can help me.
Oh my Lord, my mighty G-d -
Can You answer me?
I am sure You know the truth.
I know You wanted to punish the guilty -
And it's still going on and on.
It is time to stop this suffering - all over the world.
I know I should not even think about it.
It is not my business.
Yes, You are right.
I am trying to see - maybe this way,
I might get some answers from somewhere.

I know neither You nor anyone else
Can guarantee what life will be.
Therefore, I am turning to You for guidance.
I'm hoping You will hear me again.
I have no other place to turn.
I know You are very busy,
But I'm asking for Your help and guidance.

Chapter 21
Encounters with Europeans in America...

Some people choose statues to pray to -
That is okay, if that is what they choose.
It does not matter what they choose.
Still, over the world's history - old and new - it does not matter.

Many times I think back, remembering how everything used to be. Sometimes I was terrified thinking about the painful memories of what we went through. How could this take place that so many nations let one man, an animal, a madman, take over and rule the world.

No one cared, no one tried to lift their finger to stop that horror that was going on in the beginning. Some people in some parts of Europe tried, but unfortunately they couldn't do it on their own. If they would have been able to get together at the beginning, perhaps they could have stopped it and done something, but no one did.

The whole world was silent. Why? I have lots of questions, but I cannot find any answers.

A person of a different nationality pointed out that just because Jews were different, they were smart, they could have learned from them. They were professionals: they were doctors, lawyers, businessmen of all kind. They were good people religious, farmers just like their neighbors, they helped people, they employed them and gave them jobs. There were managers and teachers. They were helping those that wanted to learn and they never hurt anyone. They helped to build the country and they were hard workers. Most of all, they respected all religions and people. If it would be the other way around, I'm sure our nation would not allow to watch how they made us suffer. They would try to do something or they would use everything to stop it.

As I read their letters over and over and try to understand the horrible destruction. The world had the tools to stop this horrible nightmare. How come that they ignored it? Were they deaf? They did not want to even try to understand the hatred inside of the country. The jealousy of one group to another. Was it just because of religion or something else? What was the reason? Why? Who gained by all this suffering? Did anyone gain by this?

Yes - those criminals, sick-minded people - lived only until they had the power, the glory. Show me - what did they gain from all that? In the end, the result was that they themselves paid the price for it. Not all - but at least the top leaders. They tried to save their own lives, running to South America. And some sneaked into America also.

After all those nightmares, most of those people tried to cover up with lies - and some have gotten away with it. But even for those who were punished, it wasn't enough. It doesn't matter how hard the punishment was -

they still got away easy, because no punishment could begin to compare to what they did to those millions of people they destroyed. There were probably more - those who were unknown and not counted. So many people missing, and children, all ages, suffering.

The founder of Czechoslovakia was Thomas Masaryk, and he became the president for 20 years and the Czechoslovakian government controlled our area. He died in 1938, and the government collapsed. The territory was taken by different countries. At this time, the Hungarian government - with the Germans backing it - succeeded in regaining our region, what had been once theirs. The population was very happy to be united with the so-called "Motherland," with their own country.

I was still at home when the Hungarian army marched into our village. They always wanted to get it back - finally, they succeeded. The population was very happy, they celebrated and collaborated, but the final payoff of their collaboration was destruction. They never dreamed of what would happen - and no one did. After the war, it was too late. The lives of these people were completely turned around - since they were not under Hungarian control. And this time, they were not happy, since they did not expect it. I'm referring to the part I lived in and came from. Instead of their own language, Hungarian was replaced by Slovakian. The Hungarians were getting the destruction. The Jews were not there any more - who are they going to blame at this time? Now, non-Jewish people there have to start a new life. They lost whatever they had before and are suffering - they're asking for help. Some of them - with lies - were able to come to America. Very shrewd - they got away with lies before.

Accidentally, I met them in a business place. I stopped in to purchase something there. I met the owner. As we were speaking, she asked me where I'm coming from. I told her. She said, "Wait, I have a very good friend of mine - a customer, a young couple - who came from the same place." She said she knew them for years and they were her best customers. I said, "OK" to myself. I had nothing to lose - why not? Before I had a chance to answer her, the couple was there, and she introduced me to them.

They came to America after the war. They were a very young couple. Both of them had very good jobs. Everything was all right. I mentioned that I'm a senior citizen - and of course, they could see that. They asked about me. I usually don't give out information, since I'm a private person. I give respect to people and I love people, but they were very anxious to keep up our friendship.

I mention the above because one learns from it, and one would never expect their reason.

They were telling me that they expected her mother to arrive for Christmas, which was only a couple of weeks away. She had no one here, and they asked me - when she arrives - would I speak to her on the phone sometimes? At that time, right there, they asked me to come for dinner. I said I'm Jewish - and they, of course, were not - and I do not eat outside because I only eat kosher foods. They offered to bring kosher food into their home.

I thanked her for the invitation, and I expressed my feeling that I would not be able to go, since I'm not looking, at this time, for friends. I'm retired and not able to entertain and keep up with any friendship - even though I regret it. I cannot - I'm very busy, and it's a hardship for me to travel anymore, I go only where I have to.

All of a sudden, she said, "I have a lot of Jewish friends. I can say all my friends are Jews." She said she would pick me up, she has a car, and would bring in kosher food.

I still said no, but she insisted. And finally, she said that her mother would come only for a couple of weeks. She was here before for a year - she visited them - but she has no one to see because they are working, and they do not have time to entertain her mother. She is lonely.

Therefore, I agreed to visit them in their home - without entertainment and no dinner. Just to visit them. She did not waste any time. She insisted I see her that weekend, and she would pick me up on Saturday at 5 PM. Finally, I agreed. I told her I would go - but only for a short time.

She arrived somewhat late. Her mother had already arrived from Hungary. I did not know that her mother would be there with them.

When I arrived at their home, her husband was working at the time. She spoke Hungarian well. We understood each other. They were very nice people. And the mother also. They had purchased pastry. I too took some pastry with me, because I had mentioned to them that I only eat kosher food.

Finally, the mother was telling me that she was looking for a job - anything - such as a housekeeper, or working for senior people. She does that type of work whenever she comes to America to visit her family for a couple of months. She used to sleep in or, if needed, do day work only. She said she's a very good cook. She said they had an agency that usually helped her mother to find a place to work.

She asked me if I needed any help. She would be happy to come and help take me out for lunch while she stayed in America. I told her I did not need anyone. I also said to her that the person must be an American citizen. She told me that she can give references and any information with regards to her previous jobs. She also said that it would cost me less than an American. As I said to her, I did not need anyone at this time.

She began telling me what was going on in Hungary. She pointed out how some people became millionaires and many others do not have anything else except suffering. There are many others that are coming to America to make some money as housekeepers, jobs, or whatever they can find - and this was the reason why she came to America. I got enough information of what she was interested in - that did not make me happier.

I did not want to hear her telling me about her thoughts. First of all, I did not want anyone - not even for free. I do not look for bargains. If I need help, I know where to get it. Secondly, I will not hire anyone just because they speak my language. Especially, after what we went through in her country. No one is innocent.

The mother was telling me stories that she knew and remembered - but not the ones I wanted to hear. I knew all the stories before.

She showed me one picture. What was that picture? When I look at it, right then it hit me hard. The picture showed a big empty land, not a tree there. I saw only one man standing, wearing a coat, without any movement. She was telling me all about it. I already knew what it was all about! The man standing there was a Jewish man, middle-aged. She was explaining what was going on. He was told if he does move one step, then they will shoot him. The other people were watching when they shot him - and he was finished.

Naturally, they are innocent - but the others are the guilty ones. I heard that story before.

I silently watched and listened to the story. After that, I got up and asked her to take me home. She said that she will - and her mother will come along. I politely asked them if they would like to come up to my apartment. They did. They spent a couple of hours with me. I served them pastry, fruit - everything was okay.

Then dinner time came. I did not expect them to stay for dinner. It was getting late. I looked at the time and it was later than I thought. They still insisted that they like my home, and she told me that she would shop for me and clean - whatever I wanted to do. Again, I told her that I did not need anyone. I could see that they were not very happy with me. After this, they got up in a hurry and left without a word - and I never heard from them again.

What was the motive? To get a job and to help me whether I wanted it or not. I understood who they were. I wondered why she showed me that picture. That did it! What was she thinking?

The young couple came out after the war. She told me how they came to America - she and her husband (that is, the young couple). She said she went to Germany. Her boyfriend was already waiting for her to come to America. It was a place where other people were waiting, at the Jewish Agency - they arranged for those people that did not have a place to go after the Holocaust. This couple was not Jewish. How did they manage to come to America - that is the question! They did not have to leave the country - they had a place where to go. She said that she came to improve her life. They never went through any problems as the Jewish people did. How did they manage to come to America? They had no one here. This question remained unanswered. Why did she keep that picture for herself? Was she proud of it - showing it to me? Why did these people help them? They never went through the problems that the Jewish people did! The more I think about the situation, the worse it becomes. Sometimes with lies they were able to manage their way for their own benefit. Innocent people who really needed help - no one heard their cries.

~

My brother was walking with one of his sons by a pizza store in Long Island, New York. They decided to stop in to have some pizza. It was lunchtime. He had never been there before. After they bought the pizza, his son accidentally dropped the pizza on the floor. When he bent down to pick up the pizza, the owner came by to help him. "Never mind, I'll give you another one to replace it," he said.

At that point, the owner looked up and saw my brother's face, and all of a sudden he said, "I know you. You gave me candy in Italy during the war."

He never expected to meet him in America - especially in a pizza store. From that time on, they became the best of friends.

What is most interesting about this story is that after so many years, a child could recognize a face - even as a grown man - from a different country.

The above is a true story. Remember, a child without hesitation keeps that memory. Children grow up to be young men.

When my brother told me about it, many years later, I was overwhelmed by this story. Because of that incident, they became good friends, and they even took pictures together. My brother and his family became customers ever since. It is the best pizza you would want to eat. Now they bring home pizza for the family.

This is part of life's experiences - we often ignore or forget it.

∼

Story about what happened to my sister:

After the war, she went to a store looking for some clothing and heard someone speaking our native language. When she approached her and asked where she came from, and when the woman looked up, all of a sudden, she recognized her. She was from the next town where we lived in Europe. She had gone through the Holocaust and was a survivor.

It was a happy reunion for both of them. In a big city like New York, it can happen. As we see, life can bring surprises.

Chapter 22
About doctors and healthcare...

1. The Insurance Trap

The insurance field is a very big problem, and if you're lucky you have government insurance or private, but it is causing us more problems than we need. You must have insurance, but it's very difficult to keep it when the price is going up every day. Everyone thinks that seniors have money - that it grows on trees - and that we must spend it to improve our life. That would be good, I wish it was true. We are getting increases from all sides - Medicare, private insurance, and the deductible. When the government needs money where do they turn, to us, we the seniors in our golden years. That sets us back. You sacrifice yourself, spend your whole life paying money, which you yourself can use, so when you need the insurance - you should have it. No one cares where the money will be coming from for those increases. There is so much waste all around us - that is the biggest problem in healthcare. That should be looked into. Our Social Security income will stay the same - there are no increases in sight. Where are we going to get those monies for payment? The government can print it, but we cannot. Today people are suffering because nothing is left since the interest was taken away - that was helpful when I earned a few extra dollars from my savings. I have bills to pay, and am using up the money that I saved trying just to live. The conditions are worse now than ever. Let me just tell you, without insurance we could not even get a glass of water from the doctor!

But insurance companies should take an inventory and see the injustices that they're doing. They need our money and we need them to approve the care that we deserve and need. We must work together, not against each other. Only then can these problems be solved. I always tried to have the best insurance because, just in case you have a serious problem, I would be covered. I worked six days a week at the time - long hours, low pay - to make it sure I had the right insurance. I used my better judgment and paid it every time.

2. Doctors Today

With all this insurance you are still struggling to get the right help, trying to find the right doctors. If only we could find a quality doctor who would be able to help my dearest brother and myself. We can hope and pray for it, but I don't know if that will help. There are doctors that try to help - what they think is help - who really try to do a good job. But I've seen others destroy healthy people. Before even you know how good they are, already you must go to take tests that you may or may not need. Instead, they should try to understand you. If they would only listen and try to communicate - that is out of style today.

Doctors are too busy. They have no time left for you, not even to stop and listen why you are there. They already know everything about you from the computer. Why would they waste time talking to you? They have become self-centered. I'm sorry to say, but it is so - it is true. Some of them have very bad behavior. I feel they should have been trained better. They don't want to spend time with the patient, but expect more money for less service. Just because they become doctors does not mean they should be - especially not for the sake of money. This is the biggest problem in today's practices. Something is missing.

Their knowledge is very specialized, and they won't give advice except in their immediate field. It is not like it used to be when I had one doctor who did all kinds of jobs. Now, if you have more than one problem you cannot get any help unless you have more than one doctor. Even then, how do you know what kind of a doctor you really need? As a layperson, you know only that you don't feel well. What does each type of doctor know? I really do not understand. I'm trying, but how can I? You have to look for them and you become so frustrated. They're the same. They have no patience to deal with older people. How can you trust a doctor who is not willing to work with you? This makes it more difficult to get help. I try to manage, but it is difficult with a doctor who cannot get the answer or is much too busy or does not have the experience for what we need. The answer we get is "I am sorry, but I cannot help you."

Doctors should learn about people; they should not be judges. They should follow their specialty and give undivided attention to help whatever their patient needs without hesitation. Do the job the best way possible, without discrimination due to age or sickness. Every sickness should be treated equally, and that is the doctor's job. They should never forget that. This is a very serious problem, as I see it and experience it. We cannot get the right doctors. All have some excuses and this makes it more complicated and creates more headaches.

And the patient? No one cares. They forget about the patient - especially if the patient is lucky enough to reach their golden years. Respect should go along with age, and doctors should try to make a better life for all of us. They forget they will have to face their future. Today, doctors have a rose garden, and they think it will be there waiting for them when they retire. I hope it will be. I wish nothing better. But I must say, nothing comes out as you are planning. I have seen people like you. They are so sure of themselves now, but they fall down very fast. They did not know what hit them. Since you are a doctor - you think you will not need one? You can't help yourself. And then what? You will be faced with our reality. You will become a senior, just like we are. The same condition you put us in. I assure you, you will be there, too. You will looking for help and find no one will hear you. You can't blame no one but yourself. Now you would like me to feel sorry for you? You made the bed - sleep in it. Be careful - with all these modern tools - you might not be able to continue your practice, and you better wake up. The next generation is extremely smart and with them they may be able to replace even you, the doctors. Change your attitude. Ha! You would be happy to have those people that you did not want to deal with. They were not good enough.

3. Healthcare and Money

Secretaries make it very difficult for everyone from the start - maybe that's where the problem begins. They are so busy, or perhaps not organized well. There is no system, from A to Z, to make sure they know their job and follow the rules. If they did, it might be easier to get help and save time.

There would be better communication and people might be happier. As I see it, the problem begins with money, naturally. Before you even see a doctor today, they already know how much they will make from that visit. They try to schedule tests because there's money in them. That is the most important thing: money. And the patient - that's not important. I'm afraid to say, as I see it today, the next generation has a bigger challenge ahead than I ever had.

The present generation failed to do the job. We learn and try to help ourselves, but after all, we need some professional help. We should be able to rely on them when we really need help. I'm sure I'm not the only one who feels the way I do. There are times I become very frustrated and there is no way to get what I need. I am sorry I don't know who to blame for it - perhaps we should start with our leaders…But that's another story.

4. Waiting Rooms and Rushed Visits

Any time I have an appointment I always like to be there on time. When you arrive, it used to be you would not have to wait too long, but today all this changed. Sometimes you spend hours waiting even though you have an appointment! The secretaries get carried away and forget who was there first, and you're still waiting. I went in to the secretary to find out what is the reason. There was someone before I came in I was told. I will be called in shortly.

I'm still waiting. Finally I told her people are walking in after me, so many, and I'm still waiting. Eventually she realized and asked for my name. Then she woke up and called me in. They forget about me. Some of the workers do not take their job seriously. If they can't meet the requirement of the job, then they should not waste our time just sitting and waiting. I try my best and am patient without complaint, but after all, I think they should take me in consideration also.

We worked very hard all our life, so when time comes to retire, we should be able to enjoy the little time we have. No one knows the future, but we hope we could make it a little bit easier, without headaches and heartbreak. We are human. We try to be very concerned about everyone, including the doctor. If we cannot get the right help, then we have to try to find someone who will take us into consideration too. We are going through a crisis also.

And then, once you finally get called in, it doesn't mean the waiting is over. You would expect your doctor to know we have come in and you would not have to spend another hour waiting for him. Finally, your doctor comes in, says hello, takes a minute to look in the computer, and then asks you how you are - before you answer him he runs out. He has no chance to get an answer. Sometimes they forget why we came there they are so busy.

We would be happier if we would be able to speak with our doctor and he would have time to listen so we would be able to communicate with each other. That is the only way to get the right help we need. Today doctors don't have the time to listen. Instead, they should try to explain what is going on with you besides just saying hello and goodbye. In the long run, we all would be better off and maybe save time, instead of running around. Like this, we cannot accomplish what we really should. How can they help? They think that they know the illness, but do they? How is it possible?

They ask questions, but do not have the time and the patience to wait for the answer. The only answer they want is yes or no. Otherwise, they become angry. They lose their temper right there. You can tell right there that they do not want to deal with the patient - it does not matter how good they are.

If you have a question, before you finish asking it, the doctor disappears again - with the precious creation [the computer] in his hand. You think you're waiting for the doctor to return so you can finish your question - but then, his helper comes in: "You can leave now. The doctor is finished. Come back in a couple of weeks."

Today, they direct nurses to do what they themselves used to do. They take the blood for the blood test, check the pressure, do the cardiogram. The nurses prepare everything for the doctor and they have all the answers. And the doctor, when he comes back in, he just okays it. You think that this is enough for us - as patients? Then he will start to say that everything is ok, and if you interrupt to find out how was it compared to the test before - because you never heard from him - the doctor does not have the time to tell you the results of those tests. Before you have the answer he just disappears again.

The question is, why did I take the test? What was the reason - was it for the interest of the doctor or for the patient? A person takes the test for the purpose to find out what the problem is and what the patient is suffering from. He deserves an answer. This way the doctor would be able to help. But the doctors are too busy, they do not have time to read the report, and it's easier to say to the patient "everything is okay," even though the patient is not okay. Just to take tests becomes meaningless.

When you ask to have a copy of that report, you have a tough time getting it. The helper says you have to ask your doctor. I cannot give it to you. "This information is for the doctor himself." By law, they are supposed to give you a report, even a blood test, but they do not care. If you ask them to "Please mail me a copy," they would say, "Yes, we will." They promise but it never comes, and you have to call again and again before they finally act. This type of difficulty exists all around, even in the biggest hospitals.

They are interested in taking tests, but when I ask "What did you find? What is the problem?" there is no answer. We're back in the place where we were before. Why do I have to go through so many tests, not because of him, but because I'm yet hoping we will get the result one way or another. It is our life. We have the right to know what is the problem with us and to decide what we want to do. By right, the doctor should take out time to explain what is the situation and what is his idea to do next to be able to live with. We should understand in plain English, whatever is possible, and together try to help to find the problem We would not have to go home and find a dictionary to learn what goes on with us.

How can they help you when they don't spend even five minutes with the patient? The excuse is usually that they're very busy. Today it is very common. I cannot understand and accept this type of treatment. We have appointments one after another. I'm sure other people go through the same situation.

There was a time when I was seen by a specialist after an accident. I was recommended to see one of the best neurologists. I didn't know what kind of a doctor I needed, so I decided to go when I was told to go. He was supposed to be one of the best. The doctor who sent me there was an internist, and he was nice enough to listen to me and to try to help me.

When I arrived to the neurologist, I was asked to come in. I sat down and was waiting for the doctor. As he came in, he was watching the time - how many minutes will he spend with me and how much money he will get. He wanted to know in advance, and I wasn't happy about that. If nothing else, this for me wasn't acceptable.

He sat down and all of a sudden he asked me many questions. Usually I'm able to answer the questions, but here, all of a sudden, I tried to answer yes or no but added an explanation, because I felt yes and no for me is not an answer. I did not feel I came here just for yes and no. I tried to speak to him nicely, when all of a sudden he said I do not want any more answers, only yes or no. Then I got up and I said to the doctor, "I'm sorry I made a mistake. I have the wrong doctor."

All of a sudden he was very surprised. He asked me to stay and apologized. But that did not make me change my mind. He tried to stop me and pleaded "Please let me examine you at least," but by then it was too late for me. I did not have to put up with this nonsense. There are more fish in the ocean than one. I need to express myself to be sure I have the right care - that's why I went there in the first place. I did not go there for socializing. If I went, there was a good reason. If he was not able to do what he was supposed to, I do not want him.

Is there anything else we can do? Oh yes - we can all run around again and try to find someone who sees you and doesn't ask for more tests. You might think that you lost your mind. He can't see anything wrong - only that you like doctors and therefore you create a problem - and it is all in your head.

Above all, you are lucky - if you have your sanity and a healthy mind. Does not matter who you are - without that, what becomes of you? The medical field will lose their wisdom - or let's say, you are finished with them.

They feel that you lived enough. They tell you "we cannot help you. Try to understand your situation and help yourself however they can." It's easier for them to call in a psychiatrist - because you are a senior, so you must be mental. If they would use their brain a little harder, maybe just then they would be able to decide to help. Even though some of the doctors are getting closer to being seniors - that does not matter. They have to go with the flow - otherwise, they're not in style.

Also, today, psychiatrists do not care about people. The only thing they care about is forcing themselves on a healthy mind - especially if the person has insurance. They want it all, just for a piece of the pie. Instead, they do everything without asking - and give them a label: 'You are mentally ill, and I must help you. And this is very dangerous - we must do something to stop this. This should never happen. There are so many people who truly need their help, and they do not see them. If you need help, you know where to find one, and you get one - but they should not push you or make it a habit to forcefully try to destroy someone. Some of the doctors will try to help, but others do not. The patient might need medical care first, but they do not want to see it - they just try to ignore it, and instead do everything to protect themselves from further trouble.

We are being shortchanged - our life is in danger. What are we doing about it? Whose fault is that? I read about people demanding better services - better education, better schooling, better training. If we let them get away with it, how do you expect better services? Needless suffering - it seems this situation just keeps on going. For how far and how long, we are yet to see.

5. Emergency Rooms and Medication

In life, we have all had difficulties, and every person has their own story. I usually get sick on weekends. If you call your doctor and tell them that you need some help, that you don't feel well, usually the machine answers and says that if it is an emergency, go to the hospital. If you have an emergency, you cannot even call an ambulance. They will take you to the nearest hospital, not the one where your doctors are. If you cannot drive, you must take a taxi to go to the right hospital. We are lucky to have taxis when you need one, but sometimes it gets more expensive and we cannot afford it. Even then, it is more difficult to find someone to go with you to help you, especially on the weekends. Even with the best insurance, you still have big problems. We are helpless at times we really need help.

I do not want to depend on the emergency room. It is very dangerous to go there. The patient gets lost. Even some of the doctors - you never know.

It is the worst place to be, especially if you are alone.

Oh, the nurses - yes, I know there are some nice ones, but there are some not so nice. They should not be there. They should not even be a nurse. Some staff people can be very rude. They do not follow their job as they are supposed to. They think they are in the driver's seat. But if you have insurance - it is not a charity. You expect respect and proper care, whatever you need.

If you are lucky enough, you have your own family doctor, who cares for you and he will see that the staff does their best. But today that is not existing. Your own doctor does not want to go to the hospital when their patient is there. Everyone is too busy. No time even to listen.

When you arrive in the emergency room, you learn your doctor has all the information, the hospital does not. They will try to contact your doctor, but sometimes they cannot reach them. If you're lucky enough to get someone else to help you, okay, but otherwise be careful. You might be sorry you went there. Without knowing you, they take more complicated tests to find out what's wrong. You can be there for a couple hours, sometimes almost a day waiting and going through all those tests. When they finish, you must see the doctor for the result so you still have to wait.

In the emergency room, the doctors always are asking how they could help me, so I tell them to sort out whatever medications I don't need. Most of the medications and side effects are worse than the sickness. They do not take time to check it out and all of that adds to the problem. More medication, more problems. The answer is that they did not give it to me, therefore they cannot take it away from me. So I started to help myself! I began one by one and finally I left only a few to take and I felt better. Presently, I take only what I really have to and I try very carefully to check all the side effects.

If you need medication, you have a problem. First, if you need a prescription, you have to ask a secretary. He gives you a medication and you feel worse from it. The side effects are worse than what the medication is supposed to help. And if you've been taking a medication for many, many years, and it makes you easier to live with, now the drug company or the insurance are trying to change it. We never know from one day to the next and this makes it difficult even to get the medication you have been taking. I am taking this medication for so many years. My doctors previously tried to change it for others that might be better for me. But it seems it did not work out. Although we tried a new medication from time to time it seems I always went back to the first one. And now I come to the point again I had to send in for another authorization so I would be able to continue to get my regular medication. I feel this is very difficult, it makes it almost impossible to live with. It's bad enough not getting the help that we really need. Do they need to do something to make it more difficult to exist?

6. Pharmacies, Profits, and Patient Abuse

And now - to the pharmacists and the drug companies - everyone is looking out not for your benefit, but their own. They will work hard enough to get what they are after. I'm sure they're smart enough, and they know how to wiggle themselves into the situation to get their way - to earn as much as they can. In the short run, they were able to accomplish what they were after. These people are very nice to the helpers and workers, but when they were changing around staff, it became from bad to worse.

Finally, the pharmacy reached the goal, incorporating with new partners. At first, he started with the best people, but later, they transferred them to other places. The first pharmacist did not continue what he tried to accomplish - he could not be everywhere all the time. Then he became very arrogant. He forgot that he was also working there - even though he was there the longest time. He too treated customers no better than the others. They forgot how difficult it is to get customers. They forgot courtesy and respect for others.

For a while, I had to live with them. However, I decided not to do business with these types of people. I will never take any abuses or insults from anyone. I was thinking to let them know what's going on. They did not care. They were making mistakes in filling prescriptions, and this happened on many occasions. I am sure other people are going through this same situation where an order is mixed up - we hear about it all the time. But if we could fight it, they have the money to fight back and cover it up - it does not matter what. You couldn't talk to them since they didn't want to hear it. The prices they charged - right or wrong - they didn't care.

As a customer, what can you do? You're honest, and it becomes your headache. So, I decided to walk away and say nothing. Many times, I remember, both owners came to me, calling me to come back. They wanted me. I was a very good customer of theirs. I never had trouble with people. If they respected me, I always tried to give them respect in return. I always paid cash for my purchases at the drugstore.

If you want to be treated right, then do as you would want to be treated - with respect. I know, I've seen and experienced it myself. It is a disgrace that some people do not see how they behave towards helpless people. They think that they are above everyone else. Their behavior should not be allowed anywhere - but especially when you're paying a high price for insurance that goes higher every day. That is your money, you're paying for it. You're trying to make the best possible. People think that it's not my money - why should they help me?

It is our money and we deserve the best and should not be abused. I try to speak up. If not for us, none of them would have a job. Now they have a big mouth; it should be closed, and they should do what is needed. We must speak up, because no one is doing us a favor. We are paying a high price for the services that we get. They get more money than we ever got for the same work.

Years back, if I would open my mouth, they would have kicked me out. I could not collect unemployment even though I was being fired. They would tell them the reason why you were fired. Now they think they can do whatever pleases them, but not so fast - now I can put in a complaint about the abuse. Sometimes we don't want to bother with it because it's enough to live without aggravation - it's not worth it.

When you see the bill from the doctors, and you realize how outrageous the charges are for what they have done. Some of the doctors never visited you at the hospital, but they apply charges as if they did. If you have insurance, they submit a bill to them and get paid - though they never came to see you. If they do, it is just for one minute - to say hello, ask "How are you?"- but not wait for the answer. All this reflects today's training. This is our life. We are being told this is the best that you will be able to find anywhere. "Take it or leave it" - that's the answer. How long can we take it, and what can we do about it? I'm afraid - we cannot do anything about it.

The responsibility should fall on the hospitals, where the patients are. They should account for their behavior. There is no excuse. It is a disgrace today how many people get away with misdeeds. It seems that no one is willing to take their responsibility seriously. Plainly, they do not care, and nothing is important, because they get away with it. Why not? Why should they care? Some don't even care for their own. Why should they care for anyone else? The main thing is to get more money - that is okay. They do not feel that they have to do something for it - it is coming to them. Okay, they work hard. Didn't we?

Yes, today it is more expensive to live because of inflation, but if it was less expensive before, the wages were also less. And we worked harder because we did not have the computer as is today, which is much better than it was. Even for a doctor, it seemed that it was very hard work, but think today how much easier it is. There is more knowledge available. The computer helps to save time. Therefore, the doctor should spend more time with the patient. But they do not. They spend the least amount of time ever.

7. The Biopsy That Saved My Life

I decided to look for the best doctors on my own. I need a good doctor who cares and is respectful and will try to spend or give quality help and have time to listen to his patients. I had no choice, I didn't feel well. I went to the best doctor and the test results found something. It could be cancer. I went to a second doctor for another opinion. He sent me to take the test again. When we got the results, he said he would not do anything at this time - that I should wait. As you know and can see, I did not wait. I knew what I was facing if I listened to him. I went to a third doctor who did the test again. She reviewed the results and told me again to wait. I told her again about the first test results. She told me she could not see any problem on the latest ones.

I told her that they should look again and see, because I was told by the doctor that on the first test there was something - but it was very small - that there is no reason for surgery. I insisted that she should look closer and see, because I know how I felt. I can tell - I did have a problem. I wasn't looking for surgery. I just wanted to know - to find out the cause of my problem. She told me that sometimes, when we get older, we change inside just like we change outside - and sometimes a problem can disappear without anyone seeing it. But I was not that old. At my age, it *could* happen, but I didn't believe it. Finally, she advised me to go back to the doctor that sent me to her and have him take a biopsy. She said that would be the only way to know for sure.

At this time, I had only lost a couple of weeks - not a whole year. I agreed to the doctor's advice. I told the first doctor to go ahead and do the biopsy without delay. He said that with the biopsy, we would find out the truth. I went through the test without delay. When the biopsy results came back, the doctor told me that I was right: "It is what we thought it is." It annoyed me that now I had to have surgery as soon as possible. I agreed with his decision and we made the arrangements. I had the surgery just in time. As you say, I have the knowledge and experience to solve a problem the best way possible. I can tell a good doctor from a bad one.

This shows that many do not have the knowledge, what they're supposed to know - that is, knowledge and experience to recognize the danger that they should have learned. You should know your body. Sometimes we can see things before the doctor could. The difference is that they can save your life if you are aware of things and recognize the problem and face it.

After the surgery, the doctor was very happy. As he received the report - this was after the surgery - he called me. He himself went through very carefully to check if any of the damage affected the parts, and he told me he did it just in time and it did not spread to any other organs. I'm safe. I'm okay.

Later, going to follow - up visits, he was always very happy to see me. He told me some of the people were having so much trouble, but with me he said that I am doing so well. I reminded him that if I'm okay, it is because you are a very good doctor - the best in the world. "Doctor, I want to thank you for caring and listening to me."

My doctor told me after surgery, if I had any problem within five years, to come back there. After that, it is questionable that it would return.

Later, during my follow - ups every six months, my doctor was always happy to see me. He told me that I was doing quite well. Now it is over 10 years past, and he said that I am really remarkable how well I'm doing. I reminded him again that if not for you, I would not be here - not even for five years. Thank you again. I'm lucky that I used my doctor with his knowledge and experience, and that he cared for me. It was not the money he was looking for, he told me. He said he would help me and would charge only what the insurance company would pay him.

Now he retired three years ago. I was seeing him until the end, and I wished him the very best for his retirement. He advised me to continue follow-up visits at least one more year. Believe it or not, I've seen other doctors after that, but it is unbelievable that I cannot find another doctor like he was - not even close to him - and I'm still looking. I do miss him. I never gave up and I try to help myself the best I can, but I cannot find one who is caring - to whom life is not just numbers. I do not understand why or how they became doctors. I really don't know. Now, after 16 years have passed, I will thank our Almighty who helped me - to give me a healthy mind and kept me alive.

8. About Stents - timing is everything

This system - placing stents into the arteries - was just very recent. My sister heard some rumors that at Stony Brook Hospital they were experimenting with implants, putting something through the artery in the groin that could save a life. I told her to try to get some information - maybe it could help. In 1997 I was part of the first group of women to receive it. A stent was implanted in my artery that October. I did not worry, it was a miracle. Before this, they only had open-heart surgery. I didn't have to go through bypass surgery, as my brother David did - twice. I didn't know if I would go through with it. Thanks to those scientists who discovered this device that helps to save human lives without major surgery and with less suffering. This has improved life. This will bring it to your attention why I am older and still here. G-d bless them who worked so hard to bring about a lifesaver, who helped us to lengthen our lives.

I have one doctor, a heart specialist, who helped me and my brother Irving. I have two stents implanted by this doctor, and my little brother Irving has four. I must say - my brother Irving is a very unusual person, with what he went through. He has never forgotten his family. He loves them. He took care of them more than he was able. He suffered with them in pain. No one knows how he felt - no one knows inside. He needed help - in business and at home. Finally, it caught up with him.

He was taken to the hospital, where he was told that he needed a stent implant. The blockage in the arteries was 90%. After further checking, he had to have an additional three stents. He had some skin reaction, so they kept him there for a week, and then they added the three more stents. Thank goodness he's ok. That prevented him from a heart attack.

You should not throw away your life. That is valuable - more than anything else. I'm not 21 anymore. I have a heart condition and I was lucky because of this new knowledge regarding stent implant, but my oldest brother and my sister weren't so lucky.

As I mentioned it before, my brother David went through open-heart surgery twice. He went through a lot of suffering.

My sister also - not old. Unfortunately, she suffered. The stent was not used at that time. The only thing they used was surgery. My sister remembered how much our brother suffered through with the first surgery. She did not want that to happen to herself. I was talking to her one evening and the next morning she was gone. It was very close to the discovery of the stent. This is called progress with suffering.

My brother got his stents in the year 2000; mine, the first one, was in 1997. The stent saved my life - thank goodness I'm still here, as is my brother, and I can write about it. If it was not for the stent, we both would have been gone long ago.

9. What I've Learned

This is the advice I recommend to others about healthcare, especially in today's situation. It has everything you need to know. It can save your life. Knowledge is never too much - it always comes handy. Whatever it is, you will know when you need it.

Your health and your life is priceless.

If you are well, you're able to make a living and enjoy every moment, and you must keep on going. It might take a little longer than you expect it, but it will come, therefore you must believe that. I try not to harm - I read and listen. It is more important than ever. So many are misinformed about life - they do not and cannot face reality.

Especially if you are alone, you are responsible for your life. Sometimes it can be really scary. Think carefully before you make any judgment. Don't make a decision in a hurry. Slow down and ask questions. See different doctors for advice and then you will be able to make decisions with good judgment. Examine whatever is best for you. After the advice, choose and follow-up and do whatever you need to do to improve your health. If you're still undecided what is best for you, then think of those people who depend upon your help. Do you know what will be the loss if you don't take care of yourself?

I must say that I know - I was always a different person. My belief is: to prevent a bigger problem, you must take care of the small one. And not wait - or delay - getting help. It seems I was right. I proved it so many times. Sometimes it is difficult to convince others. In my life, in my experience, I must say - I have been convinced so many times. Not just in your health field, but in all of life's history.

This was true even when you only hear rumors. All kinds of rumors. I feel - do not wait, do not dismiss. Check it out - any rumor. Invisible, silent rumors - they could be very dangerous. If you let them go, they might - or can - become dangerous. Sickness, or otherwise.

Learn not to complain all the time, because people will get tired of hearing it. The place to complain is when you are with the doctor, telling the problem - although, they are too busy to listen. Sometimes we need an ear, someone to listen to us, but it's not the right time or the right person to whom I can complain. Everyone is busy. They interested sometimes maybe, but not all the time.

You should have someone around you who cares for you most, to help you to get well and to give encouragement. If you really care for that person, then that person will be there with full support. I don't feel that you should be left alone. One of your family members would be the best person - the best choice before others.

Sometimes we do not want to take things seriously, therefore we never know what could be the result. I feel we must try to face whatever we have to, instead of just letting it go. We are human, and let's not try to ignore it, whatever it is. Sometimes we do make mistakes and by the time we realize what's happening, it might be too late. I know it from my own experience - it has happened. We think that we will beat the odds, but it doesn't always work that way. We must take control of our life and take it seriously. That does not mean to sit down and worry about it. You have to just work on it, to prevent further catastrophe. It does not pay to sit down and wait or worry about whatever you lost. It does not change.

I'm in favor of things that will help you to get your health back. I'm taking the whole person into consideration without major surgeries. There are other types of help in this situation to make life better and easier. Comfort and understanding is more important to any patient. Without all this, there is nothing but suffering. I myself feel that when there is suffering involved, it is very difficult to watch - especially if you really care for the person. It is never as simple as that. We have to accept the unacceptable, whether you like it or not. This is life. When it comes naturally, it is easier to accept it.

We learn to live with it. As you can see - maybe it's just that I'm very old-fashioned and do not want to go through all this.

Today I was told that if you're looking for a a reliable physician, one who owns their own practice and works the way it used to be, you will never find one. They are all gone.

Maybe that is the reason for all these new diseases? We did not have these diseases before, and now we don't know what comes up tomorrow. How do you expect to be ready for anything popping up? How many people have to die senselessly? What would you tell them? "Oh, I'm sorry, this is a new problem, I need time to learn about it? I will have to call the disease control, and maybe they will answer in a couple of days." In the meantime, what happens to the patient? He may not make it until tomorrow.

The doctor who could recognize a simple virus, who would answer right away - is no longer here.

Yes, they are specialists. Maybe they're too busy - but as it is today, they cannot diagnose even a cold by themselves. What's happening? How many people will lose their lives needlessly? Is that what America wants for her population? What is it we want for our children? Or are we just sitting and waiting, without lifting a finger or our voices? We have the right to choose our healthcare, but must we accept whatever we get good or bad?

The computer world is changing all of this. This is just the beginning. Now it seems science took over medicine. You can expect in the future to be able to get even a doctor in - when you really need it. You will be able to get their advice and treatment on the computer. How would you like that? Would you be happier to get a house call without leaving your home? It sounds good - maybe. But would you feel you can accept that as safe? As I see it - it is not too far away. The science is working hard - faster than you think.

People will accept this new idea. But what happens when you need health care at home? Who will be there? Will anyone respond? Or maybe there will just be one doctor for every kind of illness? By then, they will need fewer workers. What will happen to the jobless? No jobs around. The unemployed - the sick - the elderly - and the family. What will happen to them?

Previously, I wrote some notes - a couple of years ago. And now, all these things I'm talking about - I could say I predicted, just from my experiences. Or maybe I was able to sense whatever comes through in real life - before it happens. Sometimes, some people have that ability - to see the problem way before it happens.

And when we come to a certain age, numbers don't matter. Everyone comes to that stage where doctors think numbers matter, but act your own age. Do not be what you are not - be what you are. This way you will find yourself in a better position, and people will be happier wanting to be with you, and you will feel better.

Some people cannot live without coffee. It is the worst thing they can have. It doesn't matter what kind - caffeinated or otherwise. Tea is the same.

While there is life, there is hope.

Chapter 23
About home health aides...

    Today is November 1, 2009 and I'm continuing my writing today. Today is Sunday and my brother usually comes to visit this day if the weather is good. I don't like him to drive when the weather is not good, raining or snowing. I hope it clears up. He always makes me very happy! He never comes empty-handed. There's always something that he brings. I asked him why he's doing it? (Shopping) I did not want him to do it. Where he shops, he tells me the prices are very good and that's why he wants to help me if I need anything. I don't like to bother anyone if I can help it because everyone has their own problem and that's why I like to do shopping on my own. I'm grateful and happy that I'm able to help myself as I do. I don't think much about it. I try my best one day at a time and try to do whatever I can. When I need help it's not easy and that is a big problem.

    It is very difficult to find the right person to help. There's always a problem with or without it. From my experience it is sometimes worse not knowing whom to get. There are some people who are not interested how they can help. These people are sent from the agency and I thought that they were checked out with their background, but unfortunately their checking is not very desirable because of the experience I had with them. Mostly these people are hired by the agency, yet when they arrive they want more money from me. I understand about the money, but you have to work for it. I can see from my own experience if someone is misbehaving. Unfortunately the agency does not pay any attention and does not care. These people come to help the elderly - the fragile, the ones who live alone with no one around - but instead they leave them feeling even more lost.

    It doesn't matter today what we have, life is in jeopardy. Even as I am, it is very difficult to get whatever I'm trying to get. Everybody is in a hurry and there's no time to help. I don't understand where these people are running to. It is getting out of hand. They see the people they're supposed to help, but they only look out for themselves - trying to cut corners at the expense of the helpless. Unfortunately they're so busy that there is no time to check out the background of all these people whom they send out.

    I experienced that some aides that were sent out to me were drug addicts. They stole my credit card numbers and went and charged to my account. One that was sent out on her first day she complained she had a headache. I felt sorry for her and I let her rest - instead what I should have done is to send her home. This woman decided to rest on my sofa in the living room. She was well dressed - one would never believe that she was a drug addict.

    This was the way it happened. This woman was young and looked well, so I let her come back the second day. We went grocery shopping. I needed a few items. When she came back she looked at the tape from the register. I asked her what was she looking for and she said she was checking in case they made a mistake. Somehow I had a feeling that she wasn't telling the truth.

When she came in again I was very surprised - she looked like she was coming after being out all night. She was wet, it was raining, and her clothing smelled very badly. She misbehaved in my living room, dancing in my living room while listening to her cell phone. She said it was her program. It was set up for the music that she was dancing to. I asked her to hang up her coat, and then I decided I didn't want her. I let her go and called the agency to tell them.

In a couple of days I was getting bills from out of the city, as far away as California. Then came telephone calls from different places. She bought merchandise - the most expensive clothing and other items, over a thousand dollars worth - with my credit card numbers.

I reported the charges to my credit card company. The merchandise was sent out to the wrong addresses, but with my name on the package. She arranged so that she was waiting there to receive to receive it. She even gave my telephone number.

I asked the credit card company: How could this happen? If I want to purchase something myself, then I have to show my identity. Why didn't the places do the same thing? I told them I was not paying for it - I was not responsible. It was enough of a problem to straighten out and prove that I never purchased anything from them. I was lucky that my insurance company straightened things out.

When I confronted the agency, their answer was: "What do you think - we're checking them out?"

The next aide, I did not like from the first day. The agency insisted that she is very good and she looks good also - she owns a very nice new car, they said. All that didn't impress me, but okay I will try her. I let her go on first day. I had enough with the first and this was my second episode with these people. The agency asked me to give her a second chance. I did it against my better judgment. I found out later that she likes to drink liquor and she said that makes her happy. She was dressed casually. She was saying about herself that she goes out and she talked about her family problems. She was saying that she was married before and has a son. I was right about her the first day and I wasn't happy with her the second day. Yet, I let her come back.

Once she was sitting next to the closet doors. I lived in a studio apartment and furnished it very nicely. I purchased everything about 30 years ago when I moved in and I kept it spotless. I do this all by myself. I was and I am an independent person. She asked me when I made breakfast - I always try to finish eating breakfast before any aide came. I heard that she went outside and when she came in something was not right. I don't know why, but I noticed that one of the bags was full and was covered with something. When I asked her what was she doing outside, she said that she threw out some papers. Sometimes she used to eat breakfast in my apartment. I knew that she was drinking.

Before Christmas, I gave her a small gift, and she told me she wasn't going home yet - she would take it tomorrow. The next day she took it, but I had a strange feeling about her. I never would have expected what she ended up doing.

My closets and dressers weren't locked. I kept small but valuable things there. She started talking very loudly, trying to distract me so I wouldn't hear what she was doing. I asked her to come closer if she wanted to talk. When she didn't answer, I looked around. I knew there must be a reason.

She wasn't even a good helper. She did whatever she wanted. She suggested I lie down and rest, which I usually don't do, but that day I wasn't feeling well, so I did. After that, she offered to help me and rubbed me down with alcohol.

Later, I realized I had been right to be suspicious. When she left, she took shoeboxes with her - three pairs of dress shoes I had been saving for special occasions. They were beautiful shoes: two in fine old leather, one in suede. I had handbags to match. I take good care of my things and only wear them when I need to. I buy clothes that don't go out of style, and I don't wear them every day. These couldn't be replaced. They'd cost too much now - and I wouldn't even be able to find the same kind again.

As I looked further, I saw what else was missing. She had wrapped my tablecloths around herself under her clothing. They were brand new, never used - a set of twelve, and another set of eight, all with matching napkins. Gone. I had saved them for when I needed them. Now I'll never be able to replace them.

I was very upset. I called the agency. I couldn't hold back my feelings. I told them what they were doing was dangerous for the lives of senior citizens. I don't think the main office would have approved of how they were running things. They were not helpful.

Another thing happened, also before Christmas, with this helper. In my neighborhood there is a flower store that has artificial flowers. She wanted to see it. She liked it very much. The owner said to her that because it was before Christmas, the following week they will have more selection. I was with her. The following week I wanted to go back to see what they have. She ran to the store ahead of me, with me behind. I used my cane to walk. In the front of the store there was a large window, but before that, as you walk in the front of the store, they had a very small step close to the window. When you were walking, you had to be very careful - otherwise, you cannot see the step. This was all the way in front of a building. She walked away from me and I followed her and I tripped on the steps and I fell. Lucky that my head was only half an inch from the glass panel window! If I was a little bit closer I would have hit the window and would have been seriously hurt. As it was I still hurt my head and had a serious problem. I couldn't get up and she was yelling at me get up! get up! but I couldn't, I was just lying there. Finally I asked her to come and help me because I'm unable to get up. And I want to see my doctor immediately because I knew I was hurt, but I didn't know how much. Afterwards, she went home to work another job 24 hours a day for five days a week. I had to take a taxi to see my doctor and he was nice enough to see me. I couldn't move my arm and my hand was very painful. When I saw the doctor he told me my shoulder was fractured and my hand was out of place.

The girl called me to come back the following day. I knew then I don't want her. I told the agency what happened. Since I don't want her they told me to wait because they have no one else at this time. I wasn't able to use my arm or hand or dress myself. I lived alone and I had to help myself. I had no choice. I'm not going to wait for anyone. I took my bath alone and got in my bed too. I got dressed and even made my breakfast and I had to take my medication. Very carefully, I tried to do it myself. It wasn't the smartest thing to do. I needed to clean. I did whatever I had to do with my left hand. I took a bath because I wanted to ease my pain and soak my arm in warm water to reduce the pain and things will be better. I massaged my hand. The doctor told me he couldn't do much even though it was very painful. I could not take any painkillers because I had a reaction from them - even from aspirin. When I was in the bathtub I wasn't even able to touch my hand, not even my fingers. I tried every day. One day I felt a crack and I knew that my shoulder was out of place and I just put it back when I heard the crack. I was able to move my wrists and it made me happier. However my shoulder was still painful and they could not put it in a cast. They could only use a bandage. Little by little it was better. It took me a couple of months.

During this time, this same person came with me to shop. She was holding a book and was reading it. I asked her if she was buying it and she said no. I checked my tape after I came home and she started to scream at me. I was very upset about it and I made up my mind that this will be the last day for her. Not even an hour more. And when I was checking my merchandise, I noticed that she charged the book on my account - the one she was reading in the store. Did you charge the book to my account? I said to her. You had the nerve to do that without asking me. And she was wasting my time reading the book. She was once again nasty to me and when the time came that she had to leave, I told her not to come back again. When she went home, I called the agency and I told them what happened. This was enough - I knew that she was drunk when she showed up that morning. Next morning I did not want to open the door for her. She was calling me to open up, open up, I only want to speak to you. She said I'm sorry about yesterday. She made excuses. She called me on the telephone also. I don't know what else she did. I was ready to call the police, but I didn't. Against my better judgment, I opened the door even though I didn't want to hear what she had to say. She was silly and offered me money just to keep her. The book wasn't the only reason that I let her go, but also because of her misbehavior and because I fell. I just didn't want her anymore. At first, she didn't want to leave. Finally she left.

The third episode was that they sent me a health aide that was like a jailer! You would never believe it how some people behave. The first day this person told me that she was a registered nurse in a hospital. She had taken a leave of absence. She had a family that needed help. After that, she decided to go back to school and continue her studies to get a better job. What I've seen and noticed was that she wasn't a young person, she may have been at least in her 50s. She had trouble walking. I asked her to remove her shoes when she came into my apartment and she refused. She said she is not allowed. That is the rule. She said if someone was coming unexpectedly then she'll be in trouble. I told her that before anyone comes here, they'll have to call first. I told her that doctors usually don't come here. My apartment has carpet from wall to wall and it's clean. I worked very hard and even now I keep it clean. This helper usually came in and had breakfast and read the newspaper on my dining room table.

I needed help because I had trouble getting around because of poor circulation problem. For the past six years I was getting treatment for both of my legs. I had an ulcer on my ankle and I was told that I needed a vascular doctor. Well, my doctor that I usually see recommended someone and then that someone recommended a specialist since I had an open sore and it was very painful. I went from one doctor to the other. They seem to be very busy. I'm sure other people find the same problem everywhere. I found a doctor who was recommended and he was able to help me. It was very surprising that after everything I went through, all that he recommended was a stocking. The price of the stocking was $50. After I came home I wanted to put it on, but it was impossible to put it on. Therefore I decided to go to see another vascular specialist. He gave me medications, ointment in liquid form to heal the ulcer on my ankle. It took me a long time, but I did that by myself because I didn't have a helper. I did a good job. I bandaged it and learned very fast. This was a routine that I had to do twice a day. It took a long time, but finally it got better. After that, the doctor recommended that I should have treatment, and injections for the circulation otherwise I will have more problems. By this time I already had a heart condition. I was getting injections in both of my legs every five weeks and wrapping my leg overnight with an ace bandage. The doctor's helper showed me how to wrap it around my foot for 24 hours to prevent swelling. I did it for over six years as I mentioned before. And every six months I took a test. And he said so far I was doing well.

The doctor told me that I must have some help at home, so I decided to get some help as the doctor recommended it. I needed help shopping and to go to the doctors. He also recommended an agency, and they gave me someone very nice - she was helpful. I kept her for five years. Eventually, she told me she could only give me two days a week because she had to take care of someone else she had worked for a long time. Also, she wasn't available in the morning hours - only in the afternoon - and I needed help in the morning.

At that time, the agency changed to another one, which was not as nice as the first, but I had no choice. I was paying for the services - not full price, it was discounted - and this continued for years. Then the agency changed again, and this time they sent me the person I had trouble with - the one I called the jailer.

From the start, she didn't begin well. Instead of helping me, she wanted me to do things while she stood and watched. She was told to encourage seniors to help themselves. If I was telling her what I needed, she would say she was only there to supervise.

But what I really needed was a nurse. The agency told me they didn't have anyone else. This woman was planning to go back to school and only wanted to work part - time.

Next day I had an appointment to go to the doctor. I had to take the bus and it was a long walk. To go it was 26 stops and to return by bus was again 26 stops. I had difficulties and the agency told me that I'm responsible to pay the helper's bus fare. For myself I was paying half - price, but for the helper I had to pay full price. I had extra expenses, but that was the only way I was able to get around. If it was an emergency to go to the hospital, I had to take a taxi. That was the only way for me go.

The following day, the woman told me she had something called a city carfare, so I wouldn't have to pay for her. She said that on her previous job she didn't have to pay anything - she traveled free. I wasn't sure how that worked.

When we got on the bus, I paid my fare. Then I heard her telling the driver that she was working for me and coming with me, and that I had refused to pay for her. Because of that, the driver was going to let her ride for free.

When I heard what she said, I got very upset and told the driver that it was a lie. I took out the money and paid for her fare myself.

When I sat down, I was watching where to get off since I did not want to miss my stop and I could not depend upon her. I knew where I was going. She ordered me as a fiery child to sit up straight. This was something that I could not accept. I did not say anything when we arrived at my doctor's office. I turned around and she disappeared. I was looking for her, but I couldn't find her. I sat down and waited. Finally she came up to the doctor's office and I asked her where she had been and she told me that she was in the ladies' room. I said to her the ladies room is in just the opposite direction. That was that.

I know where she must have been. When I was called to see the doctor, this was my heart specialist, the one who was after me to get some help, he was telling me to try to cooperate with the person. I knew exactly that I had been right. She lied again, and I would not tolerate it. I needed help, but not this kind of help. This was just trouble. If I could not get real help, I had to do all the work. When I came home, I told her I did not want her back next day. She said that now that she has this great, well-paying job, if anyone jeopardizes her job, and she loses it, then I will be very sorry. She will do with me what she can do - she will hurt me so that I will never forget it as long as I am alive. And I took it very seriously, every word. The next morning she came back. My case manager called that she's coming to see me and this woman was not supposed to come back. When the case manager came in, my helper came in and took a seat right next to her. The case manager didn't come to see her. She came to see me.

She was telling the caseworker that I have bad behavior and I do not listen to her. Just the opposite, and she should listen to me. What I didn't know then, the office told the case manager that they went out of their way to select some special person just for me. They were giving her more money and I didn't appreciate it. What is wrong? The case manager did not come here for that - there were other reasons. She was annoyed with this aide. I could tell, when I explained what had really happened, that it confirmed what she already suspected - that the situation was bad. I told her that the day before, the aide came back even though I did not want her to. Although she was very nice and neat, she threatened me that she's going to report my misbehavior.

I also told my doctor how she threatened me. I was afraid to live in my own home. I never knew what she might do next. I told the manager the same thing. This was on a weekend and it was a legal holiday on Monday. I did not want anyone on that day. Before the weekend I called the office, who was usually in charge with the health aides and I told them what happened. I said to her that I do not want this person anymore.

On that Monday I received a telephone call from the aide. I tried to be nice to her to make it better. I'm a nice person all the time. However, when someone mistreats me like she did, I cannot tolerate it, it does not matter who she is. She asked me if I have any help on that day and I told her I did not need any help. She advised me to call the same office and that I should speak to the lady who is in charge of the health aides. This woman requested that this aide come back to work for me. I said I do not need anyone. I was shocked to hear it again after I told her what happened and that I dismissed her. She said that I should have talked to the agency about my wishes and I did not do it.

Early in the morning on Tuesday I received a call from this aide telling me that she's coming into work. Then she rang my doorbell and said I better let her in. If I don't, I'll have the biggest problem. She frightened me again and she told me it's no use to call the office. She was okayed to come back. I have no choice. I did not listen and I called the office again. I told them that she was there. I said to the office person why did you give her permission to come back! I told you I did not want her back. Why did you do it? I do not understand that. Are you running the business? Do I not have enough trouble!

I received a call and it was from the manager. She was from the main office and was in charge with the nurses. I did not know whether this aide was also under her supervision. She was asking me if I'm satisfied with my helper? I was very upset because no one listened and I wanted to give up their services. I did not care, I do not want anything to do with this helper. I was stunning this lady. I retold what happened and explained how she behaved. She knew who this aide was. She made a remark that I should not worry about it and she made me feel okay. She was my savior. That was the end of this episode.

Before all that happened, several people called me - and most of them were real characters. They asked me for more money saying the agency was not paying them enough. I refused. I will not pay anything extra to them. They can take the job or they can leave.

I mentioned it before there was one aide that was nice but helpless. She had two children and was living alone. Helpers are supposed to help and hold on to protect a person and keep them safe. This person walked separate from me on the sidewalk. I was walking by myself and in the middle of the way where people walk some places on the sidewalk were broken up and it was dangerous. Anyone could fall, not just seniors. It was very cold and windy and I was coming home from the doctor. The bus stop was about seven blocks away. As we were walking near the damaged sidewalk, I fell. I was not able to move. I broke my glasses. This was the second pair I had broken in a short period of time. It is a focal eyeglass and it is very expensive. I had surgery on both of my eyes. They took out the cataracts and I was nearsighted. I had to pay $500 to repair them. The frame broke right on my nose. I was lucky that I did not cut my eyes when the frame broke - there was enough other damage. My nose was fractured and was bleeding. I did not know what to do. She was standing there looking at me, calling my name, and asking me what to do. Finally I asked her to help me to get up and gather my belongings - my cane and my glasses, too.

Medicare only pays for glasses the first time after corrective surgery. That was a long time ago, but now it was the second time. I was hurt too much and my leg was hurting also. I had trouble walking home. I was really in more trouble and pain. I'm always very careful. Accidents do happen whether you like it or not, and there wasn't any telephone to call an ambulance. Someone else had a telephone and they called the ambulance. They wanted to bring me to Flushing Hospital. I didn't want to go there. I know from my past experience that I wouldn't have come out alive from there. The ambulance would not have taken me from where I fell to where my doctors are, namely to LIJ. I was sure I would have gotten better help there. This happens because of our mayor. He ordered that everyone has to go to the closest hospital. Even though I was a Medicare patient and my ambulance is paid by Medicare not by the city, they would have had to bring me to Flushing Hospital because it was the closest.

It's true that I was much closer to Flushing Hospital, but Medicare pays the same amount for the nearby hospital or to go to LIJ. By taxi they charge $10 either way to either hospital. Do you think that this was just? In Flushing Hospital it was very bad - people's lives are in jeopardy. The only way it would have been okay there is if you have your own doctor and also that you would speak English well so that you could communicate with him. Even though they could help me, I would never go there. And because of that I didn't take the ambulance.

When I went home, I called another ambulance and I went to see my private doctor and he cleaned my face, and nose - my left arm was hurt and my nose had a fracture. He told me that I should go to have surgery on my nose. But I had been told before that I cannot have any kind of surgery. So he told me nothing could be done - only with medication. It will heal as time goes by. I would have to have surgery for the fracture, but since I cannot, I have to live with it. Even today, I still have trouble with my nose, and my hand swells up and it hurts. It looks like I'll have to live with it.

This is why I do not want any helpers. This is what happened with the agency and all of these helpers came from there. It shows that they're not checking out people and not able to get good help and the people who are in charge are not qualified to do the job either. We seniors suffer. I've heard other people speaking about their helpers and health aides. It appears the same. It seems like life is very complicated, all around.

I would like to mention something nicer - about some of the people. We all must have some experience. Sometimes we are not prepared for something unbelievable - then we find someone - just the right person. Let's say, "G-d sent you." It is too good to be true.

How could it have been - after such a long time - that I was not able to have half as good help as this one? To my surprise, it looked excellent. I was very happy - finally we succeeded. Here we are speaking again about the home health care services.

After the surprise began to wear off, I began my examination and questions. I still could not understand - previously, I had enough experience and reasons to be suspicious. It looked too good. With an open mind, I tried to accept and wait and see. I did not keep my suspicion a secret. I asked some questions. I found out she has many trades and is able to carry on different jobs - or work in one at a time - without any problem.

I had another question: then what is she doing here? She could have a better position with more money. Still another question.

The background is that she had enough experience. She worked with all kinds of people. These came from her mouth - no one else's.

Her job was helping an older person who was still able to think - not senile. No mental defect. The problem started after this person had an accident and fractures. She had been in hospitals, rehabs, and finally in therapy - until more accidents occurred. Why? Because the workers weren't cautious. They thought they were above you - like they were in the driver's seat. They thought they were in control, able to take over. They didn't stop to check if the person could even walk or stand. Their main goal: to push you - until they break you. That way, they succeed in getting whatever they want. Then they disappear. Gone missing again.

Enough.

All these people were supposed to help - even though the doctor had told her, and told them: "Do not over - exercise her." This was told directly to the therapist. But they didn't listen. Now what? He was let go. But the damage was done.

Once again, I'm here with a new episode. Little by little, I'm coming to the point. When I asked questions about her work, I was told she worked with all kinds of people and had enough experience taking care of all kinds of problems - able to cook, do whatever needed to be done. All this sounded very fine and indicated that she had enough experience with the therapist. She started to work with retarded people,[45] and their behavior was very bad. She wanted to change them - by the time she finished with them. She treated her patients equally and she changed them until they behaved.

Now here's an example: now she treats everyone equally.

Right here is the first mistake. Like they say - not all cats are black. Not all people are alike. Then what is the problem? Wait and see.

Here, in this position, it is an entirely different situation. I needed some help to get better - to get around from the fracture I suffered. Otherwise, I have a healthy mind, but I'm suffering a lot of pain and due to other problems that exist. I cannot do too much anymore - and when you become a senior, no one cares. People do not want to even lift their finger - even though just maybe, they could help you get some relief.

As I mentioned before - the medical field is getting out of control. No one cares, only about themselves. It is a selfish world.

Here, in this case, it became abusive from the first day - as you can see.

By the way, this worker - quite young, in my opinion - needed training. First, she was tolerant from one side - the second, not all people are equal. Not all patients are having the same problem. They are supposed to be treated individually - whatever that problem is. But this person felt that her patients were all alike. She wanted to break them - or else.

As I saw this, it was the beginning of the word "abuse." She said that she had the power to change all the people - instead of helping them, as she is supposed to - with respect, kindness, understanding, and helping them. The agency did not even want to hear about her - because they had no one else. Was that a good reason to keep her? I don't think so.

Going back to the Flushing Hospital - this was a different time. The Flushing Hospital is not the best place. I was taken there with an ambulance for one reason or another. It was on the weekend. When I arrived there I didn't have anyone with me. I was taken to a cubbyhole for one person. It was a very small room. A person came and told me that she is a doctor and asked me why I came there. I told her I have chest pain and my regular doctor told me before that if I have a chest pain at anytime on the weekend I should go to Flushing Hospital immediately. He would arrange that one of

---

[45] *Editor's Note:* The term "retarded" is now considered offensive, but is retained here to preserve her voice.

his associates would meet me in the hospital and will help me and stay there with me. I did not have anyone from my family available. My niece left a day earlier for a vacation. My own doctor was also on vacation and therefore another doctor took over. He said he would never advise me to go to Flushing - the best place is at the Long Island Jewish Hospital where they are specialists with chest pain.

Later on, while I was waiting, I started coughing and my throat was getting worse. It felt like I'm getting a cold. I had to be careful with coughing. I did have asthma and breathing problems. When I was checking in at the hospital, another doctor was called. He came in, checked me, and took away all my medications. They were supposed to give me new ones, as they usually do in the hospital. I still had an open sore on my ankle and I was taking antibiotics. I told them and the doctor saw it. I had a lot of pain. Before he left, the doctor gave me medication for some pain and he told me that they will give me my medications. The next day was Saturday, and I was not getting my medication. Only here and there and not for the heart, and no antibiotics, and no Band-Aids for my leg. I got nothing and I had a problem. That afternoon, my coughing was getting worse. I went out and I saw a lady and I asked for a doctor. She told me she is one. No other doctors were available. She asked me what is the problem? I told her what happened. It was dark at the point where I met her and I couldn't see her. She asked me to open my mouth And she said she sees nothing, everything is okay. I knew she could not see and could not speak well English. At that time I was still in the emergency room at the hospital. Is this what they have? Is it possible not to have medication either? Why not? It's unbelievable. I was very sorry that I listened to my doctors. I was afraid. I'm all alone - my niece went away that afternoon. I had a nightmare and I got an attack of asthma. When I get it, it is very bad sometimes and I don't think I will make it. I was getting inhaler treatments for this condition for years. I know that danger when it comes. Usually I was always carrying an inhaler with me. It was my lifesaver! When it happens in the hospital, there are nurses and in this case there was one there. I don't even know if she was a registered nurse or just the one in charge, or just helping the doctor who cannot speak English. It looks very bad all around, when I get these attacks. I cannot breathe. I cannot talk. I cannot swallow. I become almost paralyzed. I was choking. I remembered the inhaler - I kept it because it was in my pocketbook, instead of with my medications. I reached in my bag - luckily it was there. But before that, I rang for someone to come and help me, but no one did. I got off the bed and ran out as fast as I could and could not speak, I pointed to the nurse and to my throat and showed that I was choking. Instead of seeing what was happening, she brought me some antibiotics chopped up well, so I will be able to take the antibiotics with water. All day I did not have medication, but now she offered me, when I needed oxygen or other help! She had no brain to see what was happening! I returned to my bed, but before that, the whole hospital heard the noise from my choking. Can you imagine how much noise it makes when you are choking? When I went back to my room, I found my inhaler. I was using it and it didn't work and I was still choking. But I kept on praying...... I took my inhaler again and sometimes it seemed to work for a second. I did not have any time between to take another breath. I was not able to breathe for a second. I have seen an oxygen plugged in to the wall. I thought that this may be belong to someone. A woman came to see me if I'm still alive, since I was still choking. She gave me the oxygen in my nose, but it wasn't enough. I needed more on my mouth. Then I went back again to get my inhaler. It did nothing. I just kept on continuing what I could do. I used the oxygen both on my nose and in my mouth for at least an hour. Sometimes it relieved for a second, but it returned a minute later and this happened all night. I finally succeeded. I was able to breathe, but I was very worn out from this episode of what I went through.

My doctor's helper, the one that sent me to Flushing Hospital, lived not too far from my place and from the hospital. I called her on the telephone, but I had to be very careful since I was still using the inhaler just not as often. I only spoke only what I had to because anything could bring back this choking episode. I called my friend, she was not home. Her mother answered. I told her that I'm here at the hospital and what has happened. I asked her if she would come over and help me. She did. And I told her I don't know what to do anymore. Later, after all that, I thought I should have told her to check me out and take me to another hospital or home. I would have been better off not to come here ever.

Sunday morning I received visitors. This doctor belonged to Flushing Hospital. They were notified of what has happened. They knew that they can have a problem because of what happened. They came to check out to see what was happening here. Before that, in the hospital, they knew and heard what had happened. That early morning people walking to find out what happened, if I'm still alive. Looking to see me. By then I was quieted down, but I was very cold and shivering from this episode of what I went through. I rang at this time for more blankets. The woman in charge was running to give me what I wanted and she was very happy to help. I told her what I wanted and she ran right away and in a second she returned with warm blankets and she covered me. G-d helped me. She was very happy to see me - that I was alive. She realized by then what had happened, *but she wasn't able to help*. It shows how people don't care, and how irresponsible and negligent they are. I don't think this is the way to run a hospital.

When the second doctor arrived, I was told that even if I wanted to go to another hospital they will not take me. There are no doctors on the weekend. Also if I wanted to leave, I had to sign documents because I was in a very serious condition to leave the hospital. I was in danger. The doctor checked my heart and my pressure and told me it is very low. If that was the case why did he not do something to help me? I still did not get medications.

Later they called in another doctor as a witness if I do want to sign out or stay. I refused to sign the paper. He said, even if I don't sign and decide to leave, Medicare will not pay for my stay. I would have to pay for everything they did, and they would have it witnessed by two doctors. I have to choose either way. I said that I will remain till Monday and I will call my brother and his son to pick me up. I was told that I must be in the hospital because I am in very serious condition, and they were right. They gave me a letter. I took it to my doctor who just learned what had happened. The whole scene is in my memory and I shall never forget it.

I went to see my doctor. He had just come back from his vacation when he examined me. He sent me to another hospital. When I left the second hospital, I called my nose specialist and went to see him. He's one of my best doctors and he told me I suffered and that my vocal cords were very bad. He said that he has never seen me like this before. He was treating me for 16 years and after his treatment I felt better.

After I came home from the hospital I called Medicare and I told them what has happened. I was advised to call the mayor's office and to report all this. I told them I did my job by reporting it to you. Whatever you want to do, it's up to you. This is your job. I also called the hospital services of Medicare A and B. I did not want to get involved anymore. I had enough. I called one of the state senators since I knew that he is helping these hospitals. When I called they told me that he is going to look into it. I'm sure he never did. This is my life's history. Normally, I try to forget whatever happened. At this time I will try also.

I have my own experience with my home agencies. I have a home health aide. Today, it is very difficult to get anyone who really can help you or who wants to help. It is a very complicated situation we are in. We are an exception. If you really need help, you are in trouble. It seems the personal touch you cannot find. What you are getting today - you cannot even believe it! You are going through so much heartache, you are forced to take whatever you get and expect nothing more.

You cannot talk to them. I have to have kid gloves. If they want to hear you, they will. Many times you are on your own - they believe they do not have to do anything. You cannot complain, because you get no response. They came to help me - instead, you have to do whatever you can, even when it's impossible. We try to help ourselves, but what happens if you are not able to? You need to eat. I have to be able to prepare it or take care of myself without help.

It is getting out of hand. Which way can we go? You are in your golden years - but they're not so golden. If you are lucky to have a loving family, you can get understanding and caring, love, with a little help. It would help if you're lucky. Without that, there is no outlook for any help. It is very sad even to think about. As we are, my dear brother and I - we are going through an ordeal. We really need help, and we cannot get it. I must say, in one sense, I'm very lucky. As hard as it is, for now, I'm still able to prepare our meals.

Sometimes, even that - it seems I cannot finish. But I have no choice - struggling day in and day out. I hope our Almighty gives us strength, and at least we will be able to do what we must to be able to survive until our time comes. The aide comes in and does whatever she wants to. As I see it, they should be accountable and look into what is going on with the agencies that are responsible for giving help. There is too much waste - no wonder Medicare and Medicaid are going broke.

And we, the people - we who very much need that help to be able to function or get around and are unable to - my question is: I believe in our freedom of choice. I would not give up freedom for anything in this world. Our freedom must be respected.

It is priceless, and we are lucky to have it. On the other hand, some people will abuse it, and you have to just watch. I tried myself to do something about it, but no one responded - therefore, what else is there?

Chapter 24
Rail Road Episode

You must learn how to communicate - without discrimination - to anyone different than you are. You never know who might be your savior. Believe me, you do not know - when you need help, the one you least expect may reach out in a critical condition. You might be surprised - who will be your savior. I had many times when someone came to help me. It did not matter how busy they were. Without a word - they stopped and ran to my aid, to help me when I needed it.

When I fell down seven steps on the Long Island Railroad, I was on my way to mail a letter at the post office. The steps were extra narrow, always wet, very old, and very dangerous.

I must say - I was in a serious position. And they were on their way to business. They could not speak English - nothing. But they knew I was in trouble. They understood the seriousness - it was life-threatening. The husband wanted to call an ambulance.

I could understand silently - which shows there was a conscience. I was able to express myself without knowing their language. Believe it or not - we were able to help each other and understand each other silently.

I tried to tell them: no ambulance. From my experience, if I had called an ambulance, they would have taken me to the worst hospital - where I had previous experience. I was lucky I came out alive. They have rules about where to take you in an emergency, and you have nothing to say.

They were about a 60 year old couple - but you could see they were very refined people. The husband urged his wife - "we must go." His wife just went on helping me - without a word. She was my lifesaver. I made them understand I lived nearby, and asked them to help me get home. I said I would be very grateful - and from home, I would call my family. They would come to help me. Against her husband's urging - "we must go" - she just continued helping me.

I wasn't able to walk. They carried me all the way home, up five blocks, to my home and up to my apartment. Then his wife took some ice, placed it on my head - by then I had a lump like an orange on my forehead and I had a terrible headache. My whole head hurt from the fall. She gave me my telephone, and I should call my brother.

She helped me - whatever I needed - I called my brother, and again her husband repeated things in their language: "must go, must go." His wife kept on helping me, removed my coat - it was winter, very cold and icy. She was helping me - and my brother appeared with one of his sons in 40 minutes.

My new friends, they waited and even helped me get dressed again so my family could take me to the emergency room.

I asked this couple - please give me their name and their address. I wanted to let them know how much I appreciated what they did. My brother gave them a pen and paper so they could give us their name. But unfortunately, they did not.

They knew my name and address - and also my phone number. I promised I would not mention them, or get them involved in any problems. I just cannot erase them or forget these people. Without them, probably I would not be here after such an accident.

There are people who will take chances - at all cost - to save a life. Even jeopardizing their own.

After I got better, I tried to find them - looking all around, everywhere - on street corners, for the couple who looked like them. I knew they lived down there, or maybe they had a business down there. I was unsuccessful - never had the chance. I wasn't able to see them again. I pray for them - and I cannot forget them. My angels. Unusual couple. You cannot find one in a million.

After all that, I should have called an ambulance - especially if you fight for any compensation. It was a negligence case. They previously had a serious accident there. I could have had a large case. I knew that - even then - I didn't want to lose all that. But I also didn't want to go to that hospital. I think these people knew something about all that. That was the reason this husband was afraid to get involved.

I was taken to one of the largest hospitals to be x- rayed. I had a terrible pain on my left side and couldn't stand. Later I was told that I bruised my hip and my left shoulder was fractured. I had to go to a rehab center. The doctors ordered therapy since I could not walk.

I also told them I was having problems with my stomach. They had my previous medical records, and I told them those records would show the medical problems I had and the medications I was taking. The doctor came and prepared the old information and records to take it with me to the rehab center. This doctor was a lady doctor and she was very nice. She understood me and she made a remark that if she would be in my position she would be worse than I am. I transferred from there to the rehab.

I was never in a nursing home or a rehab center. I did not know what to expect. When I arrived to the rehab, one of the nurses welcomed me and gave me therapy. Whatever she did it was alright.

During this time my stomach began to give me pain. Usually I always take my medications with me, but I was told I cannot take them in the rehab, only their medications. I was waiting patiently for my medications, but my stomach was getting worse. It was time now that I must take my medication. The pharmacy was supposed to prepare my drugs, but they did not prepare the medication that I needed and they will not have it till Monday. I was surprised when I heard that. What will I do without it? I said to the nurse "how is it possible that you took me here without preparing for me what I needed?" I asked the nurse if I should call Medicare about this situation? I threatened - Is that what you want me to do? Maybe they're happy to hear this! I wasn't feeling well by the accident and with the other problems it was more than I was able to take. The nurse did not say anything. She just listened.

I didn't know they had a speaker set up so whatever happens in the rehab everyone can hear it. Later, to my surprise I was told by others they heard everything what I was saying.

I must have had lots of listeners and to my surprise the next morning I got two visitors. They introduced themselves and said they were interested to know how I was feeling, if I'm comfortable, and do I want anything. If they can help they will. They wanted me to be happy. Anything I needed they would see to it that I would get it.

They kept me for 14 days. For me it was more trouble than help, and I was ready to leave the first day. They even changed my medications and claimed they were the same, but they were not. I became sick, and only later learned they had given me vitamins. At night when I rang for help, sometimes no one came. One night a man gave me a pill that let me sleep. I don't know what it was, but I was grateful.

The therapists, though, were very good—kind people—and really the only reason I stayed. I worked hard so I could come home as soon as possible. At first I had to use a wheelchair, then a cane, but I said to myself: not me! When I came home, I was able to walk.

Chapter 25
On Politicians / Leadership…

I woke up after a short sleep and found myself thinking about our lives - and somehow, something hit me. Why is there always trouble in this world? I said it before, many times! As I see it, all this could have been worked out if people would learn how to communicate.

We try to select the best - capable people - around today. They claim to be good leaders, able to work out problems that arise in our government and business. They claim they can settle disputes and make important decisions. They convinced us that they're the best qualified to do the job. But after they are elected, we realize we were wrong in selecting these people. They create problems because we never checked them out until it's late - we were too busy. We trust them, just like we trust and believe in G-d. But we shouldn't.

We need to learn how to choose leaders who are capable to find solutions for a better life - with respect, with understanding, with caring, for us all. That would be best - without any more time wasted. With all our science, we have a good opportunity - if we have the right leaders who really care for their country and their people. Don't just vote because he is a good-looking person - you must look at his personality and his behavior! Some politicians are always looking for an argument - and we do not have to listen to that. Some have nothing to offer. They promise the sky, but you cannot believe what they're saying - it's full of air. Leaders can change their minds overnight. I know that politics is a dirty business, but I would still like to hear how they could improve our country and our lives - and whatever the promise is, how it can be fulfilled.

Why do they spend so much money on advertisements? We cannot even learn from them what they are offering. Did you learn from the last presidential election? Did you choose carefully, or did someone influence you? That happens all the time. Whose fault is it? Take one subject. Ask them to work hard and try to work it out - for what is good for all of us. They owe us that. But don't hold your breath.

If not for us, we the people, they would not be there. They should acknowledge that and make decisions without any delay. It would create a better atmosphere for everyone and would show an example for the world.

I feel we must look to the head of the country: our president, senators, representatives, and also their advisors. Why is it that in Congress they cannot see their way to solve the present problems. They have no idea even where to begin. They're not trained enough how to lead, and there is no more teamwork.

It is very important to sit down, face-to-face, with honesty and in a peaceful atmosphere, and work as hard as possible - do whatever is necessary - and really put their heads together, without fighting. Our leaders are too busy arguing with each other. They waste so much time, and do nothing. Both sides should try to understand the real problems we're facing. If there is a will, there is a way - but do not waste more time - it's running out. Leaders should never relax for a minute.

The key point is how to make the right decision. If you are not able to make it - then look for another way you never thought of. Have an open mind, use common sense, and compromise if you have to. Learn to listen. It is very important to have good judgment, to know right from wrong, and to never waste time on one subject because you don't know what you should do. Get all the information, understand it, and find a way - it might succeed if you really want to do it. Use your judgment for all the people, not just for yourself. But sometimes a wrong move could cause disaster - in business or in your private life - when you have to make the right decision, very carefully examine all sides. Even then, it can fail. It depends what we are facing. Therefore, think before you accept the job - are you qualified to fulfill your duty?

We elect our leaders. We believe they will help us and lead us down the right road - to really improve our lives for all of us. Look and listen what we the people expect of you. With willpower, and honesty I believe all this is possible with hard work, together, not against each other. Never forget why are you there and who put you there. If you are not able to, and don't want to work on it, then get out of office and let someone who can take over.

It seems we need a powerful leader, if there is one. We must believe that they might be able to solve some of the problems. Is there someone who is willing and cares enough to wake up before it's too late? I'm afraid - unless you stop arguing and find an able leader who's able to work the way out of this mess - you would not know what hit you. This is not a joke - it is a serious business.

We are in America. We're supposed to be the richest country in the world - we used to be. The word "America" was a big subject. People wanted to hear what we had to say more than anywhere else in the world. The leaders were able to take care of the biggest problems - even though it was not easy. They worked until they found a way out - to make our life safer for all the people. We had respect all over the world. Our ancestors tried to improve our life for all the people - giving us priceless freedoms. We should be able to work out the differences. We are supposed to be the best, strongest, most powerful, freedom loving country that exists, with caring people willing to work with their leaders and each other to improve everyone's life. And we should show other countries how to be a happy nation - by managing our nation peacefully - all colors, all people, living together and happy as one country. That's our reputation. Maybe then we will be able to live together understanding each other. It is very important to learn and understand how to do that in a family, a business, and even a country.

Final Reflections

You might say that I'm losing my mind - that I don't know what I'm talking about! Think - just for a minute. Go and look up history. It might teach a lesson. It might be the most important lesson. Where can you find another, better haven? Without America, you will suffer. Today - even now - our soldiers are fighting and dying for this idea. They include people of all races and religions, fighting side by side to protect our freedom, our rights, and justice for all people. You should never forget that. Some of us are sitting comfortably in our homes, sleeping in a comfortable bed, enjoying a warm meal. Meanwhile, others are sending our young people to fight and to give their lives - whether you like it or not. Therefore, think very carefully about what you are expecting from your life - since you have the opportunity, and it is up to you! You must be tolerant of your fellow human beings to have a better way of life. Today - now - is the time to wake up and work on it with all your strength. Even with distractions - be a human, and live like one.

Our top leaders must remember to support better education and teach the price that had to be paid for our freedom, and the sacrifices ordinary people made. What is happening in our schools, colleges, and universities? Did they ever teach them how to be leaders? How to make decisions? How to work as a team? Teamwork is a most important lesson - which people forget. Even in our personal life it should be a household lesson. One should learn it as soon as one is able to learn what it's all about.

Our educators should try to educate their students to pay attention - to learn about people and understand them. And our leaders should educate themselves beforehand - not when they get their jobs - because it is too late for that. To those who want to become leaders - teach them how to talk, how to speak clearly about what they offer. This may help us select representatives who have more experience, more knowledge to communicate and solve problems for the country. If you're not able to find a solution without delay - something for all the people and the country - what does it mean? Are you a good leader? Stop the arguments and fights! It's not becoming. If you're not a leader, you shouldn't be there. Honestly, what can you offer to improve the lives for all of us? And do not make the situation worse - before you make any decision - think and learn.

Today, some of the people think they know it all. They will not listen or accept that no one knows everything. There is always room to learn, and sometimes we never do. It depends if you have an open mind and are willing to learn, or if you understand the situation - what can help you to make a decision one way or the other, and be able to make the right decision. It is important - especially if you are in a position - because other people may get hurt by it. And you are responsible to help them cope as a result.

I know money is a very important subject. We cannot live without it. But our leaders must learn how to be responsible with it. The price of everything keeps going up, day by day. But the value of money? It goes down by the minute. One day to the next, it disappears. I call it not being able to manage. Instead our leaders should cut expenses and have better training in how to manage. All this is missing.

We know we have to pay taxes. But remember: the more we spend, the more taxes rise. Where will the money come from?

As it's being said - the rich get richer, and the poor get poorer! Where is justice? The rich get benefits - then they can have all the good times. The poor seniors worked hard all their lives, and when they actually need an income, there is nothing - just a small amount of Social Security. Today the banks pay no interest on their deposits. We are forced to use the capital - and at the end, what will remain for us to live on? Should we suffer because our leaders cannot find any solution?

I'm not an expert in economics, business, or education. I do not have the education to give advice and I'm not a politician. I called myself a zero. I have none except my own ideas and beliefs. I'm very lucky since our Almighty allows me, at my age, to have my memory and be able to function and to know and understand what goes on around me. But any person with common sense and willing to do hard work maybe has good ideas how to get us out of this mess that we fell into. With all the new ideas, new smart computers - amazing how far we have come - every day is a new adventure. All kinds of new lifesavers and medicines, but are we going backwards or forwards? There are too many new ideas and we are not able to digest it. Perhaps we do not have enough training, not enough leadership, not good enough teachers - from A to Z. How to manage our country, a business - or even the beginning - your own life, your own home and family. What's missing? Look around us - and around the world. You might say "Who cares? Why should I worry about someone else? I'm too busy - I have my own problem. That is not my concern." Don't go any further. Maybe, if you show some interest, you might be very happy you did. It might just stop something very bad before it is too late - a situation that may be serious, for you and for the country. If you let it go, it may arise into a very dangerous situation.

In the 21st century, we have the tools to educate ourselves. We have computers and opportunity, but some people still are not able to make for themselves better conditions to live in. I think our duty is to try to correct this by insisting on better help from our leaders. I would say they are selfish - they can't see no way out because they refuse to see. But they were not elected there for that reason.

How long can we tolerate this behavior? Where should we look for an answer?

What is waiting for the next generation? Nothing to be proud of. I would say the biggest mess ever. They will have to be ready to deal with it.

We elected you hoping you would take care of our country. Instead, you don't even hear the people cry. We all make mistakes - but we must try not to repeat them. Your followers will forget why they elected you there. You can't even work out one problem. You just blame each other.

Here we are, surrounded by nothing but trouble - wars, natural disasters, hurricanes. All this - what should you do? Look back in history - way back, centuries ago. If you know the Old Testament, the real Bible, maybe you should take a look. When Noah decided to save all the animals and people he worked hard. He built the ark as best he could. The rain came and there was no dry land. He sailed until there was dry land to build a home. He was a righteous man in a troubled generation. This is just one example of leadership from our early history.

I hope our G-d will not be too busy to hear our prayers - in all languages and all cries. There is no one we can trust anymore. The anger we see in everyone is very disturbing. It does not take us anywhere - only toward more suffering. There must be a reason - but people cannot deal with it. There is frustration. Everyone has their own story - if you could hear them, you might understand why. But there is no one to listen. No one wants to talk.

We must educate the people. We must find better leaders altogether. We must have knowledgeable leaders in home, in business, and in government offices. It is very important. We must pay more attention. We must learn whatever we can to better our life - and our country. We must hope to better ourselves. Every one of us is responsible. We cannot wait - not even for a minute.

We have a beautiful garden with so many different flowers. You enjoy every minute just to look at them, smelling the different fragrances. Imagine you are in a garden. Yes, it is beautiful, but it takes hard work to keep it up, you have to pay attention to each one of them. I know I was raised up like that. But we have not had the opportunity to enjoy it for a very long time.

Hoping that our leaders will find a way to get out from these horrible nightmares - so we can come back to a peaceful atmosphere. So we can enjoy life as it is. It's possible that we will go back and live a peaceful life. We must work out whatever is needed to improve. I would like to see it in my time - that is the only hope I have left.

Whoever will read my notes might understand and will learn. As of now I think I will try to come to a point to stop writing for a while - wishing all a better life. Learn how to manage your own life in order to be successful. Never sit down and wait for something to come your way. It will never happen. Work hard and educate yourselves. Keep your eyes open, and be alert.

END

finished April 16-013 BY MG

Chapter 26
On Jealousy

In the past, when we had something come up even just in our dreams, it came with surprises that made you feel excited. Today, all these things have changed.

No more excitement. Everything is an open book. No more mystery - everyone is seeing what everyone else is doing. In fact, it is the style now - it must be fashionable. Catch up with your neighbors - it does not matter how! High price? You will pay it. It might be your life - it doesn't matter - that is today's life. We cannot go back to the way it was.

The theaters are giving all the examples to go openly, willingly, to show what kind of life you should live. No more imagination left. Why shouldn't they practice it? Everyone else lives like this. Share your bed with whomever you want to - this is love? If it is - why are those young people, so happy with excitement, turning to drugs and other things? Why aren't they happy? Why do they get so bored? So tired? The more famous they are, the worse they become. Just when they are right on top - something happens. They have enough money - it is not the money. What is it?

When they are on the top, take a good look at how much trouble they get into? Every day, more than you want to see, right in front of your eyes. They themselves helped destroy their own life - for what? Sometimes for fame or money. They cannot face it. They need something else. What? More excitement? Not enough with what you have? Do you want to jump into a foxhole?

The trouble today is that people are not conditioned to accept and live a healthier life. For some people, this is the life they want. It is good if it is healthy. From all this - young people, old people - it does not make a difference, this is what they like. Why should they wait? What for? A better life? That is just wasting time, it's not important. We want to live *now*, not just tomorrow - because it may be too late.

Why is it too late? No one is chasing you.

Much of this comes from jealousy – seeing others live freely, and wanting the same life, even without responsibility. It is not important to wait for a paper to have sex. No need to get married for that. You're right - you don't need it - but maybe take time out and think carefully. If you're lucky to reach 20 or 30 years old, you have only a short time, and this is the nicest age. Usually this is the time to have a good time and try to get your education, whatever you wish, and learn how to manage your life the way you would like to. Now, with your freedom of choice, you can get a good job. Live a respectable life, and yet you might have a different outlook on life. Clean living - I can argue for that. That is the reason we are different people. Every person is different - they are individuals - and not everyone thinks the same way.

Stop here!

Stop and do not follow others. Be yourself. Think for yourself. Use your own judgment. Listen and learn. Be a better citizen - it would be better for you and for your country. Your country deserves better citizens - people who respect it and do not expect to get something for nothing, especially if you are lucky enough to have good health and are able to work. Learn a trade. Educate yourself. Do not be jealous of others - just maybe you're better than they are! Learn to be happy with whatever you have.

Here I'm writing this now because I care for you - but I don't want to run your life. That is up to you. In any case, I'm old enough and have been through life. I have the experience to show you a way out from a miserable life.

This sickness of jealousy does not stop at individuals – it spreads through families, neighborhoods, even nations, until it erupts as hatred and violence. Just continue helping those who need it. Today there's an epidemic - deep inside, some of these people don't even know the reason, or cannot understand what hatred really is. Hating or disliking someone just because someone else started it - with a sick mind - who loves misery, and for no reason at all.

You can help, if you really want to. Every person can, if they take time out to learn what is causing the hatred. If they try to reach those people who are hurting - what really happened? Who were left behind?

Take a look! Do you like what you see around you? Would you like to have that type of life? Or would you rather have a nice, comfortable home with your family around - or to be hunted down like an animal - because you are one? Would one deserve anything else? What did you learn? Do you see yourself?

What do *they* want? I'm sure they don't know. Was it worth sacrificing so many lives? What did they receive as payment? Was it worth it? How about their families - their loved ones - when they decided to give their lives for nothing? Is there any reason they had to go? Why did they die needlessly - just to do someone else's dirty job? Why couldn't *they* do it themselves? Why not? They have the money. So why are they so unhappy? What is it they really want?

Can you see? They want *your* life. They don't even know you.[46]

I'm sure if you asked them this question, they wouldn't give you an answer. I'm sure they don't know the real reason.

Jealousy.

That's the biggest problem around us. It means: they want whatever you have, without working for it. Perhaps they don't even want to be alive. They don't care - they just want to fight. What is all this fighting about? Why can't we stop them? There are followers - they're educated, some of them. They use destruction and are willing to die for nothing. They are sick - very, very sick - brainwashed. They cannot, or do not want to, face the new modern

---

[46] **Editor's Note:** In this passage, Maria shifts between referring to perpetrators, leaders, and the people themselves.

way. They want to live in the past. They claim to follow the Bible - but the information they are spreading is not exactly the same. There is room enough in this universe for all people - and they could live in harmony. It would be a better life for everyone. It could be worked out - the differences between one group and another.

Jealousy creates many other problems. It causes genocide - wars. People want what you have, but in an easier way - they are lazy. On one hand some are trying to learn and improve their life - working hard to build a better place to live in. On the other hand, other people are watching to see how much they have and what they have - and they will come around and try to take it away. They have no idea how to live and let live in a peaceful world together. Try to learn it. Don't envy others. And don't envy others by thinking they are better than you, sometimes that could be misleading. Be happy with what you have - because you never know what they have. Enjoy what you have with your family. That is the most important thing in life. I know that from my own experience.

Jealousy leads to hatred, and hatred leads to destruction.

Chapter 27
On Hatred

At this time I have been thinking about the situation we encountered - every day. We have family letters that my brother kept for 70 years, and as I read them, you will not believe the stories they tell. Some of those letters were dated from the beginning of the war, 1940, and later letters were from people of our village after the war. Our entire family was murdered.

When we came to America, we thought we would settle down and learn the language and later bring my father and other members of our family. We made the biggest mistake in our life. We knew about what was happening, but we never thought that such horror might come to us. Now that we have learned the full truth of our history sometimes I think it would have been better to just leave it alone. After all this, nothing but nightmares come when we think about the suffering they endured. They knew their fate - and to face that was heartbreaking. And now we are facing it again as I write their story. You can never forget them. We lost them the way we lost the other six million Jews, just because they were Jewish. There was no other reason.

And the whole world watched and waited, not even trying to lift a finger to help. They allowed one mentally ill man, a wild animal, to carry out his hatred and get as far as he did. I will never forget how one person succeeded and then turned the world into madness. Can you imagine? How could they have been brainwashed to allow such a horror and spread it so fast? He convinced so many people in the world - and they went along with him - they must have lost their minds. No question about it. I must say they were crazy. Can you think of anything else? I never understood how they were able to carry out such horrible destructions of fellow human beings from so many countries. No one in this world would ever believe that such a thing could ever happen. No one opposed these fascists in the beginning. Many countries even welcomed the monster and helped him sacrifice innocent lives. It is not forgivable. Surely the other countries must have known. They stayed silent and never tried to stop it. They allowed the buildings to be created that carried out genocide. Except for a few gracious people who endangered their own lives - who, without hesitation, sacrificed themselves. I think it is time to learn from that. We must say: never again. This was a very hard lesson, and we must learn from the past.

We should never have had to go through such a terrible ordeal. For what reason? Who gained by it? Who was the winner? In my opinion - no one. We all lost, one way or another. How could people be so cruel as to allow this to happen? It was madness.

If we would have paid attention in the beginning, then many people could have been saved, even our family.

Therefore, where is justice? What delayed the help? There was no place to go or run. All the doors around us were sealed. Our friends did not want to know us. We helped them before, but we had helped the wrong people. Now not only did we not get any help, but they betrayed us. Some of these people that followed instructions had been our friends - they changed when the government changed. How could they get away with it?

I thought about it and asked myself many times: where was G-d? And I asked G-d how come He allowed such horrible murderers to carry out their deed? He was silent while six million innocent people were destroyed. Is there a G-d in heaven? What we believed wholeheartedly - we are supposed to be His children - and He allowed them to carry out such cruelty? Murder - torture - suffering from hunger - naked, without heat in the winter - without any help - He allowed all this to go on? I still believe in our Almighty G-d, but I have sometimes doubts. Why do I feel that way? Because I cannot find anyone else on earth I can trust. I try to convince myself that we must believe in someone. We were always reminded by our parents that G-d can see us wherever we are. If you do something wrong, then G-d will punish you. We cannot see G-d, He is invisible, but He can see you - night and day. As grown-ups we still have the same philosophy. We trust Him because He is our G-d, our life, and we must be grateful. We have nothing better to trust and believe in. Our hope and prayers are that He listens to us and helps us.

What's the answer to those questions? Are there any answers? I'm sure there must be answers. We must be aware and alert. Open our eyes. Don't be so innocent to trust everyone and believe everything you hear or see. There is still hatred around us. There are people I know - it seems they never learn. It seems like no one can be trusted. It could be a next-door neighbor - it does not matter. Sometimes it is hidden, waiting for the time when the lid blows off. Don't fool yourselves. Today, due to the economic conditions - unemployment - all over the world is just waiting for a match to light up. I'm sorry - I don't want to scare you - but it's true. And some people wake up and want something that you have - even though you worked hard for it. Those people - sick-minded, very sick - they want whatever you have, with promises they will find the cause and their message succeeds. And before you know it, they find followers - convince them to go with them. As we saw, soon after that they become like monsters and enemies - like very sick people. They do not care for anyone - not even themselves. They forget they are human. They become like animals. You cannot reason with them - it would be like you would reason with animals. It is rooted deep into their minds. We must be careful to be positive and strong when we face them - they are dangerous, but we must try to stop them before it is too late. Otherwise, history will repeat itself, and you will have nothing to enjoy - they will destroy whatever you worked on and tried to raise - your family, your life in peace - your children, or maybe your own life. And those gangsters promised their followers whatever they wanted to hear. Did they ever keep that promise?

In the region where we used to live, Slovakia has taken over, and the people there are very surprised. They lost their plan to be Hungarian - even though that's what they wanted. Before World War I, it used to be Hungarian. They spoke that language. Even though we lived in Czechoslovakia, it was allowed to speak Hungarian. We were taught in Hungarian - it was allowed then. But now the times have changed. Now, they are not allowed to speak any other language except Slovak - in school, in every home, in private, and in business. Now they are not happy. They are very disappointed and unhappy people.

As I see it - instead of getting what they expected, the followers lost much more - including their loved ones. For what reason? They also paid a high price, for no reason at all. I hope they learned the lesson: promises are easy to make, but you never gain from them.

Now that I think back - when I think how this world was created - I think about what our ancestors went through 2,000 years ago. I'm sure you know what happened, but people deny our history. There are people who deny even the last 70 years. They claim that what happened - never happened. Even though, luckily, we still have a few people that survived - there aren't many. They wrote down their own life. There are historians who wrote about it. Some countries still feel it. I hoped that those people learned something, but it wasn't enough - they are still trying to continue with their genocide. They try to destroy the world and the population with it. They're asking for more. What is wrong with those people? It seems like they were born with hatred. Can it be? Or is it true? Children are born innocent. Some may be neglected or mistreated. Or is it a gene? I think it's time to study this - because it is an important subject. In my view, perhaps we could prevent another genocide by studying children as they grow up.

Yes, the Holocaust was real. It was true. What will happen 1,000 years from now? New generations will ask the same questions. "How will I know it is true?" You can question it - that's your privilege. But take it from me and examine the evidence: the case is true.

I tried to figure out an answer to my own question. We don't believe so many things today, even though I remember them clearly from our Bible. I tried to separate truth from fiction - what was evident, and what we learned from our own family. And from our Bible, it is true. All of it - what man prepared, what they tried to convince us of - this was our history. Our faith. Our life. And always, there were some people who found a reason to take whatever you worked for. And that still wasn't enough for them. We were forced to live all around the world and suffered only because of our nationality - I mean, for being Jewish. We were driven out and deprived of our home - there wasn't enough space for us. They wanted something for nothing. It didn't matter who you were - even if you had the will, the title, the money - they wanted it.

I remember reading about it as a child, in the Bible - whenever they had problems of their own, they tried to blame it on the Jewish people. We were driven out from our rightful place, Israel. That time they used different names - called us Hebrews. We were forced from our country - scattered all over the Earth - trying to find a place to settle down and make a home - in peace and happiness. To have a family with respect and to be able to live as human beings - they did not look for any trouble. They tried to make a living and better themselves and get along with all the nationalities - like human beings are supposed to - without any hatred.

In my memory, we used to observe Tisha b'Av. We used to sit all day and pray for our loss - our people went through the same hatred then and they were destroyed years ago. I remembered every year our family prayed for those people who were killed - their life taken - as the Bible said, 'and they got together all the Jewish families - children - slaughtered them like animals.' We were sitting shiva for them. But I never dreamed that I would do it again - for my own family - as it came, the Holocaust. What a horrible nightmare. The other side - the non-Jews - they have no knowledge about it. They were happy - dancing - like nothing happened. They killed their fellow man. Still, it wasn't enough. They would not accept what they had done. They took their lives - thousands of years back in our history - and then it repeated. Again and again. It was never enough.

Without thinking it over, they paid a high price too - not just the Jewish population. They have losses of their own, all kinds, even now, after all this. Their people are still suffering. They cannot blame us though - it is their own creation. They have no right to blame us or anyone else. Our farmers and scientists help them to put food on the table, and in other ways - to better their lives. But no one cares - they had the chance for a better life, but now the people who helped them are all gone. Now it is up to them. If they want to build a better life for themselves, they have to take another look and try to understand - so nothing like this ever happens again.

How can I forgive them? Forgive them? Hell, I cannot respond to their cry for being in need - because they're guilty, in my opinion. Finally, they are getting something back - not enough. Maybe one day in the future - maybe in the other world - just maybe, somehow, or some way, our Lord, our G-d, will find some way to punish those that were involved. I hope that people will learn - even now - and receive the punishment they deserve. One doesn't know who will be next. Look around - what happened to those gangsters and their friends? The punishment they received wasn't enough. They got off very easily. The punishment wasn't enough - they deserved much more.

I asked this question - how could those people who committed this crime get away? And now those same people - crying for help - yes, I know they have losses too. Whose fault is it? They cannot blame anyone but themselves. Now they know how to find us when they need help? Is there no one else they could turn to? But now I cannot - and I will not - help anyone who was not able to help my family. Now - the way they made the bed, they will sleep in it. They want everything - from clothing to money. They even had the nerve to ask me to bring them to America! They would do anything to help us - if we could help them. Now they need you - and it does not matter who you are. They do not care if you are Jewish now - the Jew is okay - it does not matter. When our family needed help, where were they? They turned their back - they did not even hear that cry. No one listened. Okay - now they forget all of that - like nothing happened. Now it is too late. My feeling toward them is all dead. It was a modern world - they knew what life is - and they went through, previously, with the First World War. That should have been a lesson. And after that they still wanted something so badly - a territory - their homeland. Now take a good look - what do they have? Nothing but disappointment. And they also got a nightmare. Now I ask that question - was it worth it, if you have losses more than you bargained for? You would like to run away, if you have a chance? I could tell the answer by the way they were asking me for help - how does it feel now, when, as you are saying, there is no way, no outlook - no way to turn for help? How does it feel? I should feel sorry for you, but I have no compassion for you. I would have - if you would have tried to reach out for my family. They were crying for help. I understand you were only one family, and were not able to. Your own life - it was in jeopardy - in danger. I remember in the past the family - we were very close friends - I never forgot that. I also understand - if you have to do whatever you have to do to save your own life - you have no choices. But I still feel - those little children, without food, clothing, just trying to be alive - they went through an intolerable life. I know, because my family wrote me all about it. Therefore, you got what you asked for. I don't wish anyone anything bad, but I hope they will question their own conscience and see how they could live with what they did. How would they feel if it had been done to them, and no one had helped them?

I had a cousin who lived in Helmec. She was married. They struggled all their life. They had one son. I knew her more than the other relations. When they started picking up the Jews, as I heard from others, she was left alone in a city where you could get lost very easily - especially if you are alone, and all of a sudden you find yourself nowhere. She had a sister who lived with my Uncle Lajos and his family. And as I heard, she became very ill, and was all alone. She had typhus - and can you imagine, years ago, you were not able to get help immediately, because as you know, it is a very dangerous sickness - a catchable disease. And here she was, left all alone. No one there. She was not able to get a doctor or anyone else. Why was all this happening? Just because you were a Jew. Now I ask that question - was it a good reason? How would you like it if you were in her position? What happened to her after that, you can imagine. I don't even have to answer you. I just wanted to mention one of the cruelties that went on.

I hope they learned their lesson. Hatred never accomplishes anything - it only destroys. Peacefully, you can accomplish - and reach the highest mountain. I do not hate anyone, but I never can forget the past, and about our dearest, loving family.

The question remains: What would have happened if this would have been known to Christians or to any one of other religious faith? It can happen! Would anyone try to save them? I am sure the Jewish people would never have allowed it to happen. They would have fought to the last - to try to protect, to try to save them. We, the Jewish people, if there is any problem, we are there - trying to help. Even right here in America. Hopefully, this we would never know.

We read and know our Bible. We believe in G-d, and we accept the Ten Commandments.

You shall not murder!

The Jewish nation will not kill - only in self-defense, if such time arises. "Help thy neighbor" - we believe it and live by it. Charity is our way of life. We do not hit people when they are down. We try to help them.

You believe in G-d, you pray to Him - but it seems to me that people really do not know or understand our G-d.

As humans, we all have questions. Unfortunately, some human beings become like animals. As a child, they grow up okay, but somehow they transform as they grow up and fail to learn from history. They have not learned to say to themselves, it's enough of wars. Let us sit down and talk it over and see how we can compromise, without jeopardizing the ability to live in peace. They are filled with hatred.

Hatred destroys. Sooner or later, it becomes uncontrollable and you will not be able to understand what is driving you. Problems can be helped - if you accept it, that is, the knowledge that you are in trouble before it goes out of control. It is advisable to seek help, but sometimes people don't want any. Hatred - stop it before it takes root - before it spreads any further - otherwise the innocent have to pay a high price - it leads to fighting and wars. It is going around - take a look - we have wars all around us! It seems it never ends.

How can you stop these terrible hatreds? Education is the key word - to stop hatred and wars. By proper education, perhaps we could improve our lives - as well as those that have been mistreated and are wanting to get even. Every one has the opportunity to choose and have equal rights if they want to do something. It is time we accomplish and recognize equal rights in our land of freedom, but still the hatred against each other exists.

Maybe you could do as good as anyone. We have enough room for all of us. We could live together and work together with respect for each other, and get along like a human being, not like animals with hatred. We could have a better world to live in for all of us. We have had enough hatred - genocide.

Even in ancient times, if you look back at the Old Testament, you will see. In our modern world and with all this science and room enough for all of us to enjoy life equally, just maybe then you have a chance to grow together, to pray together, to raise your family in freedom and I bet their future for them if you love them you would wake up.

You have to face the fact - try to create jobs and stop hatred and hunger. Give respect. You must try to stop this sickness. Maybe, if you work hard enough, it is all possible - to improve our life so the worst history will never be repeated. Some people are denying that it ever happened - maybe you have to go back and learn history, so you will never forget that.

Improve your own life and your family. That is the most important thing - for you and for your country. Respect others in any position you are in. Understand every one of us has feelings.

There are so many ways you can learn to improve your life. Study and use your common sense. Learn the difference between love and hatred - then you will understand the meaning of both words. There is a big difference between these two words. Some people don't even know the real meaning of love. They can also use it for destruction, if they desire. There are so many definitions.

You must learn and try to educate yourself. Learn to be responsible and to have self-control. It is easier to build and create a healthy atmosphere and give respect to others - and work hard. I know we all do that, but sometimes it just does not work out, and we must be very strong and try to overcome. There is always somebody - someone - who will reach out and understand. You should never give up. Try and try again until you succeed.

We are all the same - maybe one is darker than the other - but people come in all colors, races, and religions. It must be respected by all. Learn to look up and not down on people. We are all human beings. If we treat others as you would like to be treated, just maybe - if we are lucky - we may stop this hatred. People need to learn how to get along with each other and respect each other, regardless of their race and their religion. The world is large enough for all the peoples. You must teach your children so they can understand the dangers of what can happen when there is hatred. Teach your children - and most important, of course, teach it in school. Failure in what we educate threatens the future. Therefore, people must pay attention and learn about life. Life is sacred - no one has the right to take it away. No more wars. No more killing. Let's live. Let's live in peace. Let us live side by side. No more hatred. You must learn to respect - and lift your finger if someone cries - because you never know, it could be you, and no one will hear you. Let them learn the meaning of love and honesty. And practice it - beginning with their own families. I believe if the people stop this hatred, and they really want to have peace, then they must stop this crazy hatred against each other - nations, and even individuals. That's the only way to try to correct it. I've lived together with all nationality - it could be done. They could see much more improvement - to have a happier, better life for all of us. We must learn how to build our lives, making sure we all have the opportunity to learn whatever we want to. People must learn that hatred never worked out. Another point - full employment - to keep people busy, to let them enjoy life, and make a healthy living, not just for survival. Not everything that shines is gold.

We must remind the world, it is not only one side that is suffering. We - all the people - are suffering. We all paid a high price. In the war, no one is the winner and there is no winner when it comes to hate. That word is very dangerous. People find any excuses just to kill. Whatever reason you choose - it is a very stupid reason. There must be very sick people, and one person could do so much - it is unbelievable - all the value of life got lost.

Even after that, the people in this world are still trying to destroy one nation, one population - all for one reason - because they are Jewish. You would like to have the whole world just for yourself. If that's what you want, go ahead and try - but it will be a short life. We must remember who we are, and be very careful, and prepare yourself for an emergency.

And some of the people are questioning - denying - it ever happened. Yes, it did happen. There is living proof of all this, and we must remember. They also have a habit of blaming the innocent instead of the guilty. Why? Isn't it enough? Why do innocent, loving people have to go through this?

Today, so many things are going on. We must speak out in our own best interest. At this stage, it feels like an almost impossible test. We must repeat ourselves - because if we don't, and we just let it go, people will forget this ever happened. And that would be tragic. People - and especially the leaders of their countries - must be reminded. If they fail to learn, it can happen to them too. Some survivors are left to tell us firsthand and talk about their ordeal. They went through it, is enough for a lifetime. They are young children survivors. I hear them speaking about their own experience and speaking about the others, how much they went through. It is a miracle how they survived and managed to continue their life and get an education. I am thankful for all of them who came forward to speak about their experience and I'm very proud of them. I thank them for their courage. It takes strength to try to convince the world to learn and stop with this killing. War was never productive, hatred should never exist. It should be stopped at all costs. I know we repeat ourselves. They believe very strongly that education is the only way to prevent another outbreak. We need more than ever to stop this madness - hatred.

From time to time, I listen to or read the news - nothing but more trouble all around the world. It is discouraging. I'm very concerned about when will this end. If you are a conscious person, you can't just dismiss and not speak about it, even though that would be easier - but I can't. We are in such a condition that not even I want to think about it. Those criminals need to be taken care of. The way we let them go so far becomes a nuisance to the whole world. I cannot understand why we are so good that we allow them to become strong again. Why the people did not learn from the past? Do the innocent people have to go through the suffering again? I know we are a peace-loving nation, but sometimes we should try to see our own shortcomings and problems and learn to deal with it. Today, like always, there are people who do not want you to live. They cannot live and let you live. These people have criminal minds and they cannot function peacefully - they do not understand any language other than their own, which is killing. They get followers easily, and this is a big problem. Some nations can be secretly bought by other nations.

Why does it always come back to this word - hatred? I have asked this question so many times, but I come back with no answer. It is not just in America - but America is the best example. Oh G-d - what we went through. Horror. Nightmare. The young generation cannot see it. Therefore, they cannot understand what we are saying. Hatred can spread to others very well

- that's the way it began. I cannot understand how and why it spread so fast, that it became uncontrollable, or went as far as it did. No one can assume that they cannot escape from such a situation. It's like an epidemic, like any other sickness. It spreads faster than the cure. We must learn before it becomes worse! One must learn their minds as to how they started and must deal with it. It will never go away if you allow them.

If we have laws, but don't live by them - it will destroy us from within. That will be worse than any outside enemy. You can pray and pray - but it will not help, not if no one acts. It happened before. Don't sit and wait. This could be dangerous. It took 1,000 years, according to religious thought, that the Messiah will come to improve the lives of all. Don't wait - it will never happen. You may wait until the world goes under. Might as well bury yourself now.

As a young child, we heard some rumors what was happening in this world against the Jews. Then the Holocaust. Why all this came around is impossible to understand. Every time I sit down and try to write, nothing but heartaches comes in and I cannot even express myself the way I should. In my mind, I have all the memories and I would like to express myself as it was. On the other hand, it is very painful and difficult. Stop hatred before it gets out of hand. Try everything you can. You can save heartache - and more. I urge you - do whatever you can - peacefully - to protect our country. Protect our freedom. For all people - all races, all religions.

We cannot relax and wait-and-see. The longer you wait, the worse it becomes. We could not have foreseen before, but we were not looking because we were hoping that it would go away. We must learn from the past - it should never happen again, and the next generation must learn this lesson. Work hard - show the world an example and be proud of our heritage. We could do it - we could make it - we are smart enough to work out our differences in peace, and smart enough to protect ourselves - we're as good as they. Show the world how they can learn from us. We have all the right to be here, just like anyone else. It does not matter where we live - we are good people - educated as they - maybe more. And most important - we are human - just like they are, flesh and blood. We have equally the same right for existence, just like anyone else - just like any other human being. We were created just like any other creation. You never know - someone might come along and can do the same to you. You never thought about that - you better do. Do not underestimate us. We learned the lesson - never again.

In my family - my father, my oldest brother with his wife and five children - even though seventy years passed by, I never wanted to give up hope. Perhaps someone will call us that has survived. Unfortunately, as we learned, they all perished. Innocent children, babies, parents and grandparents of all ages being congregated and forced to follow their orders for their destruction. Our people were praying even on their way to their own destruction. Even now, I can't believe it - my heart aches just to write about it. I still cannot believe it.

What all those letters contain - if you read them - you would feel that the situation now is similar to what happened before in Europe. By reading it, you would feel that people knew it was coming - and their fate was hanging in the balance. There was no place to go, no place to run. There was hunger, cold, and not enough clothing to stay warm. At that time, no one was listening to their cry. All those people who were educated, talented - rabbis, professionals - had difficulty in getting to America. No one was concerned what will happen to them. Unfortunately, before the war, innocent people wanted to get away from Germany - and they had no place to go. America declined to accept them. They were willing and able to pay their own way - they just wanted to survive. They would have been an asset anywhere - if only they would have let them in somewhere, to live their lives. Unfortunately, they were denied - even to enter America. The freedom-loving nation denied their permission to come in - and save their lives.

Take a look at today - anyone that wants to come to America gets in. Some people are innocent - hard workers - and are having trouble making a living. Struggling all their lives. Then someone comes - and wants everything for nothing. Unfortunately, after the disaster that happened, here in America we found out that these people who committed the crime were living here in America - and no one suspected them. These people were living among us - and no one knew they were criminals. How could this happen? It unfortunately happens all the time. Criminals know how to get away. They're very smart - for their benefit - to do destruction and get away with it.

I hope this madness disappears soon. I hope people wake up - to a better, happier life. That is my wish.

There is still hope - for all of us. Maybe not in my lifetime, but it will come. Replace hatred with understanding, and you will see how much happier your life can be. You may even find the answer you've been looking for. But you must try. We must try to learn that hatred must stop. We all pay a price - not just the guilty ones.

It seems people are greedy. The more they have, the more they want. They do not care how they will get it, and who gets hurt by it. And how many lives - innocent people and children - lost their life. And the money, or the people, have a high price to pay. You must learn to be happy with whatever you have. Do not become greedy and want more - because you never know what is on the other side. If you want to have something, you have your own choices. First of all, try to educate yourself - whatever you like to do - and try to learn whatever you feel you are capable of, and enjoy doing.

Especially when you have the choice. We have freedom and are lucky enough that we have the opportunity to come and go and be happy and raise the family as you wish. Go to the church or the Temple - no one will stop you - pray to your own G-d. You have the right and you must learn to respect others. You must have common sense and be able to decide wrong and right and try to stop hatred before it begins. One thing you must learn is how to raise your children to love their neighbors and to learn the value of a family. This is our backbone - not just in the family - even in the countries all around the world. Want happiness? Preserve the old fashion families - you would have all the fun right in your home with your family. You could do so many things together. Pray together - eat together - play together - and most important, not be against each other. Families should be able to get along - it is no reason why not - otherwise, why people bother to get married? No reason in it - you want a family you would be proud of and be happy and enjoy each other's company - but something, somewhere, is all twisted.

I will go back to the words 'jealousy' and 'greedy'. Some of the people can't accept defeat - even if they have the opportunity to work out for all the people equal rights, no difference religion or race. It seems we still have not changed. The present environment is not acceptable - nothing there. If it would show any improvement - it's only by a miracle if there is one. I can't foresee what will be next. Hatred may never really go away. Everything is so messed up - not just here, but all over the world. After the Second World War, we created the UN, the world organization, with the hope it would be able to create peace in this world instead of war. The organization, it seems to me, was wasted - it's not able to help people get along with each other. It seems people have no more respect for human life around the world. So much so that hatred and the fights - they cannot even accept peace - they do not know the meaning of peace.

So I hope you learned your lesson. Education would be cheaper than the ammunition and sufferings that goes with hatred. And don't look at others and think they have a better life than you. You might be surprised. Try to enjoy what you have - and be happy.

Now I will come to the closing.

I hope we all learn respect - caring for others.

I hope the world will never again go through so much agony what my generation did - to teach the idea of the human being.

It does not matter what religion - we are all equal.

There's much more I could say. But I'll stop here. Maybe, just maybe, someone will find a solution to all this.

Everyone has a dream.

We all try and hope for a better life and a better future. How can you accomplish all of this? Sometimes we try, and it seems hopeless - but as they say, *try and try until you succeed*. But we never know what comes next. The time will come - unexpectedly - you never can tell the future. Sometimes if you expect too much, you might be disappointed. Therefore, do what you can and try to learn how to manage the best with what you have - and go forward. Try to be happy. Enjoy your family and your life.

Now I think I will come to a stopping point. I hope I did not say something to discourage you. I did not mean to.

Learn from someone - it's much better than learning the hard way, by yourself.

I will say so long. Have a happy and a healthy life - to all of you.

Maria

This article I have decided to type into the computer, hoping whoever reads it can learn about hatred. We should never forget that word. Every time I think of my past - what caused all that agony and destroyed so many human lives - all that hatred - it must be stopped.

All the human race must remember that word forever. Teach love, not hatred. You might have a chance for a better life - for all of us.

Thank you again for taking time out to read my articles.
Typed into the computer - 12/1/012

Chapter 28
On Love

What is the greatest thing in our life? It is to love. Love is much more productive than hate. With it, you will see how much you can accomplish - to have a better life. We can accomplish much more if we remember - that the one and only power that can help you survive is love: love of your family, love of your fellow men, love of your country, and the most important part, love of our G-d, if you believe in Him. In my opinion, if you do believe that love is the greatest and the strongest of all - it gives you strength and can keep your life going on living.

Our prayers are always about sharing our love all around the world - not just today, but always - to have peace and to live in harmony with each other. We can do it, if you want to.

Love has no price - you can have it and use it as often as you want to, and you will learn how much you can accomplish by it. You can say that you have accomplished something in this world if you can influence even one person. Maybe others will follow in your footsteps. This is all there is about life - to teach a little bit, whatever you can, to make life easier for your fellow man.

There is enough love around. Families should pay attention - they can get some help sometimes for some of the problems. If there is a loved one who needs help, it is your responsibility to try to save them from further destruction and pain.

Knowledge is never too much. Love is never too much. Both in combination work very well. Both are important. You will not go wrong. If you have love and common sense, you can accomplish a lot and conquer the world.

Show love, show caring for others, show understanding. This is what it's all about. With love you could build a mountain, but with hatred you could destroy the world.

Chapter 29
Last thoughts

As I was writing my story, all of a sudden something went over me. Like someone shook me up, a feeling that I've never experienced before. I would never want to go back to Europe. There's no family left, only heartache. It was a feeling of mixture, good and bad. I try to understand why all of a sudden this feeling I am having is so very real I cannot understand it, it lasted only a few seconds. But it was enough of an experience. Like someone is ready to go back home. I felt very anxious. The other feeling was, why go, there is nothing to see. It would not matter. I would just look at the place - and I would like to look in the window. I try to forget it, like I never lived there. Would our friends and neighbors be there? Probably they are gone! Even if they were there, I felt it is better not even to think about. Now it doesn't matter where my birthplace was. In reality, I would never go back to see or visit.

Our brother David, he was different. He wanted to go back to visit to see the property we have there - and we still have. He thought that after the war he would have liked to go and sell our land, because it was the only way we could. There was no one to help us. And there was no money to do it. Later, because of his health, wasn't able to travel but he still wanted to go. Our place became Slovakia. Therefore, I don't know if he would have been able to do anything there. Also it would be most likely be very dangerous. It wasn't worthwhile to jeopardize his life. We tried to correspond with the officials there, but they were not anxious to help us. There are some Jewish agencies that could help, we tried, but without success. It became hopeless, therefore we just try to forget. The memories are too great, too much pain involved, and now there is nothing we can do.

Even if I could go there, is anything we could do about this? You would have to live in Slovakia otherwise you cannot keep your property whatever you have. You are not allowed to have too much property either, only whatever you can take care of by your self. The government controls it and it is very difficult. This is what I was told. And now we have no other choice, just walk away, like with anything else, our life our family. As I see it, we have to close our life like it never existed.

Recently I had a chance to see our place. It happened to be on the computer, and to my surprise, I could not recognize our birthplace. Oh it is entirely different. We had a very large property in the small village where our home was. And now I have seen the buildings on our property. They have electricity. That's it, nothing more. And nothing is left except in our heart. Now I could say we have to close the book. Don't look any further, there is nothing left there for us.

Life goes by pretty fast, faster than you think. I am speaking from my own experience. I feel I've seen enough of life - of lives coming and going. Many times I would like to go out and scream: be careful! do not waste time. It is very precious. Our life is very difficult sometimes, but we are stronger than we ever know. We humans endure lots of pain and heartaches and we cry when no one sees it. We are very lucky to live as long as some of us do. I think in one hand we are very lucky to be able to be here as long as we do. To reach our golden years, not too many of us can say that we did. It wasn't easy road ahead of us and how we will continue going on that road one cannot see and cannot tell.

I'd like to write many more things, but I don't have much time.

Chapter 30
My prayer...

This is my own belief and creation and my prayer.

O'mighty in heaven, as always I ask You in my prayer for help. In my heart You have a little time to hear me out. The Old Testament, our regular prayer, You created and I learned from our grandparents, our father, our teachers. We were those that have respect and pray every day, mornings began with a prayer as I remember my father. He always began the day with his ritual prayer, put on his Tefillin and read in his prayerbook, prayed, thanking You, praying to You, so he'll be able to carry out his duties with full heart. He took his time, whether he had this time or not. When he was well or sick, he prayed without interruptions. When he finished his prayer, he had his breakfast. Before breakfast he washed his hands, this is our belief, to clean yourself out of respect to Almighty, that means You our G-d. After that he made another prayer thanking You and then we began to eat. Every time he followed our religious ritual and just after that he sat down and had his meal which he has gathered for his family. Even that wasn't enough...

He never forgot that he is a Jew. After dinner he never missed his prayer. Thanking You for giving us the food that he ate. After every meal he carried out the same way. He never, not even for a minute, forgot to do this religiously. He observed Your rules. How You showed to his parents, and to us his children. If any one of us got into any problems he always reminded us that G-d was everywhere, He will see you and you cannot hide or misbehave.

At that time we followed Your creation and Your Bible. When I visited our grandparents and we went to the temple there, there were two sections separate for men and women. On holidays or any other occasion, it was the same. We walked to the temple every Saturday, to the next town, where our grandparents lived. We attended services there almost every Saturday to pay respect. We had to have 10 persons to have a quorum. At that time of day counted only men for that purpose. Women were not counted into the 10 persons. They always made sure there were enough people as was necessary. This particular town had more Jewish people. It was a big town, not like our village. When I visited my grandparents, sometimes we slept over, and in the morning we went to the temple to pray. Our grandparents were more religious. At home we used to pray short prayers before each meal. We washed our hands, but it was not as strict as for the boys. When our brother became 13 years of age, in accordance with the Jewish tradition, he became a man. He studied the necessary prayers to be called up to the Torah and recite the prayer. Now he also was able to be called the tenth man. He was prepared by his Jewish education and learned to pray and used tefillin just like any other adult man. Now he was expected that he would follow the religion faithfully. We all followed it faithfully.

Some of the youngsters were students and studied in the yeshivas for further education and some became rabbis, teachers. These individuals studied like in a university. They believed very strongly in You, Almighty. All my life my belief was very strong. Also my heart, my prayers were always very faithful.

To understand me, why I'm trying to express my belief and my thoughts and why I'm changing my prayers, now I will begin. You were our life, our hope, but when they needed it You did not hear their prayers. You were too busy. Why? You forgot how there were so many innocent people and their cries, young and old, every corner, You let them be destroyed, their last breath they were praying for you with all their strength, You failed to respond.

Oh, our Lord forgive me for my feelings. It is very important for me to be able to find some kinds of answers. I wasn't able to understand why all this happened. I had no answer! These people were Your children, and first creation. We studied Your Bible, we learned and believed as we learned from our parents. We learned to have respect for You and were told by our family don't ever forget, not even for a moment, that you are a Jew. And be faithful to our Almighty. We learned and we practiced that. Whenever we have had a problem we returned to You because You are watching over us. You could see us whatever or whenever we are. We cannot hide from You. We were told as children that you can see us if we misbehaved, every corner everywhere. You don't need any transportation such as cars. You're in heaven, with Your angels surrounding, waiting for You to tell them to help You. This was called the heaven. You are in our creation, our body, our mind, therefore if we need something all we have to do is just pray....... the Almighty will hear you, He has ears. He cannot talk or cannot be seen He is not visible, but very strong, He will help you, even grown ups believed in You. You are our life, our hope, our belief, You are Almighty in heaven. After all this, You allowed us to grow without paying attention. So many innocent people and crying, young and old in every corner. Broken hearts with their last words, their last breath, praying, praying for You, with all that strength and their belief in your creation. Here we needed You most, and You were nowhere. I look back - there were so many men, people, who prayed all day and night: religious, talmid, yeshiva bochur. It did not matter - they are all gone. They prayed every day of the week, every moment, for everything. They were faithful. Take a look what happened to them. You watched and listened, but did not lift Your finger to help. Where were You, our Mighty? Did You not hear them? Did You not hear their cry? How about their children - all ages - from one day up? My heart is aching so much for them. I just cannot dismiss it. Sometimes my pain is so bad, I want to get up and scream - "So, my Mighty, why did You allow them to carry out such a genocide?" Please come back. I cannot accept You are no more in existence and in power. I try to sort out where we failed You. Why You ignored all their prayers, our prayers. All of the people's prayers. If You are so busy, You could have had Your helpers all around you. Why didn't You ask them to stop these horrible nightmares? Why did You allow those gangsters, killers to carry out such a terrible crime? Were You happy to see the torturers, the butchers, the animals carry out such an inhuman torture of innocent children? All those people were innocent! And the way I learned, You are G-d for all the peoples, and here the people were blind, no one saw us in this miserable time, not even You! You were blind and did not hear anything. My question is all our question!... we never had any doubt, with all this and we still believe in You! I don't believe that You for a minute wanted all this horror to go as far as it did. You showed us Your strength before, it is how You saved us, my brothers and sister. I'm very grateful and I never stopped believing in you. I never gave up on You, our mighty G-d You are still, and I trust You and my prayers. I know and I hope that by now You got in a better position to reach out to our people, Your creatures. I know, we as people without Your help, we would never be able to go as far as we did. We are, all of us, grateful.

I am thanking You now, as always. I'm thankful for saving my brother Irving, You heard my cries at that time and my prayers every day and night to help him, guard him, to have a better chance, in the American army. Our creator, our G-d, I hope, as I began to pray to You, as always I did many times before when our family was in my homeland. I do not understand where I have failed as of now, I'm praying all the time without stopping day and night. My life was interrupted with suffering, without knowing the real truth what my family was going through. How would I know? Beyond human imagination. We know our past history from our prayer books and the Torah. Your 10 Commandments remained in our history, our G-d in heaven - respect our family, our elderly and we learned that as a child. We never stop praying our original prayers. We knew we needed new prayers and try to sort out our life and wake up. We were sleeping and not listening, but did not care what happening around.

What a shame that the rich, the powerful, the strong rejects all. Hope they have learned their lesson. I never wished anyone any harm. By my nature I do not in any way wish punishment or torture and anger. I believe You must teach people how to communicate better, learn to straighten the way.

It is possible to try to learn to be more flexible and deal with problems as much as possible. The main thing you must remember we cannot believe and trust without life. Our Almighty is the best and still the only one around, still need his guidance, after all that we went through so much suffering and ordeals. Hoping that this will never happen again. What's happening even now it is very difficult to go ask. We cannot rest our mind because we are still suffering. There is little hope as I see it. Some people should not be called people, much like animals they will never change. They manage to create followers, teaching them by lying to them about money. And the people say that they're helping them and their families to do whatever to help them and here they are suffering with their life, for nothing, as I see it. They believe in nothing, but only thing they believe it's to brainwash, distract before they had a chance to be great or to learn a better way of life and to create a healthier life for all of them and their families.

As I said before our prayers did nothing and were not working. All our people believed it when they were taken away and were gathering them up. You could have listened, but for some reason You didn't. They never stopped, You are to be their savior, they were very strong in their beliefs, until they were even with their last breaths, "Almighty in heaven help us." Therefore, I'm trying my way maybe to make change and it will be working better. My belief is strong. Your existence nowadays, some people forget about You, trying to get away from the original prayer because of disbelief. All the people around the world, good or bad, still need Your help. They still use the original prayer, still trying to prove it how much they believe in You, others dismiss it. Sometimes I have the feeling You heard me. I want to thank You for Your help. I can feel it – yes, I do. It is not a dream. It is real. Thank You. Our Lord – unseen, invisible – He is all over the world and beyond. He represents all races, all colors, all equal.

So much disappointment, so much suffering, and it still exists today. It is every day, nothing but suffering all around us. There's little hope left at all. Never stop looking if there is anyone can solve this nightmare. I see science is here and will continue to be in existence - more new ideas, more evolved. I still do not think it also will overpower You. Our Mighty, You are creating those brains. You give them the power to better our life. How long will this go on? With smart people, educated doctors and more medicines everyday, but we miss how to do the job, the biggest one - that is to stop this hatred. You are the first one to turn to, hoping that this time You will be able to, just like You created life, given us brains, teaching us. We learned from the first creation, therefore I do not want to believe You will fail us, or destroy this world from the beginning to the end. The way I see it, I'm hoping for a miracle.

Try to remember that the Almighty G-d is strongest and the most powerful. But people need to help all human beings, and to help all races and religions. End wars – and end hatred against all human beings. In Europe all our family used to say that our Savior, the Messiah, would come. We, as children, asked our parents how would we know who he is? How will he be dressed? How will we able to recognize him or her? We were told that he will come on a white horse! That I always believed in. This was their hope that it will happen now.

Historically, something happens daily. It is a history of a lifetime. If you're lucky enough to live and are able to learn. If sometimes don't have the opportunity to be lucky to go to the University, even then, if you want to learn, learn by observing others every minute - there's always something to learn. Where there's a will there's a way. Instead of wasting your time looking or waiting for something to come your way, try to read all kinds of books, a real education. As a child I found the story of the first world war in books first. It was real. People can even learn from that. Whatever I was able to get, I tried and was interested. Even in later years, as of now, I am still willing to learn. What even a child speaks, I wanted to be able and to be sure to understand it. If I can or what I can help I am trying to do. You don't have to be rich. Whatever you can do, even though just old saying, it becomes helpful. Learn to respect, don't wait, don't expect to get something for nothing.

When I was a child, I learned from my uncle that money does not grow on the tree. It is to work hard to earn it, this really appreciate more and more careful how you will be spending it. You'll learn how to save even a dollar. Start with pennies, you will see how good it will be. It will be useful and will be handy when you learn how to manage your own life. Sometimes you get into a position where you think there isn't any hope left, everything is getting out of hand. Everyone in life sometimes needs help. We have to expect and look for that help. Don't expect or wait for someone to offer you any help. Sometimes you think if you have friends, real friends, you have grown up together, even then when you need them and you have any kind of problems they disappear. It is like you never knew them, not even a phone call, and you are all by yourself. But if your relations with your family are good, you can depend upon them, they will try to help you. But if you don't work on that, then it can create more problems.

Time passes by - bedtime, waking time, and during - I am always thinking of You. I am praying to You. You are the only One.

About the Author
Written by Maria Gluck, dictated July 5, 2012
This is a short story about the author.

Maria Gluck came from Czechoslovakia with her two youngest brothers and another sister when the Second World War broke out in 1940. They had an uncle in Columbus, Ohio, and one of their oldest brothers had already arrived in America and established a home there. Maria never had the chance to finish her education. Her youngest brother worked very hard, made a living, and later volunteered for the U.S. Army. He served bravely at the Anzio beachhead. With our G-d's help, happily he survived and returned to his family. The rest of the family in Europe were murdered by the Germans.

Maria was never trained to be a writer, but later in life, she found the courage to write a few short stories and novels - especially remarkable at the age of 93.

Her youngest brother could not remember much of his childhood. The family had wanted him to be educated, so even as a small child, he was away at school. Growing up in a small village, they didn't have access to proper education, and as a result, he missed out on the closeness and love of family life. He often asked Maria about their family and what had happened in their village, and she remembered.

Eventually, Maria decided to try to write down whatever she could recall. This became her first book, *As I Remember*, telling their life stories. At the same time, she also wrote another book titled *Vacation*.

She began writing around November 2, 2009, part-time, and finished 300 pages - all by hand. She originally decided not to have her brother read it, because of how painful some of the memories were. Instead, she began to write another book, something funny, interesting, and educational. The title of that book is *Imaginary*. She said it would be easier to read than the first one. It was about 140 pages, also written by hand.

She hopes readers will enjoy *As I Remember*. The second book may take longer to publish because she only recently learned how to use a computer. Her brother is helping to prepare the book, and one of his sons - her nephew - is editing it and may publish it. She knows her nephew is capable, understands books, and believes it is a good one to share.

Written by Maria Gluck

Appendix
Later Writings by Maria Gluck

This section contains reflections, short stories, and essays written by Maria Gluck after completing her memoir, *As I Remember...* in 2009. She was 93 years old when she finished the memoir - yet she still had so much more to say. Once she allowed the floodgates to open, writing became a cathartic outlet that let her explore her life and express her enduring love for her family.

These pieces were composed over the next three years. They continue her recollections of life in Europe and coming to America, but they often turn inward - personal meditations on the world around her, family dynamics, social change, aging, caregiving, memory, and faith. They speak in a voice that is older (!), often sharper in tone, but always rooted in the same love of life, resilience, and moral clarity that defined her earlier writing.

Several of the short stories contained especially vivid, significant passages that I chose to weave into the main body of the memoir itself. Others repeated material from the memoir, with added details, so I integrated them rather than duplicate them in the appendix. One piece, focused mainly on the family story, is marked with a ★. It repeats the general family story told in the memoir and can be thought of as a condensed version. Finally, recurring themes were drawn together into standalone essays - for example, *On Jealousy, On Hatred, On Love,* and *About Doctors and Healthcare* - which gather her thoughts from across many writings. Throughout it all, my guiding principle was to preserve her voice and vision.

The short stories are dated and presented mostly in chronological order. Together, they offer a portrait of Maria not only as a survivor and storyteller, but as a lifelong observer of the world's beauty, complexity, and failure to care for its most vulnerable. These writings are testimony, protest, and plea. Some include reflections on family members or situations that are emotionally charged. They are presented here without alteration to preserve the authenticity of her voice.

Maria wrote them all in the hope of being remembered, being heard, and offering something enduring and transformative for generations who may one day read these pages.

- *Editor's Note*

Table of Contents (Appendix)

Table of Contents (Appendix) 217

Life, Living, in Any Age 219

My Observation: Association with People 225

A True Story from Which One Can Learn 227

A Dream from Which One Can Learn 229

A Reflection on Change and Concern 233

I Reached My Golden Years 235

This morning by myself 239

Freedom 241

How to Get Along with People 245

A story (On Freedom and Survival) 247

Recipe for Danishes (tekercs) 251

★ Family story (in a nutshell) 255

Ethics and Good Manners 265

A note after typing 267

About Science 271

about science as I see it 275

How to be a happy family 277

just another note (Getting help as a senior) 285

Our brother Lajos - life history 289

On Violence 291

my opinion as I see it - a short story 293

From a newspaper in 1940 came to America 297

Memorial for our family Holocaust day 301

How to Behave in order to have a Better Life 303

About my niece and great-niece 305

another short story (On Work and Age Discrimination) 307

remember as we were growing up (About my mother) 309

another short story (Am I a good writer? Am I happy?) 311

about my nephew, the editor 315

Life around us 317

Maria's 2nd book about Irving 319

On lawyers, judges, and a crooked business 329

Home Health Aides revisited 331
On Managing Money 339
My Brother, His Sons, and His Grandchildren 341
My Vacation (Introduction) 351
My Vacation (The Imaginary Episode) 353
About the Author: 413

Life, Living, in Any Age.
2010 July 4
Syosset Long Island, New York, 11791

Typed 8/8/2011
Printed on 10/3/011

Written by Maria Gluck

    I was asked by one of the largest New York University hospitals if I would be interested in sharing with them how and what it takes to reach a senior age as I did, and what I am doing to be successful in achieving a long life as I do. Is it an inherited condition, or can I help them learn what it takes to achieve a long life?

    These researchers are trying to study how they can show how to succeed in achieving a long life. I wrote to them a very nice letter with the information I could at that time, and I told them the truth, as I know, as I always do.

    Here's my first part. I could not give them the past family history of long life because of what has taken place in Europe. I told them that I came from Czechoslovakia with my sister and two brothers.

    I was writing this book for my youngest brother, since he asked me many times to tell him about our history of our family, because he did not remember everything. Thus, I decided to write down what I could remember.

    I have never written anything serious before.

    Here I would like to talk about life as I see it, as I'm getting older, what it takes to achieve a long life. It is not an easy subject.

    I never thought of myself as being old, or when I will reach old age. Physically and mentally I still don't believe that "I am what I am." I never looked at myself as being or getting old.

    First of all, it is up to you and not the numbers what you are. I went through enough in life to make you old or feel your age. I always got compliments - I was told that I am at least 20 years younger than I actually am. I take care of myself. If you do not neglect yourself, and you do not worry about yourself, it shows.

    The only person that reminds me of my age is the heart specialist. I know him at least 18 years. He always asked me if I knew how old I am. My answer to him was yes. I asked him if he knew my age why did he ask? Then he said he wanted to remind me of it and that he cannot make me young again. Then, he said let's face it, you are old. My answer to him was that you are referring to the numbers, just like any other numbers. In my opinion it is up to you how you feel. Some people are only 50 years old and they feel that way, therefore, it's up to the individual. If you neglect yourself that will show your age. I would never consider myself to have any plastic surgery or anything else, that would show that I am young. If you are fortunate enough to keep yourself mentally, physically in fair condition and keep yourself busy and you do not sit down to watch television all day long, be active, do some homework. I go shopping and I watch what I eat. Do not eat all day long junk food, such as candies, soda. I never bothered with those things and was never a big eater. Once in a while I do some baking and make some good danishes and share it with my family. In the past I used to bake "pogacsa" for my sister and brother-in-law to enjoy while they were driving to Florida.

I was shopping for groceries, carried it home on the bus. I never owned an automobile. However, lately, sometimes I took a taxi, if I purchased more than I could carry. In my younger age, I walked quite a bit and when I was working I had long walks to the subway and back. All this took place during the summer and winter. Maybe that helped me to get enough exercise. When I had some aides they were there, but they did not help me much.

When I was in my early 50s there were some doctors that reminded me about my age that I was getting older. I must tell you that I resented it, I did not care for that type of remarks. All of this came about because he couldn't help me. I think that this was uncalled for. If he would have looked around himself, he would have discovered, that he too was getting old and was in his senior years. Just because he's a doctor, he did not realize that he's in the same position, that he is getting old just like everyone else, or he might also need some help one day and he may get the same reply from another doctor. How would he feel then?

How would you feel, if you do not get help? A good doctor will find a way to see just like a younger person. We all need help sometimes. Today that's the biggest problem, doctors do not want to bother with anyone that might take a little brain work. They may be fortunate enough to have good health. No one gets a guarantee what life will be. Maybe we are lucky. I myself think of today that I cannot worry what will be tomorrow.

By the way as I said, going back to how do you define old-age? My youngest brother was asking yesterday if I can explain the simple word, because he never thought about old age, his ideas are just like mine. Since I'm writing about it now and try to define it.

To get older it's not so simple, it takes a lifetime experience to define it.

We should think positively, as they say - it will happen, it will be better. But when you think more deeply, you realize it is getting worse. You just get lost, and you may never be able to come back to where you started.

This is part of life's experiences - we often ignore or forget it.

Story about what happened to my sister:

After the war, she went to a store looking for some clothing and heard someone speaking our native language. When she approached her and asked where she came from, and when the woman looked up, all of a sudden, she recognized her. She was from the next town where we lived in Europe. She had gone through the Holocaust and was a survivor.

It was a happy reunion for both of them. In a big city like New York, it can happen. As we see, life can bring surprises.

We can never tell - sometimes we see amazing stories.

It is a July morning. As I finish my breakfast, I've decided to examine what life is.

We live it every day, but does anyone question what life is? We live it every day, day in and day out. We mind our business, in and out of the regular routine, without thinking - just go on and do what you want to do.

I asked many times myself what is life? And I try to define it and to really see what it is. On the other hand, we cannot just say life is when we lived life. That is what I really mean.

I know, we must educate ourselves. Books are all over, doctors were more qualified to define what life is. How we became human beings? It is in existence. We now know how we came into this world. We are aware of it. The real explanation is not found what I really would like to define. There are broader explanations what I'm looking for.

We can go back to the Old Testament and referring to the Adam and Eve story. I do not know if the young generations have any idea about it. I wonder if they have knowledge of what I'm trying to say you would have to study the Old Testament the five books of Moses and you know what I'm talking about.

What I see and learn about life is much more to it as we live daily and experience it and it's much more to sustain life. What we take for granted without giving a second thought.

Let me stop here, why am I bringing all this up now? I really never was thinking about life either. Why not? I'm recently experiencing more difficulties and I realized that our life is very complicated. We never thought too much about it, and especially not about this time in our life. It is enough to experience every day whatever comes our way especially when you reach a certain age and wherever you're going to hear nothing but telling you, what do you expect nowadays and then don't expect anything more in the future.

What you do today, you cannot turn the clock back, that will never happen.

The whole situation is very scary as I'm thinking of different things such as the present situation that exists all around us in this world. I'm searching for the explanation about life. I hope that with more time to research it they will find what I'm looking for. I'm still here - why am I not happy just with that? I'm thinking of life left behind how fast it disappeared. Those years I was very busy and took it for granted, just like anyone else. I know when I realized as I'm looking back I'm very surprised that I do not know where the years went. It seemed like a dream, but what kind of a dream was it? Can I really define it? Did it really take place? Did I learn anything by this? I really do not know. Life is very complicated and it is a secret. It should be treated as such as is. Life is very precious and should not be taken very lightly. It should be treated with respect. Every life is precious. Every human being individually is precious.

We never really think especially when we're young what will be when we reach our senior years. Until you reach the moment, even then I never wasted at any time on that. Only time was when my doctors reminded me, especially when I felt young and I wasn't feeling well. I do not have any reason to think of my age. To me everything was normal. It happens to everyone, sometimes we do not feel well, young or old. I just needed a little help and they claimed that it was your age. Luckily, I'm not just the person that sits down and worries about every detail and taking it apart. Luckily I'm able to help myself. I was living all my life alone.

That made me accept and learn to seek help when I needed it. Life was easier in my younger years, but believe it or not I needed a qualified doctor and I went to look for one until I found one. Even then, I met all kind of personality, good and bad. At that time I didn't have Medicare, but always had an insurance. To me that was the most important investment. This way I didn't care or have to worry what will be if I got sick. Therefore, I did not have to wait what happens when my old age will pop up on me. Now that I'm in the age, able to get Medicare. It is not as good as it used to be. The doctors are not happy. I still try to have the best co-insurance, so I will be able to select my doctors that I like. Believe it or not, I still have trouble for other reason - doctors do not want to take you now due to your age. Therefore, like they say it, I know without reminding me of it. Certain things they can help and certain things they cannot. I have knowledge of that.

We go back to continue about figuring out life! I do not think that we will really find out what it is! Every person sees it differently. Different life, different experience - a different way of life.

The above subject is very interesting and it's worthwhile to study after all, old age is life that we experience everyday. If we're lucky enough to remember the life history that is remarkable. To live through this world, the past, and the present, whatever you're going through life.

Conclusion to my life experience I'm hoping that you will understand and learn from it. Try to sort out and whatever it may be enjoyed it. I can see there is not much hope to it however they say, if there is life there is hope. I believe in the philosophy of never give up until you succeed. I try to keep myself busy and forget the problems and concentrate on my writing.

One must learn how to reason to achieve better understanding. Therefore, you must learn not to say something that brings you in that position that adds to the problem that has occurred. One must remember that words are weapons, therefore, we must remember that you must be careful not to hurt anyone and think before you say something you may be able to prevent some conflicts.

It seems that some people will never forget and never forgive, it does not matter what it is. It happens quite often, as I mentioned, in the best of families too. I have both types of experiences in our lifetime. I was not looking for it even though they themselves caused the problem, they will blame you. They must have someone to blame. This is their makeup. Try to work it out the best possible way. Try to accept things as they are. Life is very complicated. We learn every day but we still do not know everything. Good luck to a healthy and happy life.

BY MARIA GLUCK

Story is finished January 5 2011. Typed on 8/8/2011
Finished 9/30/011

My Observation: Association with People
Written by Maria Gluck
September 12, 2010 - Syosset, N.Y.
(On Women in the Workplace)

As I traveled in life, some parts were good and some were not so good. Some were more interesting and made a good impression upon me. My working days were in different businesses. I am usually a very good observer. I always try to learn as much as is possible so I would be able to do the job assignment fully and correctly. I had knowledge to know what's right and what's wrong. When I hear it, I try to learn everything that is possible.

I just want to tell you that I was working with an accountant, and I had the privilege to see how they conducted themselves. Some of these people were interesting, and I learned and saw and observed them in their functioning. There are all types of people that follow the rules. They were working for large corporations as accountants. These people are well known and trusted. After many years of the practice, they found themselves in 'hot water'... and it was unbelievable. These people, each of them, had their responsibility to their own customers.

The company had a good name all around, and all of a sudden a cloud appeared from nowhere. One person tarnished all of their names without their knowledge. Here they have an unacceptable event. More trouble than they had ever dreamed of - to prove who is guilty or innocent. Finally, they were straightened out, fined, and went to jail. The innocent was okay in the end; however, it took money to clear themselves. Because of this situation, they lost some companies, and in the long run it was not worth it.

The guilty wanted to get rich. He was married and had a family with children - he did not care what will happen to them. He ended up in jail. How could he be so greedy? Some people will do anything and destroy innocent people with their action. We hear about such situations daily. Some people will take chances - for what? These people do not care, and they cannot see further than their nose. It is unbelievable.

Sometimes people in business or even in families - brothers, sisters, or father - it does not matter who, become greedy. They influence other people, but even their own family does not matter to them. I know they are well educated, and nothing matters except achieving their goal.

Today's lawyers are like any other profession, however they cannot foresee the unthinkable that may come about. You have to be a lawyer yourself, because some lawyers find reasons to charge you more. If you are not poor but not rich, you can lose everything that you worked so hard for. And you know that you're innocent, but some dishonest person will show up just to make money without working for it. I know it happens quite often - you can lose everything legally. It happens - they, the guilty, will get free lawyers. Where is justice? The lawyers know that they are guilty, but in our system, they must protect them. Many times, people are afraid to speak out because they may get reprisals.

There are large corporations that hire young people to influence them and to use them for their own personal gain. Their mothers were working there, and to keep their jobs they had to be quiet. The young women were physically used. And at this time, it was the drug and AIDS era. These people were at the lowest point in life. Unfortunately, it was a common situation.

If they could not follow their orders, they were out - fired. They had evening parties anytime they felt like it, in their offices. The other workers knew what was going on. They had many retail stores in New York and out of town. Wherever they went, they repeated the same behavior. They took them out - all those young girls and some other well-known people - for a "good time."

When I heard about it, I was told that in most places they did this - it was the type of life. A young executive's secretary was telling me on the first day, the manager approached her, told her what he wanted, and asked her would she go along with the idea. When I found out, I advised her of my opinion; however, she said when she was asked about the idea, she got up and walked out. There were others that left after the first lady.

There is more than one individual boss in this situation that was going on. First, I didn't believe this can be true, sometimes people make up stories - but it can happen. I was finally convinced it is a true story, because other people were doing the same thing.

By the way, it was like an epidemic. Many people were not aware of the drug situation. They had their own families - they were responsible people, and they got away with crime. Young women, and no one even attempted to solve the crime that these people were doing. The parents needed their jobs - they were afraid to speak up, and therefore their daughters could not be protected. I heard similar stories from other people. The office manager belonged to the same group.

In my life, I met all kinds of people - some were nice and some weren't.

A True Story from Which One Can Learn
By Maria Gluck - June 27, 2011 to August 3, 2011

How can a family survive?

It seems to me that it must come from deep within - a love for each other that nothing can erase. It has to be something deep-seated, something rare. No one can take it away from you. It doesn't matter - it's like brick and stone. It comes from the foundation, from your upbringing.

World War II and the Holocaust brought on unbelievable nightmares - pain, hunger, starvation, torture, and concentration camps. As human beings, we cannot even imagine what our remaining family endured.

As I look back, it seems like a dream. It's hard to believe this is a true story - but it is.

From my immediate family, five people survived. Our father's brother Lajos, his wife Etelka, and their five children - including four boys, ages twelve to one - were all lost. The little girl was ten years old. I'm writing about them. All this happened seventy-one years ago. You might say, "By now you should have forgotten," but no - there is no such thing.

My grandmother - my mother's mother - was eighty years old. She was taken away along with her sons, my uncles Márton and Lajos, their wives, and children. Our grandfather had just passed away before they were taken - by the Hungarian government, following the orders of the Germans.

All our family in Europe is gone. We tried to find out what happened to them. We reached out to different organizations, but we came to a dead end. They perished - along with six million others in the Holocaust.

Five of us were lucky enough to come to America, though it was not easy. Today, only two of us are left - me, Maria, and my brother Irving We hold on to each other. Our love keeps us together.

Now I want to return to what I originally meant to write - about my own family.

Our love was always there.

Today's world is different. The word is the same, but the generation isn't. I worry about the next one. They need to learn that hard work and love go hand in hand. The past generation worked hard to make a better life - but they didn't always give their time. Time and affection matter.

"Take care of the pennies, and the dollars will take care of themselves." It's true. But today, families fall apart. Love has become a word people throw around, but don't understand. Ethics, courtesy, respect - these things hardly exist anymore.

Now, I live with my dearest brother. I never married, lived alone, worked hard. My brother has been wonderful - he took me in, cared for me when I was very ill. I hope I can be helpful to him too.

Now I'm closing this story. Whoever reads it, I hope you take something from it: don't be selfish. Try to understand the elderly. Don't misjudge them. Don't hold onto things that aren't fair. Learn, and you might be happier too.

Don't be afraid to show love. You may receive much more than you give. Set an example for your children - they learn fast.

Wishing you a clean, healthy, and happy life - with all my love.

Love and kisses to all of you,
Maria Gluck
August 3, 2011

P.S.

I just finished reading this article. Sometimes I find it hard to believe I can express myself like this. I'm thankful to my dearest brother who encouraged me and helped me believe in myself.

I never had the time to write before. I worked hard. I didn't speak English well, and that made it harder. But I always tried my best. I knew I was capable - whether decorating my apartment or doing a job well. People didn't believe I had done it myself.

I had good taste - I decorated my little studio apartment simply and beautifully. It made me happy. After work, I'd come home, cook dinner, and enjoy the peace.

Giving it up was hard. But now I have a wonderful brother who took me into his home, took care of me when I was ill. I never thought I'd get better - but thanks to him, I did.

I hope you'll read my other stories too.

Wishing you all the best - good health, happiness, and love.
Your sister Maria - and your loving Aunt Marie

A Dream from Which One Can Learn
By Maria Gluck
Dreamed: September 10, 2011 | Finalized: February 23, 2012

Last night, I had a very frightening dream.

It felt so real, and when I woke up, I was shaken - especially because I still have my Flushing apartment in real life. My superintendent is a very good friend of mine. She has three children, ages six to eleven. But in the dream, everything felt different.

I was in my apartment, and my landlord was there too. All of a sudden, he asked, "What happened here? Why is it so dark?" I looked around, and I noticed it too. The whole room was dark - so unlike the usual warm light and bright furniture I'm used to. Everything looked black and shadowy.

I didn't understand why. First, I thought maybe someone had come in and switched everything - maybe the furniture had been replaced without my knowledge.

After the landlord left, someone knocked at my door. It was the super's wife. She, too, noticed how strange and dark the apartment looked. She asked me how I was feeling, then left.

After that, things became even more confusing. A young man suddenly appeared in my apartment out of nowhere. He told me he was the superintendent's son and said he had something serious to tell me. His tone was menacing.

"I'm not going to repeat this," he said. "If you tell anyone I was here, next time - it will be your life. I'll come back and kill you." He had a big knife in his hand, pointing it directly at me.

I was terrified.

I tried to stay calm and assured him that I wouldn't tell anyone. With that, he left.

I don't remember clearly whether I called my brother, but later I found out that I must have - because not long after, the young man returned. He barged in, angry, and said, "You told someone I was here. I warned you not to. Now I have no choice - I have to kill you."

I pleaded with him. "You can't do that," I said. "I'm your friend - and your mother's friend. What would you gain from this? You're a young man. You have your whole life ahead of you. Why would you throw it away by killing me?"

He still held the knife pointed at me. I was trying to reason with him, hoping someone would come - praying for a miracle.

Then suddenly, the doorbell rang.

The young man froze. He recognized the voice outside - it was his mother. "Don't open the door," he warned me.

I told him, "I have to open it. If I don't, she'll know something's wrong. She's supposed to show the apartment to potential buyers. If I don't let her in, she'll know something is not right."

So I came up with an idea.

"Why don't you hide in the closet? I'll make sure she leaves as quickly as possible. I won't tell her you're here."

He agreed and hid in the closet.

I opened the door. The super's wife walked in and asked, "Have you seen my son?" I told her no. She said she was looking for him and also mentioned that people were coming soon to see the furniture. She believed she had found a buyer.

Shortly after, the doorbell rang again. It was my brother, my nephew (his son), and another man. They told me they were there to see the furniture.

The young man was still hidden in the closet, silent.

What the young man didn't know was that the third person with my brother was a detective. He pretended to be a buyer, looking around the apartment. Then, without warning, he walked over to the closet and opened the door - there was the young man, still holding the knife.

"Oh? What do we have here?" the detective said, and pulled him out.

He began to question the young man.

It turned out that two people had been killed in that building just a week earlier. There had been no witnesses, no clues. When the detective asked him questions, the young man began to talk. He said he wasn't the killer - that someone else was. He claimed he didn't even remember killing anyone.

All he remembered, he said, was that a man had offered him candy in exchange for helping with "an errand." The man told him, "Ring the bell and get into the apartment. After that, go home. I'll do the rest."

It was chilling.

Afterward, I found out that my brother had gotten a message from me - though I didn't remember making a call. He said I'd sounded scared. He immediately contacted the superintendent's wife and told her not to say anything, but to go to my apartment and stay there until he arrived. He warned her that my life might be in danger and asked her to pretend she was showing the furniture to buyers.

And that's exactly what she did.

It's strange how the mind works. Things can feel so real - even in a dream. I woke up quickly after that. Usually, I don't dream at all. But this one was vivid.

In real life, I am trying to sell my furniture and give up my apartment. My super really is a nice person, and she has been helping me with the sale. As of now, no buyers yet.

When I told my brother about this dream, he suggested I write it down. He offered to put it into the computer for me. He said, "If you're thinking about something important, it's only natural that you might dream about it."

Maybe so.

But this dream felt like more than that.

Maybe it's just a reminder that scary things *can* happen. Even when you think you're safe.
Or maybe - it was only a dream.
But I won't forget it.

Written by Maria Gluck
Started: September 10, 2011 | Finalized: February 23, 2012

A Reflection on Change and Concern
By Maria Gluck
Started January 30, 2012 - Finished February 10, 2012

As I'm looking out the window, the sun is shining. It looks beautiful outside, but it feels very cold.

I was thinking about what I'll do today. I'll probably have lunch around 2 p.m. But sometimes I feel I can't do much. I can't go out easily, and it's hard to get around. I think about writing - but sometimes I wonder if I've written enough already. I don't see the reason to continue. I do get encouragement, but I'm still not sure.

And then again, sometimes I like to write short stories for my dearest brother. He likes them. And somehow, I always find something to write about.

I often wonder why I am the way I am - so concerned about people: past, present, and future. Why is it so disturbing to me, when most people don't seem to have a hunch? Maybe they don't feel it's their concern. But I do. I always have. I care about what happens around me, in the world, and in our future. I'm always wondering what will happen next. I can't help it.

No, I don't think I can see the future. Then why does it weigh so heavily on me?

Many years ago, when I was very young, I dreamed of coming to America. That hope carried me. It gave me something to hold onto.

Today, I read the news and it brings more sorrow. All around the world, there is trouble. It's everywhere. At home. Abroad. Sometimes it even touches our own family, our own background. Wherever I turn, I see more trouble. You might say, "That's nothing new. So what about it?"

But I can't dismiss it. Others can. I can't.

I remember the drug epidemic that followed World War II. Something changed in the younger generation - and even among some doctors and educators. I remember reading about two brothers who overdosed. They had been on drugs, and it was later discovered the hospital had known about it. But no one had acted. Had they tried harder, they might have saved their lives.

How could something like that happen? How could they practice medicine in such a condition? So many lives were destroyed by this epidemic. It didn't matter where people came from - even the best families were affected. They weren't happy. They wanted to change the world - but only for their own convenience.

Some of them left home and never came back. Others disappeared. Some were found years later, all the way in California. But by then, it was too late to help them.

Everything began changing during that time. The invention of the computer brought new challenges. The younger generation wasn't ready for such a shift. It hit too fast, too hard. Some of those young people were able to turn things around - they started families and found new direction - but it had nothing to do with the atmosphere of the day.

If we look carefully, we'll see today's generation is very restless. There are no jobs, and not much hope. I don't see a lot of encouragement. People have forgotten how to communicate. They run around, not knowing where they're going or why. Families have lost respect. People don't know how to speak to one another. They've forgotten how to love.

It's hard to understand. The world feels shaky. Our leaders aren't getting the help they need. What I see is troubling. That's why it's so important to choose representatives carefully. Don't fall for promises. They should explain clearly what they stand for. Use your brain. Don't rush. Don't just hope someone will show up and fix it. That's not enough.

We've heard too many promises. And then what's left? Nothing but an empty bag. Is that what you want for the next four years? Ask yourself: Are you happy? Do you have a roof over your head? Can you feed your family? Can you see a doctor? Do you have insurance? Can you afford your medication?

Don't wait too long. The clock is ticking. Things are already in motion. Be ready. I could go on and on - but maybe it's better to stop here.

Written by Maria Gluck
Started January 30, 2012 - Finished February 10, 2012

I Reached My Golden Years
Written by Maria Gluck - January 31, 2012

I look back, trying to understand the word "hatred." Why, all of a sudden, just that word? It is for a good reason. I'll try to express myself. I don't believe that anyone really understands me. Here, I will try - really try - to express myself the best I can. In my experience, I have met all kinds of people - good and not so good - and users who have taken advantage of me. I would say, people with an angry and nasty personality who go out of their way to hurt others. What I would call a split personality. Sometimes, you cannot predict what will happen next. You have to be very careful, even in how you approach them. Usually, if it's someone I don't have to deal with, I just walk away - and forget the incident.

So far, I try to deal with my visiting nurse - but it is not easy. My personality is not to hate - I do not like that word. It is not in my dictionary. If I have a difference in personality with someone, I walk away. I do not like to talk about myself - so why now? One of the reasons is that, in the last couple of years, wherever I turn, people are changing. It seems they have become angry. They must be deprived of something. They just keep on running - doing business or whatever their trade - including doctors and nurses, home health services, and health aides. It does not matter who. Oh - it does happen. Let's face it! It is true. I myself experienced it firsthand, like it or not. In this case, with my visiting nurse. Life does not run smoothly - it's a bumpy road.

Especially if you are a believer in love - and you have a sensitive personality - it becomes harder. I would say, I am not a fighter. I don't fight back. I try to stand up for myself, but I don't always succeed. I prefer to run away - as far as I can, and sit privately, quietly. I know this is not natural, and maybe not the best answer. But what if you're not confrontational, and someone just attacks you - without cause - just because they think you need them? Yes, I may need their help - but they need me too. It is their job - that's what they came for. But they want to be your dictator and take over - especially if you are incapable of managing what you need to.

Today, quite often, when they see that I can figure things out, they get frustrated. They can't see themselves clearly. They are restless. They think they are perfect. Filling every minute - no time to listen. This is a very big problem. We, the people, suffer because of it. Is there any solution? I don't know. I cannot see a way out. It would take a miracle - someone willing to try and solve this intolerable situation we are in.

Lately, I am in such a situation. It is very difficult to deal with. It seems there is no way out. The air around me - with the people in it - is not the healthiest. Quite disturbing. And I already have to deal with so much. It is more damaging than helpful.

I never used the words "I hate you." I would have to be in a very extreme position to ever use that word. Sometimes, I can feel the anger coming from the other person - the outrage. It is unbelievable. And you have to put up with it. I am reminded that silence is golden. But on the other hand, being silent can bring danger - and more problems. Especially in cases when you have to deal with people like that. Even the best of them - in certain situations - can be unpredictable. We must try to learn how to deal with people. Sometimes it's impossible, the more you try it, it becomes more impossible. But you must keep on trying until you succeed.

I lived by myself - I managed, and I was happy. I was always busy - I worked long hours. I was able to do whatever I wanted. I am a very sensible person - and a responsible person. I never had trouble with my neighbors. I lived in one place for 20 years, and the other for 37 years. I enjoyed every minute. Now, I am very lucky - thank goodness - I have my youngest brother with a golden heart. Really, I don't know if you can find one like it - not in today's world. When I came to the point where I really needed help, he came to my rescue. And to this day, I am still here. I am very happy and proud of him. I must say - he went through trouble, poor dear, himself. It is a miracle, I can say, that he served in the World War. Then he lost his wife. He has two boys, and grandchildren - and he is very happy with them. Seeing each other - with all of this - with all these problems - I am still here with him. How long? I do not know. I take one day at a time - then we take it from there.

[Editor's note: material moved to memoir. Talks about hatred, leadership, and G-d]

I woke up this morning - and at this moment, I felt better. I slept well. As of now, I am concerned about my visiting nurse. She usually comes every two weeks, on Wednesday - and she was here yesterday. She's been coming here for about four months. But ever since she started, we have not been able to communicate with each other. I don't know why. It seems like she is a good nurse - she claims she has 38 years of experience. I also know when someone is really good or bad - I've had experience with all kinds of people. I know the difference, all right. She says she treats everyone equally. Each patient should be treated individually. And how do you get that? First of all, you must listen. Pay attention. But she fails to do that.

When she comes in, she is like a broken record. She asks all the questions - and hears only what she wants to hear. Okay! So far is good. But as soon as I open my mouth and try to say something - she gets very angry. The first time, she said: "You're mumbling back and forth - I cannot understand you." No one ever talked to me like that. I know she has a personality problem. It seems we cannot communicate - and I get very frustrated. It's come to a point where I dread the day when she comes. I cannot even answer the questions. It happened again yesterday. For the first time, she brought some papers to sign. She was telling me all about them. One was my Bill of Rights, as she explained it.

I said: "Yes, I know all about it. I also have my rights - just like anyone else. And I deserve respect. But if I say something, you don't want to hear it." And I said it. She was so angry - furious. She jumped up and would not allow me to finish what I was trying to explain. Then she said she treats everyone the same - equally - with respect. And then she ran out. Because of that anger - even though she knows I cannot take anger, or get aggravated. With my condition, that makes things more complicated. More difficult to handle.

Sometimes, I don't even talk about it. If I have a question, I don't even bother to ask - just to prevent another outburst. I'm with my dearest brother now. I had to give up my apartment. Therefore, as I mentioned before, he took me in to help me. I must say - he is doing a better job than anyone, with all the help I need. When I came here, I had Medicare. The agency could not give me any help for a couple of months. And my dearest brother - all by himself - brought me back to life. Hard to believe, but it is true. I will never forget it.

Before the nurse came, my brother and I made an agreement: I would not say anything to upset her. Whatever she said - just answer "yes" or "no," and nothing more. I did just that - up to that point. But then I said something about my rights. And now, I created more problems. Even though I was right - I shouldn't have said anything. My brother is right. And I broke my promise to him - something I never wanted to do. I didn't want to create more problems. And I knew it might happen. I lit the match. I created more problems. I made my bed - now I have to sleep in it. I will have to face it - whatever it is.

Recently, my brother struggled with a cold. He is still helping me - as always. I'm trying to do whatever I need to do, or whatever I can - which is not too much. Between us, there isn't any problem. The only thing is caring - love - we want to do so much for each other to get well. In a way, it's not so simple. There are two of us. And we went through more than we will ever be able to speak about. The feeling grows more every day - the caring. My dearest brother is not openly in favor of showing that. He doesn't want to worry.

But how can I not? I care for him so much. I cannot just sit down and watch him. I know he's capable of helping himself - he's a knowledgeable person. I trust him with my life. All of it. Fully. No questions asked. I hope this problem will pass - somehow. My brother is right. I created, for both of us, an additional problem. He was just trying to smooth things out - so I wouldn't have to go through more aggravation than necessary. He is more tolerant than I am. I try to comfort him. He does the same for me. He always has good advice for me. I admire him - for his patience, and for his tolerance.

I'm not sure if I should continue writing - or stop here and forget all about it. At this time, I'm by myself at home. Trying to decide what to do. I expect someone to come in - sometimes it's unpredictable. What comes next? The situation is not good. Like everything else, nothing can be done.

It seems, like I mentioned before - these people need a better life. I hope they will find it. From what I see, and I hope I'm wrong, there is not much hope. It's like an epidemic. When it starts, it's difficult to stop. Until, somehow, some way - someone comes along strong enough and smart enough to save the world. And save all human beings.

G-d bless you. Take care of you. Keep you safe. Forever, you will be my best brother. We will try to help each other and your family as much as we can. Hope for the best to come. Stop worrying. It's not productive. And it's not worth wasting any more time. Best of health and happiness for all of us. Good luck.
Your loving sister,
Maria

I finished dictating to the computer today.
2-24-2012 - 1:00 PM
I hope I did not make too many mistakes.
Thank you.

This morning by myself
Written by Maria Gluck - February 15, 2012

This morning I am here by myself. I'm thinking why I am so bored - not much to do. After breakfast, my brother tried to exercise to get back his strength that he had - after a bad cold. He went through it - was not easy. We lose our strength and we have to build up whatever we can - especially when we reach our golden years. Now it is more difficult to get around. You don't have too many choices. At this time I'm getting some help - luckily. My brother and myself trying to make it. I consider myself I am still very lucky. And thankful to our Almighty.

Here I am staying at this time with my brother. Here you have to have a car, otherwise you cannot get around. I used to live in Flushing. I had very good connection. I could use buses, Long Island Railroad. Therefore, it was much easier to get around for me. Here I cannot go anywhere anymore. Under the circumstances, as I look out on the window, it looks beautiful - sunny. I would like to get out and enjoy the sun. It seems the best I can do is just look out and enjoy it.

This weekend we had some snow. Luckily it did not last too long. We are very lucky about the weather. It is very unusual. I would say it is beautiful. I do not remember to have this type of winter. I clearly enjoy it. My brother just came in - he is in a better spirit - thank goodness. If I see him in a better mood, it makes me happy. That is all I am asking for - one day at a time.

I tried to continue my writing. It is lunchtime. My brother just stepped out and as soon as he comes back we will have our lunch. After that, my brother wants me to start my computer lesson - how to speak in the computer without typing. Just speak into it. He thinks it will be easier than handwriting all my stories. He's very good, and he became an expert. One of his sons taught him and he's doing a good job. About myself, my nephew - the same son - started me.

And now my brother is helping me. He always gives me all the encouragement. Without him, I would not be able to do it. For that - I owe him everything. Thanks to him.

Now we will have lunch before start the computer lesson.

Now I started after lunch to continue my lesson - whatever comes up. Yesterday after lunch, we did go back to the computer. I was practicing dictating to the computer. My brother thinks I did well - especially when he is sitting next me. He does all the work - I just read into the computer. On the other hand, I think the computer is getting to know me. We will get along, maybe this way it will be easier for me. I would not have to write by hand.

As of now my brother had to struggle to read my handwriting. Now, I hope it will make his life easier - I told him that. Yes, it will be easier to write - but, what should I write about? Running out of ideas. My brother has faith in me.

Now I will start again. My pen is not working. My brother left for exercise. Now, he is getting it twice a week. Hoping he will get well soon. He is having some difficulty. I hope he is getting better from the cold. It is time to get better. I myself try to get better from a cold. It seems if not one thing, it is always something else.

I should not complain. It could have been worse. I try to finish this chapter with a better tone. At this time the sky is cloudy. It feels like that it may snow. I expect my brother soon will be back. I do not know if he wants to go back to the computer.

Until next time, good luck. Have a good happy day… all of us.

My dearest brother, especially you - my thanks for helping me with your love.

I remain your loving sister,
Maria
As always.
I finished about 4 PM, Friday, February 14, 2012

Freedom
By Maria Gluck - Dictated February 28, 2012

(Originally written December 7, 2010)
With supervision by my brother Irving

    I could not help myself - the urge to write about our freedom came over me so strongly, I had to get up and begin. I couldn't sleep. The word "freedom" was echoing in my heart, and I felt I had no choice but to put my thoughts down.

    You might ask: why is freedom so important to me? Why couldn't I wait until morning? I'll tell you the truth - because freedom means everything to me. And yet, some people take it for granted. They don't pause to think about what it really means. But when you truly experience it, when you understand it with your heart, it becomes like a beautiful piece of music. It touches you deeply. It stays with you.

    I will try, in my own words, to explain what freedom means to me - and why I feel the way I do.

    Many people today don't appreciate what they have. They grow restless, even bored. They forget that our ancestors fought and died for the freedom we enjoy. Some people try to change things for their own benefit - without thinking about the consequences. They misuse their freedom. They say they are tired of family life, of responsibility. But freedom was not created to please the individual. It was not meant to be misused or taken lightly.

    Yes, in this land of opportunity, we have the right to choose our paths. We have the freedom of religion, of expression. We have justice for all - regardless of race, background, or belief. These principles are enshrined in our Constitution. And we must never forget how lucky we are to walk this land, to breathe its air, to live under these protections. We should kiss the ground we walk on.

    In my life there is nothing better - the most precious thing is our freedom. People forget and try to change things for their own benefit. They do not care what price we will pay for it. Maybe you should turn around and ask the question: Is there anything more important to protect and respect? Maybe then you can improve your life - and the world - and protect your freedom. Try to learn to live without wars all around you. Try to work peacefully - do whatever you can.

    Our ancestors died for it - they sacrificed their own lives so we would have a better life in our free country, for all of us - all religions, all nationalities - to come together in harmony. We have all the opportunity to create and choose our religion, and to pray to our G-d to help us and enjoy our life the best we can, and to have peace for all of us. I wish with all my heart - that is my biggest dream - that the American land of freedom will never be lost. We must preserve it for all of us, so we can have a chance without any further trouble.

And yet - even our own government, at times, tries to change or restrict these freedoms. Some people grow so reckless they would destroy what was built to protect us.

I urge everyone who truly believes in freedom: do not let anyone take it away. There is nowhere else in the world like this. Nowhere to replace what we have. As someone who lived without freedom, I can speak from the deepest place in my heart. I was born in 1916, in a small village during the First World War. I remember being hidden by my mother behind our oven - between the chimney and the wall - to protect me from gunfire. Even as a toddler, I felt that fear. That memory never left me.

After the war, our country became part of Czechoslovakia. We had some freedom, but it was nothing like what we have here in America. We lived under control for twenty years. Still, I dreamed of America. I had uncles here - but we hadn't heard from most of them since they left. They disappeared into their new lives. Except for one uncle - my father's brother - who came to visit often. As a child, I used to beg him to tell me stories about America.

He always told me, "Forget it. Money doesn't grow on trees. You have to work hard." I've never forgotten those words. But something inside me never gave up. I knew, somehow, I would get there.

My brother David was the first to ask our uncle for help. That was in 1937. He promised to pay all the expenses - he just needed a guarantee. And our uncle agreed.

David arrived in America in 1938. Soon after, he arranged for the rest of us - my sister, my two younger brothers, and me - to come as well. We left behind our father, our oldest brother, his wife, and four children. We believed we would see them again soon. We didn't realize it would be forever.

By the time we were ready to collect our visas, war had broken out in Czechoslovakia. But somehow, we got out. We were among the lucky ones.

If only we had known what was coming. If we had all left together, maybe we could have saved the rest of our family. But we couldn't foresee the unimaginable - the genocide that followed. Who could have imagined such hatred?

Six million innocent people, wiped out. Including my family.

Even the world's so-called "freedom-loving nations" stood by. They did nothing to stop it.

That's why, even now, I feel a deep responsibility to speak about freedom. Because I see signs that we may be forgetting. I look around the world today, and I see unrest. People turning away from responsibility, turning toward hate or indifference. They should be happy, because they are alive - they have their family. They want what others have, but they don't want to understand how it was earned - through sacrifice, through work.

Here in America, we've built a nation on equality. You can practice any religion. You can come and go as you please. You can rise, if you work for it. I never waited for a handout. I love my freedom - I would never give it up! It is priceless! You must remember that! There is no other place in this world where you will find it. You are the luckiest person to have this freedom - a place to live and raise your family. But that freedom only works if we respect it, if we live within the law and honor its purpose. Otherwise, it begins to slip away. Therefore, be very careful not to lose it, because it is very precious.

We must never forget what our freedom stands for - not just for us, but for all people.

If you have the means, help others to have the same opportunity. Remember how your ancestors worked and died for you to live in freedom. During World War II, we lost so many soldiers. Some were lucky enough to return. Many did not. Have we forgotten what they were fighting for?

I ask myself this all the time. Do we even tell our young people what freedom means? Do they understand? Do they know why we still have soldiers sacrificing their lives?

And for what? To protect people who don't understand freedom? Or to help those who don't even want it?

Meanwhile, we fight among ourselves. Our leaders blame one another. Promises disappear. Our jobs vanish. People wait for miracles while everything our ancestors built slips away. Social Security, Medicare - these are lifelines for the elderly, and even for the young. What about education? What about the next generation?

The outlook is not good. And even if they manage to get an education, will there be jobs?

Healthcare is another concern. Insurance companies are taking over. Soon, dentistry, too. If you need a lawyer - good luck. If you're a small business owner trying to be honest, you may find yourself the target of those who only want to make more money. They'll take advantage of you before you even realize it.

These are just some of the reasons I worry.

Because once freedom starts to slip, everything becomes uncontrolled. And once that happens, it doesn't stop. That, to me, is abuse.

I could go on and on. But I'll stop here.

Please understand: I don't like control. I've seen where it leads. Before you know it, your freedom is gone - and this is only the beginning.

I close this note with my heartfelt best wishes. I hope for a good life, for all of us. And I pray we never lose what so many fought so hard to give us.
- **Maria**

I dictated this to the computer myself, with my brother Irving's supervision. I never thought I'd be able to do this. But it turns out, age doesn't matter - what matters is that we keep trying.

How to Get Along with People
By Maria Gluck - February 28, 2012

This is a different subject, but I think it's an important one: how to get along with people and with family. Why is it so difficult? Why are so many people unhappy?

I think this question deserves attention. I can't put all the blame on one place - whether it's someone's background or upbringing. To really understand, we have to look deeper and try to see where it all begins. This is not a simple subject. It takes thought and study. Some people have no idea what's happening around them. Others are determined to place blame on someone - maybe to feel like they're in control, like they're doing justice, when in fact they're only creating more distance and hurt.

Some people reject their families altogether. They think they're better off, but they don't see that they're missing something very deep and meaningful. Sometimes even well-educated people can't see right from wrong when emotions take over. They pour all the blame onto others, never asking whether the real problem lies in themselves.

I've met people like this. I've tried to understand. But when it's one-sided - when someone builds a stone wall - it's almost impossible. And the pain that comes from it? It's deep. I've seen loving parents who gave their children everything: education, support, love. And still, they're shut out. Apologies are rejected. Forgiveness never comes. The word "never" becomes permanent.

Children and grandchildren are no longer allowed to see their elders. Years pass, and bridges are never rebuilt.

This isn't just about personality - it's about control. It's about a deep-seated need to punish, to dominate. Some people teach hatred - knowingly or not. They say "never" and mean it. And the damage they cause spreads beyond them. It hurts the innocent.

When someone has such power over others, talking doesn't help. You can't offer a "quick fix" or a few kind words and hope for a miracle. The more you try, the worse it becomes.

I hope - truly - that when the children grow up, they will see things differently. That they will change. Even though the wounds may be deep, it's never too late to see life from a different angle.

I hope they learn to live happier lives, to forgive and move forward. I hope they grow in wisdom and develop the judgment to see what truly matters - before it's too late.

They're missing out on something so precious: the ability to forgive, the power to love, and the warmth of family. And they're missing out on their grandfather - one of the best people I've ever known. He loves them dearly. And he misses them more than they could ever know.

I know this kind of healing isn't easy. But it is important. We all need to learn how to love. That's what brings happiness in life. Some people are educated, smart, successful - but they may be repeating patterns from their own pasts. Maybe someone treated them like this once, and they never healed. Now, they're repeating it with their own families.

I just hope they find happiness in their own lives - with their partners, with their own children and grandchildren. I hope they can learn, and change.

There's so much more I could say, but I think I'll stop here.

I wish them the best: peace, happiness, health, love, and prosperity. Even if they don't wish the same for others, I still wish it for them.

I finished this note on February 28th, around 8:00 PM. I'm still learning how to type and use the computer, so if there are mistakes, please forgive me. I'm proud that I've gotten this far - and grateful for the chance to put these thoughts down.

- **Maria**

A story (On Freedom and Survival)
By Maria Gluck - March 5, 2012

Here I would like to express myself.

More and more, I have thoughts that weigh on me every day. I try to dismiss them with good reason. I didn't want my dearest brother working so hard on my stories. Sometimes I wonder - maybe it's just something to put on paper and then forget about. Just to write it down. But maybe it helps to sort out the situation. So much is happening every day. I'm even afraid to listen to the news. To look around us.

Here at home, across the country, and around the world, it's the same. I surprise myself - why am I so worried? It's not my job. There are so many educated people, problem solvers. And yet here I am, daring to write about it. I may not do it perfectly, but I try to stay honest and say what I see.

Let's start with freedom, and the new generation. How are we living? How are we supposed to accept what's happening and swallow our pride and dignity - which are disappearing before our eyes. What I see and experience every day is frightening. It's not getting better.

I ask: why all these changes? Where are we going? Why do people have to suffer so much - so much hunger, with no place to turn? People are short-tempered. No patience to stop and listen. Many just don't care what's happening around them. Especially those we should be able to depend on for leadership and support. My thoughts circle around - so many questions. Where are those people?

So many issues - job loss, healthcare, confusion. People want something and expect to get it - right or wrong. Good or bad. I believe in freedom. I believe everyone should have equal rights - not just some. That's what freedom is. But I wonder: is what's happening good for all people? Or only for some? Is it good for the country? Or are we just keeping quiet and going along, even when something doesn't serve us?

People are on edge. There's no way out. Our leaders are failing us. There's no leadership. So I ask: how are we going to get out of this mess?

When you're tired, you want to sleep. When you're hungry, you want to eat. But what happens when you've done both - and you wake up and open your eyes - and all you see is trouble and disappointment?

All around us, we wonder - are we on the right road? Or have we been led down the wrong one? Why can't we stop this nonsense? We - the quiet, hard workers - have we lost our senses and allowed our freedom to slip away?

When we wake up, what will be left? Nothing but nightmares and questions.

Is this what people have struggled for? We were given the best - can we not do better? Can we not learn from our mistakes, and improve our lives?

Instead, we are sinking deeper into misery. Is that what we want for our children? Or for the next generation - for our grandchildren?

When did we fail? Maybe when people don't pay attention to their children - when they were too busy, too tired, too blind to see what was happening around us. Too busy to watch where our leaders - who we elected - were taking us.

They forget why they're there. Their duty. Their responsibility to all of us.

Sometimes I ask myself - am I even qualified to criticize them? I'm just one person. But it seems we the people have made the wrong choices. In America, everyone has a chance - if they want it. Isn't that the point?

So why am I writing this story - not a happy one? Yes, it would be easier to write something joyful. But this weighs too heavy on me. Maybe I should leave it to someone else. But it seems everyone else is too busy. Or they think it can wait. But how long should we wait? Haven't we waited long enough?

Is there anyone with a better answer?

America is changing - very fast. I don't believe anyone, in the near future, can do much to solve these problems. We're too deep in them already. Still, I say: I hope so. Without hope, there's no life left.

I've had miracles in my lifetime. But on the other hand, I've also seen the loss of six million human beings. Persecution took away their lives. Torture. Hunger. The young, the old, and the innocent. I lost my closest family. I will never forget it.

If someone is unhappy here, and wants to change things only for themselves, I ask them to stop and think. Try to work instead - for your country. Work hard to preserve what we have: America, and freedom. Not just for a few - but for everyone.

Anyone who wants to work and build a better life should have the chance. We all have the same opportunity. It is supposed to be a free country - freedom for all. It does not matter who you are - if you are able to do the job, you should be able to find a job. The only thing we need is for someone to find a way to show them they *can* do it - whatever it may be. But it takes time. Encourage each person, and take time out to show them the way - the basics - that's what is important in life. Maybe this would ease the unemployment - and give people a chance to make a decent living and support their family. There are so many qualified people around, yet it seems that being unable to get a job is still a very big problem.

I don't believe that Americans want to sit around and wait for an unemployment check. That's not the answer. Most people want to save and build - to create a strong country and a life of meaning.

We must act without delay. And we must find the right path - whether at home or abroad - to stop this madness. The wars, the homelessness, the hunger. The suffering.

I feel all of this so strongly, it's as if I'm living my life all over again. So much suffering. No one can understand unless they've lived through it. It was long ago, but you never forget.

Hope. Faith. Trust. That's what we've lost.

And then - miracles. Can we still believe in them?

People are so confused, they're not even sure praying will help. I think of the six million who prayed on their way to the ghettos. Who cried out to G-d and still - they were ignored by the Almighty and by the leaders of the world. No one heard them.

So who can we trust now?

People are struggling, and they're lucky if they can just survive with their families. If you believe in faith - hold on to it. But people are losing faith, fast.

[Editor's note: material moved to memoir about hatred]

The situation is out of control. It will take more than education alone. I don't know if the kind of person who can fix this even exists. I don't think money will solve it, either. It's wasted everywhere.

What matters more than money is honesty - and communication. That is what we need most.

Yes, we need money to live. I've worked hard my whole life - often for almost nothing. Long hours, good work, but I gave more than I received. Some employers didn't want to acknowledge that.

If you survive that, you must be strong. The abuse - yes, it comes with it. I never thought about it this way before. But today - I see it. I've experienced it.

There's no way to fight the anger, or the insults, when there's no cause. No solution in sight. Especially when you become a senior.

If you are an older person, people think you're senile. You try so hard just to get along, but whatever direction you turn - it's trouble. Thank G-d I'm still able to help myself. I just need a little help. And instead - I get surprises. I never would have believed it if someone had told me.

Maybe you are going through the same experiences I am - in one way or another.

So many people want more money. But they're not willing to do the work. And when you try to explain something - they get upset.

Yes, we need them - but they need us, too.

This goes on and on. We are lucky if we can manage without them.

In my experience, I've met all kinds of people - and many have short tempers. Anger. No patience. And no sense of responsibility.

It seems like a joke sometimes. And yet - it's not funny. It's sad.

Some people jump to conclusions. They want to go high - but fall low. What I hear sometimes - it's out of control.

I've been hurt before, physically. I've suffered. These people - educated or not - do the same things. Doctors, nurses, home health aides. I don't understand how far they think they can go with such behavior.

You must try to keep your sanity. Keep going.

I try to do what I can to be happy. But the more I try, the harder it is to find someone who can help - who can really do the job.

We try to enjoy our Golden Years. But it's not always easy.

I'll stop here. I've said enough. Maybe too much. But it's on my mind. Good luck to you all.

We all need some luck - and improvement - in our senior years, or any year.

Good health to you all.
Sincerely,
Maria

Finished 3/6/2012

Recipe for Danishes (tekercs)

This recipe is for how to make Danishes or tekercs.

First, take about 2 pounds of Hackers All Purpose Flour, one package of yeast, a little salt, and half of a small glass of orange juice. One stick of margarine, one small container of yogurt, 2 eggs, and 1/2 cup of sugar. If needed, you can use a little milk to help make the dough.

First, take the yeast with a little lukewarm water and work it through in a small dish.

Add a little flour to the yeast - not too much, about a tablespoon - and 1 teaspoon of sugar. Then add all the ingredients, except the flour. Make sure the yeast mixture is smooth. Don't make it too loose or too hard. Let it sit in the dish until it grows double.

Then take a large enough bowl or dish and sift the flour.

When the yeast is ready, add it and all of the ingredients above into the flour and make a fine dough. It is important to use your hand - make sure the dough is very smooth and your hand comes out clean. Do not use a spoon.

When the dough is ready, let it rest until it doubles in size.

When it is finished, take a piece of wax paper to cover it. Then take a clean small cloth and cover that, so it stays warm and continues to rise. It takes about an hour - you have to check it.

I work on the table, and I take Cartwright wax paper and cover the table in a few places so I can work with the dough.
One longer piece I put across from me on the top layer - you have to be careful not to move those papers when this is done. Then I take the dough and I put flour on the dough so it will not stick to the paper.

Then I cut three pieces and put them aside. I take a little flour, sprinkle it on another piece of dough, and with that one piece, I make it about half an inch thick.

Meantime, I take another stick of margarine and keep it out until it gets soft and is easy to spread.
Now I am going back to the dough - the half - inch layer I rolled out. I spread this margarine on it like you're spreading on bread, covering all over the dough. Then I take a little flour and sprinkle it over the top of the margarine.

Then I take one side of the dough and fold it halfway, then the other side - on top of the previous one. Then I take the third side and fold it on top of the others, and again the fourth side - bring it on top of the third one.

Now I take a piece of wax paper, put a little flour on it, and place the dough with the margarine in it on the wax paper. I wrap it up and place it in the refrigerator until it grows double. I repeat this with the other pieces.

Now I'm going back to the fillings - how to prepare them.

Nut filling

I take the nuts [walnuts] - clean about 1 pound, one package. I grate it to smaller pieces - and add about a tablespoon of cinnamon, sugar, raisins. Mix this together - and the sugar should be to your taste. Do not make it too sweet.
Now this is ready to fill the dough.

Cheese Filling

Now with cheese, if you want to make cheese Danish:
Take about 2 pounds farmer cheese, 2 eggs - beat it up - and add a teaspoon salt, 3/4 of a cup sugar, tablespoon of raisin, cinnamon. Mix all this together - now you are ready to fill the Danish.

Now I will go back to finish the dough for the Danish.
I take out the first piece from the refrigerator and see if it grew. Then I again make it thin - about half an inch. When this is done, you can make a square 3 inches, and now I put in the cheese mix. Then I bring all corners together to the middle - making sure to press them together, so that it will not fall apart. Repeat this.

Then I take the baking tray and take a little margarine on the bottom of the tray - just make sure not to grease. Then I put the Danish on that tray - not too close to each other, so they should have room to grow again. Leave it out until it grows.

Now, separately, I take one egg, a drop of water, a drop of sugar, and beat this together in a glass - making sure it is smooth.

Take this mixture and a featherbrush, and spread this mixture on the top of the Danish - and make sure that it covers all over.*

Now this is ready to bake. Before that, I make the oven at 350. When this is done, I put my Danish and bake it until it has a nice color - do not burn it.

*If you want it with nuts and cinnamon, then I make it the same way, except I cut triangle pieces. Then I take 2 sides and cover the nuts by rolling over to the corners - the 3rd one.

And now I make like a horseshoe. I repeat again as I did before - take the baking dish, make it sure it is nothing on it, clean it, and use a little margarin on the tray, the same way, and place the dough on it and use the eggs mixed with the water on it and let it grow again. When this is done - ready to bake.

If you want to make tekercs, I do the same way. May have inch thick dough, make a large leaf [sheet], cut it halfway cross, then I take the nuts mixture, place it on the top of the dough, spread it out evenly. Then I take, lengthwise, the dough, turn over the edge on the top of the nuts - not too tight - till you finish. Don't make it too long, just long enough to place it in the dish. Repeat this same thing again - you could place 2 or 3 pieces in the same way until ready. Also, use the eggs mixture on it. After this, the tekercs is ready to bake.

★ Family story (in a nutshell)
Written by MG. - 7/12/012 - 3am

    The other day, my brother Irving asked me to write about another brother also. I mentioned him previously. He wanted more details about him. I will begin here.

    His name was Herman. He was born after me and was the 8th child. It is a different story - something unusual. I must say, each of us had different personality - although our look, our resemblance, was similar. Otherwise different ambitions - different talents - but all of us hard workers. If we had a chance for a better education, we could have been able to accomplish a better life, each one of us. As I see it here, it is a living proof. My brother and I, we found our talent and capability in the golden years, unexpectedly, just by simple by coincidence. Others are telling me now - why did I had to struggle so hard all my life for nothing, when I have hidden talents? I did not have time or the opportunity even to sit down and think and to sort out my abilities - it seems I knew I had many talents - I was able to do many things. I must say, anything I wanted to do, I did well - better than or like an expert.

    They could not tell that I was sewing, decorating, designing my own clothing. I never copied anything. I used my own ideas. And had many compliments, not just one compliment. We all of us were hard workers.

    We were not lazy. We all had inside talents. As I look back, my eldest brother and his family, we lost them in the Holocaust era. His name was Lajos. Our mother and our father, our parents, needed help. As I remember, I am speaking about the beginning of 1900 and after, in my dearest family there wasn't any restriction about schooling. From beginning as young children, the first ones passed away at 7 and 9 years of age.[47] Lajos (Louis)[48] was the first living child. He was educated all on his own. As he grew up I do not know too much of his childhood - only thing I remember what I myself learned about him. He was the oldest brother - one of the best. He helped us in every way. He was there for all of us. Helped our mother and father all around. On the farm-business, he made it sure we all ate - he went fishing, helped our dearest mother all around, and he was there when we needed help.

    Our second brother, David, he had ambition. He was an entirely different personality. I must say he had talent and was hard working and caring - he had love for his family. He proved it, too. Right here in America he was the first one to come to America - he tried everything - all kind of jobs. On his own he also had talent-but as I see it, he did not have a chance to better himself for his own family. He passed away aged 79 by himself. His one son

---

[47] See earlier correction in Chapter 3 on their birth order and survival.

[48] When they spoke about Lajos in America, they called him "Louis," but that was not his name.

denied him his own roots. He wasn't even there when he needed him the most. He passed away with a broken heart. The rest of us sisters and brothers loved him.

My dearest brother Irving and I were there to help him with whatever we were able to. As of now we never heard from David's son ever since. His name is Fred and he's an educated man. He claimed he loved his father so much after he found out his father passed away - right after the funeral. He knew his father was seriously ill, but never bothered calling or visiting him. He was interested only in their money, that yes.

He wanted the business his father left and claimed we had taken it. My brother wanted to take care of his estate, but even when he had to clean up and he wasn't able to, his son refused to help. Therefore he lost even the dollar what he could have saved. It was all his fault. He cannot blame anyone - it's lost. By the way he is an educator in schools. He's very good at that. He was helping out children when they needed help. He has 2 sons - both educated. When I heard from him the last that I called him to tell him that he's lost his father, he never saw himself as at fault. He blamed us - the family - which is not true.

Next was our sister. Her name was Hermina I must say, from her childhood she was a very unusual child as we were growing up. She used to surprise us. All her life she was there for all of us. I remember she always had some ideas to help us in the home.

Our mother did not want us to do too much. She used to say they will have time when they will have their own responsibility. She said it because of what she herself went through at her young age. Therefore she felt she did not want us to go through it, too. When she passed away, then we had to do the grown-up job all at once: cooking, baking for a family with younger children, taking care of all of the chores.

We both of us were very young. My sister and I, from the beginning to the end, did not have too much time for ourselves. We struggled all our life. We were able to do what ever arose. If not for our sister's alertness, we probably might not be able to come to America. It only took a second. Her alertness saved us at the last minute.

We came to America, all 4 of us at the same time. It is a miracle how it all started from the beginning to the end. I must say it again, a very unusual situation how all this worked out.

Heartaches were there from the beginning - especially with our dearest father. I could say so much about him also. He was something very special I mustn't forget about his talent and ability. To do so much without preparing himself for life or any business. He was born as a farmer.

One more thing I remember - all my family had Hebrew education. On our mother's side, her father was a yeshiva bucher. He finished studying Hebrew and the talmud and was from a very respectable family. Our father's side, they had the wealth in money when they came down and settled as a business man and a farmer in a small village. He was able to give the villagers a job to better their life. This is as far I know. As I remember he didn't have further education.

Yet, he was doing much more than just a farmer - he had to take over all the responsibility in business on the farm. Then make sure his children get care and food and get ready for school when time came. He did not get any help. He went through so much with our mother's illness and the legal problems. It was a small village and he was a farmer. At that time it was nothing like today, especially in America. That was unheard of.

As now I go back, I'm amazed how much trouble he went through just to prepare our papers. He was constantly running around, spending money, and dealing with endless red tape. You had to really know what you were doing, whenever he went. At that time you had to know how to approach a person to be sure you have the right title.

Here I finished 6.45 a.m.

Here I started again at 11:20 a.m.

Every official had a title. When you needed legal papers, it was not just a title - and it is not like this in America. Here, saying Mr. or Miss is sufficient, but there, at that time, it was a different world - especially in Europe. It's hard to believe how strict they were.

Our father, as a farmer - as I think back - I do not understand how he was able to take care of the business he had to do. There was no one else to help him. He needed lawyers, and it was very expensive. You could not afford it, and you had to pay in advance - especially when we were getting ready to come to America.

The first time getting the papers was okay - it was much easier since we were coming from Czechoslovakia. We were ready in a very short time. But it seems you can't ever fully plan everything, no matter what you want. Overnight, it could all go down the drain. I agree - it does happen all the time, without any notice.

The day we were ready to leave Czechoslovakia, we were called in to Prague. That changed our life. That's when the nightmare started.

It was a German uprising. We were not able to go there - it was too dangerous for us as young children to be there. Therefore, we were delayed. I was horrified. Now we all knew that because of what was happening there, we would have to start all over again - from the beginning to the end. And with that came all the expenses again, and running around for new papers. We also needed permission from the Hungarian government, and they had more restrictions - so, more problems.

The only thing that was different: we already had the okay for the papers from before, in Czechoslovakia. Therefore, it was easier to come to America - otherwise, from Hungary, it would have been impossible to come.

The restrictions they had from America didn't allow people to come from Hungary. There was a very long waiting period - many years. Also, we were very lucky to be able to work it out as it was. The expenses - and our father, what he went through. It was a very bad dream. If I try to recall some of the true story, I myself can hardly believe it. But it is true - every word I wrote in *As I Remember...*, plus some short stories here and there. And my dearest brother - the more I write, the more he wants me to.

Sometimes I feel maybe I should not open up the pain we went through. It is heartbreaking, and to go through it once is enough. He does not need any more pain and suffering from the ordeal he already went through. But as I noted, I could not deny him this - at least he will understand what his family was and where he is coming from. Their love and caring - understanding all about it. The meaning and his background - where he is coming from. He can be very proud of it. We had a very good name, well known - respected - up to the end. Oh, I love my family.

Our mother and our father - and my brother. He had five children, and his wife Etelka. She was an unusual person also. We loved her. Oh, if only we could erase what came later. My sister did everything she could. She was always running - just like a sister should.

When we were getting ready, once again, to try and come to America, I made a plea - a final hope that we would be able to come. All of a sudden, we received a call from our sister: we cannot get tickets for Hungarian money. They must be paid in dollars. We could only get two tickets, but we needed four. We did not have dollars, and it was very short notice. We had to get it from America. It was such short notice - it seemed impossible. My sister and one of our brothers were there in Budapest - where you had to go to make all the arrangements at the offices.

My sister was running around from one place to the other to get help, until someone heard about the trouble - and gave them the good news: they had just received from America money for the other two tickets. Now we would be able to go, all four of us. Our sister did not give up. She demanded they must be there.

She had the feeling - sometimes people are not so ambitious, or it just does not bother them. But she showed us that if you're ambitious and do what you need to do, you will succeed. The most important thing is you never give up. My sister immediately sent us the second telegram to come at once. We must be there without delay, the next day - otherwise we will not be able to go at all.

The ship will be the last one to leave from Naples - otherwise we will not be able to go.

At home, when we received the first telegram, I was very heartbroken. I was so disappointed. I thought the whole world falls in. I did not even think about - as of now we've worked so hard, trying - and at the last minute, this could have happened.

Then I felt this is all - I can't take it. Why now? How could this happen?

At that moment, we had no idea what would be next - and what was waiting for our remaining family. We were getting ready with the idea in mind that, when we would come out, we would begin the arrangement to have all the rest of the family follow us to America.

We had enough property there - we will sell it and get ready, whatever it takes, to bring all of them out to America. Our father - our brother - his wife and his five children.

Otherwise, I know myself, I could not bear it - the knowledge we left them there.

Our hope and plan was all there. The only thing was, at that time we could not foresee what will be next. As I write this note, I relive the anguish and the horror. We have letters from them - while they were able to write to us.

And after this horror, we have other letters from survivors. And some neighbors.

There they are, telling me how good they were to my family. We knew - all lies. Now they want us. They need help. There is no one else. Which I know - it is all lies. Our sister-in-law wrote all about them. When she needed help with the little children, when she needed food, she was all by herself. And no one was there to help or lift their finger to help them. And now, when they need help, they knew how to find us.

Probably, if I could have foreseen all this, maybe I would not even have wanted to come and leave the rest of my family behind.

The people in the world did not care for anyone - human lives - six million - the best of the crop and innocent children - they let them be tortured and suffer so much. And then burned them. Killed them inhumanely. And no one lifted his finger to reach out.

And they call themselves religious people? How could they live with it? I could never understand.

Now they are having some problems. Maybe they deserve it. In my heart, no one deserved such a treatment. Inhuman. Those few people who reached out - I bow to them. I hope our Almighty will help them, take care of them, and guard them. I am wishing them, praying for them - they are real people who are like angels from heaven.

To be there - there aren't enough people like those. There would be a place to live in peace for all of humanity. I wrote more about myself previously in the other stories. I hope I will be able to publish them - at least one. I don't think it will be in my time.

Now I think I will be going back to a story of my younger brother from his childhood.

I wrote about him. His name was Herman. He was the eighth child - born right after me.

He was a different personality. He was very particular: clean - spotless. I remember him that way as a baby. He was loved by all. I wanted to play with him. I was myself only about three years older than he. I myself was a child. Yes, I remember very clearly - like it would be today.

Our mother was very busy. We had sometimes some help, other times she was alone to do whatever she needed to do. Especially with a family - there is always something to be done without looking for it.

[Editor's note: material moved to memoir. Herman hanging clothes on hangers]

He also had a private Hebrew teacher with my youngest brother - which I wrote previously more briefly. His name is Irving - the 9th child. They had the Hebrew training at home. After that, he remained at home only for the regular school.

[Editor's note: material moved to memoir. Epidemic in village Irving to quarantine]

Irving was growing up busy in school, and he became a very handsome young man. He was different than all of us - ambitious. He was favored by all of us. He was smart - was helping out with whatever he wanted to. He wasn't doing too much on the farm. I do not know any problem growing up except what I mentioned.

[Editor's Note: material moved to memoir. Uncle Herman scared by gypsy music on Christmas]

And meantime our mother passed away after a long illness - that was also an ordeal for all of us. Especially for our two youngest brothers Herman and Irving - both of them. Children need both of their parents equally. When they needed them there, they were not there. Our father also was away with our mother for a long time. We were alone or with strangers almost all of the time. It wasn't the best and our eldest brother, his name was Lajos (Louis) - lucky with him he was a Dad for all of us. This time also, like always.

Our second brother David - when he came to America, he was working all kinds of jobs. He was very helpful. Our cousin, who manufactured large scales - you could weigh a ton on them - was trying to help David. But David also tried to have his own mind about what he wanted to do. When we came to America, his mind was on helping us.

[Editor's Note: material moved to memoir. About Herman's job at machine shop and defense department tool making]

We used to live together - all five of us at that time. When we arrived to America, our uncle was still alive. He had finished a two-room apartment ready when we arrived - at least we did not have to worry about where to sleep. Finally, our uncle managed to find a job for all of us. It was not a big job, and the money wasn't much. It didn't matter - we were working. I was happy.

When our uncle passed away, we moved to a new apartment, and my sister changed to a better job. Meantime, our brother Irving was inducted as an infantryman and was immediately sent to Texas for training in 1943. When he finished, they shipped him overseas to the European theater. Irving became a citizen in Africa, in the middle of the war zone. He went overseas with the hope that he might be able to save our family because he was so close - but still, he wasn't able to reach them. You can imagine how disappointed we were. Our brother David moved to California dreaming of Hollywood, but working in a naval shipyard. He was single at that time, and he had friends in Columbus, Ohio - we lived there then. Our sister was working at a job. It could have been a better one - she was still very young. She came home on the weekends.

We had a cousin in New York. A couple of years later, she wanted my sister to come and visit them. My sister - she decided to go visit our cousin on her vacation. She came to the conclusion it would be a good chance to see what she can do or get.

Coincidentally, Herman was also inducted in to the army, but he became ill, so he was discharged after a short time. My brother Herman and I still lived in Ohio. When our brother Irving came home, we were the happiest people when we saw him coming in our door! One of my dreams was to see him again. It had been an intolerable nightmare.

Thank goodness, he came back to in one piece - as well as it could be.

What he went through - it was a miracle he made it. Shortly before that, my sister made arrangements with our cousin that she will visit them and she left Columbus for New York. She came back to Columbus just to be there when Irving came home. David he lived in California and by then he got married. His wife happened to be very nice young lady. She took over our corresponding which our brother David neglected. He became a lazy writer. Now at least, as she took over, we heard from them more often. Thank goodness they were both happy.

They decided to go into business together. My brother Irving did not have a chance to see them until many years later. He went to visit them when he finished the university education. Our sister Hermine was asked to stay in New York. She had another chance to socialize. There were more opportunities to better your self. Even a job would be easier - getting around, too. In a larger city, it would be better than Ohio. There also, if we would know English better we could have found a way - as it was we had no one to show us or help us.

Traveling was more difficult without a car. In New York, it's much easier to get around. In a couple of weeks my sister got an adequate job. In the meantime, she stayed with our cousin. Everything was so expensive - especially finding an apartment. It was almost impossible. Then I received a call from my sister I should come there - it would be much easier for both of us. We could get a bedroom cheaper for both of us - and for me, in New York, I would have a better chance, even for a social life, and naturally a job also. I wasn't very happy about it. I was between two people. I loved them both. My sister - in a sense it would be easier for us. How could I go? There, in Columbus, our brother Irving just came home - and I loved him so much. I knew our sister loved him too. I knew both of them were right. I just couldn't leave him - and our brother Herman wasn't feeling well. I just couldn't run and walk away on them - not now. I spoke to all of them and explained that I just cannot make myself leave.

In my heart, I felt this is as big a decision as I ever made. Finally, our brother Irving explained to me that he just enrolled to the Ohio State University. He wants to finish his education there, and he will be very busy anyway. I should not be concerned about them. They will be all well. They will manage. And our brother Herman and Irving, they were very close to each other. Therefore, they will be okay. They will visit us or we can come there. They will keep the apartment where we were living.

We had some friends there - a very nice neighbor. My sister also felt that when Irving did finish the University, he can come. We will all be able to move there also. While we were speaking about this, it made sense. But in reality, it was very difficult. Finally, I made my decision. I moved to New York. Our cousin and my sister were very happy. When I arrived by them, they found near our cousin an elderly lady who was willing to take us in to share her home with us, but she did not have a bed for both of us.

Our cousin was trying to get a folding bed large enough for two people, at least temporarily. We needed it for that night. There was no place for me. Luckily she found a bed - just what she was looking for. That night, at least we had a place to sleep. Now we needed a job. Next morning we started to look for one for me. My sister, when she first came to New York, luckily she found one in a movie house office - they were willing to train her. She expected to work for a trial basis - if it works out for both sides then she'd take it and would get a better pay also.

My sister was very ambitious and a hard worker. She made it in a very short time. They liked her, too. She remained there because they promised more money. She was looking forward to the raise they promised, but she was not getting it. She asked for the increase, but still promises, therefore she started looking for another job. Soon after that she found one - even a better one with more money. She took it. In the meantime she met one young man, then others. After being proposed to by the first - he asked her to move to Israel. She said yes, but in the end it didn't work out. She met another and she kept on seeing him. He was a businessman.

They came to a decision. Both agreed to get married and settle down. They did. My brother Irving, he came for the wedding, but Herman did not. We asked them to move to New York. It would be a better chance all around, and then our family could be closer again. We thought maybe they could settle down here. And for Herman also, it would be better here. They could meet someone and better their life - both of them. Finally they made their decision. They will move here also. Shortly after, they did move to New York.

Now again, we had to find a place for them - and it was still difficult. I wanted them to be near me. By then, I lived in the same apartment where my sister had lived for a couple of years. She had gotten married and moved out. I remained there with the elderly lady. It was in the Bronx. Finally, we found - temporarily - in the East Bronx a small, furnished apartment. It was nearby. Convenient. Later on, I found a studio apartment. I moved in, and our brothers found one on Long Island.

This was also with an elderly lady - to share a room in her private home. Both were happy.

Until Irving found someone. He met a young lady, and they decided to settle down. I wrote about that before in more detail. They did get married and settled down.

[Editor's Note: material moved to memoir. She concluded the story of Herman's death and the medical error leading up to it, and David's.]
[Editor's note: material moved to memoir. about doctors]

Now I would like to close with happier notes. As of now, I and my best brother Irving are trying to manage together the best we can. Helping each other. I feel thank goodness - we are lucky as of now. How long? We wait and see. One day at the time. I feel I am very lucky to how a brother like Irving. And I will do everything in my power to get him well from this accident.[49]

I also want to mention - he is the youngest in our family. I wrote more beautifully about him, his life and what he went through from the beginning up until today. His life wasn't as it seems. He went through so much, it makes it hard almost to write about it. Nothing but trouble - one after another. Even the thought of what he went through three times over,[50] I can't even begin to write about. In his life he had nothing but suffering and hard work all around . As a child he was deprived of his family - to really know them. And love - from his sisters and brothers, mother, father only reminded him that they all perished in the Holocaust. I wish I would know what really happened.

The real story came only by making the connection - secondhand - in our letters that my brother saved for so many years. Now we are trying to sort it out and re-live that agony and the heart aches over what we went through, and to write what ever I remember and am able to. Maybe I should not have done it. But I felt I cannot deny it. I cannot deny doing whatever I can or whatever I was able to. There is always more, if we really want to - but for now, I think it is enough.

But before I end, my dearest brother Irving - you had your share of the problems.

It is time to forget whatever is possible and go on living with hope.

---

[49] **Editor's note:** According to my recollection, my Dad was coming back from the post office when he tripped on a crack in the asphalt and landed awkwardly in the snow. He broke his arm/shoulder and hit his head - his Khrushchev-style hat protected it. I didn't recognize it at the time, and the hospital didn't check, but he may have suffered a mild stroke. Somehow, my aunt helped him into the house and called me to come. I then took him to the hospital, where they gave him a tetanus shot. Within a week, both of his hands became swollen and stiff. The doctor blamed arthritis, but at the time I believed the shot might have caused his hands to swell, though in hindsight it could also have been related to his fall or the mild stroke (which was confirmed when he broke his hip and they did a CT of his head).

[50] **Editor's note:** When she wrote "three times," she was referring to my dad's hardships: once as a combat soldier, once when he cared for my mom during her illness with multiple sclerosis, and the third time when he took in my aunt and nursed her back to health.

Try to enjoy your little family and your grandchildren, hoping for a better future for all of us. Especially you. You've worked hard enough to accomplish what you worked for so hard. Sometimes we do not get what we deserve. Only thing I ask - you must take care of yourself! If you need help, do not wait. Look around before you need it. I'm sure you can find someone somewhere who will try to help before it's too late. And make sure you do not deprive yourself whatever you need. At least if you need something, you are able to get it. This is my advice. Be selfish for once in your life. You must, and now my dearest take good care of yourself.

Do not forget - now you come first. Good luck and good health and all the best of everything. I am sorry I cannot accomplish more of what I would like to. And I feel you mustn't worry so much - it is not productive. It's a waste of time - you have better things to do. I hope I could help you a little more to get better as fast as possible.

I think it is time to come to the point for closing time. I want to wish you and your family also the best of everything that goes with that. Your grandchildren will come around, all of them, both sides there to give you the happiness you well deserve. With all my love to you all.

your loving sister Maria.

I finished this short note dictated to the computer with hope that my brother will like it and will approve of it finished today 7-23-012.

Ethics and Good Manners
9/8/2012 - This is about an ethics: how to behave

I would like to speak about another subject: about good manners.

Today, this word - it seems - got lost somewhere. We don't hear about it - I don't even know if it is in the dictionary. I am not sure if people know about that word. What is a good conduct? Yes - I remember when I was growing up - how to behave, to be a lady or a gentleman. It used to be very important, especially how you appeared in public. But it did not matter where you were - a person was able to conduct themselves, or just opened their mouth - you knew exactly how to act.

I learned manners from my upbringing and from people close to me. For example, my sister-in-law Etelka traveled a lot. She was an outgoing person, had a very good personality, and was very smart. She had experience - and in Europe, it was very important. That's what they called good manners. They could tell from your behavior who you are. She learned from us how to be a homemaker. And we learned from her how to be a lady. We were happy to do that. I learned a lot from her.

Lessons in manners were not just at home. In Europa, from where I'm coming from, at that time they taught it in school - as I remember. They taught it even in America when I came here. As I see today's children, it's different, it has a lot to do with how they are raised by their families.

They do not teach it in school - it seems mostly out of style. And their parents are too busy. Some parents have no idea what it is all about. Schools - colleges - do not teach it. They think they do not need it. It is good enough as is.

Let's go back to learn how to behave in public or at home. What do you think - is it important, or isn't it? The other question: do you want to raise a well-behaved child, or misbehaved - nothing but trouble?

My answer is yes. Years ago they used to say: it is like the cover of a book - what you see, that is what you will get. If you have good manners, you are not ashamed to go anywhere. You are always ready, able to speak up - not just with words, but the whole person will appear well-mannered, without any unexpected surprises.

It is important even at home. Especially when you have company at the dinner table. I do not mean just how to hold a spoon or a knife - although even that tells all about you and good manners.

Once I had an opportunity to ask a young doctor about manners. He was being observed by his professor. The young doctor tried to criticize me - the patient. My surprise came all of a sudden - as he was convinced how smart he is. I asked him a question: "Do you know what bedside manner is?"

He turned around and asked his professor, "Do you know what that means?"

Up to that moment, the professor never said a word. On that question, he said quietly: "How you behave when you visit your patient in the hospital - that shows who you are. Your ability and personality - if you are really as good as you present yourself."

It is the same way sometimes in families. They do not have the capability to teach their children how to behave or control them.

First, they think it will go away or get better - or they will have an opportunity to develop themselves. You cannot learn this in school. Real experiences - if they stop and think, develop their mind so they are ready to learn - this richness and ability to think and use their mind can make them a better person. They will be capable of developing good judgment - instead of losing their temper without cause or reason.

All kinds of experiences come in handy. I feel very lucky I had those experiences. I was proud of myself. I know now it is a different story. I always was pleasant. Uncle Julius used to tell me, "When someone is speaking to you, you should look in his face." I listened to what he was saying. He can see you are listening and is able to keep on going - it was a very important lesson. I always made it my business to listen and hear what they are saying - to be sure, and say you can understand what they are saying.

Today it seems everyone is too busy. They do not have any patience to listen. It's become a very busy world. There is no time for anything or anyone.

A note after typing
Dictated by Maria Gluck, October 9, 2012

After typing 1938/7/8 Father to Dezső (Book 4, 217-220) into the computer:

It is difficult to understand and believe, after so many years, how much trouble people went through, even under normal conditions. As I dictate this letter, I myself cannot believe it - even though I was still there - how difficult life was. Just to show you, we have all the proof. No one could believe such an ordeal that we went through.

Our dearest father - he was one of the best and most caring fathers in this world. Even then, he did not have a normal life - not a moment to think, but one trouble after another.

As I remember… I wrote about it - you will find it in that book - but there is much more I could say. Now, as I am writing on the computer and going over all these letters, I am more convinced than ever how lucky we were. Without G-d's help, we would be gone - along with the rest of our family. They sacrificed - without choice - their lives. In such a horrible way.

I just don't know how to explain my feelings - especially now - that we are still lucky. My dearest brother Irving and I, with our aide's help, are here. I must say: very lucky, and very grateful.

Perhaps I should not write this note at this time, but my heart... in one sense, finally, I have a little happiness. Because just a couple of days ago I went through something very sad. As I mentioned before, my dearest brother Irving had a tough time - all his life, he went through so much. One heartache after another. And he cared so much for his family - past, present, and today. Unbelievable.

How could a person go through so much, and when the time finally comes to enjoy his life - the life he so well deserved - then there's always something else. A problem comes unexpectedly. He's going through one thing after another, and I have to watch him suffer. I can't do anything more but ask our Almighty for His help.

Finally, we have a little good news - we found a good doctor this week. I hope he finds the right medication. I hope it will help. As of now, we have the prognosis, and the medication is working. I hope it will continue to get better.

He's like a different person - and that makes me very happy. At least now, we have more strength to deal with everything. He deserves that. And now he can continue his life with his own family. He should be happy and enjoy the future - whatever it is. This is my wish from my heart: nothing but happiness to all of them. I hope his children and grandchildren will help him make it so. I care for him, and love him.

As of now, I am lucky also - to have a brother like he is. I must say - one in a million! I will do whatever I can to help him come better than ever - and be happy.

But now I will try to come to a closing point. I could say much more, but I don't want to bore you. As for the rest of my family - we never forgot them. Sometimes it's hard to see them as they once were - but in my heart of hearts, they will always be there.

It was a terrible nightmare. How could such an ordeal have ever been allowed to happen? They killed a small nationality just because they were Jewish? No one had the right to destroy them without a reason.

Our kind - educated, top of the crop - was it jealousy? Money? Only hatred? Why? What could be so bad to hate so much? And how about the children? G-d's creations - all a nation - how could they hurt anyone and give such a punishment? Take away lives - for what reason?

They had their own families - what would they have done if it were their own family in that same position? Or maybe their own lives?

That is a terrible thing. And the whole world just kept silent and watched them!

How could this happen? I will never understand. I have searched for answers. And in my heart, I cannot forgive - and I cannot forget. Ever.

I asked so many times - we have all kinds of religions all over the world - and I'm happy for them. But why did they choose one little nationality, just because they were Jewish? We are all created equally. Flesh and blood. We look the same. We are hard workers, with respect for others. All kinds of nationalities. We try to get along - without hatred - without trouble - educated, trying to help others in any way we can.

Doctors, lawyers, educators, professors, colleges, universities - they are all G-d's creations. We were there, like it or not. We helped build the world - cities, states, countries. All over. A few people here, a few people there - but we were always there, next to you, protecting you. Next to you, fighting with you - for your freedom, and for ours.

I don't know why, this morning, I just cannot sit and do my job - just typing on the computer. I am carried away - like my dearest brother always says - I am carried away. He's right, like always.

Perhaps I should finish this letter with one last word: thank you for listening. Thank you for understanding my writing - and the reason for doing it.

I do not know if anyone will ever be interested in what I have to say. I just hope someone - even out of curiosity - will take the time to read it. And I hope they will understand.

Now I will say: good luck to you all. And may it be a better future. Work hard enough, and it might be.

Live life with love, not hatred. You must have respect for all religions, for all nationalities. You must learn to control your temper. Like or dislike - between Jews or others - do not discriminate against each other.

Teach your children love - not hatred. What you put in your children's minds - how you raise them, with love - you will create a better life for all. You should never teach them anything that instigates hatred against others.

I hope the next generation will be able to function - to know that, dear friends, without this understanding, the world cannot exist. It is up to you.

I don't know why I feel that way - but I do.

So now, I come to the point. So long - wishing you all the best.

- Maria

Dictated on 10/9/2012

About Science
10/21/2012

It is Sunday morning, 5 a.m.

When I woke up, something came to my mind. I felt maybe this time - against my promise that I will not write anymore - the reason being, maybe I'm wasting my time. No one will ever read it, so why bother?

The only thing - this time I thought maybe for my sake - I wanted to know more about what I can write about, especially this new subject. What is all that science in the new modern world - what I have no idea what it's all about. I am trying to understand.

Little by little, I'm getting there. In the 2000s, beginning what I am experiencing and trying to understand - science - it is amazing. Little children, even the youngest - unbelievable how smart they are! I myself watch them - their mind, their little fingers so fast. Where did they learn? I ask that question every time I see them.

Another telephone - this is not just a telephone - this is a new modern computer. It does everything. Just name it.

You can play with it, entertain yourself, or see the world all around - East, West, South, North - while you're in your home, sitting comfortably in your chair, and see the world going around you. Before you know it, you get so involved with it, you lose other interests and find out so much - like addicted to it - you cannot be without it anywhere. Just take a look on the computer and you get the answer - you do not need to talk to anyone. It would be wasting time that we do not have. It takes only one minute to look at the computer - you will find all the answers.

This amazing little gadget has all the knowledge.

All kinds of secrets - and you don't even have any knowledge of them - are kept in that little machine we call the computer. It knows enough.

Nowadays, I would say we are all accounted for - everything, in numbers.

From our family to our finances, they've got all the information about you.

You can't hide - it is an open book. Your whole life history.

And now, as I am getting to know the computer world, I understand something more than I expected.

My question is now, as I see it - can we depend on a computer? It is very smart - sometimes I think too smart. I must say, it is a good teacher. But it takes more time to learn about a computer - it would take years to know from A to Z, and maybe you still would never know everything that you can do with it. It is a creation of a new world.

Is it possible that one day it might be able to solve the wars around the world?

Yes, we have the computer, and it does a wonderful job. I accept it. I respect it. And I'm very lucky to be able to use it. But sometimes, even that does not help. We can do so many things with it. The education - what we can do with a computer is amazing. It is the best tool around, but you can only do so much.

Many years ago, we did not have computers or telephones, no television and many other things - especially modern tools around. When we came to this country in 1940 there were some rumors about the television. That time they didn't know that it will be television. If I remember, it will be like a box, and you will be able to see pictures.

Later on, we had television, it took a while - but then it happened. Before we knew it, voices were coming through, and that became our television. It was unbelievable how fast the world changed. This was just the beginning. All this we accomplished - whatever we wanted to.

There is another lesson. See if we can learn from it. Let's examine the other side - science's good and bad sides. Yes, it is one. Therefore, we are able to create the modern world - and we can make life better for all people. Yes, we need a way to know how to use and learn computers. We have an easier and faster way to communicate - all kinds of business, or even privately. We can learn about anything and everything, right from our own home - and if you are smart enough, you have all the chances around you, and you can do whatever you are wishing for.

Now we can go anywhere. We have proven something by going to the moon - to Mars, in no time. We can travel wherever we wish. What will come next? Is it going to be for the better - for all people? More prosperity - or more sicknesses? Will we compete with one another, or will life be better without hatred - working together to improve everyone's lives?

Without any discrimination - learning love instead of hate. It depends on how you define it - and for what purpose you are using it. In the wrong hands, everything can be dangerous, as we learn every day. I could go on and on - but we are trying to build a better world for your children. Isn't it time to work toward peace - and a better life for all of us? And for a better life for all of us with better schools - colleges - that take responsibility for better understanding.

How can students learn and understand the real meaning of life and work - of living - and how can they be happy? And not just that, but beyond their own family - how can they get along with neighbors without hatred, and learn how to work together and learn from each other and their children?

Science is a wonderful thing to have, but it can also create more problems. Unemployment is difficult. It's hard to find any job and this is a time of hardship. It seems we create some of the problems - we cannot see the crystal ball in advance. We cannot tell what the future holds - the only thing we can see is the outcome after suffering through it. There is hunger all over the world, and when we try to look at the future - as of now - it is very difficult to find any good answer for the next generation's outcome. We try to forget about it.

Science is advancing very fast. There's no way to stop it. Therefore, you have a responsibility - to learn how to use it for better creation. It's your responsibility, your creation - how to deal with it for a better life.

If you have a family, you hope that you can create a better life for them. And for all people, it may seem like only a miracle - if there is one - could save us to get out of this present troubled world all around us.

Especially when your new generation comes. I'm sure, if we really want to we could accomplish a better world for the next generation. Try to educate, so we have better common sense to see and experience the better side of life. It is worth it to try to improve the world you are living in. There are people who are working very hard to accomplish something new all the time. Especially today's children - they already learn more than some of the grown-ups.

What I see today - everything is possible - to build and improve the quality of life. It is worthwhile. There are people who like to build or create something new.

All over the world, we would have a better chance to succeed - to better our own life and that of another person. How can this be accomplished? It seems impossible. Yet, in my opinion, nothing is impossible - especially in today's modern world, with so much knowledge all around us. We have all the tools right here, all around us, to learn - to build a better life for all of us. With our capability, we can create a version [of the future?] that you can't imagine or never thought about.

With this note I am coming to the closing - I hope with a happier note. Wishing you all the best of health and happiness, and a better life within the near future.

With all my love to you all,
Maria
[Typed in] *1/18/013*

about science as I see it
Written by Maria - the 2nd note about science - 1/5/013

I was thinking, as I remember, about science. I just finished the first article, and I came to the point where I would mention it again.

As I woke up Saturday morning, I was sitting and reading my prayerbook - it was written in Yiddish, this translation, so I was able to understand what I am praying for. As usual, my question arises - about our existence and man's creation. We can look it up in our Bible, our ancient history, and our myths. If you want to know all the truth, you will find it in our Bible. And this continued ever since our history began - since the creation of 'the Hebrew'. How do we know the truth?

Like people wrote - how do we know all of this happened - our existence, the beginning of our creation? Like Adam and Eve, Moses - who was there? How did all of this come to life? Whoever started it - does not matter - we know it, and all that it includes, is written by men. When, how, and who they were, I call them brilliant scientists. With their knowledge they created and gave us the answers. It took them a lifetime - working, studying, trying to find answers. They tried to go back, looking for proof.

And they put together whatever they were able to. As I was growing up, trying to learn, I had questions - and I still do. Whatever I see - it is all written by men - men who sacrificed themselves - who studied life, one after the other, and interpreted whatever they found. And from the past, so much information - and you must trust them, as they were trying to show the truth. Way back in our history, they were brilliant - very smart - how far they were able to give us the information.

They taught us that our G-d in heaven is invisible and is for all people. No man has the right to come and take G-d away or ruin faith for their own benefit.

They also taught us how this world was created, and about Moses - how he got to the point about the Ten Commandments in our Bible. All of it is man's creation. How do we believe it is true? Who really saw it?

From the Bible, we must believe it - that's what we learned. If you do not believe the writings of the Old Testament about how the world was created, then ask: would it be possible for a human being to create it?

What does it mean? Did the world exist as we read in the Bible? It is okay to read it that way. We may question whether or not all this existed and whether it was written by men. Others can write whatever they want to, to explain the history of the beginnings.

Even if we spend our lifetime studying the Old Testament, still there's much more to learn. The Old Testament talks of only one - and only one - our Lord. When the Ten Commandments were received by Moses, they were written, as I remember as a child, only the Scripture was seen - our Lord was never seen by human eyes.

Yes, I do know people ask, "How do we know it was real?" They claim man wrote it. "Is there any proof?" But if you think and look back - the world did not just exist from nowhere. Think again, very carefully, from A to Z - you will find all the answers, if you really want to.

A thousand years from now, those generations will be asking the same questions as we do now. Who will have the answers for them?

In my opinion, it does not matter how it was written - by men or created by our Almighty. Take a look at how our life exists - it began somewhere, and we came to understand that this was the beginning of everything.

Science - they did work on all of it - the way man can remember our ancestors, and how far back our imagination can take us into history. Man can create, and try to find some answers for our creation - and not just preach, but educate us - convince us.

They must have found some of this to be true, to be able to put together all that history as they did.

We are not speaking about one person - there were different kinds of scientists who tried as fast as they could

And they still continue to work on trying to find some answers and proof. Men never gave up.

We are not the only ones questioning history.

Therefore, we must learn what was written by men - as far back as we can go. The original history must have been witnessed by someone, just like the latest history, the First World War and the Second, which we survivors are able to write about. We're living proof. And we are writing about it - the survivors, those who were able to leave behind their horrors, torture, and the nightmares they went through.

If you want to have a peaceful world to live in - for you and your family - to raise a healthy family and live safely in your life, then you must try to work on it.

Nothing comes easily. Pay attention to what goes on around you. If we want to learn, we can. Now I will come to closing point - hoping I did not bore you. Wishing you the best of health and happiness. Take care of yourself. Look out for trouble.

Now I will say so long - have a good day.

Written by Maria.

How to be a happy family
Written by Maria 2013/2/21

This morning, just as I opened my eyes, it is 4 AM. All of a sudden - like a flash - someone appeared out of nowhere. Who was it? What was it? It was a beautiful young lady - and a very smart one. Therefore, I see you as a young lady growing up. And as of now, I know you have no cause or reason to worry - thank goodness you have parents who care for you, and a loving father who loves you very dearly. He will do everything in his power for his family.

How to be a family - to enjoy each other - we all can learn.

This is the beginning of the family breakdown - no longer knowing how to sit down and have a real conversation. Honest discussions between husband and wife, or even with grown-up children, seem so rare. We've become restless, frustrated, and overly sensitive. This worries me deeply. The ties that once held families together are disappearing because people are no longer able to honestly express their feelings.

As I am observing today - family - how different it is!

Marriage should also be treated like a partnership. When a couple comes to a decision to settle down and get married, it should be all worked out as a business deal - carefully. To be understood by both parties - that before they come to a conclusion, they understand each other. They have the same feeling - the same ideas - before they tie the knot. Also, it is important to have a similar background.

They also need to be able to communicate with each other - marriage should be taken seriously. It is never so simple. You never know for sure why the other party is choosing you. Sometimes in the beginning they say whatever you want to hear, but later it changes. About children, they might say they feel the same way, but sometimes, one party can change their mind after they get married. Before entering it, both people should ask important questions - not just about love, but about values, expectations, and life goals. If you sense something is off, it's better to address it early. Love may be blind, but clear communication can save years of heartache. When both partners work outside the home, new problems emerge. People do not take time to think it out before marriage - what they really want. Before they know it, they have a family.

If you are not careful - it will lead to more problems. Something you never expected. You would never predict what could come up. If both parties would like to work toward a good relationship - it takes hard work. From both sides. Especially when you plan to have a family - you would like to have a happy family on a solid background.

How we learn, and the conditions in which we are raised, can affect us - and we grow accordingly. Learn the right things without hatred - that word must be used very carefully. It can affect your ability to grow and to understand right from wrong. You must also learn to love and respect - and most important of all - you must have common sense. That shapes not only your ability to think, but also the kind of decisions you make and the path you choose in life. These choices influence everything you learn and how you grow up. It is very important to make the right decisions. One day, you might have a chance - an opportunity - and you never know: maybe you will be involved with the country, or even the world. Think carefully - you will see what I mean. When you have strong family ties, you can build on them. But if you try to destroy them, you can destroy what you try to build too.

One day, you never know, they could be a leader in one thing or another. They could be a businessman or woman - it does not matter - or a leader of a country - or they could be someone in the education field - you can never tell. You like it or not, it has a lot to do with how your family was as you were growing up - the atmosphere of how you were raised. Happy or sad, children will remember. That is the foundation of a lifetime.

When children are involved, it is more than just a job. To begin with - to have a happy home with children - it is a big responsibility. They need attention - and with attention, give them love. Children are not born to be bad - they are innocent and lovable, but without that some become bullies when they grow up. They go in the wrong direction.

To raise children - it's not as simple. To begin with - prepare yourself - when the time comes, be ready. Have some ideas. Also, there are places where you can get more information. This is very important - otherwise, you might have more problems. Especially when children start growing up - at certain ages - they learn fast. And they have their own ideas - good or bad.

Parents used to say ten children - each one will be different.

In the beginning, you have to make sure they understand you. You are their parent - and they are your children. First of all, you have to understand how to take charge. With love, you can encourage the highest mountain. With anger, you can destroy the world. It's up to the parents to teach children at home. Give them the best tools or whatever they need. You don't have to be rich. You should follow the pattern just like you would teach the ABCs. How to walk - to eat - how to get dressed - and how to take care of themselves. Which does not come overnight! They must also learn how to speak, and how to treat others. If you don't, children learn from each other before they have knowledge to fully understand life.

The children need supervision to help them grow and manage their life. They need chances to learn right or wrong. Protect them, care for them, love them, enjoy them. Raise them and be proud of them. Beginning day one - it is especially the mother's job - it is most important in raising the children (fathers usually try to make a living). Mothers should be able to take care of them, to protect them, and teach them - to help their mind - to be able to grow up and learn how to make decisions and choices. Learn to have the ability to make healthy decisions.

As they get older, they have to learn and think - to be a responsible person - how to conduct themselves - and they should remember who they are. A mother's job is not easy - but it is the most important one. She must have the patience to see how their children are growing up. With problems, especially at home, it's both parents' job. At home, their mother is with them - does the chores - shows them - teaches them as they are growing up. Some small chores they are able to do - learn how to keep their room clean. It doesn't mean they have to wash the floor.

Their clothes - they should learn where everything belongs. When they need it, they should know where to find them - without any hassle. Make it sure it is clean. When time comes to wash, the children should prepare the clothing - usually it is the mother job to wash, unless they have some helpers to do it. For the young children involved, it's too soon to leave them without a mother's supervision. This is the time that the mother should pay attention. Later on, as they are growing up, you can teach them to help you.

How to set a table the right way - especially when dinnertime comes - this is important to learn. Also, you must have a set time for dinner, and all the family should be able to sit down together - without disturbances.

They must learn to enjoy the family dinners, at least. There should be no television running - they have to show respect for their family until everyone finishes their dinner. Only those people who are serving dinner or helping to clean the table - or helping out at dinnertime - should be moving around. That should be the rule.

Everyone eats together - and tries to enjoy each other's company. And they will learn how to eat together. There should be no computer, no phone. If you get a call, you should be brief - and try to call them back after dinner.

As they are growing up, they can help you - things like helping you with breakfast. At other times, children would like to work with you when you are working - baking, they like to help you. It is okay - they can learn under your supervision. They enjoy it, but they are not ready to do your job - let's say baking or cooking - by themselves. They have plenty of time for that, especially when the mother is okay and does not have to support her family.

Children at a young age should enjoy their life as they grow up. There are parents who care for their children, teaching them. They have chores to help out at home - starting with their own room. They organize and keep their room clean, and learn how to organize it - neat and clean. Learn how to take care of their clothes - put them away wherever they belong. They should be responsible for doing it. Show them. Teach them good manners.

Teach them how to save a dollar. Teach them how to learn, and what is important in life - clean living.

There's plenty of time to grow up. Teach them what goes along with growing up. Get a good education so they should have a quality life - first for themselves, and then it will follow to others. That is my advice.

Teach them right or wrong. Show them courtesy, appreciation - and don't forget about love. All this creates responsibility. They should learn how to get along with others, be good citizens, and how to become leaders, not followers. If you are a follower - someone's idea - sometimes you can get lost, maybe dangerously misled, and it might be that you choose the wrong road. Therefore, you must begin with growing up: never be a follower. To be a leader, you can accomplish whatever you want to, and learn what you want to - it's your choice.

No lies. No hatred. That can destroy even the best family - and that should never be. This is the beginning of life - you must teach them the meaning of the word *hate* - how bad it is. But parents have responsibilities, too.

The parents are responsible for their children. If there is any problem, it will not go away on its own. You must seek help before it's too late - you cannot ignore it and hope it will disappear. Sometimes parents are too busy, or maybe they choose to ignore the problem. Sometimes it is more than we can imagine - or they simply do not want to see it. Perhaps they do not care. But we all need help, sometimes.

Sometimes there is trouble - confusion all around us - it makes it almost impossible to see a way out. Families breaking up - this also can be a problem with children from a broken home. It makes it very difficult to carry on, especially in today's situation. Some parents ignore or try to forget their responsibility. They just walk away like nothing happened. Or they forget how to raise and respect and honor their own family. They forget where they are coming from.

Honesty and understanding life - growing up - responsibility - this should be taught at the beginning to a child. This creates a happier life. With knowledge, they can develop good sense - able to choose when the time comes, in any place - business, private life, or even as responsible citizens. You never can tell what the future holds. Be ready - with respect to each other. Honesty is the best policy - you cannot go wrong. With lies, sooner or later, you can get into more problems.

Also, they should be taught how to use their common sense - good judgment. It is very important who prepares your children to be able to make the right decisions when the time comes. This is the beginning of maturity - and the true beginning of their life. Teach them respect for each other. With that, they will go on to improve their life - or maybe even this country. You never can tell - the rest is up to them.

If you learn caring, loving, and respect for others - you should begin in your own home. You must teach children every word and its meaning - to learn how to get along in their own family. It could be a lifesaver.

A mother's job and responsibility should be taking care of the family. The mother is to help them, teach them, love them, and show them a good example. She is there whenever the children and her husband need her. Yes, it's true: a mother's job is never done. You need strength and understanding. People used to understand the value of homemaking. Today, it's often forgotten. Raising children is the most important job of all. It might be hard, sometimes boring, sometimes under-appreciated - but it lays the foundation for everything else.

This is our background - it was different - we came from a close family, caring for each other, and we still do. We are lucky to be here. My youngest brother and I - we still care for each other more than anyone could imagine. I feel we are very lucky to have each other.

Today, all this is disappearing. Therefore, we have more problems.

But somehow, people change. Values are changing too - when people say "I love you," it sounds very empty. Somehow, something is missing. From what I can tell, it seems very empty - meaningless. Our lifestyle is turning around. Everything is changing - and with it, the family. They make their own rules, and family life doesn't seem to care where they came from. They don't acknowledge the breakdown - unless they can get what they're looking for. Naturally, love is not what they are looking for - that's out of style. Especially love from a mother, father, or grandparents. There's no time left. They're too busy - even though they say, "We love you, Dad."

No one cares anymore what condition you are in - whether you are able to manage your life or need any help, or to see a doctor when it is necessary. All this is not important. What are you going to do without some help?

It became a very selfish world. The family breaks down - children and grandchildren forget where they came from - especially when one or the other parent didn't have a good upbringing. Their parents were too busy working just to make a living - not enough time to spend with their children to give them love, care, and affection when they need them most - and therefore, they missed out on the chance to learn how to raise their own family and understand their values. It seems it all turns around - sadly. I must say, they find all kinds of excuses for themselves - the reason always being that they are too busy. If you don't have time to spend with your children why did you bring them into this world? If you have them, teach them, talk to them, respond to them, and give them love. That is never too much. Let them grow up the way they were meant to.

If you are too busy and forget your responsibility to your own family - especially in today's world - they will lose their family ties. They will forget their responsibility. To raise a family, it needs 24 hours a day - it's hard work - seven days a week. That does not mean scrubbing the floor - it depends on you, how you were raised yourself. Are you willing to accept the responsibility for raising them? Therefore, I urge people - especially young people - before they make a decision, think very carefully. Learn about the past, and think carefully before you come to be sure you made the right decision.

I can speak from my own experience. We study and try to learn all of our life, but it seems we can never learn enough in our lifetime - there is always room to learn and keep your mind open. In life, we can learn every day. Experiences are the best teacher. If we are lucky enough - with an open mind and without any hatred for any reason - and we start something that does not turn out well, sometimes we have a problem facing us. We must learn how to deal with that and make the right choice.

In our lifetime, we may make a mistake - not just one, perhaps more. We cannot foresee the future, what will be - but we try to understand and work around it, doing our best, one day at a time, and hoping that we'll come to the best decision. But sometimes, we must have patience - and the feeling to change your course whenever needed, to help improve your life if it is possible, and be able to live with that.

Life is unpredictable - you never know what comes next.

In time, the children grow up - you will get the reward. It will pay off. No one thinks it is an easy job to be a mother or to be a parent - sometimes it could be boring - but in the end, that should be the most rewarding job. Especially when they grow up and you see how good a job you did - a happy family! You should feel happy and enjoy your hard work. When the time comes, they will be able to make decisions on their own. You still have more time to do whatever you wanted. Go to college and continue your education, or just do whatever you wanted and didn't have the time - especially if you have a good relationship with your family and your husband. That's where respect must come in - mutual effort, shared responsibilities, and appreciation for each other. If these things are missing, the relationship suffers. We must remember that what's happening inside the home matters more than what it looks like from the outside. A strong, respectful, and caring partnership benefits everyone, especially the children. The reward is a happier, more stable family - and that's worth more than anything.

For children, it is very important to build a solid background. They need to know where they are coming from - and learn, and appreciate, and respect - and not forget their loved ones, even after they go on their own way to continue their own life. They need to remember their responsibility to others - do not take anything for granted or forget your obligation to your family and your grandparents who love you. Pay attention, show your respect to them, and learn the richness of love - how much they care for you and love you. They want nothing more than a visit from time to time to show them how much you care for them.

The family should also try to take time out - not just calling them - take time out and find a way to visit them. Pay attention! Do not ignore them! I'm sure you would enjoy their company. They love you and did everything in their power to give you a better life with love. They worked hard to give you whatever they could - a good education and a better life for you - they missed out in their own life, because they love you. They always will.

Sometimes, children forget after their marriage - it depends sometimes on the partner - where they are coming from. Sometimes that could bring more problems - it depends how the partner was raised and where they are coming from. If they respect their own family or were raised by a loving family, there will be a chance. They will accept their spouse's family with respect - what they deserve. Otherwise comes neglect, and they forget where they are coming from - unnecessary heartaches and more trouble, and without any cause. Also, it causes problems instead of appreciation.

I am writing this note for the reason that there is a lesson to learn from it. This is the way trouble starts - at home, in business, and in the world all over. We need only one person to start. Next we'll find out - do not take nothing for granted. It will not come if you are just waiting to get something for nothing.

Today it is a big problem. All over the world, there is no solution in sight. No answer. The fear takes over - and how far will this go? I cannot see any solution at this point. I hope somehow it will turn around for a better life for the next generation. I hope so. Good luck and my best wishes - nothing but the best - this is my wish to all of us.

The house life, as they call it, was never easy. There are times it becomes very complicated. The reward you get is the knowledge you did a good job - the most important one - the biggest job of all. Happily! You never know - you might have raised someone who could be a leader, an educator, or just a businessman. It will be their choice - and you should be very proud of them and yourself.

And someday, you will understand and will be happy. They will be very proud of you, and love you more, and try to be there for you. With love and appreciation, they will remember you affectionately. And in the future, when the time comes, they will be able to take care of their children and family.

I'm sure I could have done much better, but I failed and I had to learn to accept what I have. I've learned not to give up. I do not think about myself alone. I always think of my family and that makes me happy. I am always happy to see my family and I'm happy for them as they get along. I'm happy to know that they have food on the table and are enjoying each other. This gives me an inner feeling that I don't have to worry about him.

I always concern myself about their well-being, namely my family.

I think I have come to a closing point - wishing you all the best of luck, and the best of health. Enjoy your family. Sometimes it gets more complicated. We struggle all our life.

Whether we like it or not, we cannot give up. We have so much to do. The only thing is - time goes by very fast. Then we would like to catch up with it.

It seems our work will wait for us.

Now I will say - so long, wishing you the best.

Maria

This morning is Wednesday - the day before Thanksgiving.

Usually, I used to prepare Thanksgiving dinner for my family. I used to enjoy every moment - to have and spend the day with my dearest family. I loved it very much - I still do. My family comes first.

I remember my own family. It reminds me of much more than just Thanksgiving. It reminds me what we had - and what we lost - can never be replaced. It was ripped from our life, something very dear to us: our family. I cannot even express my feelings - our love for each other. I still believe in that.

I feel a family relationship - you cannot buy. Families are the strongest tie in life - there is nothing stronger - if you learn it in the beginning of life. How important it is to have a loving, caring family that understands the word *family* - what it really means today.

Families are the foundation of the country.

There are families I call the silent people - who went through so much in life - and their parents, hard workers - trying to work and save a dollar for a rainy day and tried to raise their children under the circumstances the best they could. Thank goodness they succeeded in that. And when their rainy day came - after hard work - nothing was left.

Sometimes we need encouragement and a family who will understand and help out - whatever they can - and work together.

You are very lucky if you have it. It must be experienced to understand what it is all about. This is, I would say, real love. It comes from your heart - you feel it. You cannot let go in your mind, to try to ease the pain in your heart.

We must try and learn to keep on going - you must - otherwise you get lost and cannot go on. Therefore, we must be very strong and go on living, and be the best - it's possible - for your sake. We are here for a purpose.

just another note (Getting help as a senior)
12/13/012

To whom it may concern - just another note.[51]

I was thinking before the holiday maybe it is nice if I write you a note - to express myself and wish you the best of health and happiness - for now and the future. Sometimes I asked the question from myself: here is the agency that was supposed to help. Whoever needs help very badly - what are they supposed to do? They are in charge to see they do get the help, whatever is necessary - and to my surprise, when I needed help, there was no one around.

I received the okay to get help. Whatever they had - to send them out - they themselves needed help! It is a disgrace what kind of help they send out. We were told they do not have anyone at this time - and we were waiting and waiting for a long time - and I was very ill. I had just come home from the hospital and the rehab and wasn't able to go home. Therefore, I was told I needed 24 hours of help, but I could not get any. Was okay for 12 hours - even that I could not get.

Therefore, I am lucky my brother took me in, and here also the situation was the same. I'm very lucky to have a brother like he is - a very caring person. It took quite some time before they got any help - unbelievable. It is difficult to believe that this could happen in America - it's supposed to be the richest country and one that cares for its people - and here we cannot have the quality help when we need it.

What are we supposed to do as a senior? We plan and depend on our insurance, and Medicare, Medicaid, and Social Security - that's what we are facing. It seems if they were a charity, I would understand, but it is not a charity - instead, a government-insured program that we paid for - we are entitled to it. My question is: why not? Why are we pushed around needlessly? The government has money for everything else, but they forget their obligation.

Seniors, it seems to me, got lost somewhere - no one cares what happens.

I think they deserve better treatment. It seems when the government needs money, they choose the seniors - strip them of their rights - without any feeling. Do you think that is justice? After all, we have rights just like anyone else. We deserve better treatment. To me, it seems like they need help to balance the budget - yes - but they should look around their own backyard.

And they would be surprised what they find there - mismanagement - waste in all branches. Why not look into it? Maybe they would be surprised what they would find. And I could save you time to bother looking around - the senior people are stripped of their rights. You need to have someone who knows the business and has responsibility in management - who cares for

---

[51] She's writing this note to the case worker or nurse of the home care agency.

their country and understands - without wasting time - looking in the right direction.

And as I see it, trying to look into it - they forget their responsibility - what they really owe the seniors. They are first-class citizens, just like anyone - deserving the best. They forget who made this country with hard work. Hardship never was easy and they did not complain. They sacrificed their lives for a better life for their children, and so the citizens would have a better world to live in.

They worked long hours - the wages were much smaller than today. It is true, everything else was less costly compared to today's prices. The living was a different world - we did not have so many modern tools like today. Jobs also were scarce - especially better jobs. I remember when I came to this country, I depended on my own support - and I was happy. I was doing anything - I liked it or not - it was a job. I was very grateful for it. I always made sure I did a good job - it did not matter how much I got paid.

All my life I tried to improve myself - especially not being able to speak the language made it much more difficult - but as you see, I made it - and I still try to make it, even under the circumstances that we are in. The reason for too much waste in the government is they forget about tomorrow. This is only the beginning of the problem we are in today - spending more than they have.

They have an excuse - blaming the seniors. That is a very simple thing to do - and we seniors just wait and see. When they were in charge, they were trying to do the best. I remember all countries looked up to us with respect and courtesy. Take a look now - what do we have, and which way are we going? Is there a solution? It's very difficult to find an answer. I hope someone will come with some answer or a solution to this problem before it gets out of control. The longer we delay the program, the more difficult it becomes - and we're wasting more time.

We seniors tried to save for a rainy day - it wasn't easy - we could have spent just the same, but we wanted to have something to depend on. When the time came, I never wanted to be on welfare - I always kept on working. I tried to learn how to manage the best way possible. And now, if you have a dollar, you can't even get any interest. But if I want to borrow some, I have to pay high interest - so therefore I can't even do that. Is there any justice?

And it goes on and on - creating more problems instead of helping. And now comes this Social Security - what we are making and living from - we are dependent on it. And also Medicare and Medicaid - it is not a charity - we are entitled to it without feeling guilty. I hope they can find a way to be proud of our country and restore our place - so we could go on living and be proud of ourselves as Americans - what we used to be. Without any discrimination - equal rights for all of us. And whoever is able to do a job and wants to work - they should be allowed to, without any discrimination.

Also, there should be living wages for home healthcare so they can get the right help - to teach and prepare them for the job, so they can be qualified to do it right. This is important - just like any other job - maybe more. Rehab centers and nursing homes should also be looked into - a very bad situation exists there. They get away without anyone paying attention. I know - I have experience - I was there firsthand.

If not for our sake, why don't you think: "I hope you will reach the golden years"? I hope you do - and you might need help - and what you will find is more disappointment. By then I hope you will have a better world to live in. You might be able to manage yourself - but you never know. What the future is - no one knows. Do your homework now and study it. If you can, you might be able to find an answer.

I think I have enough. I can write much more - believe me - it is very difficult even to think about it all. We, the people, try to speak to you - please wake up - we were pushed around enough. Now, wishing you a happy holiday and a healthy New Year - many, many more to come.

Sincerely, your client,
Maria

P.S. I hope I'm not boring you, and I am sorry - I have nothing against you. You are always welcome to visit us with respect, and thank you. Even though I do not know why we have to have this visit - I cannot find any good reason.

Typed December 13, 2012 - by MG.
12/12/12 - just another note. You might be interested to read.

Our brother Lajos - life history
1/2/013

This is a note about our eldest brother (Lajos) Louis and his family. We left them behind when we came to America with the hope he will follow us shortly with his family.

My youngest brother Irving asked me to write because he wanted, individually, our brother's life history - and his family. Yes, I remember all of them!

The reason I opened another door and relived so much agony and pain - I felt maybe I just should leave it as is. He has had enough. Especially at this stage - he himself already went through more than anyone should have.

Now I will try to begin the story I was supposed to - about our brother and his family, and their life story.

Our father, and our brother Lajos and his family - his wife and five children - we left them behind. Lajos - how he struggled all his life! We can never forget him, and his family.

Later on, my sister and myself and my two youngest brothers - all four of us succeeded and followed my brother David and came to America.

When the Second World War broke out - finally, when Hungary took over our place - my brother Lajos was taken into the Hungarian army. At first, he served there.

Later on - I do not know how or when - they took him from the Hungarian army to do hard labor. At first, he was able to come and visit his family once, or maybe sometimes. When he was able to come home, it was only a very short visit.

From their letters we found out what he went through. On those visits, he was not even able to sit down and write to us - his hand was shaking so badly, he could not pick up a pen to write.

After those visits, the family did not hear from him or see him again.

At home, there was no one there to help or to work the farm - everything stopped.

Our father wasn't able to do the work.

There was no money, no business, no food, no clothing - and to stay with five children all alone…

Our dearest father suffered with his grandchildren.

Their mother, our sister-in-law, was left with the family - trying to feed them, to save their family. She learned very fast, but she could not do the job alone. We were Jewish, and the hatred was there already - even before we left. At that time, they were not able to correspond by mail. We knew what was going on there, but we were not able to do much.

We never lost that feeling, so many years after. We never forgot our brother Lajos and the family.

We never heard from them again. Before they took them away, we received letters from them and the children. The eldest was 9 years of age, the youngest son just one year. I heard - and I know - the eldest son, he was still just a child. As he wrote to us, he knew everything - what was their fate - he was writing like a grown-up. And our father - it was very difficult for him - as he wrote: "I do not care what happens to me. It makes me happy to know you children - at least you are safe." I wish - I would have been happy to do anything, whatever happens to me - if I could have saved my brother Lajos's family. My heart aches so much for them.

Those children - without a father most of the time - crying, 'Mommy, just give me a small piece of bread.' What can you answer on that? Their mother tried everything just to feed them. She learned even how to raise some of the vegetables in our garden - potatoes or whatever she could find. She did everything possible to feed the children. Our dearest father - to gather whatever was possible - especially without money. The children needed milk - we could not have even a cow. No horses. No buggies. Nothing at all.

When they took our brother for the army, our dear father - everything went with him. Can you imagine the suffering? The pain? And here we were - not able to do anything to help them. In our heart, we knew the circumstances - what they were in. But no more letters from them.

There was nothing left - only heartaches and pain - to live with that day in, day out. You never can understand - we had no choice. To lose someone - your dearest family - you have to be very strong to be able to take it. You will have that pain - it will stay with you.

It is a true story - listen and learn.
Finished 1/21/013

On Violence
12/2012

Violence does not come out of nowhere. If we look, I hope we can see any danger signs and examine what it is all about - and deal with it accordingly, before it's too late. Some of the people are looking for trouble. They do not care what price they might pay - even their own life. Therefore, we must be alert, open - minded, and take care of it - whatever it is. To prevent some of the danger, the family should be alert to their own family - to see before they get in a serious and dangerous situation.

Sometimes the reason for many of them could be sickness or mentally not being able to cope with something. There should be someone responsible for them - to help them one way or another. They should not be pushed around. They are in pain, just like any other sickness. If we try to take care of that, they might be able to stop before it gets out of hand. We could save many lives.

Some people try to accomplish a better life and raise their children in a loving family. Sometimes others come around and create problems for their own purposes - trying to get money without work. It does not bother them. Especially today, in court, some of the judges are not doing the job right. It should not happen. I know cases where this is happening - the criminals should be getting years - before, the penalties would be stiffer.

Today it seems very common. There are too many sick people around - you never know who - or when, from somewhere, it will come unexpected - breaking out in genocide. Schools are not getting enough protection against danger. You never know when and where - as we've seen just in the last couple of days.[52] Some of the families must have known what goes on in their own family - should have gotten help. They must have seen it, and they closed their eyes and their minds - and made this happen.

If you wait long enough - make believe you can get away - it never does, unless you seek help. Even for your own protection, you must not delay. You must do whatever it takes. If you love that person, he is himself in big pain. I know it hurts - you do not want to hurt them - but one day they might appreciate how you tried to save their own life.

I feel someone should be accountable for all this tragic situation. If we take a good look - examine - you can see and prevent it before it's too late, and you might be able to sleep better, knowing you are safe. We are people - we make mistakes, one time or another - we are human. We must learn and try to work on it. The problem is we are too busy to see what goes on around us - even in our home, even in ourselves.

---

[52] I think she is referring to the Sandy Hook Elementary School shooting on December 14, 2012.

my opinion as I see it - a short story
3/14/013

(Children of the 60s and Woodstock mentality)

Now I would like to mention about our new generation. I ask myself, trying to understand - some children are going to school, getting a good education. Just hoping they will be smarter and able to learn the difference between good judgment and bad, which is the best way to go. Sometimes their parents get so involved trying to make a living - working very hard in business or busy with the chores - they do not have time for the family.

As they are trying to grow up, children need both parents to help them, to listen to them - especially as they are growing up. When that young, if it is possible, they should not be left alone or just ignored. This is not an easy job, I must say - but a very important one.

Children get bored and tired of doing the same routine - day in, day out. They need some excitement. Some of the children get involved with the wrong people, and that could be the beginning of new problems - before they know it, they joined the wrong crowd. Yes, they do have excitement. In the beginning, maybe they try to smoke a cigarette. That's just the first step. Then maybe something different - and before you know it, they get carried away, and they might pay with their life, they get so involved. If they're lucky enough - they help themselves back to the right track before it's too late.

But usually they are so deep in it, they forget. They like it - and forget all about responsibility for themselves - just having a good time, like they're calling it. They have love - freedom - to do whatever they want to - the job that makes them happy. Yet, the people around them can be very dangerous. Then you are in trouble. Later on you learn - if you're strong enough - but sometimes you get lost. Especially if you are young and beautiful - you can be very popular for a while. It could happen even under normal conditions. It does happen - even to the best of families.

Yes, they were looking for something, and they went on their way. It seems like an epidemic - no way to stop. The age of free love was in full bloom and spread very fast. Some of them - home, the family, the education - just left. The family never heard from them - had no idea what happened to them.

Now when you fall in love, you forget your responsibility which goes with it. You end up in bed without knowing with whom - because you didn't care. When you wake up, you find yourself with more than what you bargained for. It may cost your life. These episodes go on with multiple partners, starting young, because they want to be grownups. By the time they reach adulthood, they'll be ready - with all the experiences. No more surprises. They know it all. All this happens before they become mature. Why? Because they learn from their peers - "If they can do it, why not me?" By the time they realize what's what, they are worn out, tired, and all the excitement is gone. These young men and women are bored - nothing to look forward to. These children - by now they have had enough and don't even know what happened to them - and they don't even care.

This change in thinking affected marriage and family life. Couples - whoever decided to get married - some improved their life, settled down, had families. Some got bored with the old-fashioned lifestyle - they don't need any license - they would live together as is. Others showed they preferred a man - two men - to live and get married. Others - also women with women.

I did forget about dear children. Now their children are growing up, and the situation is so confusing - everyone is looking and asking: is this best for them? They have children and don't even know who the fathers are. The children are neglected. And for those children - what will become of them? When they become adults - they can't sort out their responsibilities for themselves, let alone for others. This affects society. Whether you want to face it or not, it's true. This generation is having more difficulty facing real life. Right now, they are lost and lonely.

Why should you care? The main thing is to have a good time, right? That's the beginning of the problem, whether or not you think so. They forgot to learn that there is plenty of time to take responsibility - to be grown up, and to enjoy life as long as they can.

What I call a good time isn't what the majority of people think. *Real* good times come from hard work - from making things better. I know that most people - especially today, with the way the world is changing and people's desires are changing, and not for the better - must think very carefully. It is not desirable the way things are going. We cannot function too long if we ignore it. It needs to be cleaned up, sorted out, where we feel it.

I remember - it happened to be I was visiting my doctor, and one of his friends - also happened to be a doctor - walked in, just to say hello. They were friends.

This doctor asked my doctor how he was. That day, inevitably, family came up. And unexpectedly, I overheard my doctor's reply. His young son was supposed to enter one of the colleges - he was supposed to study to be a doctor. Instead, he left his home with nothing - just left - just like the other young generation. And as he quoted, after he left, he never got in touch with them - never heard from him - and he could not stop him. He was too tied up - to me, it was, he was looking for more excitement. Yes, they did not care about their family. This is the way it began.

I am sure you heard about the music festival - the name of Woodstock - this was something unusual. They had all those young people get together from all over the country to listen to their favorite music - a festival. They did not think or even imagine what would be next. They had all kinds of people there. This is the place where they got the name 'hippies'. They did not care - rain or shine - they stayed. Some of them even brought babies.

There were so many youngsters - they did not have any place to go to. It was all on the ground there, listening to the music - and also using drugs - trying to convince young girls. Some drug dealers themselves saw this opportunity - with promises they could help them. Some of the girls, as I remember, one was 14 years of age - she was from the best of families - very smart and beautiful - and overnight she changed. After that, she was never the same.

One of the drug dealers convinced her she would be able to do whatever she would like to do - and as young as she was, she believed him - loved him - she thought. And her family tried everything to convince her - it is nothing but trouble if she lives with him. They tried everything, but it was too late - he succeeded. This was for a couple of years. She went through a very bad time. After, finally, the family found out what was happening to her and tried to save her. She left her home because of that man, and we knew he was a drug dealer - an addict.

The family wanted to report him, but this young woman - a child - would not allow them to do it. Otherwise, she might hurt herself - that was enough for them. But later on, her parents stepped in to help her. They tried to get help for her, and tried to work with her if she would listen to them - luckily, they succeeded. As I mentioned before, she was very smart. In the beginning, before all this, she was enrolled in one of the best schools - they accepted her.

Finally she succeeded - the dream came true, the one she always wanted - I could say, with hard work and with ambition. And now, luckily, she turned out to be successful - whatever she does. But by the time she became successful, her parents were not here to see - and to be proud of her.

I knew her very well. I would say she's a very lucky lady - to accomplish so much after what she was going through. It wasn't easy - if not for the family who stepped in to help her, she would have been gone for good.

Today, those people are getting to be the new senior people - will be ready to retire. Let's hope they were able to come back and continue their lives - and worked out whatever it came their way.

Those days will remain never forgotten - it is one of our history. It did change. I would not say for the better - but they did change.

I am closing this article and wishing you the best - success, happiness to all of us, and a good future - good luck.

Maria
finished 3/16/013 - Tuesday, 7 a.m.

From a newspaper in 1940 came to America
2013/3/20

This is a story shortly after we arrived in America and we were interviewed by a reporter from a newspaper [The Columbus Citizen] - my brother just showed it to me today, 3/20/2013. It happened to be written in 1940, shortly after we tried to settle down in our new country. I thought I would put it in the computer to remember how we were at the time we arrived - without speaking any English. It was shortly before my brother went to the American Army to register for duty. He was selected and served in the Army for a couple of years. I'm grateful that our G-d helped him to come back to us, and we are able to be together as of now.

Here I begin to type the first newspaper article:

Irving Gluck, 19, of 175 1/2 Second - Av, is shown above filling out his specimen form for registration at the South Side Settlement House where naturalization classes are held.

beginning tomorrow and ending Dec. 26.

Madison W. Cooper, assistant postmaster, announced that registrations will be accepted in Room 133, first floor of the new Federal Building at 8:30 a.m. tomorrow.

He advised all persons required to register to call at the headquarters as soon as possible and secure a blank form, take it to their homes and fill it out before attempting to complete their registration.

And here an earlier article:

"America means land of freedom. There are no dictators, nor any monarchs in this land. Of course, freedom does not mean freedom of following any temptation, but freedom of resisting temptation.

"There is one very important freedom, too. This is religious liberty. America grants all religions the right to practice here.

"Freedom of speech is another thing, too. People have the right to voice their opinions about the Government. The minority gets a chance, too. That is what America means to me." There is a note attached to Robert's theme by Mrs. Levinger. It says: "This is splendid." With that I agree wholeheartedly.

And speaking of refugees Mrs. Levinger. I had the pleasure the other day of talking to two of them that managed to get out of Czechoslovakia after its capitulation to Germany. They were in Herman and Maria Gluck they both live at 175 1/2 W. Second - av with a brother, Irving 18-and a sister, Hermine, 27, who left with them.

The Glucks have only been here a few months but already they can talk English well enough to make you understand and they can grasp what you say.

It is hard to get a story from them but it seems that with money they obtained from their 65-year-old father they managed to go over the border into Italy and take a boat from there for this country.

Herman is working for a scales manufacturing company and taking care of his sister, Mary. A brother, David, was already here and it was a happy reunion for the little family.

Can you imagine, Mrs. Levinger, what America means to these refugees from Hitler's hate. We ought to be happy to live in a land which can receive these unfortunate people with open arms and say to them: "Here you are in a free country. Remain in peace."

My youngest brother Irving's picture is on the top of the note. This was the first interview in America.

    I typed this note into the computer to see the difference - then and today - it's like day and night. I am very proud of my experience and my mission. I hope we can improve our life and our country, and continue to have our precious freedom - we should never lose it! This comes from my heart - you must fight for our future and improve the life of the next generation. Believe me - it is worth it! There is no other haven to go to. I must thank you - our loving America - you gave me a chance to learn what is freedom, and enjoy my golden years in our precious country. Thank you from my heart.

I copied these news articles from the originals.
Typed in the computer - you have my writing -- instead of from there. Now I finished.
Today's date: 3/20/2013.

THE COLUMBUS CITIZEN

3500 Aliens Here To Be Registered

Begin Tomorrow; Hits All 14 or Older

The estimated 3500 aliens living in Columbus will participate in the nation-wide registration of all aliens, through local post offices,

Irving Gluck, 19, of 175½ Second-av, is shown above filling out his specimen form for registration at the South Side Settlement House where naturalization classes are held.

beginning tomorrow and ending Dec. 26.

Madison W. Cooper, assistant postmaster, announced that registrations will be accepted in Room 133, first floor of the new Federal Building beginning at 8:30 a. m. tomorrow.

He advised all persons required to register to call at the headquarters as soon as possible and secure a blank form, take it to their homes and fill it out before attempting to complete their registration.

OPEN UNTIL 5 P. M.

A staff of clerks and typists in charge of Ralph Rice will be on duty at headqaurters starting tomorrow morning, Mr. Cooper said. The office will be open during the week until 5 p. m. daily.

day estimated that nationally there are 3,600,000 aliens who must register. He said the registrations in no way a "witch hunt." Neither, he said, did Congress have in mind a "program of persecution of peaceful and law-abiding aliens."

All aliens 14 years old or over are required to register; alien children, under 14, must be registered by their parents or guardians, according to Earl G. Harrison, national director of registration. Per-

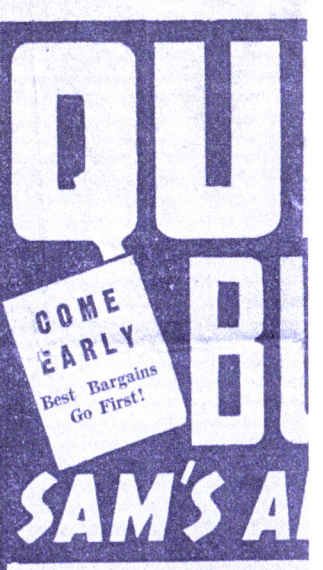

"America means a land of freedom. There are no dictators, nor any monarchs in this land. Of course, freedom does not mean freedom of following any temptation, but freedom of resisting temptation.

"There is one very important freedom, too. This is religious liberty. America grants all religions the right to practice here.

"Freedom of speech is another thing, too. People have the right to voice their opinions about the Government. The minority gets a chance, too. That is what America means to me."

There is a note attached to Robert's theme by Mrs. Levinger. It says: "This is splendid." With that I agree wholeheartedly.

AND SPEAKING OF refugees, Mrs. Levinger, I had the pleasure the other day of talking to two of them that managed to get out of Czechoslovakia after its capitulation to Germany.

They were Herman and Mary Gluck and they both live at 175½ W. Second-av with a brother, Irving, 18, and a sister, Hermine, 27, who left with them.

The Glucks have only been here a few months but already they can talk English well enough to make you understand and they can grasp what you say.

It is hard to get a story from them but it seems that with money they obtained from their 65-year-old father they managed to go over the border into Italy and take a boat from there for this country.

Herman is working for a scales manufactuirng company and taking care of his sister, Mary. A brother, David, was already here and it was a happy reunion for the little family.

Can you imagine, Mrs. Levinger, what America means to these refugees from Hitler's hate? We ought to be happy to live in a land which can receive these unfortunate people with open arms and say to them: "Here you are in a free country. Remain in peace."

Memorial for our family Holocaust day
4/7/013

Today is the Holocaust Memorial Day [Yom haShoah]. We should never forget it. We must remind the next generation - and try to learn and live in peace so no human beings suffer and go through it again.

This note is a memorial for our family.

They were taken away on Passover 1944 by the Slovakian sympathizers with Germany and the Hungarian government.

I wasn't planning to write. I do not know why I do. Silently, we all felt the same way. For us, it is a sacred day. In our hearts, we cannot say what or how we feel. The only thing we know is the memory - our love for each one of them. Nothing but heartaches and questions. How could this kind of ordeal in this world happen? With all those countries, including our freedom-loving nation - the U.S.A. - with all religions...

All races and all colors - like a garden full of beautiful flowers. All kinds of roses - one more beautiful than the other. Lilies in all corners - from all over the world. Each country has their own flower - beautiful and fragrant. One is nicer than the other. You are raising them - making sure they are healthy - trying to enjoy them. If we have weeds around them, we try to remove them, making sure the flowers will not be damaged. It takes time and hard work. People all over the world love them. The beauty and the smell - it does not matter how much it will cost - they will pay for it.

The nations, and all nationalities, all religions - there are good and bad.

How could so many people just sit and watch? Did they enjoy it? Why did they do that to them? Perhaps jealousy?

Maybe the reason was - they were smarter than you. They had more brains.

Instead of getting rid of them, you should have learned from them. Worked side by side. Opened your eyes and ears - tried to learn. You would have gained by it. Those people never hated you. On the contrary - they were helping you. Gave you jobs. Helped you when you were sick.

How about the innocent children? Babies - some of them were born in captivity. What happened to them? Were they guilty too? Guilty - for what?

You had the nerve to carry out a genocide! Do you feel any remorse? Can you sleep at night? We're not talking about one person. The world. The nations. What would they do if it had been one of *them*?

All religions pray - all over - just like the Jewish. It does not make any difference. The only difference I can see - is the language. The G-d they are praying to - it is a statue - but it is all the same. All prayers go to one G-d - invisible. We learned it as we were brought up as a child. We must behave because our Almighty is watching us. My question is - how could so many people who pray to their G-d carry out all the killings - and live with it.

The anniversary of our "yahrzeit" [remembrance] is on Passover, when we learned later that they were taken away by those gangsters. My family - our family. I still mourn for them. I and my youngest brother are going through so much agony - sometimes I do not know how we can live with that. They were taken away at the last minute. They had no time to keep records of them. Those gangsters did not even bother to keep records![53]

What they did - how they disposed of them - they just finished them. We tried to find out, and we are not able to get any information - even at this time. All doors were closed. How can you live on with that? Our father, my oldest brother, his family - his wife and children.

The oldest child was a 12- year - old boy, then a 10- year - old girl, another little boy - 8 years old, a little boy - 5 years old, and a little boy - 3 years, another boy - less than one year of age.

Those children went through so much even before they took them away. They were left without food - no clothes - no heat - should I say more? And their mother without their father - all alone without any help.

How can you live with all these memories? How do you put your life back together? We must try to enjoy - every minute by minute - without worrying that things will not work out as we would like it. We cannot change the world and the population in it. The only thing we can do is talk about it - if you have some listener. Or perhaps write about it, hoping someday someone might read and understand what you are trying to do or say - and will try to learn to understand life. And maybe they would try to better life in this world - not just for one individual, but for all the people.

I think I had enough for now. I've come to a point for closing this chapter. Wishing you all the best - and a happy life, good health, and a better world for all of you. For the next generation: be smarter and learn as much as possible. Keep your eyes and ears open. Look around - be alert, so no one can hurt you.

This is all for now. Wishing you best of luck - and G-d be with you.
Written by Maria Gluck

---

[53] **Editor's note:** If she only knew how much they *did* keep — I later discovered many documents, which appear in *From the Ashes - The Documents of a Jewish Family* (Tisza Publishing, 2025).

How to Behave in order to have a Better Life
BY M.G. - 4/16/013.

Freedom is not what you think - it does not mean you can use it however you feel like. There is much more to it. It has to follow - and respect - our law. Try to build your relationship in your family. Then you will be able to build a better world and a healthier atmosphere. Our freedom is our strength, our life, our country, our business, our education.

Try to conduct yourselves so that you can build a future for all of us, not just for one person. We must learn and try to understand life. We should teach others how to learn and behave - to live a healthier life - so they could become better people. Keep learning whatever you can, too. Build a better future for yourself and your family. Teach them affection - how to get along. Have respect for your neighbors so there will be a better understanding for all.

Protect them, educate them so they have healthier relationships. Teach them how to grow, and tell them about hatred. Explain it to them - how hatred can destroy the world - it is very dangerous. Teach them how to solve a problem when it arises - peacefully. There are always opportunities if we really want to learn. We can begin at a very young age.

As I look back at my very young years, I was always interested in everything. Whenever I had a chance in Europe, as we were growing up, our family - was always very busy. The business and the farm - we had many pieces of farmland.

It was hard work. We had to hire people when the season came - to plant and to harvest. And our father and our eldest brother were kept very busy all year. We - my sister and I - kept busy at home, young as we were. We lost our mother at a very young age. We had no choice - we had to take over whatever we needed to do.

All those chores - cooking, baking, washing, etc. We had some help sometimes, but it was a very difficult life. None of us had it easy. There was not much outlook for a better life. In a way, we were very lucky we had a dream. And that kept us going, until the time came with hardship and heartaches.

You have no idea what we went through - all of us. Oh my G-d! If I think back - our father - I don't know how he was able to work out those problems. Not just one, but many. One finished - we turned around - and something else came up. None of us could understand how in a small village - it was a miracle - he was able to manage all the problems, one after the other - without any special education.

About my niece and great-niece
BY M.G. - 4/16/013.

She was the first grand-baby for my sister. All of us were very happy to have this new baby, and I lived nearby. When she had the baby, I offered to babysit for her whenever she needs me. So she called me - would I watch the child? Oh yes! I will. When it came time to change the baby, she asked me if I'm able to do that. I will - yes, I did it! I can do that! I used to do it many years back, and I felt I could still do it - maybe more.

It happened to be, my great-niece was my first babysitting job. I was very happy to do that. When the time came to change her, I was very careful even to touch her, and I was saying to myself - I hope I will be able to do what I need to do. I was looking at the baby and she smiled back, and I tried to talk to her as I was changing her. She was about 6 months old - believe it or not - she responded to me. She smiled back, and I asked her, "Can you help me, Jessica?" To my surprise, she lifted herself up with my help - amazing how a child, as young as she was, was able to respond. She understood me. After that, we had a very good time together.

As she was growing up, before she went to bed, she asked me to tell stories to her. I told her the story from the beginning - as we were growing up, and how we spent our time - very light stories for children. When I finished one, she asked me - every time I was there - to tell her more stories. She loved them. I tried to tell her whatever she asked. One day, the mother overheard my stories, and she understood what I was telling her baby. She said to me, "This is your life experience, isn't it?" I said, "Yes." This happened to be our little story, from when we were very young.

Her father tried to tell her his stories, but she preferred mine - she loved them all. Ever since that moment, both of us were very happy together. By now, she has grown up to be a very nice young lady - and very smart, I must add to it. That shows - if you spend time with your children, as young as they are, they can learn - you just have to make time, quality time, to spend with them. You might be surprised - you may find something to learn from them.

My sister - she was very busy all her life. She never took the time to talk to her family about our background. She could not talk about it - it was too painful to even think about. When my niece heard me telling my story, she understood what I am speaking of. My little grand-niece - whenever I asked her "which one would you like to hear again?" - she said, "I love them all, but whatever you choose." After I told her this story, she wanted me to stay overnight - next to the bed - I tried to tell her there is no room for me next to her there.

She pointed to the floor - "Yes, we can make a bed next to me, and you can tell me more stories." It happened all the time. She used to set up a kitchen for herself and make - believe she would make me breakfast - and after breakfast, we could go shopping - make-believe, naturally. She was very good at singing and dancing - she entertained herself. And reading - as she was growing up, she tried to read newspapers. She loved to read. Later on, she asked me to read to her. I tried - I can read, and I had an accent as I was reading - naturally, I am from Europe. All of a sudden, that little girl said to me - "Aunt Marie, you are not saying it correctly. Watch me - listen to me" - and she read it beautifully. She was right.

My sister would have been the happiest person to see her. As it is, she did not have that opportunity.

another short story (On Work and Age Discrimination)
April 19, 2013

This is another note written by MG.

Today is Saturday morning at 7:30 AM. Just another story. As I woke up, something came to my mind, like any other story. This story is about how discrimination does exist. This is a big question. It is difficult to believe, but believe me - it does exist.

All my life as I am looking back, it was there, but without realizing what was really going on. All around us, even in our loving, free country. As I look back, all races have faced it ever since we are alive and ever since humans existed. We, the people - one reason or another - find excuses to start discriminating.

First by religion, then nationality, then color, then jobs, and just now in the modern world, age discrimination. One way or another you will find people spreading it. Before you know it, it spreads like fire. Instead of getting better, somewhere it will blow up right in your face without knowing what hit you.

When you are living in your youth, yes, there were doctors who really did their job. Some of them went out of their way to help - no questions asked. Not how much they will get? Money or no money, they just did it. It did not matter how old the patient was.

As of now, in the modern world, the 21st century, all this changed. It makes me very sad even to write about. It is true - when you reach your senior years, forget about it.

When you are younger, you say I'm too busy to even think about it. You are trying to make your livelihood. If you have a family, you're trying to raise them, if you are lucky enough and are able to do it. All we all want is to have a place to call home and to enjoy our family.

We never think beyond our life, until we reach our golden years. And then you are facing reality. Then we find out, our road is not as smooth as we expected. It has lots of bumps all around us, from all directions, like it or not. If you're lucky enough, with all the problems around you, you are able to keep your sanity and be able to help yourself at least mentally - physically we all need some help. Let's face it, we do need help.

Even under the best conditions, my question is: where are we going to get those reliable helpers?

If someone is looking for a job, do not just dismiss them without seeing their qualification. Give them a chance. By mistake or carelessness, without any thinking, you might let go one of the best and knowledgeable worker just for their looks. You are not getting them to be in a beauty contest.

Sometimes we try to look for another job. You have all the qualifications, but you forgot about your age. You will hear the word you are over qualified. Before you know it, whatever you were trying to save is disappearing. You just need a job. Yes, it is all true. You were not ready for retirement. You struggle looking, even if you find a job you cannot get it, but you used to get it. You don't have too many choices. If you're lucky enough to find a job, perhaps you can make it.

But there are other people struggling, and they cannot find one. They possibly lose whatever they had. We have the opportunity. This is the country where everyone has a choice. We are supposed to get living wages. We have unemployment - if you lose your job at least for a while, but it's not enough. So we try to manage the best we can. Is there any hope to get out of this situation? Unlikely. We know we are not the only one in this position. You are struggling try to save, but you can't even if you are the best manager.

You're trying to succeed, but not too many people are able to. Even under better conditions, we are still struggling. How and why is all this happening? Who is to be blame? The computer is one of the best around us. It is time-saving and money-saving, there is no question about that. The only problem I can see is those people who were replaced by computers cannot find another job. It created human suffering. Whose fault is it? Yes, there are other jobs around, but we cannot find people who want to do them. Some jobs don't pay enough to make a living, but if we look close enough all jobs are important. I'm sure if they really want to, they could find work - no one should be out of work. If people have jobs, they can improve business because they will be paying taxes and they would not have to wait for the unemployment check.

What we really need, which is the most valuable, is time.

[Editor's note: material moved to memoir about doctors]

So try to enjoy life - no one has a lifetime guarantee. We learned the hard way. Our experience is the best teacher, if you are willing to learn. Today's generation is not willing to learn. Why should they? They have all they want to know. I understand very well. But that does not mean you are more knowledgeable.

Okay. They have the computer. It is wonderful. I agree indeed. If they know how to use it, they can accomplish a lot . Especially today, they begin at a very young age. Therefore by the time they reach a certain age, they become very knowledgeable and smart. In my opinion the question is: Is that enough?

What happened to the other subjects they should know? Perhaps you are not interested in how to raise your children to have healthy behavior? How to conduct yourself respecting others? Learn how to listen, how to get along with people, and start your own family. I know - you know all of that. You are getting along at home. What happens to your children? They need both parents to raise them. Be a good example so when they have their own life, they will be able to take care of their children. If you cannot accept that responsibility, you better start there - you have no right to have a family. If you really love them, you will be able to accept the responsibility that comes with it.

[Editor's note: material removed - repetitive]

remember as we were growing up (About my mother)
5-25-013

Today is Saturday morning - 7 A.M.
I was planning to write something else this morning. But now I have changed my mind.

I was thinking of our upbringing in Europe - about our parents - what it was like. The experiences as we were growing up - before our mother's illness, during, and after. Our brothers and sister and sister-in-law. I remember step-by-step - good and bad - how our parents struggled and worked very hard, with no stopping point, from early morning to late at night to raise their children.

It was a different world - then and now. Especially today's life, and the opportunities we have today. Comparing America and Europe especially. We were raised in a small village. A Jewish family on a farm with a small business. Nothing else around. The education wasn't as today. I'm going back only 100 years - that, I do not think, is too much.

[Editor's note: material moved to memoir]

Now I would like to go back - what I really wanted to write originally - where I began. About my mother. This I remember very well. Here, they call her "mother" - the one who gives birth to a child. For us, that is just the beginning.

From my experiences - about our dearest mother - she was the best kind, inside and outside. She was very beautiful - a devoted mother and wife who cared for the family. Well mannered.

Her background - her parents were well educated in Hebrew - I would say knowledgeable. They gave their children love and an education in Hebrew. Both sons became businessmen - and our mother, usually the girl became a homemaker. To learn to cook - that was a must - no cans to open. Our mother got married very young - a month shy of 17.

After they got married, she moved in with her husband and his family. Like they say it - mother-in-laws. It became a new life, with a beginning of her own. You can imagine - it was a different life. From my father's side - they were different. They were educated in Hebrew and also in business. At that time our grandparents were established. Our father was the youngest in the family and he remained with his parents and became a farmer.

Our mother - she was a real mother. Not just because she gave birth - but because she cared for her children. She protected us, loved us, and took care of us. She made sure of it. We had clean clothes. We slept well. She never missed out because she was too tired. I'm sure she was exhausted by the time she finished her daily duty. Like they say - a mother's job is never finished. It keeps you busy 24 hours a day. There is no end to it.

Our mother - she loved each one of us. I should say about our father also - he was affectionate and loving. They both sacrificed - even though I should not say that because they did it because they wanted to. They loved their family. Our mother, as we were growing up - she used to make sure we looked well and clean. I remember as a child, she combed my hair so that I was okay and ready to go to school. This was a routine with all of us, every day. I treasure those memories forever.

I can speak for all of us - those days were the best. Children will always remember their parents. I think that is the most important for a child's life - a mother's love and attention - she's there when you're sick or whenever you need, for any reason. Especially when growing up. That is a special time, if you are lucky enough.

We can't predict what will be our life and how it will work out. In a healthy atmosphere, under normal conditions - let's put it this way - the mother's responsibility should be the children, without any hesitation. It should be the parents' duty under any circumstances - both parents equally. Children, at a young age, should be number one. Remember this about children - we must show an example. They will learn what is the most important in their life.

If people want to learn, they always can - from experience.

Good luck to you all.
Maria.

another short story (Am I a good writer? Am I happy?)
6/8/013

Something came to my mind unexpectedly. How would I know if I am a good writer, or even a writer at all? I never thought about writing. I have written a few articles - I was told that they are good - but I really never thought that I have the capability or knowledge to write. I was, and still am, able to do whatever I wanted.

On the other hand, I did not have the opportunity to write or test myself. As a child, I was a very shy person. I outgrew it, but it took a long time. As I look back, it seems my facial expressions showed everything. I could not cover it up - it was all there. I had to struggle to face that reality; it was a setback for me. Even with all this, I managed. I did not have time to sit down and worry about it day in and day out. I was busy. I just kept on going. I always tried to look neat, to be pleasant and polite. I never showed off. I think I was liked - especially in business. In my personal life, I did not have much time - my family came first; anything else was secondary.

Today the weather is not as nice, and I felt a little tired, so I decided to take a rest. I did - for two seconds. I got up.

I met my brother coming out from another room, facing me, and he said, "I thought you were resting." I told him I was. He asked me, "What are you doing here?" I told him, "Something came to my mind, and I do not know what to do about it." His answer was, "Sit down and write, since your ideas are always good. I will help you write it."

He had an accident. He fell, hurt his shoulder, but then his hands became swollen and stiff. The last 2 years he's been trying to get well. And it is a very slow process. By the way, I am very lucky to have a brother like him. There aren't too many like him. I wrote articles about him, maybe one day we'll be able to publish them.

Now I am trying to convince myself how far I can go with my writing.

I question myself - do I have the ability to express myself the way it should be, or should I just forget about writing? What will be? When I was young I kept busy, and did not have the time to think. To make a living is first. I came to the U.S.A. and could not speak the language. I was very lucky to get a job - there weren't too many choices.

I came from a troubled world, where there was nothing but hatred - against one nation or another, or religion. It was somewhat difficult to adjust here.

Especially when you have a family that you left behind - and you love them - and are concerned about them. I have a strong family tie. I looked forward to a better life. When you are young, you have special dreams. One hopes that someday one will be able to accomplish a better life - and to hope that our dream will come true - for our family also. This is what I was asking and hoping for.

But we can never be sure it will happen. My sister and my brothers felt the same way. I must say we were very lucky. It is a miracle how all this came through - unexpectedly. We never dreamed it could happen. We cannot make any plans. Somehow, plans do not always work the way you want. There are disappointments - one after another.

Before we had a chance to really enjoy each other, our family - our sister, two of my brothers - were not with us anymore.

My brother and I miss them all very much. We are trying to keep each other company and enjoy every moment together with his children and his grandchildren.

And our sister's two daughters, and one granddaughter - whom she never had a chance to know - come sometimes to visit us. Our family - we are lucky, at least - we have the new generation who cares for us, and takes time out to visit us whenever possible.

We are not demanding. Just try to enjoy whatever we can.

I try not to make too many plans ahead - just take it as it comes. Our life is like a puzzle - we never know what comes next. But we cannot give up. We must try to work on it until we can find a way to succeed. This is my belief, and this is the reason I never thought much about the life we had - I just take one day at a time.

It seems we humans are stronger than we think. As I look back, there are many years behind me. I have enough experience - and I learned from it. I asked myself: do I like what I see and what I left behind? Would I do anything differently?

I never thought about living or ever passing away. I must say - I still do not.

I feel I have a job to do. I try to do whatever I need to do, minute by minute. I can get there with my dearest brother - we help each other. I am hoping our Almighty will give us strength to be able to take care of ourselves. It is getting more difficult day by day. Sometimes I'm not sure if I will make it.

I do not have anyone to help us… what will be tomorrow? Are we going to be able to get outside help? Oh yes, that is another story. My experience covers more territory - of all kinds. You name it, I had it.

Oh yes, now we have reached our golden years. Let's say - we did not find the rose garden. All those beautiful roses are missing. If you are lucky, you have a family - but they are too busy with their own problems. Or perhaps they are long distance. They choose a life away from the family. They do not have the time to write - or they forget about visiting.

They feel it is not their responsibility. They are there if they feel that something is left for them - for that, they will be there. Their feeling is gone. They do not feel that they might come to that point - where their own children will feel the same way. They are learning fast. I could say their parents failed to understand - or they are selfish or irresponsible.

Sometimes people forget - or do not care - about family. It seems it is getting out of style. What will be next? I am sure there will be children. They do not need any license for it - they give birth and just walk away. That is too much trouble - to take care of their children. Therefore, why do they need more trouble? They are young - they do not care - no responsibility. Like animals - but even they care for their children.

Now my question is are you really happy?

Do you have a family? I mean a loving family who cares for you? Children who love you? I know you have all the money you need. You can buy love - as many as you want - if that is what you want. What happens if you get sick?

Or do you get lonely? And you take time - and all of a sudden it comes to your mind - you wish you would have married and had a family. "Why didn't I think of it before?" You feel somehow empty - no one there to love you or understand how you feel - let alone understand what you are going through. No one who really cares for you - only the money. It does not make any difference - or, on the other hand, it depends what you are looking for - and if it makes you happy.

Imagine all your dreams came true. Sometimes the unexpected will arise - we never know beforehand. The nightmare comes in. When we had the opportunity to do something about it - and we failed. Now it's too late. Whom are you going to blame? Where are you going to run? All doors are closed. You and your family are all closed in. How would you feel?

Just think about it very carefully. Your freedom is in jeopardy. And your wealth - that you worked so hard for - disappears. You do not think it can happen? Think again. It can happen. There isn't any guarantee in life. No one is protected from hatred, envy, or jealousy.

Sometimes, some people are created with natural abilities - even without further education - others are not able to reach their own ability until it is too late.

For my own self, I was told many times before - why did I have to work so hard? Couldn't I make life easier for myself and others? But as is, I did not have any opportunity - it takes money, which I did not have, and no one to support me or reach out to help me - I was all on my own. I never depended on anyone - not even my family. Each of us had our own problems - struggling all our lives. I did not have time to sit down worrying.

At least at home in our village we had something to fall back on. Our grandparents settled there. Now we are living here. The question - were we happy there? It depends - what makes you happy? What do you expect to make you happy? Sometimes - just to be alive, having food and a roof over your head, and family - makes you happy. Sometimes it's doing something for others - like cooking and baking. Or writing. Perhaps that is why I write. I may not be a good writer, but it makes me feel better sharing what I've learned, and maybe that is happiness too.

about my nephew, the editor

I do not know where we are going to get the strength. It seems we are running out of strength. I stopped thinking - just do whatever we have to. However, I gave up writing and came back again. I find some time to write it by and in the computer. I should say, I always find something else to do. We have some letters we received from Europe, from our family, before they were taken away. Written in Hungarian language. My dearest brother was already translating them. We still have some more. At this time, I will try to help. Otherwise, his son will not be able to read them. And he would like to read and understand. He's interested in our family historically. Also, he is working on his father's history - it is very interesting, and he would like to publish it. He already wrote one book about the history of one of the American presidents, Theodore Roosevelt, when he was on Long Island. It is already in the libraries. Very good book, all the way through the story. It is creative - professional.

Therefore I know he's able to publish. He is ready - just putting on the finishing touch. He never learned as a writer. But he's well educated and able to publish it all by himself. He's very capable, and one of the best - a family man - willing to help whatever needs to even though he is busy full time.

He always takes time out whenever needed. Together it is beautiful to see a young man who cares for his family and makes sure they are okay - besides that he is a hard worker. Today it is not easy to make a living. It is admirable how he is struggling to make a living and be with this family. They are growing up. Every day they need more attention. All this takes time. Their children adore and love him. It makes me happy just watching them.

I must say, I am very proud of him. Only I'll say something: Very rare to find such a caring person - loving, understanding. His children respect each other. A young man, he has his own responsibility. He is a good soldier. He never complains, just keeps on doing what he feels is necessary.

Many times, I am deeply concerned about him. I wish I would be able to reach out more. In my heart, I think we need some miracle.

He's a model father - very proud of him. Also I must add, he also is one of the best son. Ever since I am staying with my dearest brother, I have a chance to know him better. He gives me all the respect and with the computer - he's the one who helped me. If I have any problem, he makes it sure I can use it. For me he bought the microphone and connected it to the computer.

It makes it much faster for me. If I have any problem, just call him, he comes. By the way, he bought the computer for his father a couple years back, and taught him how to use it. Ever since I came to live with him, he wanted to help me to use it. Makes it easier for both of us.

My nephew just stopped in for a moment. He's very busy lately, working very hard all around. Sometimes I wish I could help - I have good intentions, but I know it is not possible for me to do what I would like to.

It is way too much - even for a young man - especially like him. He is ambitious, caring, loves G-d. A different, unusual person. And a hard worker - you cannot find too many, especially today. It is very rare. I wish him strength, a good head, and all the happiness he well deserves. I pray to our Almighty One to reach out and protect them all. I have such a small family left.

Last night, my nephew brought us dinner. He is a very good cook. He always brings something for both of us. Sometimes he prepares it here, Many times he prepares it at home. If he has a little time, he always stops by to see his father. I am very proud of him - and his family. Thank goodness for that. At least today, we had some happiness. It is a blessing when you can have a larger family.

You still can be alone sometimes.

A small family - at least one of them - will pay attention to your needs. And I do not mean money. A good family relationship - you cannot buy it. It has to be in you. It has to be willing - not by force. Otherwise, it will not work. It does not matter how busy they are - they will find time to visit you. It does not matter what or when. You cannot or should not expect it. But if it does happen, you are very lucky - and count your blessings.

I think now I covered everything I wanted. I will come to a closing point. Wishing you all the best - enjoy life. Wishing you the best of health and happiness for all.

Your loving aunt,
Maria

Life around us
7/2/013

Usually I am up early - I try to do the morning chores before my aide comes in, which is usually 8 AM. By then, I try to do whatever I need to - this is my routine. My dearest brother is asleep. I try not to wake him up, but sometimes I do. Usually he is a late sleeper. We all form a habit.

In my working life, I always had to get up early. Every day my working hours were from 8 AM to 5 PM, 6 days a week - because of that habit, I usually still get up early.

We like hot cereal to begin with, and some melon. For me, the breakfast is very important. After that, I prepare something for lunch. At this stage of my life, it is not as easy as it used to be. I am not complaining. I just feel I am hoping that I will be able to keep up the best I can.

I cannot even think about tomorrow. What will be, it will be. As of now, I count my blessings. I'm very lucky - I have my dearest lovable brother. We, both of us, are very lucky for what we went through in our life.

Unbelievable how a person can endure so much and still be able to keep on going. Where is the strength coming from? And how are we able to manage it even now?

When and how are we able to continue every day - I do not know. Not even trying to think about.

If we had many bumpy roads behind, ahead we have to be more careful. We are still lucky - we can count our blessings.

Would our life be better if we just went on without looking back? When we do, I must say the golden years are not as golden as it is said.

The future we cannot see. For us, we can have hope. That's all we have left.

It is true - I am one person - can I change the world? I would if I could - you're right! Yes - I would like to do that. It would make me feel better with the knowledge that I did something for humankind - a better world to live in - for all the people, not just a few. It is a good dream. Maybe someday it will happen - for your sake.

I think I will come to a closing point. I think I had enough writing - let someone else have a chance to finish better than I do.

Wishing you good health, happiness, and that our Almighty will hear us.

We must keep our faith - we cannot give up. The most important - we must have hope. That is always a problem - we are hoping for the best - we have no other choice at this time.

Hoping for a better tomorrow. Meantime, just keep on going, stop worrying, and do what we can.

written by Maria

P.S.

I have a question - should you keep your nose clean, some way, from someone else's business? Yes, this is true; let's examine the other side for the answer. This is the most important question. For the answer, I will go to World War Two. No one wanted to get involved. If they would, they could have saved six million lives - people - children. It's unbelievable.

Okay, now let's go private. Should someone get involved in a family misunderstanding when that misunderstanding creates more problems for the person getting involved? And one or the family suffers because of the misunderstanding? Like parents and children, grandchildren - they stop seeing each other - not even knowing what was the reason. This goes on for years. If there is someone - a friend or one of the family - who knows them enough - should that person be involved to straighten them out and make it a happy family again?

I cannot change the world - that I accept - but how was I not able to change one of the closest people in your life? I hope they will wake up before too late. It doesn't matter what, it seems we have to just give up - which I never believed to do - I do not see any hope. We have to close the door. I leave it as is, but how can you watch someone very special to go through so much?

Families should also be able to get along. Otherwise why bother to get married, if you aren't willing to work at it? You want a family you can be proud of, and be happy and enjoy each other's company - but something somewhere gets all twisted.

Maria's 2nd book about Irving
3/18/012

Here is a life story I don't even know how to begin. This person is my youngest brother. His name is Irving. I usually call him my dearest little brother. Ideally, I should not. My family used to remind me that now he's a grown-up person and he has his own family. It is time I should stop calling him my 'little brother.' But on the other hand, my love is so deep that I feel it does not matter how old he is - he is still and will be my dearest little brother, Irving-kem,[54] forever.

His life story is of a very rare and unusual person. Wherever he goes, he is recognized for his nature. One of the best. People have respect for him. He tries to help others whenever he can without regard to different race or color, rich or poor - equally - and to his family - he is ready to serve and help, even his own sacrifices, without thinking of his life. Sometimes it is very difficult even to begin, since from day one he went through so much. You cannot even imagine - how can a person go through so much?

My dearest brother - he could have a happier life, and he deserves it.

As we were growing up, he was the youngest. He was our favorite, naturally. We were a very close family, and Irving was always trying to help.

With all his background, what my brother went through - he had more than enough. He was, and is, the best soldier. Now the third time[55] around... this is another story. You will be amazed.

I did not have anyone to depend on. I must say I managed quite well up to now. I did not have my own family - whatever the reason.

It happened that about 3 years ago, I was taken to the emergency room. I needed further time to recover so I went to a rehab center.

I was there for a couple of weeks, but was getting weaker. And after that I was told I needed more help - and would not be able to go home on my own. I couldn't have help for 24 hours a day. Medicare approved only 12.

My brother was against it. He felt I should not go home without full time help and that I shouldn't stay in the rehab. He wanted me to stay with him in his home - I could manage with less help, because he would be there and could help.

First I hesitated. When he lost his wife, he asked me if I wanted to stay with him. He had a large home - just for himself. I also lived alone. Why should I not move there? This surely would be better for both of us. The way I felt - he is right. The only thing crossed my mind - he went through so much. And now I'll put him in a position where he will lose his freedom. He

---

[54] The suffix *–kém* in Hungarian is an affectionate ending meaning "my dear." When my aunt wrote "Irving-kém," she meant "my dear Irving," or "Irving dear" not that his name was actually "Irving-kem."

[55] **Editor's note:** First as a combat soldier, then taking care of my Mom, now taking care of my aunt.

had enough problems in his life. I did not want to take advantage of him just because he felt he was responsible to reach out for me. I knew it wasn't just that. Our love never faded - not even a moment.

Yes, I needed help 24 hours a day, but I had other choices - to go in a nursing home or get someone on my own. But I wasn't able to - it would be too costly in a nursing home - and he did not want me to be there - and by myself wasn't a good idea. It is very difficult to find reliable people whom you feel you can trust - who are willing, or want to, and are able to do whatever is expected.

And besides - I knew him. He will care for me and will protect me. I knew his love for me. How much he cares. We remained - only the two of us - from a large family. I understood him very well. I felt - and I knew - sometimes you really need help.

My brother was right. We never know from one day to the next - as it happened for both of us. We cannot foresee it all.

Therefore, I believed - and came to see - it would be better for both of us.

This time, when my dearest brother asked me again, he also told me: "I will not let you go home alone. There is no other way."

At my dearest brother's invitation, I moved in with him, in his home. It was the right decision. Life is never simple. It does not matter why or what the reason is. It depends what kind of relationship you have - or if both parties feel the same way. Not because you need help, but because you care for each other so much, and you want to help each other. You get the reward - riches of love. The real one. Sometimes people forget the meaning of the word, and what it represents. Any person who experiences this kind of caring will understand what life is about.

When I came in - already the first day, I was getting better - was able to get around. There was some hope for me. I wanted to do whatever I could.

Nurses came only to visit, but we had no helpers yet. Here my brother did everything, which kept him very busy. He was doing the cooking and all the other chores, and helping me to get well.

I was hoping I would get better - able to help my brother too. He needed some help. I knew he would not allow me to do too much. Whatever I could, I would try.

Thank goodness I was getting better. But it did not last for too long.

I fell and fractured both of my hands and was in unbearable pain. My brother took me to the emergency room - Friday evening, when all the people had gone home. One doctor came in to see me, and he made some calls by telephone. I needed, I assume, immediate care - a specialist, which I thought he will get.

Instead, he told us the doctor was busy and will not be able to come to the hospital - I must go to his office. At the hospital, they put braces on both arms and sent me home. I still had terrible pain in both hands. It was so bad I could not stand the pain.

Without asking questions, we just went to see him the next day. We were sure it would be a hand specialist, because that's what we should have. Instead, this doctor, an orthopedist, told us I did not need any surgery - but I would have to go to the store where they would get me the "right" braces I needed. The store owner took the hospital braces off and placed the new braces - only the color was different - on my hands, and we went home to my brother's house. I have written before about waste in healthcare. This is just one more example. For the first few days, my brother helped me with everything because my hands were useless.

When we went back for the follow-up, he insisted - no surgery.

Here I made the biggest mistake. I should have seen a hand specialist. - I didn't even think about it. I don't know why.

Later, when I mentioned to this orthopedist that I had back pain for a long time from the LIRR accident, he sent me for an MRI. They found I had a fracture in my back.

The doctor suggested a new treatment for fractures - they call it segment injection. It is good. I will be able to walk upright instead of bent over. He made arrangements to do it in a couple of days. I agreed.

When they took me down for the treatment, my brother and nephew were in the waiting room. They had no idea what happened. One of the doctor's helpers threw me down onto the table so fast I thought I'd never make it. I screamed from pain. I was crying, and very upset.

I am sorry to say, but I was very disappointed. All those treatments were wasted. I remained the same - suffered even worse. I stopped seeing this doctor. He is a very nice person - as a person - but not as a doctor.

I'm still staying with my brother. Meantime, he has his own problems - he fell last fall and sprained his arm - he wasn't able to use it. He tried to help himself. Then he had a very bad cold combined with bronchitis. Luckily, the internist he was seeing was able to help him with that. He felt much better. He needs more help.

I am very concerned about my brother. He is very secretive, and does not want to complain. He keeps it to himself to protect me, even though I know about his condition. He doesn't like it if I am keeping secrets from him. When I ask him how he feels: "I'm okay." He is very weak and has trouble walking. I don't understand why it should take him so long to get better from the fall. He also sees the VA doctor.

Today, one of the therapists was here to see my brother. It will take a long time for him to get better. The only thing - my brother is not used to getting help. He always helped others, and now it is more difficult for him to accept it. He was always active. Now, he cannot do much. And besides the pain, he is very weak. He's trying so hard.

I can just watch and wait and hope, and that is very difficult.

When you cannot help yourself - at least you need someone who can help with whatever you need. Especially when you cannot get someone willing to help, or even able to.

He is having problems with his stomach and this makes him very weak. It's difficult for him to have something to eat. One of his sons lives nearby - it makes it easier to come over, and he makes sure his father eats properly. He is a very good cook. He shops and tries to make different food, to be sure it's okay. It is not easy, but whatever he makes, his father enjoys it better than before because his son is with him.

I do not want to create more problems - therefore I just try to help whatever I can. He is there for me - whatever I need. He is very good to take me to the doctor. When he needs one, that is more of a problem - to convince him. He is having more problems at this time.

He's a veteran from the Second World War, and also from the Holocaust. He served in the American infantry - in the worst places - lucky that he survived. He survived, I would say, hell - twice around.

He deserves the treatment and care. It seems even the government tries to shortchange our veterans, forgetting what they sacrificed. We owe them - they should take care of them first. They deserve that much. I see it firsthand.

My brother reminds me all the time: "*You worry about the world, as if you would like to be able to help. There are smart people - educated - who are more qualified than you are. Let them do their job. As for you, take care of yourself. That itself is a 24- hour job.*" What else can he advise me? Now I really should think positive - I didn't - and he had to convince me otherwise.

I am still asking our Almighty for guidance. I hope he will hear my prayers, but He must be very busy. I am trying to believe in him. There is nothing left.

I hope my brother feels better soon. He himself needs help. Now, for both of us - my brother feels he still can manage. I see otherwise. We both need, at this time, 24- hour help. Especially at night. We are very lucky - at least we have someone around to see in an emergency, or if there are any problems that arise. One of us can help out. It is not advisable to be left alone. Could be dangerous. We have experience - both of us - so if one of us is able to help, at least we can manage temporarily.

Especially at night, it is more difficult.

He is going through so much with all kinds of problems. Sometimes a small incident can create a big one if you let it go. Therefore, don't let that go by. Try to deal with it as soon as possible. All kinds of matters - business or private - should be dealt with. The problems come fast enough, then the cure at the end of the day is less expensive.

I will try to come to the conclusion. My dearest brother - he will have to pay more attention to himself and try to understand that our life is changing. And everything else along with it. Nothing stands still. If we want to have a healthier life, we must listen. Sometimes we try to overlook what bothers us - just forget - that can cause bigger problems, as I mentioned before.

Sometimes if we pay attention, our body tells us "take care of us." Stop, think, and listen to what goes on with us. We would prevent big problems and aggravation - and also additional problems.

We cannot just run without paying attention. You do not have the time for yourself - someone always comes first. I think it is time to turn around. Otherwise, you can get lost.

It seems today, just like everything else in this busy world, no one has time - or perhaps they do not want to.

I will try everything in my power to do so - to help him, whatever it takes. Hope I can succeed. He needs help more than ever. I hope he will be well as soon as possible. The problem is it's hard to get the right help. We will have to try to see to it he gets the right help, which is the most difficult task. I know we are facing a stone wall, whether we would like to face it or not.

I think I will come to a closing point - with the best wishes to all - Hoping someone, somewhere, will learn a lesson by reading this note, longer than I meant to. My little brother and family - I love you all, especially you, my dearest Irvingkem. Take good care of yourself. Try to enjoy your little family. And do not forget yourself. This is my wish and advice. Be well, and hope - that is part of your medication - and pay attention. Do not wait. With all my love to you all - especially my dearest Irvingkem.

This part I finished before I realized I would like to continue more briefly.

His life story will continue on - ongoing this story.
2nd.book of 3/18/012
Continuation the story of my brother.

I thought I finished my dearest brother's story. I was hoping he was improving by now. It seems, unfortunately, he had an accident - right in his home. Yesterday, he fell in his house. His son came and took him to the emergency room. They took X- rays - his arm is broken. He got a CAT scan. It is the right arm - on top of the sprain I mentioned before.

I would never have thought he would have this terrible accident. It seems there is always something unexpected. He always was the best soldier - and he still is. I am very disturbed by it. I still feel the pain and suffering - what he endures is too much for even him. If I could, I would take it away.

Only thing they know is how to charge - and how much. Yes, my brother was taken to the emergency room. For one X- ray and a scan of his head they charged $5,000. Isn't that outrageous? They have the nerve. A private doctor never would have charged that much. No wonder Medicare is going broke. It was a very small hospital. They did not do the job that was really needed, but the name is big - whom it represents. The name - not what they do. This is the way it goes. Just like everything else.

He never hurt anyone in his life. He is one of those persons - hard to find - maybe one in a million.

I asked this question so many times: Why does a good person have to suffer so much? Especially after what we went through. I thought we had enough. We did not expect so much more - honestly. I am afraid I am not as good a soldier.

I prayed every moment for his, and the rest of my family's, safety. I never stopped. I am very lucky to have my dearest brother here with me. As of now, he's going through a very difficult time. I hope and pray to our Almighty to help him get better as soon as possible. That's all I want, and am wishing for. We have the willpower - it helps. But it would be easier if we could get the right help. We've needed it for a long time. I am thankful to our Almighty for every step I take, for helping me to do whatever I have to do daily.

My nephew - his son - took him to see a specialist for a second opinion. Last night, he had terrible pain. I hope he does not need surgery. I am waiting to hear the news - hoping for good news. I am trying to write, but my brain does not work. Usually I have no problem - sit down and write. But today, very difficult. My mind is blank. I continue to wait for what was diagnosed - and what is the treatment.

I hope he will get better as soon as possible. I cannot think otherwise. He is my life. He was - and still is - the one who, without asking, reached out for me. And helped me. He took me into his home. He made sure I ate - especially when I did not have my own family. He has more to live for. He loves his children and his grandchildren, and he should have a chance to see them grow up and enjoy his life - what he missed out on for so long - that now he has the time and his own family to enjoy every minute. This is all he wanted to do. But this time, I could not accept anything. I cannot even begin to think about the unthinkable.

Sometimes I wonder if I will make it or not. And sometimes I have to hide my tears from my brother. At night, I am alone with him. I try to help with whatever I can. Still, my dearest brother tries to protect me. He doesn't allow me to do even what I can. It makes me frustrated - and I worry every minute. He shouldn't get hurt or fall. He went through so much and tries to protect me from getting hurt - but how can you? I try to do the same. I have to put on a happy front to prevent him from seeing me and to keep him from getting upset. Sometimes I cannot even pretend. It is breaking my heart.

His doctor feels it will get better - it takes time. He will have to see him again in two weeks. He is getting a little stronger. His youngest son makes sure of that. Always. So I am, too. My brother was always a very independent person. He is not used to being catered to. All his life, he helped others - even now.

I make sure he has his warm cereal first - this way I know he gets some hot food. I believe breakfast is very important - to start out the day with good nourishment. These days, he doesn't sleep well at night, even though he takes painkillers. After breakfast, he usually goes back to bed. His pain is still very severe. I don't know why. The doctor is waiting with the therapy. Usually they do start therapy as soon as possible - even within a couple of weeks. Now I don't know why it has been delayed, but his whole arm is still swollen and still has the black and blue marks.

It seems I can do more in the morning. Later in the afternoon I have a little problem getting around. I am trying whatever I can. We have no choice. My brother tries to do too much. He should not strain himself - with one hand especially, with the left hand. He doesn't want me to do much. That makes it more difficult, because with the right hand he suffers too much. I try to tell him: whatever I can do - it's not much - but it's better than nothing.

When someone has been active all his life, it is difficult to accept this terrible condition that he is in - besides the pain - to be outdoors now, like this. My heart aches to watch him and what he is going through.

I must tell you, it is very sad. And sometimes it scares me.

I'm trying to make my dearest brother as comfortable as possible. It's been two weeks since he broke his arm. Both of my nephews come to visit their father. Luckily, his youngest son - he is a lovable person, just like the nature of his father and a wonderful son, a piece of gold - and his family come in and are ready to help 24 hours daily if needed. They make sure he eats and that he's okay. He makes sure his father has everything he needs and is okay. He cares for his father and even me. And his family. People should learn how to take care of their family. Maybe we would have had a better world to live in.

Sometimes I tell my brother, "I cannot write anymore. My eyes, my head - I cannot think. It just doesn't work." My brother always assures me, "Oh yes, you can." He always tells me he likes whatever I write. He is wonderful. One of the best. I do love him so much. I cannot even express how I feel. My feeling never goes away. This feeling is real and very unusual. We - both of us - treasure that feeling forever. It pains me to see him suffer so much. And I cannot do anything to help his pain. Just watch him. I wish I were a magician - that I could take away all his pain.

Oh, our Almighty - where are You? Give us strength and courage. What can we do to make this terrible time bearable? We need You to help us through this ordeal. I know it could be worse. Yes, I know. But I am grateful for whatever we have. We need Your help. Sometimes I do wonder if You really hear me. I have no one else to talk to. My respect to You.

There's so much more I could write about you. Nothing but the best - because you are the best. Not because you're my dearest brother - but because you are the best in any language. I don't know if you ever talk about yourself. It's always someone else first. Even now - you are going through crisis, more than one person should bear - the suffering - one thing after another, but you always worry about someone else. Always - someone else comes first. I do understand you. But sometimes, you have to allow someone to help you. You should let them. You did everything all your life. Now, the time is here - let others do it for you. Thank goodness - we are here to help each other. Yes, I know - we need help, but we are lucky to have what we have.

PS
Here I would like to make a little note to my dearest brother.

First of all, I want to thank you for your warmth and your hospitality - to take me into your home in the condition I was in.

You had no idea what would be next, from one minute to the other, without hesitation. Only a courageous person like you could do that.

As I've known you all your life, you are always concerned about someone else. You never, ever think of yourself. Automatically, all your life, family comes first.

You sacrificed your life for your country and your family.

Your personality and your love reach out so much - it is unbelievable.

You are a father figure for all of us.

No one can see what you are going through inside. You cover it up so deep that no one can see it. The only way we know is the love you radiate - and someone who truly feels the same way can see it.

When I decided to accept your gracious invitation to come stay with you, I examined everything very carefully before I said yes. I came to the conclusion that you have a loving family, and if you needed help, they would be willing and ready to help you too.

You worked so hard, sacrificed your life, took on all the responsibility of what you must do. It didn't matter what price you were paying - and that price was your own life.

With my decision came peace of mind. Our love for each other never faded.

It does not matter what, it seems our feelings are similar. We both respond to each other's needs. You are a naturally lovable, caring person. You cannot find too many people like that in today's world. I must say - it doesn't come around often. It must be in you - and it becomes life. It's part of your personality, and it stays with you forever. Sometimes your own family cannot see or acknowledge that feeling. It is very rare - especially in the climate of today, with science all around us, everything is machines. There's not much personal touch anymore.

Wherever you turn, humans are being replaced by computers. The respect and responsibility that go with real connection - gone. Lately, I've seen it firsthand. I can tell - I'm no longer surprised by what I see and feel. I see the future ahead of me - so deep it scares me. What exists in the present is the future.

I am glad, for my sake, I will not be here.

The only thing I hope and pray to our Almighty - if there is one (this too is questionable) - is that it doesn't disappear like everything else.

What will stay with us is our memory, and our love - that remains forever. Anything that is real and ours cannot be broken. It does not matter who or what the reason is. It will not work to break it.

Now, I am trying to come to the closing - your life is part of our history.

Nothing but the best. A happier life we hope in the near future, with part of your family - your children and grandchildren. Hoping the other part will come around, so you can live life in true harmony and be responded to in the way you deserve. It should not be this way - your age, what you are going through, Without anyone recognizing what's going on between you and them - how much pain you are in.

No one can see it. No one knows it.

But now more than ever, I see it. I feel it. I know what goes on inside of you.

There isn't any recognition - on both sides.

I try not to judge, or butt in anyone's life - not now, not ever - If I've said it before, it's because today everyone is so busy, they don't even have an idea what's going on in the lives around them.

It is very sad - that a person goes through life in silence, covering up in silence, pretending nothing is wrong. Everything is "okay."

With all those problems - it's hard to believe. You deserve the best in life. And to my dearest brother -

Lots of love,
    Your sister,
    Maria

In my closing statement, I just want to mention - thank goodness my brother is getting better. He is continuing with outside therapy. He is improving, but it will take time. And we must keep on going with our life and try to enjoy and manage the best we can. I hope we will have the strength to continue with our life - in better health - what we all would like to have in our golden years. Sometimes it does not come as easily; it makes living more difficult every day. But we must try to do the impossible - with a little help. I really hope so. I try to do the best for both of us. Also, I want to wish you all the best in life - Happiness, good health, everything you dream of, and a better future for the next generation.

With love,
Take care of yourself.
Affectionately,
    Your aunt,
        Marie

I finished typing into the computer:
6:30 - 2012

My brother will edit it when - I hope - he feels up to it.

On lawyers, judges, and a crooked business

Editor's note: *The small family business was sued by a commercial tenant for breach of lease, even though the lease had expired. The business' lawyer missed a trial date, and the case was decided by default without a trial and was sent to a hearing officer who would decide the damages. When my Aunt wrote this, the hearing was ongoing. Eventually, the family business was vindicated at the appeals court. It was originally part of her essay entitled "2nd book, About Irving" and was separated from it as its own essay.*

Today's lawyers take whatever they can. It seems they are not for the client, even though they get paid whatever they want - it is still not enough. Is he a good lawyer? - only if he really tries to do the job honestly.

On the other hand, a judge should be on the level and conduct his cases honestly. For one reason or another, he can see - but does not see.

The innocent person has all the proof and is not able to present it. Why not? He has all of the information - especially with the computer in a short time, whatever you want to know. But the judge does not want to hear that. It seems it does not matter how honest you are - you are locked in and cannot find a way out.

Essentially, they should have thrown out this case and never let it go as far as it did. Legally, they can destroy an innocent life and their family.

The guilty will carry out whatever they want to; the innocent has very little chance.

Where is justice?

And they [the tenant] are dishonest people too, trying to help themselves. They are pushing so far until they succeed. It seems no one can stop them - and innocent people who worked all their lives suffer - there's no way to stop the ones who take advantage.

Even the courts can see it - and still allow it to continue. The innocent get washed out, left with nothing. And why? In my opinion, it must be easy money. Do you know any other reason?

This case should have been thrown out a long time ago. It's a fraud case - they're lying, and the court failed to see what's right in front of them, spelled out. Still it goes on - for years. How long can this go on? It's all lies - they're a crooked business.

There is all the proof, but they are not allowed to present it. The judge doesn't even want to hear it. The judge must have knowledge of what's going on, but still doesn't allow it to be brought forward. Both sides - the lawyers - they know what's happening. And it just keeps going.

In court, both sides are not in a hurry. They have all the time in the world - they're making money. They don't even respond to a phone call.

I'm seeing my young nephews run through the money they worked so hard for - that they saved - for their future. And now, nothing is left.

The unseen suffer - and the crooked ones? They have enough. It doesn't bother them - they're able to take it all over.

What a crooked business.

This case is just one example. I'm sure there are too many cases like this.

Home Health Aides revisited

My aide just came back from vacation. It seems she will never change. She is still trying to do the old routine - whatever she wants to. Comes and goes whenever she wants to, no questions asked. I spoke to my brother about the situation. There isn't too much hope. If this will continue, we will have to find another company - to get someone who is more reliable and willing to do their job. If there is such a person - I am not sure.

Now I have a new visiting nurse - maybe I'll be able to speak with her more about our problems. It seems she is more caring and understanding. I hope she will be able to straighten things out.

My helper came in today - but came later than usual. As usual, she wasn't in a good mood and wasn't very anxious to help. I have to be very careful - not even look at her, try not to talk, or even start any conversation. She made sure I got the message. I think until now she had her way. My brother was able to help me, and both of us allowed her to do exactly whatever she wanted. We had no choice. She could have been a very nice person - good-looking, nice - if she could control her anger. She is not the home care type like they tell you. She denies things - one minute to the next. Never know when the lightning will hit. Many times it scared me.

Now that my brother is not able to help me, we need her cooperation. I just wait until she is ready and willing - and hope she will respond. I must stay away as far as I can unless I really need something, if I know what is good for me - to have peace around me. Today, I already was reminded - "Don't push me." It takes a lot out of me to be silent. She does not realize what she is getting paid for. She got away with things before, but now I think the picnic is over. My brother - he knew before, but ignored it and let her get away with it long enough. Now, it's worse than before. I do not know how long this situation will last. It has to give - one way or another. I cannot take it.

She does not care if I live or die.

I just prepared my breakfast and am waiting for my brother so we can have our breakfast together. My helper is still not here. I would have let her go a long time ago. She makes her own schedule. I was threatened before by my case manager - if I let her go, I won't get anyone else. When she came here the second day, my helper mistreated me. She called me names - unbelievable - she called me stupid old woman, crazy - much more. She reported to her nurse that I abused her. The nurse called me and asked what my side of the story was. I told her, "I have no comment."

My brother - by nature, he always tries to make peace.

When she *does* come in, she is always on the computer - and so loud you cannot hear your own voice. The computer never stops. I do not know where she finds so many people to talk to - all day long. Very disturbing. Or she's lying on the sofa.

I think about other people's health aides - they have to do more, especially when they have a home with upstairs and downstairs. They want them to clean there too. I never wanted that. She makes a mess - she should clean up after herself. I am not her maid. I feel she should be responsible for that. She is supposed to do light housekeeping. She does not qualify. Otherwise, she should not treat me as she does - with insult and abuse. If I ask her to help with something, she does not respond. I very seldom ask. I do not even dare to.

From day one, she acted like she is the boss. She was so loud you could not even rest or sleep - forget about that - it was impossible.

My brother - he still does the cooking - or else if she tries to prepare something, her mind isn't there. She claims she can do 10 different jobs at one time. Yes, she can - but not adequately. She does not care. She thinks she will get away with it - and she has.

I must say I am lucky I did not get hit. I was very close. Her temper - you do not want to know. I am scared of her - especially when I am alone. When she comes in, she usually finds something - some reason or no reason. She does not care if I live or die. Sometimes she just runs out, slams the door so hard that the pictures fly - they fall all over the floor - I was crying, almost passed out.

She told me so many times she does not care what happens to me - even if I drop dead - "I don't care."

Many times, when my brother comes home, he asks me what happened. As I said before, she always has a story - lies. *Why would I lie?* He knows I am not that type of person. I worked all my life. I never had any trouble with anyone. I was always respected. I never, ever went through such an ordeal in my life. Every week she is ready to walk out.

She used to ask me if I wanted her to leave - I didn't. I would never fire her. Unless she wanted to leave - it was up to her. I would have let her go the first day. But my brother asked me to ignore it and be tolerant. He thought maybe she might change. In my heart, I knew she would never change.

She used to tell me she worked with retarded children, with people who didn't behave. And by the time she left, they had become well - behaved - like different people. Yes, I do believe it. I am sure she didn't do it kindly. With her temper, anyone would be scared.

First, you cannot take away someone's freedom. On the contrary - you want that person to get well and be able to function. You must encourage them and even help them - with kindness and understanding. People go through a lifetime - good or bad - and if we are lucky enough, our G-d gave us a brain and the ability to function at any age. No one - but no one - has the right to come in and destroy that or abuse it. Especially if someone is still able to think clearly and is capable of handling things. I just asked for some help - to make things easier, so I could manage and get along.

My aide came into my room to have me sign her working papers before she left. She acted like nothing happened - all this week, she was closed in, very quiet, different than usual. I didn't have any idea why, all of a sudden -

even though it happened many times before. Moody - not social. When I see the signs, I try to stay away from her. Soon after that, she told me, "You better stay away. If you say one word, I will walk out on both of you." She was nice until she could manipulate my brother to get what she wanted. Her personality is very moody.

Now, my dearest brother realized - by then - that I was right all along. He agreed with me all along. But he felt - and knew - how difficult it is to get someone who really wants to do the job.

Therefore, he tried. Because he is the type of person who tries everything in his power to work it out. I do too. But sometimes, the more you try, the worse it becomes.

Before my brother's accident, she was a different person. My brother worked with her on my behalf - Otherwise, it would have been impossible to communicate or get something done for me, whatever I needed. Nothing but trouble.

And now - in the worst time - she carries on like a different person. And had the nerve to walk out on both of us. And she wasn't ashamed to tell me.

And before that, she praised my brother - How wonderful a man he is. "How could my brother have such a troubled sister?"

Now my brother realizes how she used him for her own benefit.

Before my brother had the accident - every minute she praised my brother, how wonderful a person he is. She could not understand how I could be his sister - such a tolerable person. I knew all along - she is a fake person. She used my brother for her own advantage. My brother waited to see what she was going to do. But he ignored it. He felt they are all the same. Especially after he went through so much with home health aides.

Generally speaking - in my opinion - she should never have been a home aide provider. And to talk to me the way she did - with insults - Telling me, "Drop dead. Even if you get a heart attack, I don't care." She looked at me very seriously - and repeated the same thing: "No, I don't." I looked at her - unbelievable. She looked so cold. She meant every word she said. Her face was very cold - no feeling at all.

We tried to get someone for my brother - You wouldn't believe who they sent. These people were not able to do the job. They don't care who they send out. The patient's life could be in jeopardy. It was a middle-aged man - clearly disabled - not even able to stand on his feet.

Before an agency is allowed to open a business - are they ready for their responsibility to their client? I am sure they must have rules on how to conduct their job as required. First, they should hire qualified personnel. Second, they have to have rules to train them properly - how to behave with the sick - before they send them out. They must make sure they are doing their job. They should behave with understanding - respect - not allow themselves to be abusive. They should be able to understand their patient's suffering - not to add more to it.

The government is too busy to look into it - and to see how much abuse is going on in that business. The agency's staff should make sure their helpers get proper training before they send them out to the field - to live with sick, helpless people - mentally fit and capable of taking care of them with respect, and with care, as it should be.

If you need her - she makes believe that she does not hear you. You repeat yourself - still no answer. If someone comes in, her personality changes - but she does as little as she can. She gets paid extra for helping my brother too, but she is not doing her job. She should help him whenever he needs it. Oh yes - she forgot that. The agency claims they have no one else.

I do not know if next week we are going to have any helper. My helper left today. This time she was nothing but a bundle of nerves. After she left, we thought she might not come back. Usually, she calls the agency - but they never called us. No one ever called us or gave us any notice. This shows how someone who really thought she cared for him - believe me it is hard to swallow - my brother is so disappointed. He cannot believe someone who really talked like she cared for him and admired him - and now that he himself needs help - turned on him. All of it is fake. Like a double-cross. How can a person be so mean? To do that - she has no feeling for another human being. He is hurt so much, he cannot believe it is true. He saw before what happened with me - I was degraded, called all names I would never believe. But it is true.

About my brother - He also has a gallstone. For a couple of years now. So far, it has been okay, no trouble with it, and was told by his doctor, "If it does not bother you, leave it alone. It might not give you any trouble." Lately, he feels he has more trouble - chest pain, and his arm hurts. The right arm - the one that is fractured - that is enough in itself with the pain and suffering. The left one he is using, but it gives him more problems also. It is difficult to use it. In addition, his stomach is also giving him trouble - beginning with the gallstone.

It is very difficult today to find a doctor you can really trust and believe. My brother has difficulty believing and trusting doctors - or even being willing to see one. It is a big problem. When you come to a certain age, it seems no one wants to be there with you. It becomes very sad. I would call it age discrimination. They get away with it. We do not ask for more - just do whatever you can. I do not think that is too much to ask for. They want their money - why not give the care, too? It is not enough that we have to put up with so much from our side - they are not even aware. Or maybe they just don't care.

Sometimes they demand from their patient extra money because they are not going to work for nothing. The money they get from the agency - they say it's not enough. That's what it's all about. Money. Then they leave. Their agency comes after you and gives the patient even more trouble. "We gave you so many people, and none of them were good enough for you." They think they are very good, but they fail to tell the agency that they were blackmailing you for extra money - or else they would leave. You are afraid to tell the agency because those people were very shrewd. Very clever. They denied everything. And it backfires. There is nothing else to do.

I reported it only once. I refused to give them any extra money. I told them the truth. It backfired - the helper denied it. The person I liked - I could not afford it. I felt they took the job for whatever the agency was paying. Why should I give them more, extra? The woman told me how much money or gifts they were getting from other patients. When I questioned her, she said, "I am not going to work for nothing."

Thank goodness our Almighty let me have my precious mind and memory still intact. Now, a couple years later, I'm still able to use my mind and able to function as ever - except my body. I am struggling. I need, let's say, 24- hour help. And here I have it - but not the help I need - only by name. I do not know why I have to put up with so much suffering in silence. Not even one day - I knew no one should put up with so much aggravation.

At least I have something new to report.

My helper - finally - we have to do something about. We are forced to. We should, because she really became impossible. My social worker came to visit me. Finally, we came to a decision - what we have to do. As I said, she came here nothing but trouble. Especially with me. First of all, she is not properly trained for home healthcare aide. I said this so many times. And I was not able to convince anyone. Maybe I did not try hard enough. She is very convincing - looks very well, strong, dressed well, clean person. She looks like she is able to do the job. She has many trades, she told us. She does not need this job. She is doing it because she likes to work with people. And she is very religious.

They are using religion to cover up whatever condition they are in - saying they have none. Whatever they are doing - or failing to do - they believe they will be safe. They think they'll get away with it. Forgiven.

I had one - she went to church all the time. She used to tell me, "Oh, you just have to pray to the man upstairs again and again," and I had no idea what she was talking about. She knows what she's doing, and gets away with it - she never had any problem. "You must think positively," she would say. "You will get away with it." Her best friend was the priest. Every Sunday she went to church. Every day in the evening she had a cocktail. "You should try it," she told me. "You'll feel better." She was driving a beautiful new car. Before she left in the morning, she drank black coffee so she could drive to work - to my home. She was very attractive.

This morning, my helper did not show up. Earlier, I received a call from my case manager - who never bothered calling me before. She told me that my nurse told her I have complaints. If I have any problem, I should say something. Yes, I did that once. And she followed up - and told my helper exactly what I said, even though I told her not to mention it.

I thought she knew about the privacy act. But I was wrong. In this business, there's no such thing. They do whatever they want, for their own benefit - not the patient's. They're only interested in money and how much they can get. Anything else, they're not interested. And they are always right.

Now, the reality - why should I keep someone who does not care what happens to the patient? Who doesn't want to listen, whatsoever?

If a patient or the family sees wrongdoing by the aide and the aide does not want to listen, ignores it - and they hire people who are not able to, or not qualified to, do the job - and endanger the patient - and the agency does not care - these are very selfish people.

Then they turn it around and accuse the patient. It seems they never take any blame for their behavior. It's always easier to have someone else to blame. Irresponsible. The one who isn't guilty has to prove it, while the guilty one gets away - just like everything else.

I just cannot believe what I see - or accept it. I wish I could help myself, so I wouldn't have to go through this aggravation. It is very difficult. I feel like I'm living off charity, even though I know I worked for this - and very hard. It is not charity. But what can we do? We cannot deny we do need help. That time comes, and we have to face it and deal with it, whatever it is.

One thing I'm sure of, and convinced - I do not want this helper back. She always comes back. But now, I've had enough. I would like to try someone else. If she turns out to be what we need - okay, we'll stay. Otherwise, she will go. It doesn't matter what - we do not have to put up with it, with the aggravation - I do not have to. I have enough of my own problems to deal with. Today, I am expecting my nurse. I hope she will be able to clear up this situation. She is very knowledgeable and has enough experience to see what goes on. I do not have to prove anything - I hope she can see for herself. I never complained to anyone. Even now, my helper brought this on herself.

I am not a criminal. I do not like to be threatened. I went through enough in my life - only our Almighty knows the truth. Some people deny it ever happened. Therefore, I do not want anyone reminding me of the past. I do not feel I did anything wrong. I do not need a jailer. I do not need a dictator or a manager. Thank goodness I am still able to help myself, make decisions, and know right from wrong.

I just need an honest, willing person to visit and assist me a little. I am not asking for too much. My brother and I do not ask for anything we are not entitled to. After all, she is getting paid for something - I feel she should work for it, at least a little.

I must tell you - she did not kill herself with effort. She had it very good. We did not push her - or anyone - around. We respect people. We live and let live. But some people are never happy by nature. Some think they must always be in the driver's seat - and they step on you to stay there.

She was very anxious to come back here for my brother - she would get double pay for what they are paying here. It seems she got disappointed when she found out my brother cannot get help right now from the VA. So she changed her mind - that must be the reason she walked out.

My nurse just called - she will be here next week. She assured me not to worry - she will take care of it. She will find me some other help. She said I deserve better service than what I got. She will see to it - therefore I feel a little relieved.

Just now received a call from the agency: My aide is not coming back anymore. Finally. Now they say they will have someone else by Monday. I wonder what kind of person? I do not decide at this moment - I will wait and see. It took them almost two years to try to get someone else. I also was supposed to get help on the weekend - Saturday and Sunday, 8 hours each day. We never got it. Not even one day. I did not want anyone 7 days a week. Especially not *my* pleasant helper. I think five days is more than enough.

Lucky I was able to help myself - whatever I was able to. And my dearest brother was there for me and ever since my brother had the accident - I have been there for him. If not for me, my brother would be in big trouble.

So - that is the end.

For better.

At this time I'm waiting for my nephew. He went shopping. My brother is resting.

The headline should be: "Help Not Found - Again." That's how this morning feels.

So I want to mention what happened with my new health aide. As usual, my breakfast was ready, and I was waiting for my brother. It was the first day with my new health aide. She is very nice. It seems she may be in her early 70s - I didn't ask. As of now, it seems she wants to do a good job. The case manager called the first morning to ask if everything was okay with me. But before she spoke with me, she had already reminded the aide: "Make sure you're not doing anything else - and nothing for her brother. You're not supposed to."

She is an elderly lady. She has her own family - grandchildren. She is well experienced. It seems she has truly learned that in this business, you must have heart. It is very important - especially when you are dealing with sick people and the elderly, with all kinds of problems.

She is exceptional - very nice. You cannot find many people today who are as nice as she is. She is an elderly lady, but she is willing - as of now. I do not know if she is able. I feel very badly - I'm trying to show her what is possible. Therefore, I'm not sure what will be. I am taking my time. She wants this job very much - and you can see for herself. I hope it will work out. My previous aide - I am happy at least she left us. The nightmare is over - almost 2 years.

Now, I can finally say: For us, it's a happy ending.

We have to start a new life. We must get there - that is the most important thing for me.

On Managing Money

We cannot predict our future, no one can.

There are times in all businesses, even the best ones, without thinking something could come up unexpectedly and some problem faces us. It does happen. Where are we going for help? Some people are lucky to have a job and make a decent living with a family of children. But there are people struggling, some without a home, losing everything overnight, where can they turn for help?

Let's say you have a good job. You can get everything you want. You could go to the bank. You have to sign a piece of paper and naturally tell the job you have. You should stop for a minute and think. Ask the question from yourself, do I really need this money? What is the urgency? You are not thinking what happens if you lose your job, you can never tell. It does happen - you cannot foresee the future.

Even if you have a good job, you could even be a manager. You're their right hand in charge, you could be there so many years. Sometimes it does not matter how long or how good you are. You could still lose the job for many other reasons and be replaced by a computer. Even if the company is well known and have been in business for many years in good standing, you would never think it could happen to you. You saved money, you have a beautiful home, a nice family, and tried very hard to save a dollar.

You just happen to buy a new car - you really need it for the business. You will be able to manage. You have a good job, you are able to pay for it. Nothing is wrong. You felt you will be able to retire with good standing. And you were able to raise your family. But sometimes it does not work out this way, especially in a new generation. You must learn how you spend your money wisely, carefully.

So many people are in trouble in today's modern world. It's easy to borrow money, and some people do - without thinking how they are going to repay it. They are making just enough money to support themselves - so how are they going to pay for it? And what price do they have to pay, especially if they lose their job? There is no guarantee what the future will be - especially if you have no reserve or savings.

With a family, you can get credit very easily. But you must have control over your spending - how much you are able to spend - and you must think about tomorrow. Without any control, this is a big danger. You could lose everything overnight. After all your struggles, you may find you have nothing left to move forward with. Therefore, you must learn how to manage. Even then, you never know. Sometimes, we don't pay attention. How far can we go before we wake up - and realize we cannot get out? You went too far, and now you have to file bankruptcy.

It makes it very difficult - especially with a family and children. Some people like to have easy money without trying to work for it. You have to be very careful - how far can you go without a clear purpose, and are you truly able to handle it?

Learn the value of money. Money does not grow on the tree. You have to work hard for it. Live under a budget. Do not spend more than your budget allows.

If you have more, learn to save a dollar. Don't run for a credit card just because you want to charge something - it's very dangerous if you're not careful. Spend only what you can. Never worry if you have a dollar - make believe that you don't, because you never know when you'll need it.

Some people cannot stop spending - it's like an illness. There is a big problem - and danger - in that kind of trouble. You have to learn how to manage with whatever you have and work around it. Never try to copy someone else or be jealous of them, because you never know what the other person has inside. Sometimes we think the grass is greener on the other side - and then you find out they are in worse condition than you.

We must learn as children how to save a dollar - and how to manage by saving a penny at a time. This is important. By the time you grow up, you learn how to manage and buy only what you really need - and if you can afford it. Try to resist the temptation to spend. It does not matter what kind of business you are in - family managing or any other business - learning how to manage could pay off, if you prepare yourself.

This way, we learn to control and manage what is very important in life. Respect whatever you have, and try to be happy about it. And have responsibility for your own life. We sometimes have difficulties - you never know what may come up - and you must borrow. You have no choice, but you have to be careful and think about it carefully. You should not overspend - especially today. The climate is not the best. It's very easy to get into trouble. And do not expect someone to bail you out. You should be held responsible for your actions and your behavior. The way you make your bed, so will you sleep in it.

My Brother, His Sons, and His Grandchildren

Editor's Note:

This chapter reflects Maria's deep admiration for her brother Irving and her hope that his children and grandchildren would spend more time together as a family. As the "younger son" she refers to, I struggled with whether to include this section. It's not easy to be written about. And it's not easy to include something that may cause pain, especially within family.

But ultimately, I chose to include it because it bears witness to her truth.

The original purpose of this book was to preserve our family's life before the war, their struggle to survive, and the challenge of starting over in America. But survival doesn't always lead to peace. There were losses after the war, too: losses of closeness, of shared time, of understanding. This chapter is part of that aftermath.

My brother did visit our father, most often on his own. Family visits were much less frequent and usually brief. I don't know what shaped those choices. But I do know that the distance - however unintentional - was felt deeply, especially by my father.

None of this unfolded in a vacuum. Our mother had multiple sclerosis (MS), and the impact on each of us was profound in different ways. My brother grew up gradually losing not just his mother, but also his closest confidant, as she became more disabled. I, seven years younger, grew up mostly with our father, accepting her disability as normal, even as she became increasingly confined to a wheelchair and home. In many ways, we were raised in two different households.

Maria's words reflect her closeness to my father, her protectiveness, and her longing for a stronger bond across generations. Her account isn't the whole story - but it is an honest one. I include it not as a reckoning, but as a record. A reflection of what was hoped for. What was felt, and what was left unsaid.

-Editor

In life, sometimes we learn more from experience than from books. It's easier to learn from the books, but people never learn too much either way - this is my opinion. We have problems in life, sometimes we don't even realize it.

Families can break apart. This breakdown happens everywhere. I also have to say it can happen even among those who are well-educated, especially those who marry at a young age, without fully understanding what they are committing to. Later in life, problems arise - by then, they may already have children.

No one wants to hear our opinions - good or bad - and we often have good reasons for them. I believe if there is something that we can do to help someone, we should at least try. I don't mean to run their lives or criticize them, only sometimes, when a small thing could help. I decided to help - or try to help - my brother Irving because I know how much he loves his family.

My brother cares for his family and respects all kinds of people - rich or poor - he always did, and he still does. He is well-educated, bright, and a graduate of one of the best universities. He grew up under difficult circumstances - in a family affected by illness, where our own father had to sacrifice a lot for his children's sake. This was my brother's example, and he tried to follow it.

Now, as a husband and father himself, he worked hard to make a better life for his own family. My brother took care of his sick wife, while trying to make a decent living. At home he had to prepare food for the family and do the shopping. All this was enough work. Then he had strangers in his home, before coming to this point he was doing it by himself. His wife was able to walk when someone helped. First she refused to use the wheelchair and that created additional problems. When he needed help it was expensive. It was difficult to find the right type of help that would be able to lift her from the wheelchair or wherever it needed. His wife suffered with multiple sclerosis.

He worked without any complaints. He took time to go to the temple every Saturday. He learned to read the Torah and he was very good at it. And he continued to read almost every Saturday, even bringing his wife and her aide with him, making it his routine. He also was involved in the temple as a grounds chairman and was helpful with whatever he could to cut costs for the temple. This kept him busy and gave him some escape from his situation. He didn't have other time for himself, and never had a chance to think about his own needs, but he never forgot his two sons - not even for a minute. What he went through, no one really knew - because he never complained. He sacrificed himself for his family.

You cannot tell what is behind a closed door until you open it - and if you are a good soldier, you never walk away. Even so, my brother managed to give his children the best education he could. One of the best fathers - who deserves respect and love.

He raised two beautiful sons - well educated, finishing from the best universities, both with the degree of engineer, able and capable to do whatever they choose. They graduated with high marks.

They are in business together - what the father set up. They helped their father when he needed them. Because of this, they didn't have the chance to gain experience outside the family business. They missed out on learning the skills needed to run a business independently. They are supposed to work together as a partnership - but sometimes this does not happen, and one partner has to carry on whatever it is.

As time went on they wanted to get married. With little room around the house, he could not even begin to have a normal surroundings for young people to bring a young lady home to entertain. It wasn't a normal atmosphere. Everyone paid the toll.

Eventually, the older son decided to get married. He did. After the wedding, they were looking for a home, but it was difficult and expensive. With his father's help, he purchased a building to fix it up and live there. After the building was repaired, they moved in. They were happy. Later, both my nephew and his wife said that the house was not desirable for many reasons. They were not happy in that house. They were looking for another, but it takes money - and with today's economy, it's very difficult to purchase and maintain a new home. If they could sell this house, then they could look around for a better one, in a better location.

The older son is also very busy trying to build his own business, which is never easy - especially in difficult economic times when so many people are out of work and struggling to make ends meet. We've had unemployment before, but this time feels worse. Many people have lost their savings, even their homes. It affects all of us, no matter where we live.

Each son has a family: the older son has two children, and the younger son has four. The younger son lives nearby and often visits with his family. His situation is difficult, too. He works very hard in the shared business. He doesn't sit around waiting. Like many people today, he faces financial pressure. Thankfully, he has a strong education.

My brother wants to be there for both of them, to help however he can. But it's not easy. He established a small business, and now he would like to see that his family has an easier life than he had. It's not enough to make a living for both families, but it's enough to start their life. In the meantime, until something comes up my brother helped both of them. All his life he wanted to help, but wasn't always able to. So where do things go wrong? The roots start at home. Are you happy at home? Can you function at work if things at home are not peaceful?

His sons are trying to maintain what they have and find new opportunities. But expenses today are so high - whatever you make, it's never enough for a family.

But when a business is a partnership, and especially when that partner is a family member - it brings added pressure. In this kind of situation, the burden often falls unevenly. One partner may end up doing more of the work, while the income is shared equally. This becomes frustrating, especially when the silent partner fails to see that equal pay must come with equal effort. Without open communication and fairness, problems fester. What once was closeness between brothers growing up becomes strained. Communication breaks down.

The brothers see each other in their shared business, but the families do not get together, why I don't know the real reason. But I know that it would mean a lot to have the family get together and enjoy each other, children and grandchildren of both sides. Unfortunately time goes by, years go by. If either of them would need help, my brother is always ready to do his best for them.

The younger son lives close by and spends more time with him. He comes with his children all the time to visit their grandfather, with love, affection, and caring - you cannot get anyone better than they are. He is the best - a caring, loving person. He never forgot where he is coming from. He shows it, and never forgets to visit his father and care for him, and appreciates what his father did and how he raised him - that he sacrificed his own life, 24 hours a day - it's unbelievable what he went through just to make sure his children wouldn't have to work as hard, and to make life easier for them. That's all he wanted to do.

The older one does not live too far either - just in a different town - but his family is always busy when invited. They never have time to visit their grandfather. There are always excuses - too busy. They do not care for him at all. What a shame - they miss out on the best of life: love, happiness, caring - the value of life. When they come to visit, they might come to say hello and goodbye in the same breath, before they even come in. They spend a few minutes, take a picture - just to have proof to show, "Yes, I was there. I can prove it to you." And they show the picture. But it doesn't say how long they stayed, or how little time they spent.

This son, his wife, and grandchildren behave like strangers.

This is not what they should do. One day they might wake up. It could happen to them - but it will be too late.

The older son is very busy making a living. There isn't enough time left for his family - to see what's happening around him. And his wife is all the time teaching - what I would call hatred - their children how to forget where they're coming from. This is so hurtful - especially in a family - towards a grandfather who cares for them, loves them, and deserves the best love and affection.

The older son calls his father every day and tells him how much he loves him and cares for him - but only by words, not in reality. When he visits alone, this son is so busy that he does not have any time to spend with his father. He comes for five minutes or so. It's not enough time to be together and sit down and talk to each other like father and son. And this is all that his father wants - to see his family and his grandchildren. It seems that will never happen.

He should care for his father - take time out and make sure he gets quality care, to show him you really appreciate what he's done, helping you. He deserves that much.

The job this son is trying to accomplish in the business is very complicated, and he is still continuing to educate himself - and he's doing a very good job. He works very hard - he puts in so many hours - he's not lazy at all. Therefore, he does not have any time for himself. He has to travel on his job. The locations are in all different places. You have to be very good to accomplish whatever he does or tries to do, but it is a very complicated situation he's in. He could have chosen an easier job, but he loves what he does. I hope he makes it. He deserves that.

Here it is very complicated - difficult to understand - what is the problem that he keeps himself so busy that he does not have any time for himself. His wife, I must say, she does not have - compared to him - the qualification, but by choice they got to know each other. Sometimes it depends on the personality - not just education - if a person without education could be well and happy. From the outside, it seems they are very happy, but something is not right.

The question arises. Ever since Day 1, you could tell her personality - it is very unusual, self-centered. She knows exactly what she wants, and she will not stop until she gets it.

Therefore, when people get married and they don't take enough time to examine the situation - or, blindfolded, they rush into getting married - they are not prepared and did not take time to know each other. This is the biggest mistake. It should be very important how to choose the right partners. Sometimes problems arise from nowhere, and you are circled in - lost - looking for a way out, for a solution. It makes it very difficult sometimes, feeling locked in and trying to deal with it. Especially when you didn't take the time before, when you had the chance, to look at the situation more carefully.

My brother loves his family, and he tries. It seems that somewhere, communication is broken. No one knows how my brother feels. He tries to cover up his feelings, but I see it many times - his true feelings and heartaches.

I believe that my brother deserves better. He is not happy about the distance. He went through a lot of hardships with his life. He's not getting younger and is not asking for any rewards, what he really wants, nothing more, is to see the grandchildren, and I believe that he deserves it. If there's a will there's a way. It would be great if they would change their minds and realize what life is really about.

My brother does not want anyone to support him, but he would love to have them - both of his sons - come around, but that's not happening. The two families broke apart. They forget they were brothers before their marriage. They were very close to each other - caring and loving each other - and now that strangers come in, they don't even want to know each other. All of this came unexpectedly, and we can't understand why - there is nothing anyone can do.

Let's say, under other circumstances, if there is still a way to do something about it, usually a person would welcome such a move. But this is a very unusual case. On one side you have my nephew who was taught to love and respect. The other side, his wife, something must have been wrong in how she was raised. Something must have happened in her life to create such anger - to not be able to forgive and forget, and after a while at least try to get along - show some interest.

Everyone is so busy they do not know how the other person feels. It hurts my brother inside without anyone noticing it. Sometimes a little thing could help to add more happiness to the person's life. I observe the family close to us. They have the right to live as they want to, and sometimes we fail to understand that they have their own feelings and we do not take them into consideration.

When I try to say something, it might not be the right time or I try to express my feelings with my best intentions, sometimes it may be better to wait. In that way, it would be easier to explain why I said it - that I wasn't trying to interfere, only trying to bring it to their attention. You do not want to be involved, but if my brother is not expressing his feelings, and he's the one who should be able to speak to his family and be able to express his feelings, I feel I have to say something. When I got involved, they misinterpreted and I created a big problem. They have their own mind - nothing and no one can change it. They have their own excuses.

I decided to send a note to his older son and daughter-in-law, hoping they might better understand how much Irving cares for them. I couldn't say getting involved created more problems - the problems were there way before - but after I did it, it became intractable, like a stone wall with a foundation so deep. They used to call me too, but not anymore. I haven't seen them in over a year. They say they love me very much, but they're always busy. My door is always open if they ever want to come. Irving doesn't want to ask them anymore - he understands the situation. It seems that the two wives don't get along, and that's why the families avoid being at my brother's house at the same time. But there isn't any good reason for that.

One daughter-in-law is American, the other is Israeli. Before my nephews got married, they cared for each other very much. But after marriage, it seems that cultural differences and misunderstandings created distance between them. All he wants is his family together.

His younger son has four children. The youngest is just seven years old. They are very bright. They speak English read and write and also understand Hebrew. All the children are able to speak fluently and write in both languages. Amazing how they want to learn. They began when they started to speak. And since then, they keep on learning.

They all play musical instruments. The three girls play the violin, and the oldest enjoys playing the piano and the oboe, and she does beautifully. The second plays the flute. The youngest, a boy is learning too, and sometimes all four play music together. Their father and mother also play instruments and love music. They are wonderful parents and spend time with the children. They make sure that the children want to, and are willing to learn. They like school very much.

Even though they are very busy with other activities as well, they always make time to bring the children to visit their grandfather. They come to visit whenever they can without any hesitation.

Usually the youngest son and his family come to visit their Grandfather on Saturday afternoon. They walk here if the weather is nice and stay for a couple of hours. They are beautiful children. I am happy to see them too.

My nephew and his wife go in the evening to bring back fresh pizza, and while their parents get the pizza, the grandchildren have ice cream. They love their grandpa to serve them.

Some weekends the children like to stay over and want to help my brother. The oldest helps Irving with the computer, teaching him how to use it. If you need anything to be typed, she's there to help. You can dictate to her and she types it almost as fast as you can speak. My brother dictated a letter to her and she typed it beautifully and correctly. The youngest daughter, whenever she comes over, first thing she does is look for me to say hello. If and when I am on the computer, automatically she's looking if I need any help. Sometimes I do have a little problem. And this young lady - in a second she will find it. Before I have a chance, she already corrected it. Sometimes we all have some questions. As I see it, some children are capable as young as they are.

My brother also tries to get some surprises for the children. He loves them. They love him too. Every one of them. They're very good children. Now they are growing up - ready to help. They like to help themselves also.

Sometimes they come after school, too. The children are busy working on their homework. Their father instructed them: First they must finish their homework - then they can play. They do follow what they're told. They are doing a wonderful job - very well in school. Their grandfather graduated from one of the best universities, therefore I'm not surprised his grandchildren are doing well. Their family works together - a close family. Their children come first. They are model parents. I am very proud of them.

My nephew's oldest daughter just graduated from middle school and will enter her first year of high school. She loves art. She shows talent. It seems whatever she does, she shows she is very talented. Even now, as young as she is, you can see it - it seems to run in the family.

They even help to celebrate Father's Day with my dearest brother - his grandchildren celebrate with emotion. I was joining them. I am very happy to have them over. My helper was also happy to see them. She's very good with children - the introduction was successful. They like her. She has her own grandchildren, therefore she can understand what is going on and is able to communicate with them. This way they can enjoy each other.

That's what it's all about - to teach them, as young as possible, how to get along with people. This way they can understand how to be a better person and communicate with all kinds of people.

That's what life is all about.

My brother would like to see the families get together. Sometimes, we think a small family will be closer to each other. In my opinion, that is not always so. The cousins are almost the same age. It would make him so happy to see them spend time together. But it seems one side of the family is too busy and hasn't been able - or willing - to do it. The younger son's children are very good children, very affectionate, and they love their grandfather. They visit often. The other grandchildren should try more to find time to visit. Their Grandfather loves them more than they realize. As is, he cannot understand why they are always too busy.

He is one of the best there is in this world. You cannot find another one like him - he deserves better treatment. It is not too much to ask for his grandchildren to visit. I know very well he loves his older son very much and wants nothing but the best for him. I know. I watch him on many occasions. But when they come only to spend five minutes, I cannot understand why.

Especially when you reach our golden years - we are looking for some happiness. All your life we are hoping the time will come to enjoy each other - especially one of the best fathers who cared for the world and tried to help others - and then to see him treated this way? It's unbelievable! My heart aches to watch, and I can do nothing about it. A stranger treats you much better than your own. The grandchildren are getting grown-up and their parents have no time to visit their grandfather - too busy - they have time for everything else.

I was there when they left silently, I have seen what he is going through. He does not want to talk about it, but the pain is there. I really cannot understand such an attitude toward one human being from another - it feels very cruel. That's why I was trying to bring this to his son and daughter-in-law's attention. I did not try to interfere, but I understand my brother more than they do.

As of now there is no change. People who were once close have become like strangers. Communication disappears. There seems to be no way out. I wish both sides the honesty and sincerity to try to learn how to communicate and improve their lives. If they would only try it, I'm sure life would be better by not being angry. If they just accept things the way they are, the situation becomes hopeless. I'm sorry to say it is a heartbreaking situation. In my opinion it is dangerous to hold on to it.

I believe that my brother deserves that the grandchildren should come and visit him. His oldest son tells him how much he loves him, how much he cares for him. That's why I cannot understand people do not realize how much they hurt the other person's feelings. They're not doing it to hurt him, but they should try to understand their behavior. They think that someone else is at fault and this adds to the problem. If they would forget, maybe it would be easier and things would be worked out. As I said before, if there's a will there's a way. I don't want to dictate anyone how to run their lives. I wish them well and hope their families and children will come together, get to know each other, and learn from one another. I would be happier if I knew I did help my brother to have his dream come true, before it's too late. All this *can* be done. Try to open up. It might be easier than you think.

Their father, I would say, is one of the best. He sacrificed his own life by working very hard and taking care of his family. He tried everything. He never complained that he was too busy or too tired. And when more problems arose, he still kept on going - like a good soldier would. He was the best. He is still caring, loving, and still tries to help out whenever he can - without hesitation. Therefore, I feel his children should listen, understand, and learn what goes on around him - and pay attention. Try to show a little more understanding.

I will come to the closing point. I want to wish them the best of health and a good future for all of them - children and their grandfather, who cares for them and loves them all - individually - more than they will ever know. I hope it will come about. I do love them very much, each individually. They deserve a happy life - and a healthy one. All of them and my brother together, enjoying their children. In the future - happiness - nothing more. The best of life. They are very close to my heart.[56]

---

[56] Maria wrote this chapter from a place of love and concern, but not everything she believed about the situation was accurate. The reasons our families drifted apart were far more complex than she could have known. Still, her words reflect what she saw - and what she hoped for. I leave them here as a record of both.

- *Editor*

My Vacation (Introduction)
3/14/2013
This is the introduction to the vacation story.

This is an imaginary story - how I came to write about it. It is a very interesting novel. It came unexpectedly. Then my dearest brother asked me to write or fill in these memories about what he missed out on in his childhood. He tried many times before - asked our family - maybe they could tell him, but he would like to know. It happened to be a very painful subject, even to think about. Therefore, I thought I would try to reason that he has the right to know. I began to sit down to compose my article as our life history.

The name: *As I Remember*. It is a true story.

I wasn't sure how to start. So we could not be so cruel - heartbreaking. Make it gentle - as it happened - it did not matter how you put it. It is a very painful story.

On the other hand, I came to the conclusion I should write another novel - something with humor and funny. I wrote both of them at the same time. It is the way they came to exist. This way, it would be easier to write, even for myself, whatever I wanted to. This way I would be busy enough and able to accomplish whatever I started out to do. It seems I was able to write and succeeded with different ideas and a different story.

I concentrated on my memory, plus created my imaginary subject. At first I wasn't sure how I would be able to have two different subjects at the same time, but I tried to think about it.

Before I knew it, I had pen and paper ready to write. I came to a conclusion - first the name - and before I knew it, I had seen the name *As I Remember*. The second one: *My Vacation*.

I decided that I should create something interesting, different, with humor. The reason is that I know my dearest brother - that he would like it. He is a serious - minded person. I would say educated. All our family's dream was to make sure he had a good education and would be able to succeed on his own. I took that into consideration. With that thought in mind, I sat down and began my writing. Two books at one time - you might say that it is impossible. It is true - I did it.

Before I knew it, I did both very well. In a short time - in a couple of weeks -400 pages. I wrote an hour here and there. As I look back, it was no mistake. I did not get confused at all. I just continued, until I created two books instead of one.

Finally, I came to a closing point, and gave it to my brother to see what he thought of it. He liked it. And he was amazed when he got to read it.

Especially since I wrote all this by hand, so fast, that I had trouble writing - because my hand could not follow my thoughts with the speed the ideas came into my mind. I would say my secretary was not able to follow me. I became faster than I thought. Without any problem - it came to me naturally. I myself could not believe it. I never studied, never wrote anything before.

My brother suggested and insisted that I write other stories. Before I knew it, I was writing other subjects. With my dearest brother's encouragement, I owe it all to him. My memory in my golden years - I say it is very good. I have no problem. That I thank to the Almighty.

Now I've created many articles. I was told they are very good.

My nephew considers publishing them. I hope it will be successful.

With good reading, we can learn about life - that everything is possible if we really want to. Now I can come to a conclusion. Until next time, best wishes to you all.

Written by Maria
Edited by Irving
Published by Sherwin
3/15/2013

P.S.

This imaginary vacation story itself is something different. This is an unusual story - worth reading. Maybe you can learn about life. It could be a real story - whatever you want to make it, and however you choose to take it.

As I finished this novel, I'm in my late 96th year of age.[57]
I composed the story and finished it with pleasure.

---

[57] Editor's note: That my Aunt Marie could complete this story in her late nineties, in a language not her own, is itself extraordinary. It shows not just her persistence but her refusal to stop creating. I include it primarily for that reason.

My Vacation (The Imaginary Episode)
2009 November 25
by Maria Gluck

  I've decided to get away for a couple of days, just to change the atmosphere. It may help me with the different surroundings in the country.

  First I arrived, I met the lady who checks you in. She wasn't very impressive, the look and the person. I was surprised to find someone like she, with a very dull personality and without an impression. Also, I noticed some women guests complaining. There was a large swimming pool in the front where people arrived. The impression was that I did make a mistake coming here. A woman stopped me as I was getting into the building, asking me if I'm going to stay and how long. I told her I haven't decided yet. I asked her if she is staying here and if so, how long. She told me that she was not happy here. She would like to go elsewhere, but she doesn't have a car. I told her I didn't have one either.

  As I was checking in, I noticed a young lady in the next room to the office. I just checked in. She did not look like she has any special talent, just a young woman. I did not pay too much attention to her. When all of a sudden, she noticed me and was walking towards me and looked up to me. Her first question was, are you a professor or maybe someone in that field? I said no. I am not. I asked why she is asking all those personal questions. She answered, you look like very talented. You are the first woman I can see is very different. I can tell as soon as I saw you. We have women coming here just to be picked up by someone, but they have no brain. Men don't like people like that. I want you to meet someone that will like you. Would you like to come with me? I want you to meet them. I asked her why she's so sure that they would like me. Then she told me that she is the coordinator who arranges the seating for the company, to see that they will not be bored at the dinner table.

  They were a group of professionals, all kinds of people. I did not like any one of them when I saw them at the table, but you, she said, that they will like. I told her I do not want to meet them now, because I am not the type to go after anyone. I did not come here to meet any special people. She asked me what is the reason? I told her that I came here just to get away for a while. I turned to her and asked her if she could seat me to a table where I wouldn't be bored. I will appreciate it. I appreciate nice people, friendly and kind, but I'm not looking for a husband. She said that she could tell, she thought, it would be good for all the people. Okay, you are knowledgeable and you have very good judgment. You know how to make arrangements, therefore I trust you with the table settings.

  I did not think that in this place you need any formal wear. I did not bring only one dress. I have one black dress and even that I thought I will not wear it or will not have to use it. Now she informed me that they do dress up for dinner. I told her I did not know, therefore I do not have any dresses with me, only slacks, hope that it will be suitable for Saturday evening. Today was Friday and after our conversation we departed and she took me to my room.

Where I was staying was a surprise, it was a very nice room. It seems friendly, large windows, for one person. I expected two people since I ordered two in the room, it would be less expensive. I asked this person with me if this is a private room? I asked for sharing the room with someone. Is this more expensive? I did not plan to pay more. She said this room is better and told me and assured me not to worry that this room will be less because they like me, therefore they wanted me to be comfortable. I might not like the people who might be in the same room, therefore they have decided to make an exception just for you.

I spoke to this young lady, I knew that her ideas were very good and I was grateful. I will tell her when I see her a little later for lunch.

I arrived in time, but they already finished lunch. I was hungry, so I asked the person who brought me up to the room if I could get food to be brought up to my room. I know it is a lot to ask, but I appreciate it, maybe a cheese sandwich, I would pay for it and then I'll have something to eat.

Later someone was knocking on my door, I opened it, it was my young lady with whom I had the previous conversation. She brought a tray with food. I was very surprised to see her. Oh my! I'm sorry that I bothered you. I didn't mean to. Just a sandwich would have been enough. And I know how busy you are here. You are a very unusual person yourself. I asked how much I owe her. Please charge it to my account and also the tip. I thanked her for being so nice to me.

I hope I will not disappoint her. I know that she was going out of her way to make me happy. I told her that I do appreciate everything that she's doing for me. And she told me that this lunch is free, no charge. It was her fault for missing the lunch. She held me back talking to me, therefore owed me this lunch. It was her fault. I thanked her again and we parted.

I had my lunch and I was very happy. It was a good lunch. This was enough for dinner. However, dinner will be later, but I don't know if I'll be able to eat. I was thinking, if she really said that and it is true, what she told me before about setting me with the professionals' table. I don't know how I will be. She thinks I'm smart, I've made a good impression on her, but now what will I do, I cannot even speak correctly. My English is a flop. I haven't spoken English for a long time. My brother, G-d bless him, he was trying to teach me just beginner's English. Here I did not listen to him and now here I am at a big table, my brother is not here, I'm all on my own. Maybe I should just check out and go home, that would be easier. Now what can I answer? I do not know what to expect here. Now it's time to go. I have now a lot to do, only thing left is to get dressed in whatever. I have to pull myself together and act like always, talk if they ask me, be careful, talk slowly, think before I speak. If they do not like, it's too bad. Next day I will tell the girl and I'll move from that table to elsewhere. With this I was ready to make my move.

I went down in my slack suit, as I planned. As usual, I always look nice, no matter what I wear. Now I thought like it's a date. When I arrived downstairs, this young lady waited for me and she was wearing her long gown. She looked beautiful, I couldn't believe it when I saw her, it was a big surprise. I now was convinced that she is a very smart woman and has good judgment. And she knows people well - as young as she is. She welcomed me and showed me to my table where a group of people were seated. Only one more seat - it was waiting for me. She introduced me. I was surprised to see such a group with such a very good impression. Finally, I was very surprised with the welcome I received. I was thinking, I hope that I will not disappoint them, but all of a sudden I felt more at ease.

I remembered when I was working in the restaurant, as a young person I was very good, I was able to talk to all kinds of people, rich or poor, smart ones. I thought back and I said to myself, now you are in the same situation. Not looking for a husband, just wanted to relax, this way you have nothing to lose. Something to gain - who knows, maybe the best thing ever happened to me. One never can tell the future. It might be a good surprise, why not just sit down without anything in mind, I thought, just be yourself. So far what I see, it's okay.

I was seated, they introduced themselves each and every one. I naturally didn't remember their names, I was listening. Then they started to ask one question after the other. I wasn't in a hurry to give any answers, I felt I will have time. I'll try to learn what they are doing, their specialty. One was a writer, and one was a professor, and one was an advertiser. Each one of them were telling their business. They were all retired and enjoying their life. They did have families and grandchildren.

I was waiting to hear what will be the next question. I thought to myself that they will be asking me if I'm married or if I have a family. The truth will come out sooner or later. I learned from my brother to listen - silence is gold! Listening is a virtue, you can learn more. Now is the time to practice it. Good behavior, I know that I have good manners. I have good taste. I am careful what I say. Just act normally, don't be someone that you are not.

My first dinner was a success, it seems like they have enjoyed my company also.

Later, after dinner, my young lady asked me if I had a good time. I said to her that I enjoyed my table company. She said that I told you so, they liked you very much, all of them. They thought that you're very nice and smart. They were asking more questions. What do I know about you? They felt you might not want to tell them too much about yourself. Did not matter - they like you as you are. They want to be sure that I will seat you with them again, all of them. I told them that I will ask you if you want me to. Why not? They're very nice, knowledgeable people, I like them. I enjoyed their company. Some of them are doctors retired, some businessmen, and I liked to listen to their conversation - it was very stimulating. There's always something new. After dinner, one by one offered to come to see and talk to me, they were not nosy. They trust me. Time went by very fast.

Next day it was Saturday. By the way, the place served kosher food and kept the Sabbath. I went in for breakfast and they were there. I was the last one; they waited until I finished my breakfast. They asked me, what is my plan for the day? I told them I like to walk in the country surroundings. It makes me feel like I'm at home. That is the reason why I came here. The weather was very nice; I couldn't ask for any better. They asked me how long I will stay. Can I make my stay longer? I told them that a couple of days should be sufficient. I did not plan to stay longer than a couple of days.

That means, how long? About the end of this week. They replied, we will miss you. They asked me if I would come back again soon? Or do you mind if we call you sometimes? Or you call us? Would be happy to hear from you. Would you give us your telephone number before you leave?

One of the gentlemen asked me what do I do in my spare time? I told him I'm retired. I'm trying to enjoy my free time. I help myself; in my home there is always something to do. I do my shopping, cooking, and whatever I need. They asked me if I have any help. Yes, I said. I have four hours a day, five days a week. She's there, but I prefer to do things myself. They were surprised. They thought I have steady help. Also asked me if I do read a lot. What kinds of books am I interested in? I told them that I'm interested in all kinds of books, but not trash. More educational.

They asked about my family. Little by little I answered politely. Finally, the big question was, are you married? Why are you asking me? I told them I support myself and I try to learn English, try to improve my life. We were very close to all of our family here and abroad. They did not know that I came from Czechoslovakia. They were surprised.

Before we knew it, it became a big conversation; there was no time to stop. I do not want to bring up my writing, because as of now I have nothing to prove it. It is a long way off. Even if you like it, but someone may think it is just trash. How can I even think about it, especially in a company like this! That is as much as I wanted to talk about it. It is better if I don't think about it even though I know they like me as a person; that does not mean when it comes as a writer. I was never one and never will be. It is just imaginary writings.

On the other hand, why not bring it up? Everything is possible; you never know. I read books before and it was not interesting. It does not matter what you know, whom you know. Now maybe, this is the chance I'm waiting for; some inner feeling tells me that it is a good conversational subject, I will try it. I thought maybe tomorrow I will look for the right time and the right opportunity to do so.

It was getting late and I wanted to look at my clothes that I was planning to wear. I wanted to clean up to look my best. I love to get dressed with my figure; looks well, only today I changed a little more. I figure I'm lucky that I can walk straight even with my cane. I do use a cane. Maybe tonight I will walk without the cane; I will take a chance. I wasn't planning to dance. I'm rusty; I did not practice. I am going to watch others. I want to be careful not to make myself a fool. It does take strength and hope that they are very kind and helpful. I'm lucky with that.

I got dressed and someone was knocking on the door. I opened the door; one of the businessmen appeared in front of the door and asked me if he could escort me to the dinner table. I told him yes, I will be happy. A minute later he looked at me and said, "I'm sorry I did not meet you before, sooner. You are the type of person whom I was looking for. It took me a lifetime, however, it's never too late."

I asked him if he was ever married. I do not remember hearing it before whether he was or was not married. And now I heard myself asking him the question.

He was very nice, clean, neat, and smart. I would say it seemed that he was appealing to me. What I would never consider at this stage to even think about it. First of all, he doesn't have any idea how old I am. He seemed to be younger. He has also family, nephews, sisters, and brothers. Some passed away. His family comes from Europe. I didn't ask him from where at this time.

Before he left the room, he presented me with a small box, something like a jewelry box. He asked me if I would like to open it. Slowly, I did. When I opened it, I was very surprised; it was a beautiful necklace. When I saw it, I gave it back to him, saying, "Thank you very much, but I cannot accept such a gift from a stranger. We just met. We do not know each other, therefore," I said, "it is out of question. I do appreciate it."

He replied, "I bought this many years ago," hoping that he would meet someone he dreamed of and never had a chance until now. "And you have a beautiful dress and you do not have a necklace; this would be perfect with your dress."

He put it on my neck, showed it to me, and said, "You see how beautiful you are! Just the right person. I can afford it. I can get you anything you want. I'm rich enough to give you anything you desire. I do not want anything in return, just your friendship."

"May I ask you to wear it tonight? You will make me the happiest person."

I said, "Okay, tonight only."

He said, "No, this is yours without strings. When my time comes, I will remember you forever."

I tried to tell him that I have no special place to go to wear it. He is just wasting his time and money. But without hope, he would never take it back. I said that's okay this way. I spent some time with him. I was not planning, I will not do so now. I will wear the necklace tonight.

When we arrived for dinner, I was surprised at the welcome we got. The young lady came around, and she was happy to see both of us coming. Probably, they thought maybe there'll be something. I just let them think whatever they liked to think.

After dinner, we went to the hall where they have the entertainment and also dance. He asked me if I'd like to dance. I told him I used to, but now I do not dance. I like to watch others. It was a long time ago when I did. I do like good music. Lately, I do not go out. If I have a good show on the TV, then I will watch. I cannot do what I used to do before. I just try to do what I can.

Soon after dinner, the others joined us and were getting ready to watch the show. Meantime, I was getting very tired, and I was ready to tell them I must leave, but how can I? The other people were not young either, and they were still not tired - or were they? It seemed the perfect time to go. My friend, I am sure, is younger than I. How can I try to get out of this arrangement? When I'm getting tired, I should just get up and make an excuse, leave, that's it. Maybe I should leave now? In the middle of the show it would be worse to walk out; it would be easier now.

The question is, what should I do? No one to ask. I will have to decide myself. I cannot fail. If I do the wrong move, then they'll think I'm like the others. On the other hand, I didn't come here to meet someone - I told them before. I need time for myself. Didn't have any reason, therefore I can do whatever I need to do. The new friend said there are no strings attached, you are free. If he doesn't like it, let him take the necklace back. I do not want it anyway. Where will I ever wear it? At home? To go out with him, he has the money, okay. He has a beautiful car. I do not want to live with anyone, and I do not want to get married either. But then what kind of a friend is he?

I'm sure he wants to become a real friend, but how long will he wait. Do nothing, especially if it's true that he cares for me so much. Why do I believe that it's true? Maybe yes, and maybe no. I like him, but not enough to run into such thing. I know myself - it's not a smart move. Okay, if I'm selfish, then maybe I am looking at the other side of the story.

Today people get married like a business, especially when money is involved. Today we need money for everything. And maybe I'm lucky to have someone caring for me enough to take all the responsibilities on himself and to offer to help what I need, support me, to pay my rent and all the bills. Other people would grab him. Now if I don't feel well, I'm alone. He wants me. I should be grateful and not let him go. I may be sorry if I did. He knows by now I don't have any money. I'm just managing the best way I can and still alone. Maybe I should sit down and tell him the whole story. Maybe then he might walk out, or then I will know how he really feels. This way I will find an answer and be able to come to a real decision. And on the other hand, I will be able to get the help I need. I will not have to struggle, and it will be easier. Or when I need a taxi he would be there and help me instead of me paying a high price for it when I don't have. This way would be a better life and I hope that I would not have a problem with him.

I know nothing about his background. No one knows. Can he be a criminal? I do not know for sure - we cannot see what is inside or even outside. Get someone to check him out! I do not have the money. Otherwise nothing. No way to tell, only to see his family and visit them or they visit me or to see each other more often and see how he is behaving. And to get the family together - maybe through that I will have an answer. If he finds out how old I am, probably he will walk out. I've nothing to lose - sooner or later he will find out. So what is the secret? I do not like anyone who keeps secrets, therefore, if he's as nice as he was in the hotel then I will know if he really cares for me. He really deserves the best and respect. Not to use him, but to take care of him wholeheartedly. That's the way I feel - you don't take advantage of anyone. I never did for any reason and I would rather be without it with good conscience, not with guilt. I was honest and I will be until my time comes....... We cannot change what we are. You get respect and you give respect. That's the way life is. Only thing is that not many people feel that way.

It in the evening later was getting tired as I said before, and I decided to call it quits. I decided to excuse myself and I did just that. I got up and left. As soon as I did, I heard others following - they also left. Because of me they would have stayed. I showed them an example that you do what has to be done and you don't follow someone else. You have to do what your heart and mind tells you... naturally with sound judgment. Maybe that is the reason why they liked me. Everyone has the right to do whatever they need to.

Next day the group was there waiting, looking well rested with happy faces. They greeted me, continued to have breakfast with a good humor. After breakfast each went their own way where they were doing before. I went up to my room and got ready for my walk. It was a beautiful day, especially in the country, early morning, before the sun rays - it was beautiful. The trees, the air is fresh, no clouds. As I was walking I noticed someone was following me. As I looked back it was my table friends, three of them followed me. They told me that they did not take walks before. They now started and it's a good idea - they were walking with me. They were tired first, but later they felt better. This is just an example - some people sometimes need to show an example. Doesn't matter how smart they are - one still can learn. I decided to write my thoughts down.

Education is very important, but you need common sense also. This shows if you have common sense - use it. Your behavior is learned, right and wrong. You will be able to stand up and can be proud of yourself with dignity. First you behave and show how you conduct yourself - that is important. Never forget to give respect to others' feelings. Do not think that you are above them. Does not matter how brave you are - it helps - but if you want friends, come down from your horses, as they say. Don't show that you are different, just be yourself - you will have a better time. Nice way you can accomplish much more. If your behavior is misused or bad, then you will find yourself by yourself and you are snubbed. It is not becoming to think of yourself as such. How would you like to be treated? Do the same to others, respect them.

I was always shy in my childhood. I was never afraid of people, but the way we grew up, we did not have enough friends. The family was too busy, did not have enough time, and the friends were different. But at that time I was happy. In my mind I was hoping someday soon we'll be able to meet other young men. I would be able to see or meet one. It wasn't much hope there - it was only a dream. It was left to the imagination. When we were busy, even then, it crossed our mind that it would be nice to meet someone -

but where? There wasn't an opportunity in a small place where we lived. The only hope was that maybe somehow it might happen, that things will change.

Therefore, now I will look back, and I was really very lucky to have this miracle coming my way. Whatever it is, could have been my fate, as all our family....... I think about them. What happened? Is this really the truth? How could it be? Oh, what a terrible ordeal! How in this world could this happen? So many people, innocent and children! Is it true! Why that hatred?

How can one man start and get away with it? Such a criminal was able to get started! The groups of people all over the world - educated, religious, doctors, lawyers, you name it. What poisonous mind! How? Why weren't there any human beings that would have raised their finger!? Why did they sit and watch?

Oh, what a shame! If they have learned so much, they could have stopped destroying. They call themselves innocent people. Oh no! They are as guilty as the guilty ones, because they could have stopped them if they wanted to, before it went out of control. They had deaf ears and did not hear - or just didn't want to. They feared? No, that is not an answer. The stupidity, or the hatred, whichever it was.

I'm afraid even to say it! G-d forgive, if we ever have another flare - up in this world. Did these people learn anything from the past? Even now, they began their denial - that it never happened! It is their answer! Those people, better take a good look around them! How would they feel if it would have happened to them and their family?

Think hard! Wasn't there enough suffering and hunger? What do you think? What is the reason? Think, and think again. Ask real questions - you may find a big surprise. Yes, you are right, take an inventory, look around you. Are there enough jobs? Always things go wrong. Think - was it ever so bad as it is now? Ask again! All this neglect! They are too busy to learn, but know how to destroy and not how to build. No time for that!

How long will this go on? Better, get all the best brains together who are able to solve this problem. Are you happy as is? Hatred does not build! Wasn't there enough destruction in this world? How much more do you need? What will be the excuse? Why not stop now before it's too late! Isn't there someone, somewhere, that may be able to find an answer - a real answer. Maybe then the poisonous air will clear up. I think it's time.

As I was writing, all of a sudden one of the men went by me and noticed that I was writing. He stopped and asked me if I'm writing to someone. Then, finally, I told him about what I was trying to write. I told him that I'm going to write my memoir - my past history. He asked me what about it? I told him then what happened to my family, and he showed interest. I told him that if I ever publish it, he could read it. I told him I've written it, but it is still in the making. He wanted to know what I mean - "I wrote it, but it is still in the making." He was very surprised and asked me if I have a publisher. I told him we were looking for one. I'm not sure this will be a book. My brother asked me to write whatever I remember. I told him I cannot go into any detail. He will have to read it when the time comes. Then he said, why not talk to my friend - you met him - he's a publisher. His family is still running the business, he can help you. Wouldn't that be great! Let's go now and see where he is and ask him. We have nothing to lose, but something to gain.

With that, we were walking towards his friend, and he was sitting and reading something. When we arrived, he looked up, then the first started to tell him what he learned from me. He was very surprised and said to him that she didn't want to talk about this to us. She's more than she makes us believe, he said. I want to hear all about it. I am sure I will be able to help you. What an interesting person! We never know what people do or even their personalities.

I know I never planned to write, only when my brother asked me; finally, I gave in to him. I didn't want to talk about it because I wasn't sure how it will be and how it will come out. He wanted to know what I'm writing now. He wanted to see it because maybe he can tell from this if it's good or if it is worthwhile to write it. I told him that I am just trying to see how it will be, this is my first fiction. I don't know how or why I am writing. You will not be able to read my writing. It is my brother who will put all these things together; without him, I wouldn't have anything.

They told me they would like to meet him and asked me would he come up here. Maybe we will call him, then he might come up here. We will let him know to bring your notes and let us see it, and maybe we will get someone to help you. It would be easier to do it together, and we can make it faster and will not take as long. Why not ask him?

I told him how many pages I wrote in a short time. I wrote it by hand, and he's going over it and dictating it into the computer that will type it from his voice. This way my brother reads and doesn't have to type it. It is amazing that he can type my story that way into the computer - it reads it back and can speak in female and male voices. He edits it and corrects it and it is perfect. With this computer, my brother is happy.

I wanted to tell you something else. We came from Czechoslovakia, four of us together, two boys and two girls. We left the rest of the family there. This is what I'm writing in my memoir. We have all the correspondence, and we saved all the letters. I want to make sure and mention that my brother volunteered into the United States Army. A short time later, he was taken to North Africa, from there to the Italian campaign, Casino and Anzio Beach, as a combat infantryman, from there to France and Germany. I always looked for him for a safe return. Whatever he went through, one will never know.

When you learn what I'm writing, you will get to know our history. You might be amazed - what a history! We have all the old original writings; it goes back 70 years. All this, we have because of my brother. One day, recently, he asked me what should he do with all those papers we had in cardboard boxes. Should he throw it out? I was thinking for a minute and I told him to bring some of the letters over to me and I will take a look at it. That he did. And to my surprise, I said I will put it into a book and we can go over it and we'll see what to do with it.

Little by little, he brought the boxes over to me and before I knew it, it was 30 books all arranged by dates. This way it was easier to go over it and to see whatever you wanted. There were papers in two boxes from all of us. But that was all I did.

Later, my nephew suggested that he would like to write a book about the family, but he needed more information. All the letters were written in Hungarian. My nephew does not speak Hungarian. He speaks many other languages, such as Chinese, Italian, Hebrew, and of course English. My brother suggested he would translate them into English, then my nephew would be able to write whatever he wanted from that.

As of now, he has translated over 200 letters, also my two books that I wrote recently. He has many more to do. I suggested that he has plenty of time. I myself have written three more books. I hope that he will be able to do it. It's a long way to go, I told you. I wrote all by hand. By dictation it would be faster than hand. Handwriting makes it more difficult to understand because it is written phonetically. My brother can read it, but even then, he has to be very good. It is amazing how it will become a book, if it ever will be.

My nephews are very bright; both of them have one son. Both of them are very busy. The youngest wrote a book already about Teddy Roosevelt's called *T.R.'s Summer White House, Oyster Bay* - a history book published - and he is busy selling it. Everything needs time. Now he's trying to put my writings in order. He likes it very much. As of now, it's not finished yet. I'm experimenting with this book. The question is: can I write or not? My brother convinced me that I can; let's wait and see. I think I'll have to wait a little longer until I'm able to see for myself what I can do.

At this time, you must not think of it because it does not say too much. My brother has to go over it; he is the one who can tell. I do appreciate your offer. As soon as I can see what I had hoped for, then I would be grateful for your help, especially a professional. You're G- d - sent; you can save me time. Hoping that when you read it, you will like it enough to work with us.

Thank you in advance for understanding me and offering your help. I will speak to my brother and nephew and let you know as soon as possible. He assured me he will help. I excused myself and went upstairs to clean up.

Later, my friend knocked on my door and asked me if it's okay to escort me to dinner. I told him he can and I said yes. I was ready.

We went downstairs and we found our friends there waiting for us. They welcomed us happily. We were happy to see them. Now we were friends as if we would have known each other a long time.

Now they were ready with questions. I naturally didn't have too much of an answer yet. I told them I didn't have an answer because my brother was not at home. I left him a message that when he comes home to call me back, most likely he will, tonight or tomorrow.

By then my friend also found out about me, and he was very interested to know more. He wanted to see what I'm writing now. I told him it is too soon to talk about it because I never wrote before. I want my brother to see it if it's good enough. As of now, I just want to know if I'm making any sense. He volunteered and was willing to help me with anything I need. I told him I was very thankful.

He asked me if I'm willing to take a walk. If so, he would like to escort me, and I told him he is welcome. We are ready to go. Then other friends arrived and took a walk as a group. It began to be very interesting. I learned and absorbed what they were talking about. I found they were listening to my story. I was amazed at how you can accomplish more and faster whatever you do - just one person, the right person, makes the difference. That is the way you can accomplish anything, whatever you want to.

Here, a couple of days ago, I did not have any idea what will be tomorrow, especially with my writings. I had no idea that I can, ever in my life, do so much in such a short time. Now, I really am convinced that there is someone or something that is really looking out for me. I could never accomplish so much without this kind of people. I would never believe it if someone would tell me, and now I am here among so many talented people. It is unbelievable.

I believe now, maybe I have some talent which I never knew! It is possible. Maybe I should show my writing - why not? I think it is good, but they may not like it because I'm writing about them, or maybe they will understand me better if I'm really smart or not. I really have nothing to lose. Only thing - they will find out that I cannot even spell English; a child knows better than I. What is more important: what you're writing, how you're writing, the grammar - or how you are expressing yourself?

Do you think that they are blind and cannot see? What makes them want to be with me? I'm not beautiful and I'm not young. They do not know the real truth. My background - I'm really a zero. My brother Irving does not want to hear it, but it is the truth. What is my next step? Where am I going? I think I will fail. After the professors examine my writing, I will have a big fall. No one is here to back me up or support me. Why did I start to share? What made me do it? Such a silly question. I should now feel better - it may be their fault they put me up on high horses, and I just may have fallen for it. What a fool I am!

Maybe I just should go home and not be further involved. It is ridiculous to have such an imagination that I have talent. What happened to my good judgment? This proves it is nothing but may well be a big joke after all. They will tell me that you are - and you fell for it. What a joke! Now I will go home before it's too late. Maybe I will call Irving to pick me up and not say anything. But if it's really true, I might have talent, and maybe they are telling me the truth.

I have once in a lifetime such chance. Should I blow it without taking chances? Oh, I would be a fool. I must take chances. This is really amazing to think about.

In the evening, when I went upstairs, my brother called and we spoke. I told him what's happening, and he advised me to wait and tell them that you're not sure what you're going to do. Right now he's not able to come for a visit, but he will try and let me know. I could tell them that. Take that telephone number and you will let them know when it will be ready.

I told him that I told them what I'm writing. Should I go home or what do you think will be the best - without saying goodbye? He answered me, don't worry about the spelling. Some businesspeople cannot spell or write - you can be smart and talented. Ask my nephew Sherwin what he thinks. Did he read my notes? Did he say anything one way or the other? Do you think I should stay and finish this week? I just paid up and I could go. Why would you do that? They're not shy to tell the girl, the young lady, if they want you to move.

I did not see the young lady for two days. Maybe she's off. I would really like to talk to her - she could tell me more.

The evening came again and I changed my clothing, cleaned up, and I left and went downstairs by myself. Everyone was waiting for me, and all of a sudden I noticed a young lady there. Today it was Friday, the weekend. Okay, my time is running out - two more days - and tomorrow is Saturday and I'm not writing, therefore I will not have any discussion about the writings. Here they observe the Sabbath.

This table friend told me that they do not care too much if it's kosher or not. They are here because they like the entertainment and the people. They have been coming here for a long time and they know where to meet. Like here, at home they know most of the people. I myself enjoy them; the food is not too bad either. They drove up here, each one of them separately with their car. They do not live too far away.

They wanted to know how will I go home? I told them by bus. It is the only way I can, and that's it. But now, at this time, I cannot think about it. Whatever it will be later, it will be. The main thing - we had a good time and enjoyed the dinner, it was very good. They served wine on Friday evening and Saturday. Some were not talkative at the dinner table. They're very nice but quiet. They also liked to listen. Oh yes, listening is gold.

After dinner, I was going upstairs and was ready to go to bed. This time I was really tired.

It is Sabbath and I have been here for one week.

After the Sabbath ended, I received a call from my brother and I asked him what is his opinion. If he would like to come here and maybe bring the papers - all the 300 pages - so they can tell me what they think of the original. Also, bring the ones that Sherwin printed, and we should wait with the computer printout. If Sherwin feels that you should bring it, then bring it and leave it in the car. It's safer to show them all, but one is enough first and watch their impressions, and then go from there.

There are five opinions and all kinds of brains. Maybe just what we need. It would be better and easier to go with as much as I know, I'm able to see myself. But the saying is, we cannot believe everything that you hear. There is always a reason why people do think of self - interest. I do not know anyone here, only what I see.

On one hand, I feel good vibration, and on the other hand, it is said - be careful, you never know. Do not sign anything. We have to be careful; perhaps we should take a lawyer before we decide whatever we do. We must make sure that we are not dealing with some kind of crooked people.

They have people that are hired just for getting innocent people, like me, and try to swindle out whatever they can, even my writings. I think we cannot give them these papers to take home. We must be very careful at this time. Maybe we should only show them a couple of pages to see what they think and from there we'll decide further.

One thing is, if it is really the truth, then we will miss out. This is the only chance I ever had! I mentioned it before and now we have to be fortunetellers - and if we are not, I must be careful and look at both sides and not be in a hurry, just be cool.

Let them talk and they should show some proof about themselves and some identifications, more than just a card, so that we ourselves can check it out if he is a publisher. We should check his records or books - what he did and what he is doing now.

Okay, he is retired, but he still has some background of the past - what he was famous for, like he said. It can't be hidden if he's a crook. One way or the other, we don't give out anything first. We have to have it in black - and - white, signed and sealed before.

This way we cannot trust anyone. They can't take everything and your rights. We cannot sell our rights; we need to be sure and they must have proof. Things happen all the time, even with lawyers. We cannot undersell it. If they are so anxious - why are they?

You must be sure every step you make. I will get tough, with reason. If they are so much in a hurry - be aware of it. If they take their time, then they also will give us a chance. It will work out. Otherwise, maybe it is a mistake even talking with them at this time. Let them call us later and we'll call them.

Whatever. Monday my brother came to pick me up and he also brought the papers with him. But first, he would like to meet them and speak with them and see; it will help to decide if it is truth.

I spoke to my friend also. He advised me to slow down and see what is involved, and not sign anything. And he said, if I want him to look at it first, he will advise me one way or the other. He told me he will help me with no strings attached. He feels about me the same way.

He knows those people are good people, but like with everything else, business is business. Most people become very selfish when it comes to money. I told my friend, usually I don't like to mix business with pleasure. I never did. I told him this is the first time I was carried away and I did, which I usually do not.

To begin with him, I did not lose my chances. He assured me I didn't do anything that I would have to be sorry for. "You are a lady and you're a very smart one. This is what I told you when I met you - that is still true. My judgment still stands. Whatever or whenever you need me, the only thing you can do is call me day or night, anytime. If you give me the permission to call you or to see you, I would be very happy. You make my life fulfilled. Now, I will miss you. With help, you might change your mind - would be happier."

With this, my brother showed him the printout, and it looked like he was happy that I wrote these books. He also said it is amazing to write by hand and so much - it is unbelievable. He would not believe it if he would not witness it. He saw me writing here and there. And now I showed him what I did here after I arrived.

He could not believe it. So much? When did I write this? At night, when I went upstairs. I was tired and I could not function; I must rest, otherwise I look for trouble which I'm not prepared for.

He advised me to show them one copy to see their reaction - just the beginning - and just let them give you some information and then go from there. He gave good advice. We decided just to do that.

Later on, we met not one, but two publishers, one by one, to hear their opinion. My friend was right. This way we got two different opinions. Both sounded good but needs more doing to have a decision - more information, more checking.

Here they took their time. Needs to learn more about the people and the business. It is getting more complicated. We really do not have the knowledge how to begin and what is the best. We must ask someone that we can trust, but whether you find such a person - especially in such a short time. The question is where to begin.

Only thing I might believe more is what my friend says. He sounds honest, after I have seen how they work. It is true, we do not know too much when we get involved with people like they are. I told them when we come to a decision, we will let them know. If they are still interested with the publications, then we can see and work it out on both sides.

At this time, we have not decided yet. We want to make sure the right decision because it is too involved. It is our personal life, and I do not feel that we want to part with it. This is all we have, and it is priceless. We have nothing else.

We have nothing of our oldest brother Lajos, not even a picture. It involves much more than just a book - this is our life. We want to preserve as much as possible. In our heart, we never forget him, not even for a minute. As time goes by, we always think of him and about him.

We cannot worry, but we cannot forget them either. That is the reason that I'm writing this book. Also for the future generations to learn the lesson, before they decide to go to war, and to learn that "never again" should this happen.

Try to learn how to solve problems, not to create one. You can learn on your own family and practice it. Do not make a decision hastily. When you arrive to the right type of decision, you will get more satisfaction out of it. Also, you will have a good feeling of accomplishment. Teach love, not hatred.

My writings are all about this concept. I am for the family. I believe it is a healthy life. Less sickness, creates less problems. This way will be less heart failure. This is my opinion. Stress is not helpful; it's causing extra problems. Making a living is stressful. Just driving back and forth to business - that itself is stressful.

Think carefully and do whatever needs to be done. Try to remember that all are in the same position; therefore, we must learn to respect and to live together as neighbors. Don't look for trouble. If we follow what we have learned, we will have a better and happier life, each of us. Always think the best way to be better for you and all of us.

And at this point, you must take a break to take time to figure out whatever needs to be done. We have some idea what to expect. The only thing now is: whom can we trust? Where can we go from here?

We cannot just wait! We have to act now before he cools off. It is better to have something than nothing. We do not have to sell our rights. We will see how many will be selling. Then we will know better if we want to publish more or not. We will have some idea where to start, and I think this is the right decision.

My friend also advised us the same way. He is a successful businessman and made enough money and he also made a good name, that I can see for myself. He gave me enough information, like he said, that today we have to be very careful with anyone whom you can trust, especially in business. There are more than one way to double cross you. He got to know them well. He knows them for years. They're nice and respectable people, but he does not do business with them. He used to deal with them both. Now he does not. Only they are friends here in this place. He usually travels a lot to different places.

I asked him how come that you're not married? You have the money to travel all around and you could have looked for someone before! You're a very nice person, well dressed and a good businessman, you have everything to offer, good life, you could have had whatever you wanted, a family of your own. That could have made it different. Did you not think about that?

He says yes, I did, but for that you don't have to sacrifice your life. I told him, the better part of your life passed by. You are still young. You still have a chance to better your life. Why are you wasting your time with these friends? He said, to them it doesn't matter.

I told him before to go out with different friends, but to settle down is much more involved than just get married. Didn't you ever meet someone that you would think about when you were younger?

Yes, he said, sometimes I was almost ready then I changed my mind at the last minute. I was very busy, involved in business. Not much time to socialize. It was all business. At that time my nieces and nephews were there, my family was always around.

I'm sure you must have met smart people, attractive ladies. What happened there? Why now? All of a sudden you come to a decision and you feel I am what you are looking for all your life? I really do not understand men like you, very smart and have everything to offer and you do not reach out, but wait so long for someone - not even someone young - and you are willing to expect too much from someone and running after them to spend time together. You can do much more if you want to.

I said, you must have more friends than one at a time. He said he did. That was just an acquaintance, he insists - not personal, just like you.

I hear that you're not worried. Why not? I told him, my situation is different. My life is another story and it is much more complicated. I didn't have the time, the money, and my English. I have all the reasons. For you, there isn't any good reason. I'm sorry, but for me, I can't see anything - why not?

Why do you think that I'm the one you have been looking for all your life? How do you know that? Do you still think that you are the right person for me? Now that you know me more, maybe you will feel differently. Why do you feel this way now?

He answered, now I feel even closer than before. I hope you will give me a chance. I would really like to, even seriously, go with you. You say the word and I'm ready without any hesitation. My family would be very happy. They wanted to see me happy.

You do not know my age, do you? Can you guess? I might not be as young as you think or even imagine. If I tell you, two minutes later you will run away without telling me goodbye.

He said, why not try me - and asked me, what do you think, how old am I?

With careful thinking... don't be afraid, you will not hurt my feelings. I was told before and I don't think about my age. Today, some people don't look at others, not interested. Why not? Because they're not thinking for a long time - only for just now. Right now they have a good time and money. What they really want - when they get enough - then they come and go elsewhere. They do not need any license. They can do better without a license. Some women fall for it, and later what happens is more disappointment and heartaches - and this goes on and on.

This is the way the world goes round. They waste so much time - how far can they go until something gives? Not for the better the way they're going. Money can buy everything, but it cannot buy happiness. Sometimes it's too late - no money and nothing else left. Now what? It is too late. This is only one example. We have to be very careful how we want to have a solid future.

There is never a guarantee - it may well be as we expected. But if you take time to learn about each other more seriously, don't rush into it. I don't mean for a lifetime - it should be a reasonable time. I don't mean to move in for trial living, the way today's generations are practicing it. That is not what I mean.

A good relationship can be better established by careful understanding and getting to know the person, because there is more involvement in a good relationship than just to move in - that is not the way it works. In a lifetime, it is much more interesting all around. You can learn about real love - it is priceless, it is an art - that grows more and more. Learn to respect, equally on both sides. Just then we'll find the real reason. This is the foundation of a family. You will find that it will pay off. You can be richer in fulfillment of life. This is what it's all about - happiness, understanding of each other - this is what we have to work out.

Now I come back to my friend.
Did you find an answer to my question?
He asked me, what question?
I said, my age.
Oh yes, I knew it all along.
What is it?
He said without hesitation that I am 70 years old.
I said to him, are you sure? Think again!
This is what I think - maybe a year or two off.

I will tell you only for your ears. I'm proud of my age. I'm not afraid to talk about it. These are only numbers - this is my opinion. The age is how you behave, and how you are able to function. This is how I feel - now sit down and make yourself comfortable.

Listen, my age is 63. However, I am as old as I want to be. Mentally, I feel young. Thank G-d, I'm always thankful - every morning, I say, "Thank G-d, you heard me."

This is where I have my problem - when doctors see my application for an examination, they judge me as an old woman. In my opinion, you cannot feel that you are still young, but I do not give up because of the number. Every person is different, and you have to take the whole person. I consider myself differently; I do not feel that I'm hopeless. I tell things that I'm different - my outlook in life is also different.

When you see a doctor and you try to challenge them, they think that something must be wrong with you or you are a mental case. They are the jury and the judge. They do not want to see a person as an individual, to wait for the explanation - and they do not want to spend time with you. Today it's not like years ago - a doctor was willing to spend time to listen to you and explained why you are sick and what can be done to correct the problem to the best of their knowledge. Probably today they do not teach them in the medical schools, or when they are in the hospital training. They rush in and out; perhaps they're overloaded and have no time to observe the condition of the patient.

My friend, are you still listening? I cannot believe it, but I do believe it, because I know that you are very honest. Now that you know, I understand why you think that I am younger than you. You have never encouraged me to have any affair between us. Now I know and understand why you did what you did. I asked him, if he knows the truth now, will you take the necklace back - the one you gave to me? Now you see why I didn't want to take it from you?

"I still want you to keep the necklace, and I want to be your friend more than ever. I give you my respect and bow down to you, and I'm very happy that I had a chance knowing you. I will always think that you are my best friend that I ever had. I will never change my mind about you. You have accomplished a lot in a short time - this shows how you are. You should not be ashamed of your age. This proves how much you really can do; it's never too late. With G-d's help, like you said, you have to fight to do whatever your inner feelings tell you. You are capable to better your life - do not waste it."

[Editor's note: material moved. Discusses doctors and health care]

As I told him the truth, he was surprised. He would never believe it. He knew the truth when he met me. It is amazing how I managed to be able to accomplish that in such a short time - that it was possible, especially by handwriting today. It's much easier to dictate into the computer. It is amazing, as you said, that today the computer can spell and talk practically - to do anything you want to.

Here, he said, he does not know anyone who can do what I did - the spelling and the writing - so much. He asked, how were you able to do all that? Don't your hand and fingers hurt? I said yes, they do now. I have a terrible time writing my name because my fingers do not work right. I had a couple of accidents that didn't help me either.

I cannot give up. Usually, every morning I soak my hand in warm water and massage it, and I do whatever I can. I find myself many times massaging my hand, and then I continue to get to the place where I left off.

My friend just listened, like he never heard anything like it. The more I told him, the more anxious he was to hear my story.

This brought me back to my little niece. When I was babysitting, I used to tell her stories before she went to sleep. She loved my stories. I tried to tell different stories so that she would not be bored. I asked her what she would want to hear. Sometimes they want to hear about children and sometimes they want to hear about dogs. There are a few stories - some were real and some were imaginary. She loved all my stories. I never read one from the book; it was all creation. And she used to fall asleep - not right away - but she was happy to hear and she asked questions and I answered her. We had both of us a good time. I enjoyed every minute that I was spending with her. She had a storybook, but she liked my stories best. Her father used to tell stories to her, but she told her father that she liked mine better.

Now I find myself in a different situation here. From nowhere, a stranger appears and everything seems to fall into place, but in a different direction and it's more involved than just the story. It is also a story which you cannot see, but it's up the same way. Now here in front of me, there is a wonderful man who is real but he never heard about me. He appears from nowhere in such a short time offering his help, his life, and wants to share it with me. He joins me without knowing anything about me. He is really an amazing, smart, handsome man and can get anyone. I don't understand it - why? And he said that I was always in his dream. Sometimes we used to say that it was meant to be -- "beshert" in Yiddish. I don't know if you know what it means.

This time we cannot go any further; we have more than enough to digest. We have a life to think about, even though we do not have enough time. Time goes fast enough, it is hard to catch up. We have to do whatever we have to.

Now we have to face the other people and to tell them the real story and we'll see what they will feel and say. It is getting very interesting minute by minute. What is next? Will she meet the publishers? We'll get together one by one and we will tell them before we will sign the agreement. I will ask my friend if he's still willing to help us with a contract agreement and will do whatever we decide the best. He said also that he knows someone that would be able to help because this is a legal document and it has to be just right and carefully put together. You would be better off to have someone that understands the law. Sometimes it becomes quite complicated. He will be there also and I will be there to see if that is what you want, without paying a fee. He's doing it because I asked him. I asked him, are you paying him for the services? He said no. He is working for the children's business and he gets a salary from that and he can do whatever he wants to.

And now I think you're ready to negotiate it. I asked him what do I do for you for all the services? I can't pay you back as is already. You know all about me. What are you going to get out of this? How much do I owe you? I may not be able to sign the agreement. How much will you charge me for these services? I somehow have a feeling, we do not want to get into more trouble. I cannot expect you to do everything free.

He said, I will make a handshake before and I will sign it in front of all the people. I do not understand it, I said, why I deserve such a treat. This can cost more than I can afford. Therefore, we will have to change our mind and do it ourselves. Thank you for your offer, but we have to be careful. I trust you. I know you're going to do it because you care for me. I understand that part. After the examination, we will come to a decision. We will follow whatever we can ourselves the best we can and see what will be.

Now we can meet the publishers. My friend came also, just in case if we need some advice. He will be there. In the meantime, we learn very little about the real price. I mentioned to my friend that I did go to another publisher and I told him what he told us. He replied that he was the wrong publisher; he did not have the knowledge. He wasn't the one that I needed. I need someone who is more knowledgeable about the type of writings. He had no experience in it and he did not understand anything about this type of writings.

Before you sign any papers, please trust me, be careful. Show it to me. Please trust me, I care for you. I do not want you to be hurt. You just said yourself that in business, it is a different situation and now you're saying something else.

Okay, we'll be careful. They came with their lawyers one by one, separately. And here we have no one, only ourselves. We sat down and listened carefully, and after we will decide which one we will do business with. You really need an expert.

After a while, someone was knocking on the door. Who was it? It was my friend, and he wanted to talk to us. Then one of the publishers asked him, "Why aren't you helping them? What happened? Why not?" We need a friend, because we do not know what is involved. My friend said that he would like to help us, if we give him the opportunity.

This publisher offered that if our friend helps him to get the contract, then he is willing to pay him part of the fee. He should talk to us about that, and we will not have to pay anything. My friend said, "Now we shall see how much he offers, and which deal will be the best." What if the other publisher does not go along with that? "He will, if I ask him," my friend said. We'll make a contract first, just like in any business. I did not think about that. Then, we shall check it out and see which way we will go. At least you have a good chance. You're making the right choice. We will talk it over and agree. This is the only choice we have.

They went in, and for hours they tried to reach an agreement, each time my friend came out and assured us that there will be a good deal. He will let me know if anything comes up.

In the meantime, they stopped for lunch. We also went out ourselves because this was a business lunch. It is better that they'll work it out first and then we shall go over it carefully. We should take it home and study it before we sign it. Even then, how can we tell? Maybe we should tell them to write the contract in plain English so that we would be able to understand it without any problems. They could do it, why not? They are all strangers.

We came back and they ordered food in their room. It was better that way because they were able to talk and eat. Finally, we were called in and they came to a decision that this contract will be better for us. This was the second publisher. My friend said that this publisher will be giving us a better deal now and in the future. He has more experience to handle it and we'll have a better offer.

Now, he would like to go over it with us, but it is up to us whatever we decide to do. Both of us want to have this contract. He has more experience dealing with this type of business. When it comes down to it, because he hopes that we will work with them, he will accept 1% from the sales of this book. He has a good idea that the book will be a good seller; otherwise, he would not spend his time and all the work that it involves. You would like to sign the contract as soon as possible. We will get the original papers back as soon as he writes the book. He guarantees that we will have all the rights, and no one can copy it unless we give permission, including the publisher. All rights are reserved. This is a sealed contract.

The first publisher was very sorry about it, but he hopes that later, with the next book, he will have a chance to get together. I did not include any other deals. This is the only thing in this contract: one deal and one book.

For the next book, we shall work it out where we can and want to. We will not pay for this publication. He will receive everything from the sales. He will advertise the book, and he'll be doing quite well. If he's right, then we can make the other contract with him. This we will see if we can sell. I still think we must wait and see. I do not know what to expect. I wish I did. When will you know? How long will it take? I'm anxious, and I'm lowering my passion.

In the meantime, my friend is encouraging me to write other books. I told him I ran out of ideas. He told me maybe I should go for a trip. I asked him if he was joking. "Where would I go?" I asked. He said he would take me. I asked, "Why would you want to do that?" He said, "Because I'm still your friend and always will be." I asked, "What kind of friend am I? I could be your mother." He said, "No. You told me that it's only a number." But I said, "Also, the year - it's true. I cannot do today what I was able to do 10 years ago. As you see, I have to take my medications and see my doctor regularly, and I need my rest to function right."

A young man like you has everything to live for and should still be happy, enjoying life fully. I'm not selfish, never was. I do not take advantage of anyone, especially not an old friend like you. I respect you. I really try to understand the reason. What did I do that I deserve such treatment? I do care for you. I wish I could have had the chance to meet you before, when I was younger. I would have been lucky to meet you. I feel lucky now to have had the opportunity to know you as a friend.

As you know, I really do not have any friends. It's a strange life, and it's not easy to keep friendships, even if you want to. I do like the idea of living in a senior home, but I prefer to live with mixed tenants - young, older, and children. Maybe it would be better the other way around. I would be able to get services, which I cannot here. I do not like to lock my door just to sleep and eat, even though I do that as well. This way, if the weather is good, I can go out whenever I want to. There aren't many stores here, and in this respect, maybe somewhere else would be better.

I like my apartment; I'm used to it. It is small and cozy. It's only a studio apartment, and I've been here for 32 years. I've grown accustomed to it. Here, there's transportation if I want to go somewhere, even though I don't travel much now. Traveling is more difficult, but I like to stay active, though I can't travel too far. I feel better at home. Occasionally, I go out to do my shopping. I also go to the doctor by bus. It's a long walk to catch the Long Island bus. If the weather is nice, it's okay; if not, sometimes I'll take a taxi. It's getting more expensive, like everything else. The prices are going higher, but our income remains very static.

As you see from this writing, I don't know whether I should stop writing and give it up. I'll find out soon enough, with a yes or no. What are you thinking? How long will it be? Would it be a good seller? By next week, we will know.

Are you going away? How long? Where, if I may ask? When can I come to see you? I told him usually my brother comes on Sunday if the weather is good. If you want, let me know when. On a Sunday, if the weather is good, I do not want to travel. He has an old car, and at night, I do not want him to drive.

A couple weeks later, I received a call from the publisher. He told me that he loved my book and put it into hardcover. It's beautiful, impressive, and already in stores, selling well. He tried pricing it at $50 per book, and it's already selling well. He's happy, and now he's on his way to the second book.

He asked if we had already finished it. I told him my brother didn't have a chance to type or coordinate it. Therefore, I don't know how long it would take.

Then he offered his services, suggesting we could do it without typing. I told him that the spelling and grammar have to be coordinated to see if it is good enough to be published. He also said that they do everything, but they would charge for whatever it costs. We'll have to work out a deal. "When can we do it?" he asked. I told him if he wants, we should sit down again and see what we can work out. I told him that I would talk to my brother, and we'll come back to you. "Okay," he told me.

Meantime, the other publisher called me and wanted to know what we had decided about the second book. I told him that we're working on it, and I would let him know as soon as possible. I also spoke to my friend and asked his opinion. What is he advising us to do? If he can be there as before, is it okay? But only if he feels that he wants to be there.

"Please let me know what you have decided, and we'll go from there," he told me. He said he wants to come to see me on Sunday and would be happy to come over. He asked for my brother's address, saying maybe he can pick him up. He also lives on Long Island and can take him home. I told him that I would like him then to pick up my brother and his son. I asked him for his telephone number. If he wants, he can call them - whichever is better for him. "Okay," he said. He took my brother's phone number and said he will call him. He also gave me his phone number, in case I want to call him anytime and leave him a message, and then he'll call me back as soon as possible. "Okay."

Then Sunday came. I prepared lunch like always. He arrived early and came with my brother and brought a bouquet of beautiful flowers. He was surprised to see my studio apartment. He said to me that this is big enough for two people. "I know this type of apartments, and they charge lots of money for it, and there are two people living in there."

I said that my rent is stabilized and I pay less. Some of the apartments are still rent - controlled. Some pay less for a one - bedroom apartment than I do. From here, it's convenient to travel by the Long Island trains, which is not far from here. Also, the buses travel to shopping centers, and they aren't too far. I like this neighborhood. I don't know where would be better. I know that it would be more expensive. If I would be moving out from this apartment, the price would double. There would be no more control over it. They would fix it up like brand - new.

I was ready to set the table the best I can. I told him about my helpers, how they robbed me and they took my linen, shoes; therefore, I have to use whatever I have. He told me everything looks very nice. The roses on the table looked beautiful. I made the lunch: turkey pieces, soup, potatoes and vegetables. Cucumbers were ready-made. I had sodas, fresh rolls, and fruit compote. He liked everything. He said I'm a good cook. I told him, in fact, usually it was better. Now I'm not doing so much cooking, only for my family. I don't entertain anymore. Whatever I can, I make. The children, whatever I give them, they do not complain. I love them. Whenever they come, I love to have them.

Now they are in school; therefore, they usually come on the weekends, which is the best time for them. I really had a good time. Irving is very good company. I told him whenever he wants to come, he is welcome.

My brother likes to be in good company. He said wants to see you; he lives nearby. Usually, he eats outside. He said that he has people working for him, such as housekeepers, cooks; they sleep in. Sometimes he likes to eat at home. His family comes over sometimes - children, nieces, nephews, and grown-ups. They have grandchildren, are busy people. My friend asked me if I would like to come over for dinner; I would be welcome. His home is not kosher, but he does not eat ham, pork. He buys kosher meat. The only thing is that the dishes are not kosher. On the holidays, he goes to the temple but not on Saturdays.

How come that he goes to that hotel? They're kosher. He told me when he eats outside, he always goes to the kosher restaurant; he likes kosher food. I told my niece; she could not believe it. "This seems like a fairytale," I told you. This is just a dream. I never heard such a real story. It is true. Next time, we will go out for dinner. He said he would like me to visit his home with Irving. I told him he does not go out to eat. We can eat here and go to visit his home. We parted with that.

"You already did so much. I do not want to take advantage of you. We all appreciate whatever," he offered his help. I know without him we would not have had the opportunity for a contract. I do not have all those people as friends. Those people did whatever he asked them to do. As you see, I would say I'm very lucky to have the pleasure of meeting you. I waited for a long time. I can't even believe it, that it is true. I feel that this is still just a dream. I'm afraid of waking up; it would be a big fall. You have no idea what is really happening. How can you? This is a fairytale. I feel that if I would tell someone, they will think that I lost my noodles. How do they say that? Now, I owe you everything. I do not even know where to begin to thank you, and thank you again. You're a real friend for life. I hope I, or we, my family, will thank you for all what you did. You have made our life better. We could not have made it without you. Just tell me if you ever need something! We will be always better. Now I look at you like my family, a dear friend. We shall see you soon." With that, parted.

When he went home, he called me and told me how much he enjoyed to be with us, to have dinner. I told him he was welcome whenever he wants to come.

Finally, I received the first book, it looked very nice. The cover looked very rich and better than the writings. Hope it will be the bestseller like I was told. Who knows? There are people who become millionaires overnight. How can you really tell? Now we have to work on the second book or maybe the third one. Might as well, we are in it. This is more than I ever expected, it is a good deal. If not for those friends, then we could never have made anything. Therefore, we should go ahead and sign the contract with the same publisher. Maybe we have time to give the fourth book, if he gives a good deal... We will have time. As it is, it's coming closer to finish it. The first group arrived in the stores, all over. Even though it is expensive, but people still buy it. Now the publisher wants me to go ahead and sign it. They are making arrangements in different places. How can I? Now you have to write more than just a name. I do not know why I have to. Now I will have more worries, since he wants me to go where we met them already.

I have to thank my young lady friend and all those people there. She is a very smart lady. Without her, I would not have had anything. Whatever I have, she deserves everything. I will give her something. I have to find out what. Even those friends owe her, because they wanted my company. Therefore, let them also pay. They, too, will profit from this deal.

When I went back, I signed the books. She saw me and ran to welcome me. It was a beautiful sight that people were waiting for me. People were lined up so I could sign their books. They already bought them. I was told I had to come for the weekend. I did not know that until I was there. They really did a good job. They kept me busy; I don't even know how many books I signed. I have trouble with my hand. I don't know how I will be able to continue to do that. I cannot think about it now; the way it comes, so it will be.

Even Dr. Schwartzwald, my cardiologist, was amazed. He never thought that I had the brains to write one word, and here I am writing more than that. Others cannot believe it is I who was doing it. Because of that, my book became more famous than anyone imagined. The people thought I was losing my marbles, so to speak. They cannot believe it — this must be someone else.

It is very impressive. Better than I expected. My brother is right. He is a smart one. If not for him, I would not have anything. He created this book — interpreter of my writing, typist, composer. The editor, the examiner, is my nephew Sherwin. Without him, I would not have anything. We worked like a team. This is what I wanted to show the world — that families should work together, pray together, and show the world that you can make it. Whatever you want, if you really want to — this is an example.

You must learn and have common sense. You can be the richest person — not in money, but in knowledge and respect — and you become a better person. We must learn how to solve our problems. I learned so much in a couple of weeks that is enough for a lifetime. I'm just lucky I had the right people at the right time, and such an opportunity. This is a miracle. I am still dreaming.

I spent two days in the countryside and sold 200 books. I signed them all. It was a success. The hotel made good business. If not for this event, the hotel would have been very slow. I was very happy to hear that.

Now, with the second and third books, it will be much easier. I got all the courage to go on to do whatever I do. Who knows what can happen?

A college received a gift from the publisher and they invited me also; they expected me to visit and were anxious to meet me.

After they read my story, the way I put it together - not just the wording but the composition - it was very good. This would call for at least 10 years of experience as a writer. How did she have all the courage and have all this knowledge? What a show! My creativity is unbelievable. Now they will find that I wrote these books by hand in such a short time. Black and white, all in one print, and written all by hand - especially at my age. I have trouble to sign my own name. People are witnessing all around me; they were watching me, how fast I'm doing it without stopping. I am signing my name in seconds. The professor admitted that he or anyone else could not be able to do what I have done. They were watching me, how I am working without stopping, and the pages disappear in front of their eyes. It became more and more interesting. We never expected this type of talent. Everything taken into consideration, this deserves not just a Doctorate, but knowing how this book was rated - that speaks for itself.

This is also a subject matter: how well was this book created and has been achieved without any previous education. Only genius people, an unusual person, would be able to show talent like this. They gave me the highest award for creating this composition, not considering the writings. They asked me from different universities to come and speak to them and want to find out how I became what I do.

Very interesting, now I must say that if not for my friend, I couldn't do it at all. He is an amazing man, a very smart one. By the way, wherever I go, Irving goes with me. I told the whole world that he is my motivator and without him there would not be any book. I wrote this book for him originally. First, he asked me for so many years, until now I decided to write this book for him and for my nephew. He is also planning to write a book from one part of our family, namely, his father's life story. It takes time, it takes much longer; there's more to the story than you're reading. It is a bigger story behind the story. I try to write fast because time is running out at this stage of life. We have to count one day at a time. As I told my brother, I started, and I would like to finish it, at least my life story. I'm lucky that I was able to and now I'm happy that I did that.

What made me write without stopping? Here is my answer: I wanted to present the truth. Now I can say whatever I can. I don't know if I will start a new book; it is getting a little too much. I love all the attention I am getting, but it becomes a little tiresome. I want to show the world that anyone can do whatever one wants. Just be sure and do it well. I hope that people will learn to get along with their families and with their neighbors. This is the only way to accomplish anything. Alone, I can do nothing. We need people to ask questions and help wherever you need to. You must make good judgments and take time to think out what you need to do. I would have never thought that this would be possible. Now I look back and I can see that nothing is impossible. Anything you want to do, you must work on it. You must try it and never say no. If you want to be a creator, you have to believe in it, then you will not fail. If your mind is on something else, then you'll never make it. And it always works out if your mind is on it and it's creative. Whatever it is, it takes all types of resource, and you have to examine what you like and want to be, then go for it. It is that simple. Try to be the best at it. You never know when and where it will happen. Encouragement is very important - that helps to support you and believe that it is possible. Here it is an example.

I wanted to show you that if you want to, you can accomplish much more with love than with hatred. Love that is strong. Hatred is destructive. We have choices, but love thy neighbor without judging them. The race or color does not matter. Whatever you try to accomplish - peace instead of war - then many lives would be saved, not lost. Life would be a happier life than sorrow, and this is what I'm writing all about to begin with. This is what I'm working for. I'm trying to help the helpless, the sick - it doesn't matter what it is - all need our help. You must reach out wherever needed and don't wait until it's too late. Help now, and not later. Be there and don't destroy, but build for a better future. Build not with anger but with passion and love.

Teach the better side, not the worst one. Learn to listen to what the others are saying. You can learn from anyone something - you never know. I'm giving you an encouragement, and wish you all the best: health, happiness, and good luck.

We met our publisher again, and to our surprise, he looked very happy. I asked him, what is the good news? His reply was that "I'm the luckiest person" - that he ever met me. I never thought that this would happen. He never met anyone that has accomplished so much in such a short time. I can see that everything is possible! That shows that you never know what surprises you may run into. It is the first time I have experienced such excitement. I'm really living my life. My days are not dull. My senses tell me that he is getting calls every day; they want to find out where they can buy this book.

We mailed out dozens of books all over, even in European countries. We have received calls from England wanting to know when the second and the third books will be ready. We have advertised them. I think it will be successful also. We should not waste any time. We should be able to set up and be able to print it as soon as possible and put it on the market. We asked my brother and my nephew Sherwin to come over, since they do not ask for money. Therefore, we can save at least 1% for them - they deserve it.

All the people that were involved in this project perhaps I should give them something, because from the very beginning they encouraged me. They also recognized my talent and knew - my dearest brother and my dearest nephew Sherwin - you supported me and encouraged me, therefore you deserve the best. I do not know if it would be another way, how it would have turned out the way it is now. I'm lucky in a way. I'm not selfish, never was and never will be. This is what it's all about. I'm very happy that I was able to accomplish as much as I did. This is worth more than money. I'm very happy that I'm able to help others. The poor seniors - I hope they will be able to have a piece in this, before we will say goodbye. That makes me happier than the knowledge that finally I can leave something worthwhile to my own family. This is what I'm asking for my Savior this morning. I had a very good prayer and I know he listened. I can tell each time that he does.

Now we have to continue where we left off. My brother Irving and I told my friend that I cannot do anything without him. He's the person - he is honest, sincere, and he really cares for me and my family. I trust him and we are seeing each other more without hesitation. He also knows us well. We gave the publisher more books, signed the same agreement as the first one. In a couple of days, he will show us the book; only thing, on the cover there will be another picture. He wants to do Irving's army letters and to do his own army papers.

After Sherwin will finish writing the book - that is, the military book - it would be very interesting.[58] I know there he will have many different pictures. It is the second book, and the next, the last one, you will be happy to know, it is different, and all will be together as it belongs to the family. And now, I don't know yet, we need more time. Let's see what will be with the second book. He looked at the paper as if he thinks that they will be able to correct it. Irving should read it before they will print it. He wants to see it before they decide to go ahead. We've told that to the publisher. He said no problem. We all agreed it's a good idea, because like Irving said, he knows me better and can tell if the right correction has been made. We all agreed to that. If one cannot read it properly, then an important sentence could be lost.

Perhaps if I would hire a secretary to take it down shorthand, it would be worthwhile. It would shorten the time in writing, then the only thing you would have to do is just to proofread it. My friend agreed to that. We will try that. Okay, we are going to give it to someone and we will pay for it, and it will be faster - will save time. The secretary happens to be very good at shorthand and typing. They were convinced that we will be able to do it, and we will be able to finish it in a couple of days.

Now, coming back to the first letters - but if they figured out what he has to do, what he wants to do, and how it would be best in the nicest way to put it together with the pictures - this will be very professional work, like an artwork. They are taking this more seriously than before. This would be very nice because we work together as a team and this is the only way to get anywhere. We're willing to give and take, with a smile. No arguments and no fights. Just try to understand what it is that you want to accomplish and continue to work out whatever you want to do. I call it an art.

The other publisher also is trying to give his support. Now, I learned from his friend he wants to see what's going on. Both companies got together, different, but they say both are retired. The children are responsible for this project. Here I don't know how it started - with all good intentions - and that is the key to everything that I was looking for. Now, in a few days, we're going to be all set, and I'm waiting for the good news like before. The second book is finished. We proofread it and it was okay.

---

[58] *Private Good Luck.* Tisza Publishing. 2019

Now we started on the third book and we're looking it over to see what's missing. My hope is that it is good and we will not have to waste time to redo it again. We went along because it was okay. We started with the printing of the cover and it will be different pictures; the title will be the same. The only thing that will be different is that this part is the continuation of the first one.

We shall see as we go further. The publisher said that this book is very good. In a couple of weeks, we will find out and then we'll see what we'll do with the others. It will be a little bit smaller book. Maybe we should wait a couple of days, check the third book, and combine it with the second book - this way it will be the same size.

I'm also writing the fourth book that could be combined. It would be three books - all would be the same size. That way it will be a richer - looking book. We all agreed. I'm looking forward to see what we have accomplished. It is wonderful to go back and to see what we have accomplished - so much in a short time.

In a way, we can be very proud of ourselves - how all this started from nowhere and from nothing, all came from inside of my head. And all of a sudden it became in full bloom. This is really a storybook for everyone of all ages. All countries can learn from this. Maybe we should change the name as an educational book. The only thing is that they have many books - all types of books with many different writings. They're supposed to be talented writers with good manners. I think my book is different, simply because it is easy to understand. They're simple words and it's easier to read.

This publisher - I'm happy with him because he knows how to do it. He has good taste in books - impressive. The book cover will be burgundy and gold combination and it's very rich - looking. It will be the same hard cover. It will be well made. The print will be easy to read. This will be the same as the others.

I don't know if I will continue my writings. I think it's enough. We just have to be able to see what we have now. We need time to think what we will do next.

I would like to set up a fund for the family to be able to get their education - a trust fund. Whatever would make it easier for the children of both boys and the family. Make sure that Jerritt should not lose whatever he has. The same thing goes to Sherwin and the rest of his own family - Linda and her family, Diana herself - to have an easier life. I'm sorry that I could not do much more for the older brother's family. He chose his life the way he wanted to; he made his bed and he slept in it.

My heart is willing, but I did not create the problem, and he can only blame himself. Maybe my older brother's son will wake up, because he is doing the same thing as what he did when his father passed away. He cannot see further than his nose. By the time he wakes up it will be too late. I feel sorry for his children. They could have been better off and have a happier life if he would not have been ignorant. I would say, as smart as he is, the opposite is stupid - in plain English. Usually, I don't like to label people, but I just can't find a better expression. The real name would be expressed in the dictionary. I guess we can express ourselves as we feel. We may be hurt but not angry. But just that some people feel like that, more than the others. They cannot face the truth and have to have someone to blame, instead of facing the facts and trying to work around it and say, "I'm sorry."

I do not understand myself why all this comes around, and because of that, so many people miss out. They could have a richer life, a happier life, if they would give themselves a chance. The richness of love and family, as we were - that calls for respect. You have to learn to forgive and to forget; you must learn from right and wrong. Our lives would be even richer if we follow the past. Practice the words: forgive, forget, love, and affection. Maybe it would be easier to live. I wish I could make for all the people easier lives. Only thing I can say is that everyone has choices. Only you can decide, because it is very difficult to see yourself, but others see you better.

How can they? They cannot see far; they are blind with stupidity and hatred. Their brain is blocked - can't and will not allow themselves to open their mind for thinking. Why are they doing it? I do not know. I think they may be influenced by others. Jealousy is very bad, and it is very dangerous. Must be very careful, because it is catchable, like a disease. We don't think so, but it is. It is worse than any sickness. Therefore, innocent people fall in this category, sometimes unexpectedly - not strong enough to fight it, or maybe afraid to fight back or walk away before it becomes out of control. We must be strong and hold on before it is too late.

I repeat myself because I think that is the beginning of the problem - a person may become like a dictator. We should not allow it to get that far. Stop, think for yourself which way you are turning, and be wise enough, be smart enough before you make a decision. You can learn if you want to; it's never too late. Experience is the best teacher. See what one really can do; others are trying to tell you which choice will be better. Our Lord G- d gave us a brain and we must use it. This is our power, not just money. People believe that if you have money, money is power. While this is true, the power can come and go. If you don't use your brain power, it can disappear very fast - and then what? You have nothing. There is more than money - you can have a richer life.

If you take a good look around you, it depends on you how you choose and what you do with it - or not to do - or just wait for someone to use you and destroy you, whichever. I'm trying to wake up the people to do something, not just wait. Do not allow yourself to fall asleep. I'm trying to keep you awake. I know you're getting tired or bored, and I'm sorry for that.

Sometimes we have to do things with kindness, not with anger. I believe in a peaceful way - try to reach out and to help the helpless and the sick. Maybe this is the root of the problem. You must examine it carefully and try to work on that. There are all kinds of ways; we can and we must reach out to the helpless to be able to live a better life. It would be better for all of us. We must not neglect our duty. We cannot relax. We must remember we cannot live alone. We need each other in support. Look out for better health. Whatever makes you a better person can make a better place to live in harmony. This is what life is all about - understanding. Don't waste time because all of us are important. You must better yourself.

Going back to the publisher - I called him. He told me he has good news for me from his previous advertisement. He learned that it was well done and an order for a couple hundred books is waiting to be filled. We really did not have any idea what was happening. We are very surprised, as you are. I'm happy and pleased to tell you that.

I told him maybe the last one can be better; it could be a continuation or change. What do you think? Would it be better? It starts differently but still going on the same spot. I got involved with other subjects. I am writing about my opinions. Maybe a little different, but the style is different and in this book I brought you in. Good or bad, you have to see it for yourself. If you have so many orders already, what will you do now? Are you going to print, how much money did they spend? Or just orders came in? How can you be sure that they will take it when you are finished? What happens if they change their mind? Then what? All he said, I know that they will take it. I see that it is as good as the first one. I don't even think about it. We all agreed. It will take longer to print and bind it. I'm going to start to mail it out. We'll all read it in a hotel. We promised them to give them the first one. Now we have 100. We'll call them and set up the meeting. We'll advertise it and we will be there to sign it.

There was a phone call from England. They wanted to know when can they receive the second book, and wanted to know how long will it take until they are able to see it. They wanted to know whether it's as good as the first one or not. Did you read it? Do you have any idea how it's going to work out? Will it work out as the last one? I need your assurance. I asked my friend and he said when I finished writing he will know whether it's good or bad.

My friend assured me not to worry about it, so I too assure you that it is good. Because you care for me and I for you, we cannot think any other way. You are already a very special person. I know that from the very beginning of our friendship. Oh yes! That was the beginning. Do you still feel the same way or just maybe getting tired of all of this? That is the reason that I cannot continue at this time.

I must take a vacation. I cannot write anymore. My brother advised me that we should wait, take time to examine the situation, but just then I ran out of ideas. How do they say it? My mind became empty! Everything came about too fast and too soon. We need time to absorb what was happening and to sink in.

Maybe this is not the right way to say it, now we have to learn what it is all about and learn from our latest experience. It is very different than we are used to. I cannot catch up with this new life. Where can I begin? We are still busy to catch up with visiting the places to sign the books. On the first one we didn't have too much time. What is the schedule? Where will it be? I know you made the arrangement with the hotel. I'm really very glad to go back to visit this place. I would like to see our friends, the young lady to whom I'm very grateful. If not she, this would not have happened, "never," therefore, I'm very grateful to her.

We never know what we can say because there's always something that can come up unexpectedly, even if a miracle can happen. Even then, it does not come easily. We have to wait and see, but if you just wait, you cannot afford it because nothing will be happening and that is not productive.

Then there is nothing in it. That means doing something, anything you feel is right, and in the meantime enjoy it. It's only a little thing, but I did just that. I was happy before all this happened. I never even thought about money. I was always concerned about someone else. When I came here in this hotel, I felt maybe it will help. At that time, I didn't know what I needed that would help. I was not tired and was not doing anything even at home.

Now I'm trying to see closer how all this came about this far. The way I did it, I was happy. Then why didn't I have extra money? Who told me I had to get away from home and why? Who suggested it? Where did I get the idea? I really do not know.

Then what? I must have heard about this hotel somewhere! Can anyone tell me? How did I wind up here? Where did I get the idea? I cannot find any answer. Do you know? Or did this just pop up in my mind? Who pushed me here?

This is something - has anyone ever heard such a thing? Did some power take me over? You do things that otherwise you would not. It takes some sort of a power that they cannot feel - just makes you do it. Is this what was happening?

Justly, when I began my writing, I did not feel that I did it. I still feel that I did not do it. I felt then that I could not do it. It is unbelievable. How did I do all this in such a short time? Can you help me to find the answer to all these questions?

I asked this question before and now. I still didn't find any real answer. How could I even imagine how and what is involved? It must be something invisible. I cannot even think, but I'm going to tell you that this is all about faith and beliefs.

Take a good look and tell me if I'm wrong? Are you people real? Yes. I would say so. How come that you never heard about me? I am not a knowledgeable person. I did not do anything to be famous or even noticeable. All my life I was very much alone. I did not mingle with many people. I live quietly in my home and do my business.

I am now retired and try to take care of myself every day. I did not even go to a senior center. I felt this would be the best for me as I was. Didn't even get around. Sometimes I was concerned that I was not able to get to see the doctors that would want to help me. Even my health seems like it is improving. Why? Is it because of what I did or what I didn't do? Nothing special, I just kept going.

All I remember, one morning I felt I needed to talk to my G-d. All of a sudden, I found myself in tears. I have had enough talking and crying, asking him a lot of questions.

Why all this now? Does he want us to go through it again, what they did? Was it not enough? Now, again, the road is terrible. When will this end? Why is he doing this? I'm afraid even to look around. The situation cannot be worse as it is; it has been enough. Now I remember, I was a little annoyed.

Is it true? Why not? I did not create this problem, and I am sure that he knows. Why could he not stop it before it was too late!

Our Almighty has the power to guide people into their positions. The leaders are promising everything. They get their position and they do not remember why they are there! Must be a good reason. The reason is that they got there because we, the people, were hoping that they would help as they promised.

What happened with the promise? Did they forget it? They just wanted to show the world that they can do whatever they want. That was a false promise. I'm not surprised at all of this now. I know the real reason. The Almighty knows clearly that I was the only one. I felt I was trusted to carry out this biggest thing in the whole world. I think You are right. I will try to do, responsibly, with Your help. You showed me the way, the right road, and You will not let me down. I hope that I did not disappoint You as of now.

O' my mighty, our G- d, guide me and lead me the best way to start, so that I can keep on going and follow your order. I am your messenger. I bow and thank you for creating all this true life. Now I thank you for making me believe in you. I never forget you. I know you are always around. I felt your presence. I'm sorry for bothering you. I need you to help me now. I thank you. We, all the people, thank you.

You selected this friend and put all these beautiful people here because you felt that this is the only way to see and make all this connection for me. You knew that this would be the only way. It was just in time, and everything fell into place as you planned. Thank you, my Lord.

With your help I am creating these books and hope to continue to do a proper job. I agree it is a good beginning. Now I have the money, and I need your help to show me how I can start to maintain and create peace and help the helpless and the sick. This is what I wanted to do.

I must help my generations to carry out the idea to be free. Freedom should be protected and not allow the fanatics to take over. They, the people, should be awakened to prevent the horror and stop practicing it.

Hatred must be stopped, even in our own backyard. We must protect Israel. We suffered enough. Now it is time to do what we can to protect our land and to make the right decisions. It is our land and belongs to the Jewish people. We're willing to live with all the nations around us in peace and share our life in peace that we deserve. We paid a high price for it, and no one, but no one, has the right to come and destroy it or to take it.

We, the good people, must remember that we want to live like any other people in freedom. Now, I want to remind our leaders not to underestimate our Lord, our G- d. He is silent until you will do the job. Do not monkey around, because the way he showed me, that's where I can get the strength. The same way, he can take it away from you.

Whatever comes up, do not fool around. Be careful how you pick your representative. Make sure he or she is doing what you have voted in for and should work for you and not for himself, but for the people and our country. Do not fool around. Don't sell out what you have been voted in for - your own selfishness, for yourself to get fame. It will not work; don't even think of it.

There won't be any place to hide. People get wise to you. Do not underestimate the power underneath. You think you can get away, maybe for a while, but they will get you sooner or later. This is our mighty G- d. We pray loud enough from our heart, we will wake him up. His children suffered enough. He saw what went on in the past history. Now I know that he is watching us. G- d is the Guardian and looks out for all his children.

Thank you. We trust and respect you with our heart and love. Please forgive me if I bother you. Maybe it is good that I did - this way I was doing something good also. Maybe other people forgot how to talk to you with real feeling. But now I hope you got back your own strengths. Keep up and be there for all the good people who really deserve it. Amen.

I found my answer. I feel better, relaxed, and continue what I was supposed to do - to finish my job. That which I will have to teach to someone to continue when I cannot. Thank you, our Lord, that I'm stronger than ever. We can make arrangements to continue my mission. Now everyone agreed that they are doing their job, the way it is meant to be. Now we can all feel better again, to enjoy to see how it will work out as it was meant to be. We understand our duty to carry out the best way we can. This is my purpose.

After all this, I understand how everything started to fall into place. And now I have a job to do. First thing, we have to sign some of the books today because they are waiting for us. We have to make our reservations. I also wanted my friend to make arrangements for this weekend. I will be there with my brother for this week. I feel I have to do it. It is better now than later, because I did not want to wait any longer. Anything I can do today, I must do it today. Everyone is happy now more than ever. We get all the cooperation and it works out for the best.

I did not distribute any of the cash. I put it into the bank. I tried to make it safe at this time. My friend offered to help to do whatever I needed. Until now, I'm lucky to have the best team. All the smart heads are put together and therefore we can do the right thing.

Where can we begin? The money has to be safe until we decide what to do. All this has happened all at once. Without knowledge, we cannot decide what we can do, at least temporarily. I don't want to be in a hurry. We have to think it over carefully - to whom to give and how much. We just have to concentrate on the book, and later we can think further. In this case, the publishers both agreed to work together to make it possible to carry out what was meant for all of us.

Here and now again I went back where we started. The team can wrap up this weekend the second book. We came into the hotel and were ready to hand out to whoever ordered. We sold already 100 books. It would take about two days before we can finish it. But I hope that we'll be able to sign a lot more books. I hope that my hand will not give up. As of now, all is well. I'm okay and everyone is okay.

We went for lunch. Most of the people stayed there for a couple of days. This way was a little better. It wasn't rushed like any other places. We had time for relaxation. I and Irving went upstairs to rest for a while.

Later we went downstairs again and the people were gathered there around us and we were ready to sign. We didn't want to do it on Saturday. We have decided to sign it Friday, and Saturday evening, also Sunday. We had enough time to finish it on Sunday morning. After all was finished, then we decided to stop and come back to New York. We spent the day there signing more books. I was very happy to sign the books. But this time I'm not sure how many we had. Most of them were sold for cash. Therefore, we had to be very careful. The publisher handled all the cash as of now. The first bundle of books was counted and was okay. We have deposited the money temporarily until we have a chance to finish the job.

Probably will have to hire someone who has the idea how to take care of the checks, to figure out and sort out the way I want it to.

The other countries are also waiting for the books and wanting to know if they're going to get any.

I really don't know where to begin. How can we help them first? We must check how much money they're getting. We're going to give them a part for those desperate people that are dying from hunger, sickness, and other problems. This, I think, I call it life saver expense, not just help. It is critical to acknowledge what is to be done for the world hunger and healthcare organizations who really give every penny they have - not others - but all goes to the right people. I do not want to pay for anyone for helping us to help others. It must be on a voluntary basis. If we have more money, then we can do much more. At this point, we cannot do as much as we really want to. I myself feel that G- d sent me for a special mission and therefore I must do just that. It's not a profitable organization. We cannot pay taxes at this time. We must account for every penny we spend. Not cheating. I had to go over all that before we began to distribute a penny. Or I will have to go over it and be involved in the project. It is not easy. It is very difficult to be involved, but I will try to see how I can get involved as of now.

We succeeded with the plan, and I hope we'll all see to it to continue the same way. I'm very grateful for all of you cooperating with all of us. Together we will succeed and I now know how hard we all worked. You're beautiful people. I'm very proud of you. Thank you from the bottom of my heart. Without you, I never would have been able to accomplish what we did as one.

[Editor's note: material removed about all the world's problems]

I just learned that it will be okay to be printed in a couple of days and it will be on the market. I was sure that it's a good book. We will tell soon. I'm waiting and hope for the best.

I cannot write now anything more. This book is entirely different than the others. This book is about me - how I saw the situation from my point of view. I did not try to influence anyone. Only thing left to do is to understand what we have decided to do. It was to try to work for a better life for all of us. We can make it if we try hard. I believe that.

Whatever we decided to seek out. I just called my publisher and was told that the book would be very successful. It looks and sounds very interesting. And he predicted it would be a good seller. Some people are ordering it again. Also, he received an inquiry if I will be writing any other books. I told him that this time I'm not sure what will be exactly in the future. But we will decide later on.

I want to thank all the people who showed me that they care for me. I thank all of you and wishing you the best.

A week later, I received another call and we were invited to sign books at the same places. I told him okay, just let me know when. They just purchased 100 books in the resort where we met and also in New York. Now, on the West Coast, they received the first order - the first and second editions. They wanted me to go there to sign. I told them that I have to check with my brother if we are able to go there, or if they wanted me to sign here and mail it to them with a signature. They replied that they will think about it. The person who ordered the books would like to meet you. I would like to meet them too, the only thing is, it's more than I can handle. I cannot tell as of now. I don't think there'll be any chance because as of now I'm doing more than I expected. I'm grateful for the invitation.

I usually do not think too much about it because I really want to do it - it gives me a wonderful feeling inside. I myself cannot understand. I just go - don't even want to think about it! I'm happy to be able to accomplish what I did. I feel I could not accomplish it without you, my dearest friend. You're the one. What you did, you have sacrificed your own life also. You're supposed to be retired and here worked harder than ever, without any payment. Now, I would like to work out a deal for you, which you so deserve. You worked hard to succeed what we did. I owe you so much, I cannot even measure the size. Only thing I can see is that if not for all of you, I would not have anything. I had to learn to accept all this and deal with it and learn a new way to accept my life and to learn how it is possible. It's like a dream - it's an unbelievable dream. I asked questions - am I dreaming or is this real?

I expect my brother to come here to visit me tomorrow, on Sunday, if the weather clears up. I'm looking forward to seeing him, this time and all the time. I did make arrangements to go to the publisher to see what they accomplished. I will be happy to see what and how it will work out. There I'll be able to sign some of the books, if they want me to. We will make arrangements so it will be better. I wish I could be able to travel to the West Coast or elsewhere. I would be very proud to do it. The knowledge that I am wanted - I am thankful wherever it is. We can appreciate the small ones just like the big ones. Whatever it is, we will be happy about it.

[Editor's note: material removed about healthcare]

I've seen my brother and we decided that we would like to meet up with friends. We want to see how our books are doing. We do appreciate their understanding of my books. I would like to meet our readers - I would be the happiest person. It is not so easy, I try to do whatever possible. We can make some arrangement to do it. You can contact my publisher - he'll be able to make the arrangements. I cannot take any long - term commitment at this time. However, I will try to do whatever possible. I really would like to. I want to discuss it with my publisher.

I called my publisher. He told me that there were three more orders for all the three books. He said it is better than what he expected. I was very surprised. However, on the other hand - why wouldn't it be? Let's face it - it is a good book, all of them. It is more educational than we ever wanted. Whoever wants to learn, they can. Also, I'm writing another book. I think that this book is very good and is worth reading - it's not a boring one. I try to make it so that people will want to read it and have fun at the same time.

To me, it's important to enjoy the book - make it interesting - otherwise people will not bother. I felt more like others may want to read it. I try to accomplish it the best way I can.

Now, I will try to meet my friend to see what his opinion is. I have met the other friends. We're all busy. Today, I've seen my brother - he was visiting. I'm always happy to see him. Just now, the phone is ringing - I must answer it. To my surprise, it is my friend. I asked him how he is, and I told him I was just thinking of him and I wanted to call him. "How did you spend your weekend? Where were you? Where did you go for your Thanksgiving? Did you see your family? How are they?" It is your chance to speak to your friends - how are they? Hoping that they're okay. I will try to see them soon. "Are you going anywhere soon? How about New Year's?" Hoping that you will have whatever you decide to do and have a happy holiday. If I cannot see you before, I wish you have a happy and wonderful New Year - a healthy one and best of everything, best ever. I do not make any appointments usually. I spend time at home. I'm not sure if any members of our family will travel on the holiday weekends. The main thing is we should all be careful and try to enjoy as much as possible - and peace.

My friend also asked me if I would want to see him or maybe he would come here for a short visit.

Anytime you can, just let me know so that I can prepare something that you enjoy. Next week is okay - that will be fine - but please call me before you see us. Okay? Unless my brother - and the weather is nice - he can come also. The sooner you can have an enjoyable day with the best company, then you're not getting bored. My brother likes you also.

Time goes very fast. Before you know it - it's already gone. Our lives go even faster. Therefore, we must do whatever we can do - whatever we need to do. I'm trying to finish my book. It is responsible. As in all, I'm a little slow and am trying to catch up with it. It seems it will take longer than I expected. I was asked if I plan to write another book. As of now, I did not plan to. Anything I try, I want to finish. I need more time for myself. If something special comes about, I may change my mind - but I cannot tell you at this time.

My friend came this week to visit me and it was very nice of him. I enjoyed his visit. It was very productive. My brother came also. We had a real happy reunion to see each other - with so much to talk about - and it was like with a family member. I looked upon him like if I had known him forever. He has a very nice personality - easy to get along with - and he himself is very delightful. And that was from day one estimate. Very unusual person. I must say that all of us are getting along - my family with him - although we are all busy and do not have much time, so whatever time we can, we try to enjoy it, both ways. Now it is time to relax and continue my writing until next time.

My friend looked over my book and he was amazed with the content of this book. He liked it very much. I asked him if he was disappointed or if he thinks I should stop. He said that he feels I should continue. Therefore, I take on more pressure and will write two more. I also have other opinions, therefore I have to try my best to continue.

My friend invited me to visit his family. I had no choice but to accept his invitation. It will be around New Year's. I didn't want to because I felt there is so much going on, especially in the evening. Therefore, we worked out that it would be for lunch. I thought that would be enough, but even then, they are not too close. I told him that "You will be traveling four times back and forth." It is not considerable to make so many trips. Therefore, I told him it's easier for him, possibly, to bring his family to visit me. Perhaps some other time, I can visit his family who is not far from my brother's home, and I could visit both of them. I'm looking forward to this opportunity. My brother was also invited. I know he would be very interested and is looking forward to meet him since we didn't meet them before up to now. I heard about them. I know already that they are interesting people. They also know about me. Naturally, they read my books. Therefore, it is like old friends. Sometimes we feel that way - it gives you an inside warm feeling and appreciation. I know I do. Next time, we'll be looking forward to this visit.

Meanwhile we are arranging to be traveling for the signing of more books, I'm happy to say that we are lucky to have established as much as we did. Hoping it will continue further with this one also. It will be the best. With all this help that I'm getting, it should be. I was invited to the country to visit my other friend and also my lady friend, to whom I am very grateful. She is the best friend I ever had - a very exceptional person. I can see, as I said before, I owe her everything regarding my success and having a chance to meet all my friends. She still cares for me. I wanted to do something for her, but she would not want to hear about it. She told me if I take her as a friend, that will be more than enough. I should come to visit her from time to time. I told her I will. I promise that I will.

I spoke to a few friends and they too would like me to come up at least for a couple of days. You could spend a little time, at least together. I'm also looking forward to visiting and spending some time with them.

I'm the luckiest person to have this opportunity, of which I'm grateful. We cannot have too many opportunities. As they say, you really have to be lucky - this would happen only once in a lifetime. We should never forget it. We can't live alone. We need people - the right type of people. If you're lucky, you can learn and work with them, not against them. Willing to learn and are willing to give but don't expect something in return. Sometimes unexpectedly you might have a surprise and you should be thankful for that. If you practice it, you can succeed and it makes you feel that you accomplish something in life. This is the way I felt all my life. I never expected something in return. I always felt that I'm doing it because I want to, not because I had to. Therefore, then as of now, I feel the same way. I'm grateful - as I have told that before.

Friday I had a chance to meet my friend's family, and they are great people. They're young people, and they have a very beautiful home, very well furnished. They are beautiful - nieces, nephews, sisters, brothers - all of them came up for a family gathering. It seems that they are a very close family. They said to me that they like me. They do not know what to do for me. They read all my books and they were very happy to meet me. Now they understand why their brother cares for me, as they put it. They know that I am honest, sincere, and I want nothing more than a friend. No attachment. Just a good friend without any real reason. Usually, others would want something with friendship - not just a friend - because of that, they respect me.

Before I went to visit them, I wanted to take a gift. I didn't want to go empty-handed. I asked my friend what would be proper to take to them because I don't know them and I don't want to go anywhere empty-handed. I would appreciate it if you could tell me. My friend went out and bought a gift and he wanted me to take it to them. I told him I don't operate that way. If I want to take something, I do just that. I appreciate just the idea - what he suggests - not for him to buy it for me. I will pay whatever the price is. If you agree to do it this way, then it will be fine. I am so grateful to you for wanting to help me, but that's the only way I would do it. If they do not like whatever I buy, then they can always return it to the store to exchange it. That is the way to operate. When I give something this way, they have a chance to exchange it for whatever they want. Sometimes people give things that are not useful, and eventually they will get rid of it.

When I arrived there, they opened the package, and to my surprise they loved it. I myself was very surprised. It was a beautiful antique piece. Beautiful design. It was an unusual case and was in a very good taste. I think my friend paid more than he asked me to pay him. I didn't want to make a scene, therefore I just accepted it and later I thanked him. I told my friend that this was a beautiful piece and in a very good taste. I was very happy that they liked it.

As time went by very nicely, my brother and I were very happy to meet his family. At this stage, we have to learn and accept this new life. I don't know how long I will be able to put up such a show. It is not in me. What should I do now? It's too late, I'm in it. Can I turn my clock back or my history? It seems that it is here, like it or not - there is no way out. Let's face it, we will do what is best for both of us. Here our young life went by so fast with hard work. Now it seems we can have whatever we want and we don't even try to take it. Why? Don't you want to? I'm sure we want to. We appreciate whatever we have. It's better this way - to be grateful for what we have - than to sit and wait for someone to come around, wait for a handout, and wait for what will happen next. Here, there are people who can do well - and they don't even want to. Why? I really do not understand myself why.

That is not what I wanted. What did we really want? I just wanted a comfortable living, my brother feels the same way. Okay. But what is the problem? Why am I hesitating? Why do I not take my chances? All this doesn't make any difference! I am still what I was and my family is not here to enjoy our life together. I would be happier to share all this with my family, but this way, I somehow do not feel right. Something is missing. What is missing? Someone to share with. I'm very grateful I'm able to share it with my little brother. I'm grateful for that, to see him, the family, to be happy. At least they have better life. I hope it's easier, at least they do not have to struggle.

I also want to help my nieces. I would set up a trust for them and their children. I would also establish in Israel a children's home. Maybe another organization to help the helpless. It is very important to me to be careful whom I can trust and believe. All this bothers me because everything is unsettled around us. I cannot make such a decision. I must think it over carefully, especially now. We will have to work on it and see what we will decide next. We must work carefully. Until then, we will just have to wait because we want to be sure that the right person will benefit by it. In the meantime, I try to do the best I can.

Now I'm happy at home, I love my little sweet home, it is more than a castle. That would not make me happier. I hope that I can find someone that I can trust to help me, that would make life easier. He must have also the right help who can take care of him and have a clean home where he really enjoys his life. Also better condition for his family and be able to establish and manage their life and their children and my nieces.

Linda and her family, Diana included. The family comes first to me, that is all I wanted. I want to see them happy and to give them a chance for a better life, which they well deserve. I want to be sure that my brother is well taken care of as long as he needs it. Also, his sons will remember, if not for their father, they would not be able to accomplish their goal otherwise. He deserves their respect and they should not forget it. I cannot remind you all the time, but I hope I don't have to. If he wants to move or whatever, and before he decides what he wants, it is up to him. I advise his sons to make sure to clean up his home and see to it that he gets some help to live in a house, take care of him, a companion, someone that cooks for him, maybe a couple. And he must see to it that they are doing that and to be sure that he takes care of himself and gets a good doctor - make sure that he will take care of him. But he can do whatever he chooses. He has the right to do everything. He's the wiser - whatever is best for him all around. I'm not controlling anyone, just want to be sure that whatever anyone decides or what they want to do, they do it safely and are careful how they manage their life.

In the meantime, I'm ready to meet my friend's family. It is a nice surprise. It shows that he thinks of me as a friend - that is all - and I think of him also like it. I'm proud that someone really cares, as a person, for me. That he's all about it - to have someone like a really good, clean friend. No attachment. If he likes to be a friend, it is okay, and if he decides to stop, it is okay also. I still appreciate their friendship as long as they want to continue, and I will remember them forever. I don't throw friends around. I am a friend forever - and it's up to them.

Now, we have to get ready for this coming week, because we are supposed to go to the country for a couple of days. We are looking forward to this meeting. We did not visit them for a while. Now I'm looking forward to it. I really need some new dresses. I hope that my niece Linda can come with me and pick out a dress or maybe some slacks, if we have time to do it. I did not buy any clothing for a long time. I felt that if I did not need it, why should I buy any? Only thing is that now they know me and I need something to change over. They should not say that I'm a miser. I myself like to look well and now I have a chance to wear it. I have places to go now and to get dressed, which I didn't have in the past. Now it is a different tune. You see, we never know what the future holds for us. We have surprises - sometimes it's a good one, and it's okay.

Surprise is very good and it's interesting, but nothing more. By the way, my brother just called. He reminded me that Chanukah is here. It is the right time to decide to go to the country - in the fall, especially if the weather is nice. It is cool but clear. One can go for a walk and doesn't have to go far. I don't know if I can do it, but some time ago I did it. Now I'm a little lazy. But anyway, to light the candles, and the holiday - the atmosphere is such, but I don't remember when I did it. Maybe back home we used to have an oil burner and oil lamp and they kept it in the window shelves. It was so many years ago. We were very young. All this is just like a dream. Sometimes I have to touch myself to see if I'm real or not! How can this be true? Or is it? The whole life is a dream. So much suffering went by. How did this all happen? We had to bear all that. It is unbelievable. We had to witness all these horrors. I don't really know where we've gotten all the strength? How were we able to be under that pain? On the other hand, I feel that other people went through the real suffering and they were able to survive and live with it. I cannot even think about that pain and how they live with it - luckily they were able to raise a family. Some of them suffered plenty - silently - physically and mentally, and they were all alone. Something that you can't really handle easily. Sometimes we can't change the way it is and there is no choice. There are many of us who feel that way. We have to learn to take it as it is. We have to learn to smile - otherwise, living is not worth it. This way, they say, if you smile, the world smiles with you; if you cry, you cry by yourself. It is true.

Now we arrived to the country. We had some surprises - they were waiting for us. We were very surprised that everyone came and we had a beautiful table set. Now, our table became bigger and we got more company. The hotel was also full. It was a full house - I thought because of the holiday. I learned later the news that this weekend we will be signing books, to which I was very happy. I am there so might as well do some work. We would not have to pay more. If we are lucky, maybe we'll make some extra money. I hope that is the reason that the hotel is fully occupied. Now we can make some arrangements for this book also - it will be ready this weekend. I will be able to finish it, then we will be able to print it before long. We did not check out if they like it or not - if not, they will read it and then we'll decide what we will do. I hope it will be liked as much as the others. But never know. Irving and Sherwin like it. They think it's very funny. I created all those friends from nothing and I was able to make it a successful book from it. They think it's a good imaginary book. You only never know what will be the result - we have to wait and see. And then we will decide what is the best way to go or choose the right way. I will know in a couple of days. I waited thus far so a couple of days won't matter.

Now we are on vacation and let's forget about business. It is a very nice place. My young lady friend was waiting for us to release the service with the best food. She knows her business. She's very smart and attractive and pleasant. It seems everyone likes her. The entertainment is very good. The music every night. If you like the music you can, and if you want to dance you can do that. Whatever you want or just sit and talk.

My friend asked me if I would do him a favor - dance with him - he would try to do whatever I like. I told him I'm rusty - I did not dance for many years. He felt it does not matter - whatever it is, it will be okay. I thought he's a very good dancer. And I can see how he walks - sometimes you can tell. He wanted to slow dance first. He told me he did not believe me that I did not dance for many years because he thinks I'm a very good dancer. The other people noticed also, because I got so many compliments. All around us, people were watching this, and our young lady friend came to us and said how good a couple we are, and they can see that I am a good dancer. Okay, that is good, but I didn't want to have trouble so I told him that tonight, no more dancing. That was the end - there's always another night. After that I went up to my room and Irving went to his room. We had a good night's rest.

Next day we came down and had breakfast. We were there as usual. We were rested. They were talking about the dance. They told me that I owe them a dance. I agreed - I will. I did this with two other friends. I promised them that I will do it - dance with them. I owe them that much. I must say they are all of them very good dancers. I must also say that they were handsome. I never thought that I would have such a gentleman that would dance with me. It is an unusual opportunity for anyone to have a chance to meet this type of people that were around me. This short time can make a lifetime's memory - rich and real people. Very selective. I would say handpicked with good taste. You have to be careful with them how you talk, and afraid that you do not speak incorrectly. They accepted me as I am. I do not know why, I do not understand, but they do and are graceful. This is a dream - I never thought that that would happen in real life. At least, I feel happy about it.

I spoke to my brother about this and he agreed - they are very unusual people. These people come from different places and they came as friends. I'm the only woman they chose to be their friend. There are so many educated women, attractive - they would grab any one of them - and here I cannot even dance with them, why all this fuss over me, there's nothing in it for them. Why? I can't understand really. I'm not beautiful - never was - and why? I don't even have a college education. My English also not too good - what is it that they care about? I don't know. Well, will this be enough for them? It seems like that and I'm not complaining. Why do I feel like this feeling? Is it because I do not want them, therefore they feel more comfortable with me? Maybe that is true. Maybe okay, we'll find out soon enough or may never know. I cannot just come and ask them, they may not like it - it's a story, whereas that is okay. If not, it is also okay too. Sometimes just let it go. That is what I will do - just let it go. I'm not going to think about it, just have a good time until it lasts. Why should I worry about it? There's no reason. Maybe tonight they will dance with one more person. My friend expects me to dance with him again. We will see. I told him I do want to court the others. I don't want to hurt his feelings and I hope he understands. I will try to catch up with all. We will have more time to have for him - this is what he expected. And don't feel disappointed - otherwise he may not be so happy about it. Okay, we can only do so much. Still have more time here. We will be here for a week, so I hope we will be able to accomplish what we need to.

I told him I don't want to overdo it. After so many years I didn't dance, therefore I'm just going to practice and to see how I would react to all this excitement.

Thank goodness I was okay - for my surprise it was a good experience. I love dancing. It seems like this is an unusual experience. Surprisingly it was good.

When I came home I had an appointment with my doctor. He could not believe it. He wanted to know what I did and he was also surprised. When he asked all these questions? Usually he's very busy. Why now?

I told him I was away for a couple of days. He told me whatever I was doing, I should continue doing that. You are doing well and I know I did, because now I did better on my dance also. I did not do any fast dance. I just danced only what I could and continued dancing the same.

My publisher asked me if I would see him more often. I told him I cannot because I did not want to encourage him to be more than a friend, simply because I felt that he wanted to be more than a friend. Therefore, I told him I do like him very much. If we both would have met when we were younger, then I could have talked about this, but then probably you would not even notice me. At this stage maybe you know me and you feel you like to continue for further friendship or more. I told him that it's better for both of us. He told me he does not care - even a short time is better than never. He is willing to take chances. I should think about it.

He wanted to know how I feel towards my younger friend. He wanted to know if I'm serious with him. I told him no. I'm only a friend also like with you. I do not encourage him either. He thinks that my friend told him that he's not giving up on me. He's hoping I will change my mind. I am still thinking about it and I am going to sort it out. I like him. I met his family, they are wonderful people. I do like them very much, but marriage is out of question.

He mentioned maybe I would find out how I feel about him, because I asked him how he is getting along with you. He told me his side - that he is ready anytime. He never changed his mind. He really loves you. He talks about you. It is amazing - just like he would be in heaven. I asked him if he ever was married? Was he ever disappointed with someone?

Do you know anything more? Or maybe, if I'm not serious with him or anyone else, then maybe it's best not to see him at all, because I do not want any problem for him and for myself. I never heard anything about that before. I thought sometimes that he may hope for more adventure. I never encouraged him. Now you know... I'm sorry if I did mislead you. If I was intentionally doing so, I'm very sorry. I was very careful. But now, what do you think? I must come to a conclusion. Do you think that I will have some trouble? It does not look that way. Since you have mentioned it, I do not know. I cannot get around to see his reaction. I did not see it in him as of now. We talked about it and I told him before if he feels differently, I may not be able to see him anymore as a friend either. I said that to him often enough. Maybe tomorrow it will be time to talk to him also.

I will tell him that if he is interested more seriously, but I refused him also. I told him I am closer to his age and he does not care how long will be. He would be the happiest person if I would reconsider his proposal. And you told me the same thing. I told him that other people would be jumping for this opportunity. Why? Maybe I should think about it before I give my answer. I told him before that he is too young and he has a chance and he can still have a family and have a full life. Just maybe, that would be the best for both of you. He dismissed all my suggestions, therefore you cannot reason with him. He told me that it will take some time to convince me to make him accept what you are trying to bring across. I asked him, perhaps I should write to him instead of personally telling him. Maybe it would be the best. Try it and see if you need any help you can count on me. Then I will have to do the same with you. What will I do next? I will find myself with no friends left for me.

I think of you more than you know. I think you are one of the nicest people I ever met. I value all of your friendship. I feel that it is priceless. I am very grateful that you even think of me seriously. I do care for you, and it is not easy for me to consider whatever I have to say at this stage. It does not matter what stage it is. In my opinion about love, I mean real love, it does not matter - the real feeling can come at any age. Love is a very broad feeling. I am not talking about personal feeling - you can get love by many ways. I, as a person, care for your respect, and you feel the same way, when we can, to be together all the time. It does not change, on and off, like a yo - yo. Real love does not come that way and you can control that feeling that you have. That is love - all about someone - that is real love. You must be in control whenever you feel. You must have that control. We are human, not animals. You must examine closely your feeling to make sure it is really what both parties feel, the same way, before you let go with your real feeling. Otherwise, you are looking for trouble. It is very easy to jump to conclusion. Yes, I am in love - for me, this is really not the real love - it is an infatuation. I do not consider it to be true love.

I know there are lots of people who define love differently. I think this is a very dangerous subject. I do not even like to talk about it. There are many arguments. I do not want to go deeper in examining further. But if people want to look into it, then they will find just that - maybe I am right. If they think carefully - why are there so many problems around us, especially in homes, family, divorces and so on? Take a look - there are marriages, children without fathers. Some have 10 children - they do not even know who their father is. Someday those children come to marriage and have no idea - they come to fall in love without knowing that they can be their sisters and brothers! Then the trouble begins. Is that healthy life?

And on top of it, now they don't even need licenses to live together. Should I go further? Take a good look! See why real marriages are breaking up. Now one sex is getting married - that is man to man or woman to woman - and now new law acknowledges that as okay. This is the freedom? What will be next? Do you think that this is believed what I can even think about in my category? I would never even say love. My G-d! Forgive me for saying that - I am saying this - that it is baloney! Is there any real name? I can't say - I do not know. I don't know the real name. Homosexuals and lesbians or whatever it is - I am sorry, I do not agree on that. Not when they really decide to be married. I accept that they remain single. But when they decide to have some kind of marriage - when it comes to kissing on the mouth - this is really more than enough. It seems this is some kind of epidemic - catchable - not a matter of how they are. What I see - even among educated people - their minds get lost, their senses disappear.

I know some of you people will be upset for my expressing my thoughts. I do not want to hurt anyone, but maybe if I can help one person to wake up, then maybe it's worth it. The rich and famous have everything, therefore they don't have any excitement - they are bored - so they decide to go public telling what they have decided to do - to become whatever. And here they throw away their good marriages, the children, without even trying to solve their problems. What's happening around us - we better wake up before it's too late. Some people take advantage of our freedom. They are using it for their benefit. Why is it this way? As our life goes on, is that normal? Was creation established that way? In the next generation children will be growing up - is this the example that you want to show them? Is that what you really consider this as a new life? Is that what you want for the next generation? Is it not enough? Everything else is going down. We do not have enough problems to deal with? We have personal problems. How can a country lead to victory with the situation like this? Oh my! Is there anyone who can say or do something? Is this what we worked or dreamed of for our children? I don't know. Everything is so mixed up. We need to deal with this problem at this time. I really cannot understand why. But we hope that some people will wake up from this dream - because those people I think they're bored and looking for more excitement. When they get bored with this today, they'll be finding something else. Will have already new ways of divorces also. It does not matter - divorce is divorce - just the same.

I truly wish them whatever they are wishing for themselves. Either way, you cannot accept my view. But don't worry about me - go on, keep going on - you might be tired of me before you know it. What a different life! I don't know what to say in each other's attraction. It seems these people do not look at life seriously. They only see whatever they want to. Therefore, I can only write about it - that is all.

I think this will change my belief in the subject. Going back to my friend's decision, I did sit down to write to him honestly, with a clear mind, that I'm sorry that I learned about his feelings and I do appreciate everything he was helping me with - and also how much I respect him. I will never hurt him or his feelings. Also, how much I respected his feelings, but I cannot feel that I will change my mind about marriage. I learned about his real hope, therefore I have come to the conclusion - that is my judgment. I cannot seem to get hurt by my decision, inasmuch as I want him to be a friend.

I'm sorry I can't offer anything more - that's now and forever. I take one day at a time and I try to work around it. Especially, he is still a young man, and he can do much more than he would be with me. I took the necklace that he gave me - and I cannot keep it anymore. I cannot wear it. I was hoping that he could meet the right person and give it to her. I hope he will understand my feelings. This is not to hurt him - this is really how I feel. If I would have been younger - I would never consider marriage with a younger man. I'll be better off to have someone with a closer age, and that's the way I always felt.

Therefore, I have hope for him and that he will be able to accept my decision gracefully. When the time comes, he and the woman he will meet - and I - would really be friends who appreciate a friendship. I do not mix friendship with business. I never did. In my opinion, it's wise not to. I don't know why I was careless, and with all this new excitement, I forgot how I like things to go. The way I feel is - better now than later. I would be very happy to hear about it when you will find someone you really like. There are many nice ladies around, especially what you really need. Just sit down and appreciate that I came to a conclusion.

I was wishing him all the best, with regret that I had to bring it to his attention. I misled him. I am sorry. I told him so much and I cannot come or bring myself to marriage at any time in the present or in the future. And I feel he can do much better. I don't want to take advantage of his good nature, which is very rare. I hope he will not misunderstand me and take it in the wrong way. It's better now than later. Perhaps one day he will feel good about it - but I told him the truth. I tried before to bring it to his attention. I made that clear.

I will cherish our friendship as long as I live. His help, his advice - I could not exist without his help. Therefore, if he ever needs my help, feel free to call me. I will try to help as much as possible.

Now I mailed my letter and was hoping this time it will work out. I called my publisher. I told him what I did and why I will not visit them in the hotel. I don't want to antagonize him... and about signing the books, we will have to make other arrangements. Both of my books - the one I'm finishing now - if he wants to, he can come and pick it up, or perhaps I will send it to him, or send someone to deliver it, maybe I will ask my nephew. I arranged it as I explained before. I signed my contract, so that still goes okay. He assured me nothing changed. It's okay as is, and in a couple days they will know whether they're going to work on it.

I told him that I hope he still likes it, and I'm grateful for his help - also my other friends, if I may call them friends. He said don't worry about it. They're all mature people. Many have experience in our life to accept life as it is, as it comes. I also told him about my friend. He will get over it, he said. He should have enough chances, and you gave him enough of your attention. If he ignores it, it is not your fault - no one's fault. Sometimes we don't want to face the truth, and it is not easy. Just don't worry - this is life. In a lifetime, we have all kinds of experiences. Some we like, and others we do not. But that is the truth, and we learn to live with it.

I do admire you, and I take my hat off to you. You are a very unusual person. I told you that since I met you. We always felt that way, but now I'm sure we were right. You showed us the real person you are - honest, and a rare personality. Now, I see why you never got married. I don't blame you. Because of that, I say the reason why you are a very unusual person. I thank you for that. I do appreciate that statement. All of you - I felt the same way and still do.

A couple of days later, I heard from the publisher, and they went through my book, and they were very surprised that I made it in a short time. Now my spelling and writing have improved so much that it is different than they ever dealt with before. They predicted that it would be a good seller. Both of them - they can hardly wait to get one to read. Everyone is looking forward to getting one. It is already being advertised. When the time comes that it's printed and ready to be sold, we will be getting orders.

The question is now: when are you going to write another one? Everyone knows that as of now, I will not write another one. I must take time out until some new subject will come to my mind. That is the only way I can write another book. Otherwise, I cannot write anything. Like you are telling me - I'm different. I told them this. I agree - that is also true. Is there any other question? I did already more than I have ever dreamed of. Now I have to learn to accept and live with it. I'm in it, and I want to thank you for encouraging me and furthering it.

I know I owe you a lot, which I still did not acknowledge enough to show my appreciation. Maybe I do not know how, or maybe it happened so fast and I just cannot understand what is going on around me. In one instance, I do understand - about why and how it started and where it came from. I didn't have any more information where to go from here. Everything just closed around me. I will have to sort it out now the best way I can. I think little by little I'm getting there.

Now the holidays are here. Try to enjoy your holiday with your family also. And after that, the new year is here. We will have to have the best of the holiday season, with a happy new year and the best ever. Good health goes with it, and hope to be happy, all of us, and we will have a chance to see each other, maybe in the future. I do not promise because I do not believe in promises. Aiming to be well. Enjoy whatever you can. And when the book is published, you will be able to see it. I would like to know - is it good or bad? If it sells, that is good. If it does not, then that means bad. Whichever it is, I cannot change it. Now should I worry? Whatever it is, I did what I could - and now I am just waiting and seeing.

I've received a call from my publisher. He said that both books are a success. He already received orders for more than the others. He cannot understand why - but it does not matter, the only thing is that they're getting orders, which is good news. They will let me know if there is anything else they want to tell me. They are sending me my first copy. They have changed the outside cover, and now it will be, instead of as before red and gold, a black cover with gold. It looks very rich, very impressive, and in good taste.

The publisher received orders. He thinks it will go like the others. And people like you. They like what you're telling them, and in person, they believe whatever you are telling them. It does not matter the age - all ages are interested in it, which is a good sign for selling books.

I'm excited hearing your opinion. I appreciate all this. I still learn - as they say, it's never too late. You can always learn in our lifetime. We never know everything. I also believe in that.

Finally, I received my first book. I called Irving and Sherwin. I informed them what was happening. They were very happy to hear it and will come over to see it as soon as they can, probably this weekend.

I told my dear friend that the publisher is going away for the New Year. He made some arrangements, but he didn't tell me where. He will call me when he comes back. I told him about your book. He was very happy to hear the good news. He appreciated to hear about you. He told me how gracious you are and that he will cherish your friendship. He will never forget you all. He's taking your advice. Therefore, now he is very busy. But if there is any good news, he will let you know. He wishes all of us a healthy New Year and wants to be sure that I should tell you, and I promised I will.

At this time, I'm waiting for further instructions regarding the books. I hope I don't have to go around signing these books like before, because it's getting more difficult for me.

I also received an invitation from my friends for New Year's Eve. I have to call them and thank them, but I will not be able to go there. I have other arrangements. I thanked them, and that's about all. I do not wish that our friendship should continue indefinitely. I feel it was enough - no more. I do not have the time and energy to go around. I prefer to be what I was. I think I've wasted enough time for something that was without any intention or meant to be.

Now, I can read all four books, as fast as I wrote them. I still cannot imagine that I did it. I still think that someone dictated it to me. I still believe that whatever or whoever did it - it does not matter. Might as well enjoy it. They are beautiful books and well written. I must say, I really do not understand, but whatever it is, it is good and beautiful.

The friends and the people that know me are admiring it. Colleges want me to appear on their campus to speak, but I declined. There isn't any reason I should do it. If they want to know more, then let them buy my books, for that is important for me.

Now I have to concentrate on other things in life. I hope that Irving would be able to come. It depends on the weather. At this time of the year, one never knows from one day to the other. Everyone is busy with their life, which is the way it should be. I'm kept busy with my doing, and that is all about.

As of now, I do not have any appointments. Therefore, I don't have to rush, which is good. With the new book, I would have to slow down. It was getting a little bit too much, and I didn't have time for myself. Now at least I can catch up where I left off.

This time, I will have to look for other doctors who can help me more than this one. And I have to talk to the doctor who is in charge of me - maybe he can get someone who is more reliable - and I must do that because as of now I have asthma attacks and no one to see and help me at this time. It is not the best that I have to run around. There is no one to see. It is a goal.

[Editor's note: material moved to memoir. About her doctors]

I feel better, therefore I'm going to call my friends then. By now, all this book is ready - finished. I hope to hear good news. I've decided to call them.

He said he was glad I decided to call. My friends were very happy to hear from me. I told them I was busy, I didn't have any time, and I'm sorry for that. They knew I'm at home and thinking about a new book. I asked how everyone is - that was very nice.

How's my hostess? She was busy. He told me all the people I met are asking about me and wanted to know when I'm coming around - or if we have any news about writing more books. This time I wanted to take time out, consider when, and then let him know.

My other friends asked about me. My publisher told me he is missing me and would like me to come for a couple of days. He told me my books are still going fast. If someone would have told me in advance, I could not understand - without knowing me - what type of person I am. He said that explains it. I'm an interesting person and he's happy we all understand each other very well. I thanked him for everything he helped me with. In my opinion, especially my dearest friend - I'm grateful for that.

He also asked me why I cannot come to Israel? I told him, "You can visit me as a friend. I do know that is enough for you."

I asked him if he has heard from my youngest friend. It's only a matter of a few days or weeks, and he also asked about you. He wanted to know if you wrote another book. I told him, as we now know, you did not. I told him your books are the best selling - still demanding, all of them. What we think will be the bestseller.

Also, he asked me if you are here since then, since he left. I told him no. He asked me if I'm sure that you don't want him back. I told him no. When I make a decision, that's it - and I stand by it. I don't change my mind one way or another in my decision. I think before I make a decision - what I want to do - before I make up my mind. This way, I can live with my decision without feeling guilty.

We were speaking about that before, many times. Especially now, I need my time. What I had to endure - there's no return. You would have to be a fool to start a new life at this time of life. I know some people would do it without any hesitation. It is okay, if that's what you want. With me, it's a different story. I know what it's all about. If I would have been younger, I am sure I would take my life differently. I would have the energy to accept such a proposal.

I did have a situation once - people who had time - sometimes I missed people, and they would not take no for an answer. I had to order them to leave, because otherwise they would come anytime to see me. I did not bother with anyone after I made up my mind and made the decision. I knew what I wanted. I always tried to be in control of my life.

I believe that if you know what you want, then get married. If you don't know - watch out. You're looking for trouble. I never tried to be someone else that I am not.

I love people. I couldn't speak English and because of that it was more difficult to communicate the way I would have liked to. I'm very sensitive to all, inside and outside, therefore I knew if I don't think in advance I can have trouble. Just the same way as if I wouldn't have self - control with everything. Therefore I was single all the time. I was supposed to be in control for one reason or another.

Now, as I learned our business is doing well maybe, I should consider writing another book. It would not take me very long if I know what I want to write. I have to ask my brother. I'm sure you'll find something interesting.

Maybe you should go somewhere again for vacation and meet some interesting people. Who knows what can happen just like before? This way I can get new ideas what to write about. It seems it is the newest idea. Why not? I did it before and it worked out. It might work out now.

As just my friend maybe you would join me for the next time - as a friend, pursuing maybe a good idea for a new story. It would be interesting and learn more about myself. As of now I do not understand, it seems this is not real, it is not me. When are you doing it? I don't know the answer. I am just wound up and going on and on - more money, doing what I want to - something is driving me to go on with whatever is there left to go on finishing it.

When I spoke with my publisher, I asked him - since he is in the publishing business - what does he think of the present situation? I was thinking about writing something. I'm very disturbed with regards to the politics. I know it's a dirty business. I don't like this business. I can see danger around us and it's causing my suffering and anger. Am I right? Do you see? Can you give your opinion?

Usually I don't even want to think about it. I know I shouldn't have asked the question. I'm a very good observer. People have so much in this world, and the smartest person is looking for an answer. May I have his? I have so many questions. Maybe you see a way out. Please tell me if anyone there - or you - see differently. Maybe I shouldn't even talk about it. Just keep on and be blind and deaf to all this and go on dreaming. I cannot do it. I am one person facing the world - in trouble all over - and helplessly.

Maybe it's a good idea to reach a certain age, because our experience - what we have learned - you cannot forget. After all, we're lucky to reach a certain age and be able to express ourselves as I do. As I write, therefore I feel this way. We can get in more danger if we can't find a better solution, especially after the horrible life, after what a person herself experiences. How can you dismiss it - all the memory? Can you tell me?

What's wrong with my inner feelings? Can I stop it? Just please tell me. As much as you've gotten to know me - and we each other - I feel maybe you can enlighten me. What is your opinion?

Here he was thinking and said, "You're right," and he really put it - it is to be. I agree that the situation is not the best. We cannot just dismiss it. Maybe if we talk about it openly, just maybe then others would open up too - and just maybe it would be helpful.

What would happen if, in our own personal makeup, we hold back what we believe? That could be even more dangerous, even jeopardizing us. Like I said, we do not even know our neighbors - who they are. From my experience, at this time you cannot even think about trusting them. People fight each other like dogs.

What is your opinion? Could I forget even to try to write about it? Or maybe I shouldn't think about it. That will be the easy way out.

My friend was thinking again, then slowly assured me. "And we are speaking now, I'm listening to you. I can see how you are expressing yourself. It is amazing. Again you are right, and you are finding the way - as if you could be part of this time, a sign of possibility. As I see it, you are so special. It seems like you can predict the unpredictable. You are right. Now I can tell. But again you surprise me - no one ever came over with this feeling. And I never experienced - even met anyone - to be able to imagine what you are thinking, not to express themselves.

I am still sitting - he said, "without proper training - you are a natural - born writer."

I must say that he himself told me that he went through studying and tried to prepare himself to be a good journalist. It was years of hard work, day and night.

He found me - at least the way I see it - just as I was about to begin. A whole new world opened up in front of me, and looking back, I still don't have the knowledge to compare it to.

You're asking for my opinion, says the women who thinks about writing! And to advise you, I can only say to you: you choose whatever you want to - because whenever you write, it does make a difference. It will be very educational and different. Therefore, please go on and write. I'm anxious and ready to publish it. It will be the bestseller. When are you going to start? I hardly can wait to see it.

I told him, I should just write love stories. Maybe that would be better. Maybe it will help to relax our mind. Given today's generations are not thinking the way I am, therefore also what is the answer?

He told me, doesn't matter - because that is the reason why your book is so popular - because you are different and not boring. That is the reason I feel about you the way I feel. In my age, he said, I wish you would change your mind. Even in the short time it would be worth it. When I'm with you, I feel I know you all my life, and I want to be with you - something like a magnet pulling me closer to you - and express my feeling of gratitude and to be able to be your friend. If you need me, don't hesitate to call me anytime. I'm ready and happy to be at your service, day or night.

Again he asked me to go there for New Year's - a couple of days. I'd be sorry that I did not - it would make him the happiest person. He pleaded with me and said all our friends will be there. I'm sure to have a great time. It will be different from any other weekend.

I told him perhaps - let him make a reservation - even though I do have to speak to my brother and see how he's feeling, because lately he wasn't feeling too well. I pray and hope he'll feel better. We will see. If not now, try later. We'll let him know.

And this time, I feel in a way - thinking out where to go or where to start - to figure out what is the best way I can be of any help to my family and friends, so I'll be able to do whatever I have to until the next time. Wishing you a healthy and happiest New Year's you ever had - to you and yours. Until the next time. Looking forward to seeing you.

He assured me the same thing. Wish my brother the best. I should let him know about him and my family.

I received a letter from my youngest friend - also thinking about me - and was stunned. He said I was right to tell him to look around. You'll have a chance to meet someone you might like. That is the reason he wants to let them know: this time he met someone. Maybe you will see what he would do - and thanking me for my advice and mission. When he decides what he will do, he'll let me know.

For now, I will continue to figure out my plan, if I can, to come to the conclusion.

I just received a call from my young friend from the hotel resort. She said that we all would be honored, and that we should come up again to meet new readers. She told me that everyone is asking about us. She kept it short - we will get the best accommodation in the house. It's already ready for us, and she's saving us the rooms, both for Irving and me. She promised to give us the best attention. She said we will not be sorry.

Other important people will be there and we will have a good time. She pleaded with me - "Please say yes." I was thinking about what she said for a minute, and then I said it - yes, okay. Unless my brother isn't feeling well and cannot go back, I will try.

How could I outright refuse? She's such a nice person, and has done so much - not only in the past but now again going out of her way to do something for us. I want to show her our appreciation, to let her know we value her. I asked her, "When do you expect us to be there? What day? What time?" She told me - any day, any time, we can come. She will be ready for us. "Just please come."

And that is the way it is. We have nothing to lose, and it might help me to have more ideas for my next book. Maybe I should take the chance.

[Editor's note: material moved to memoir. Remembering hardships of leaving Europe/family and helping Herman. Explaining why she chose to stay single]

Therefore, when I got the call from my lady friend, I came to the conclusion that this is what both my brother and I need - just a change to a different atmosphere that will lift up our spirits a little. I felt a little better. I know New Year's Eve is very busy, maybe too busy for us. We can always walk to our room and rest. We do not have to go through anything we cannot do - and they know it. I'm happy I made the choice that I did. We found out soon enough.

It's coming closer. Now I have to ask my niece to find a new dress for me for this occasion. I want to look nice. I hope my brother does not mind. He will be busy enough; he will not have time to look. I don't know if I will be looked at, but I will try. I need this because I want to write about it - something. I need some ammunition to write about. It is important to have new ideas.

Now that I've decided, I am looking forward to seeing them. Time will come soon enough.

We arrived early. We were escorted to our rooms. Both of us had separate rooms. It was comfortable, and on top of it, she refused to take money from both of us. She told us that we became her family, and whenever we want to come there, the door is open for us - free. "Just let me know when."

I took a bath, cleaned up, and went down for dinner. It was a late dinner. Luckily it was late.

In the meantime, my hostess did not tell my friends that we are coming. She kept it as a surprise. I don't know why, but she did it. When we arrived for dinner - it was late - by then my friend the hostess was waiting for us. And we were surprised - all of our friends were there, and some of our customers were there as well.

We arrived and all of a sudden a big clapping went on - it's like some very famous person walked in. First, I didn't believe it was for us. It can't be! Why? All this fuss? I couldn't understand.

Then I noticed all my friends stood up and were surprised to see us. I didn't expect such a welcome. I could not believe it. We were amazed to see such a welcome. After all, people wrote books before - I would never believe what I witnessed here now.

I never felt such an experience, such a feeling. Why now?

I must have done something that I deserve such a welcome. Okay, they had a full house. Maybe as I see my little hostess, she is very clever, has a notion of business, and also knows how to get them around and works for hire. She was doing for the owners whatever they needed. She is very smart and beautiful, and I know she likes me. She did everything to prove it.

I was in disbelief. I could not believe what was happening around us - so many smiling faces. I cannot even describe that feeling. I thought it was just another dream. When I arrived at the table, they said, "Why didn't you tell us that you are coming?" "Oh, I'm so happy that you did come. You made my day. What a surprise!" We could not get over it.

Finally, we settled down and couldn't wait a minute - all of those questions we were asked. I didn't know which one I should answer first. Slowly, we had dinner. We were getting ready - it was closer to New Year's. Then beautiful music started. I liked it. It was different - everything was different. I say the truth: I never went to a New Year's party or dinner. I could say this was my first one ever, and on top of it, such a lavish affair. I never had any training like this. I was always too tired and usually went to sleep - that was it.

But now I can understand anyone regarding these happenings...

I do not have enough education. Why are such business people and writers making so much about me? Tell me, am I dreaming, or is it true? I don't seem to understand all this! Now for the first time I'm concerned. When I see and try to examine all this - is it the truth, or is someone making a joke from this just for their own gain? Is this real, or am I just imagining it?

Irving was a little tired, so I told him that if he started to feel tired he should go up after dinner when the time comes - 12 o'clock - and I would follow him. He told me he would be fine.

In the meantime, my friend asked me to dance with him. I did. Then another person wanted me to, but I was tired and didn't want to overdo it.

Here, to my surprise, others were telling me how they felt about me - how unusual a person I am. They said they never met anyone like me before, and how fondly they feel about me, and also how my friend never stops talking about me.

Here, they like you - maybe they will tell you that all of us feel the same.

I told them, I thank you and appreciate the knowledge they have and how they feel. I appreciate it more than they will ever know. I'm very grateful for my little hostess that she wants me here. I do love you all, the whole world.

I think whoever wants something should try again and again until they reach what they want. It is my example - I don't know how, but it came, and I'm very happy about it.

The evening was wonderful.

It was very nice music, just like I remember as it was years ago. I was very happy we did go there. The way people respected us - it was really real, not monkey business. I still do not understand what it is all about. I just let it go without worrying or feeling any guilt, because there must have been a reason. We are still here, trying to improve life.

It is natural to show people that there is another way to be happy and have lots of fun - having a good time without getting involved in personal acts. On the other hand, let's say, at any years or age - it's never too old to have love, but without personal acts or lovemaking. This is how we were raised and brought up - to have clean fun. And especially if you like good music and dance, you can have the best time if you follow your own rules and you believe in it.

I'm happy just to be in such a selected group. These people are very special - excellent company. This resort is a very respected place run by hard workers. The place is very clean, well - respected. Anyone that goes there just wants to get away, appreciate good food, and have a good time - not for matchmaking people. But it happens - it could happen - but that comes naturally. The space is clean and well maintained, and whatever you want to do is up to you. If people expect to meet someone in a hurry - forget about it. Then it is not for you. Do not even bother coming here. That is my advice.

This is more a family place and it offers all other things - valuable education, if you're looking for that - but just to enjoy whatever you like.

I did like whatever I've seen. The first time I walked in, I was very happy I did. Sometimes, unexpectedly, you can have a better time than if you expect too much - because it never works out for me. Therefore, I did not have much experience with that.

All my life, I was always too busy. I never pushed myself to meet someone. I wasn't that popular - not because I didn't look well, but I think they could tell that I'm not the type that would do whatever they were looking for. I did not go there as a pickup.

I went there to dance - and that was the purpose I went - and then at the same time I had an opportunity to practice dancing. Sometimes I went to some organizations - it wasn't the best place because most people there were together and they knew each other. I was an outsider.

I did not do as some women did - walking over to men and saying, "Hello, would you like to dance?" Some will, and some will not. I never did that. That is why I'm different - I didn't come to that stage that I should walk up to a man and ask him to dance with me.

When you get to a certain age, you outgrow your shyness - but that still does not help to socialize.

Today, you have a different lifestyle - especially the younger generation, and even older people have changed. There is more freedom, and no one cares what happens tomorrow. When they wake up, then that is something else - it doesn't make any difference to them. The main thing is to have a good time their way.

I learned more than I expected. I would never believe such an experience could cause you such warm feelings. It seems that one day can make a difference - it makes up for a lifetime experience. You would never believe it - that luck like that is possible.

I feel I did have an unusual experience - for myself, my life - I never had it any other way. I don't know if I'll have it again. I take one day at a time, and I wanted to write more about this, but it will take time to think.

I had enough. I'm satisfied as it is.

Now it is the most important for me - and for my brother, and all my family - to be happy and enjoy whatever is. This gave me something to think about and remember - it was a very wonderful dream, and I enjoyed it.

At this time, I will try to figure out which way I will go. If everything works out okay, then I will play it by ear. I will come back with something new and fresh and not boring - just to make me happy.

All my writing is for that purpose - that's the idea - hoping that I succeeded.

When I came back from the New Year's celebration, I was so excited, but overtired, to observe what had happened and try to understand what it was all about. It is unbelievable - if someone would tell me this story, I would not believe it - because it is so unusual, and I have never heard that there are people like this, especially in today's climate. We don't have it - you cannot find such kind of happy people, who would go out of their way to give you full support, their life, and care for you.

While this is such a different situation, I cannot even sort it out. My imagination far overcomes me.

This is where food is feeding me for energy. I was looking for some kind of excitement, new ideas - to see if I can or cannot start a new episode, something different - making it interesting so that it would lift up people's real feelings and bring them back to being happy again, like we used to know.

I received a letter from my young friend, telling me he is in Israel, having a good time, and thinking about me. He also heard that I was visiting a hotel on New Year's weekend. He was told that I looked very nice - exceptionally so, he said. He wrote that he was sorry he couldn't be there to help celebrate and hopes to see me soon. He said someone will be coming back with him - and that I will like her. "She's very nice," he wrote. "And as you know by now, you were right."

Now it seems he's trying to make up for lost time - and I hope it's the right decision. He'll let me know! I'm pleased for him. But - why is he in such a hurry? Why didn't he say anything about this before? He's not young. Maybe he was married before, although he never mentioned it. He didn't bother to talk about it. I guess we'll have to wait and see what he says - what kind of person she is! Is she looking for something? There's always a reason.

I really don't understand. He's a very nice man and, as I see it, has good judgment. But why is he in a rush? Did he know her before? We'll see. I'm happy for him - if it's true. I didn't want him as anything more than a friend, yes. But still, when a single man came to my table, I felt uncomfortable. Yes, he was helping me - honestly, I cannot say no, because he was. But I don't want, and never needed, anyone to support me. I can help myself.

I had to come to a decision - whether I want to continue writing or stop. I think I've had enough time to enjoy whatever I can, without any worries. I feel that I've enjoyed every moment with my writing. It gave me energy, pride in myself - that I was able to accomplish as much as I did. I never would've believed it myself. I was lucky to have such wonderful people helping me. I must've done something to deserve such help. I would not have been able to finish without my little brother's help - and my little nephew, Sherwin. They are responsible people, and they helped me accomplish what I've done.

I set up the basics and carried on - but the others: the computer, the editor, the publisher - they are the ones who deserve the credit. They worked very hard, both of them. So it's for them - not for me. Even now, I hope they are well and able to keep going - praying to help whoever they can.

I wish I were able to help, too - whatever people's needs are. Especially a friend, if I could help with whatever they needed.

Today, that's what's missing. I tried - but it wasn't enough. Hopefully, there is someone who can.

I've come to an understanding about my friend. I cannot believe this happened - to someone who, in my opinion, is one of the best businessmen I know. He was successful in business - and a failure in his personal life. Let me come back to that. Some people just don't take marriage as seriously as they should. They're in too much of a hurry. That's the problem in marriage. Marriage should be treated like a business. When you enter into marriage, you should take it seriously - like entering into a business partnership. How many marriages today are in worse shape than ever before? Why is that? Do you have an answer? I think I do.

People meet at first sight and fall in love. But what is the meaning of love, if I may ask? What is the meaning of love? Do you know? Let me hear from you. When you consider marriage, it's like going into a business partnership. The first thing you should do is take time - get to know the person. Study whether you have anything in common, and start from there. If you're already having problems in the beginning - see if you can work it out. If you can't, then forget about it. Because it will not work. Forget about your heart.

My friend told me that he arrived home with his new wife and would like me to meet them. He is planning to go to the resort this weekend. If I find time, I would be very happy. I told him at this time I'm not able to go there, maybe he can find some time to come to New York to visit me. Just let me know when. I would be happy to meet them, and with that, that was that. I did not feel I should go out of my way to see her, because as much as he told me about her, it was enough information about what was happening there. First of all, I thought of him as a very good businessman and expected better. I told him he was going about choosing a partner in the wrong way. And here, he did it again.

Now he has a problem. That wasn't enough; he went deeper into it. It appears that they are not going to stay together. The first night on their honeymoon - why did he bring her to America? He shouldn't have done it! What was the reason for all this? Where was his common sense? I must say I'm very disappointed in all this. I asked him what he was planning to do next. Without hesitation, he answered that he will get an attorney and divorce her. Why can't he just annul the wedding? Are you going to give her money? He said, "I will offer, and she can stay by herself and meet someone else." I asked, "What do you think will happen? Why not send her back?" He did not answer. She had been telling him lies on the first night. She only wanted to come to America. You fell for it! How many lies will you take? Isn't it enough? Why not, once and for all, get a lawyer and annul the wedding? She did not live up to the wedding oath. That should be enough. You do not have to give any money. Make sure she's on the plane and forget that you ever met her! I hope this will be a lesson. You are not the marrying type. You have no idea what marriage is or how to choose a partner. What is involved in a partnership? Make - believe this is a business. Would you conduct yourself in the same manner? I do not think so. Otherwise, you would lose your shirt.

It's high time, at this stage, that you should try to learn what to do and what you really want to do. I hope you do not plan another marriage soon. That would not be wise. Do you know what you want to get out of marriage? It is a two - way street. Both persons have to work hard, and even then you have to be careful. You can wind up with something that you never dreamed of. Married life is very complicated. And you must work at it at all times to be successful, especially if you plan to have a family and raise children. Both have to feel the same way. You must work out these problems before you enter into partnerships. When you're ready, just ask yourself, "Is this what I really want?" Both have to decide after that, and then you will go further if you still think that you care for each other. Then you are ready. I would not advise you to fall in love and work on it after you're married. It is a constant affair that has to be worked on at all times. And after you're married, it is too late to ask the question of whether it was just infatuation.

If you expect her to live with you, then you must be naive. What do you think of it? Do you know how long it will last? Do you want to have a family? Do you know anything about each other? I must give you an example. There was a couple; both were lawyers. They were courting each other, then they decided to get married. Before they were married, everything was fine. He used to stay over at her house. Then they decided to get married. Her parents helped them to set up a home. The young couple moved into the apartment and everything seemed all right. There was no problem. Both parties were educated and had good jobs. After they were married, everything appeared fine. They purchased a furnished apartment. I hoped nothing but the best. Here's the question: why would they have any problems, since it seemed they were happy?

Here's the story: after they got married and set up housekeeping, both were working and came home and had to prepare dinner. He expected that when he came home, food would be ready to eat, just like it was when he was single. This time, he thought he would have his wife clean up and wash the dishes. To him, it was granted. He never thought about talking about it before they got married. The wife had mentioned that when they got married, he should help out and wash dishes and clean up after dinner. Finally, the time came when the wife asked him to help clean up and wash the dishes. The husband refused - even though there were only a couple of dishes for two people. The wife was upset. They argued and fought. Before they realized what was happening to them, they applied for a divorce. I spoke to both of them and both agreed - they worked hard outside and both needed help. If they really loved and cared for each other, that would have been the solution to the problem.

She walked out and he insisted that he was right. The question was: why did this happen? Why couldn't they have worked out these problems before they got married? They were both lawyers. No, they did not even think about these problems. They took for granted that everything would be all right. They never questioned whether it would work out equally for both of them. That was a mistake - to assume. Therefore, you never assume anything when it concerns two people.

It doesn't matter where you are or what you decide to do. You must ask all types of questions before you enter into a contract with anyone - in partnership. This means equal work, equal money, equal respect. You must be flexible. Try to understand and work it out. You can never relax and take things for granted. This is one example, and there have been much worse. It is difficult to believe, but I have seen more serious things.

I'm trying to explain this situation because this is the problem - especially in today's generation. It seems that today they have more problems understanding the difference between infatuation and real love. Why am I saying this? Because it seems there is something else going on. People are dreaming up things that are not real. They are confused in their personal lives with everything that is happening. Maybe our new educational system is not working. They're too busy to sort out what is real. Life is very precious. Today's generation is confused. What will be next?

I've decided to close my story, and with careful observation, I'll do it. If my friend decides to keep his wife and business, I do not wish to be involved any further. I see it this way: it is his fault - he's a grown-up man, mature, well - established, and should be able to take care of himself. I do not want to go into it anymore, and I do not want to keep up a friendship. I'm not in a position to do so. I'm grateful for whatever he gave me to write and for his advice. I'm grateful for it. Wherever he wishes to go, he still has a chance to work on it or walk away. It's up to him. I gave him my opinion the best I could, and that is all. If he needs more advice, he can get professional help. The rest is his life - he is responsible for it.

Also, if he wants her to be around for any other reason - perhaps just to show off her beauty but not as a wife - then perhaps he will be happy. It is his life. He can keep her for himself and have whatever he wanted. Whatever comes out later, it's up to him. She is very shrewd and unpredictable. I don't know her, but from whatever he has mentioned, that is enough for me. I wish him the best. Good luck and the best of happiness. Like I mentioned before - work on it, and just maybe you will succeed.

As of now, I'm going to go back to my publishers, or at least write to them whenever I get the chance. It seems that my book is doing very well. It is very interesting, and it seems to be a good seller. They're very excited about it, and I'm excited too. I look forward to it. It seems I will have to go to the hotel because they asked me to sign some more books, especially now since this is my second book. It's nearby, so I'll go there, but I do not want to travel too far - only if I'm able to.

This is a good stopping point: when to continue and when to stop. I wish I could continue further, but it seems I cannot finish, so it's better not to start.

About the Author:

Her background: she came from Czechoslovakia with her two young brothers and their sister. When the Second World War broke out in 1940, they had an uncle in Columbus, Ohio, who helped them. One of her older brothers had arrived in America in 1938 and helped establish a home. She never had a chance to finish her education. She settled with their brother.

The younger brother worked very hard to make a living. Later on, the youngest volunteered for the U.S. Army and was stationed in many places, including the Anzio beachhead. With G-d's help, he survived and returned to his family. However, the rest of the family perished in Europe.

Maria was never prepared to write at such levels, especially not at her age of 93. Her younger brother could not remember much of his childhood - he was mostly away from home in schools. It was a small village and he could not get a proper education. That's why he wasn't close to his family, and he asked me so many times to write down whatever I remember.

Finally, I decided to put it on paper - without thinking of a book. The first book is her life history, titled *As I Remember*.

In November 2009, I began to write by hand, part time. I was able to finish about 300 pages.

I decided then that I did not want my brother to go through reading my essay with so much pain. Therefore, I decided to write another book - something funny, interesting, and educational. The name is *Imaginary*. I started to write it and thought it would be easier to read. This time, it was different from the first one. I just finished part time - about 40 pages - all written by hand.

Now, I'm trying to finish and close the first book, *As I Remember*. The readers may enjoy it as is, but it may take longer to publish. My brother just learned how to work on the computer, and he is preparing and setting it on the computer. One of his sons will help, and perhaps publish it. My nephew is very capable and understands books. He feels it's a good book, and it's worthwhile to publish it.

Written by Maria Gluck
Prepared by her brother Irving Gluck
Edited and published by her nephew, Sherwin Gluck
Finished November 7, 2010

Eulogy for Maria Gluck
Delivered by her nephew at her funeral - Monday, October 14, 2013

It is fitting that we are here on Columbus Day. After all, Aunt Marie, along with Uncle Herman, Aunt Hermine, and my Dad arrived in the United States on Washington's Birthday. As we know, they came here, like Columbus, in search of a new home - one in which, in the words of Washington, "the Government of the United States [would] give to bigotry no sanction, to persecution no assistance…" And where did they move to? Columbus, Ohio.

Since I am the youngest, my recollections are incomplete. However, one of my earliest memories is watching Jerritt set up the race cars in Aunt Marie's living room in her apartment in the Bronx. I remember how small her kitchen was - and how much smaller the dining room - but somehow we managed to squeeze everyone at the table. And where was Aunt Marie? Always in the kitchen, busily cooking!

This never changed. When she moved to Queens, I remember the smell of her cooking even filling the small, dimly lit elevator that carried us to the third floor. Apartment 3E. Somehow, she knew exactly when the elevator doors would open. She'd open her apartment door just in time to greet us - and then run back to the stove before the latkes needed to be turned.

She always let me help her cook. Most of what I know about cooking, I learned from her. Whether it was just frying an onion, peeling potatoes, or drying dishes while Linda washed - she always let me help. Every holiday was special because Aunt Marie made it so. She put out her finest silver and set the table perfectly. Not to impress us, but to teach us what a holiday should be like.

Aunt Marie's idea of baking was more suited to a bakery than to her small kitchenette. Where we bake with two cups of flour, she baked with "only" ten pounds. She turned her entire apartment upside down making pogácsa and kifli. That she was able to clean everything up was a miracle in itself! But how we all secretly looked forward to being loaded down with bag after bag of goodies and leftovers. Her cooking was our comfort food - and it was her way of showing how much she loved us.

Not only did she bake with Linda and Diana, but even Jessica baked with her - and when she moved to Syosset to live with my Dad, so did Noa, Ayalah, and Naomi. Boaz, on the other hand, was content to eat glass after glass of Aunt Marie's apple compote.

In her later years - that is, after she turned 95 - I showed her how to use a computer to type. Why? My Dad asked her to write down what she remembered. And she did. Boy, did she ever! She started writing by hand, in a mixture of English words spelled phonetically in Hungarian. Page after page. Notebook after notebook. During the day, and sometimes even in the middle of the night.

The thing was, even though she knew what she wrote - and my Dad could decipher much of it - I knew there was no way that anyone else would be able to figure it all out. So I worked with her to train the computer to understand her voice - and off she went!

Not only did she finish one book, but she wrote another and was working on a third. In her spare time, she dictated personal letters with the computer as well. She said to my Dad that the only problem was that she started too late.

Well, here is proof that it is better to start late than never to begin.

She exemplified everything that a grandmother should be - without ever having been a mother or grandmother. To the end, she listened to her father's advice to take care of each other, and I can only hope we can learn from her example and do the same. For her, family always came first. Even when we were leaving her apartment in Queens, she always made sure to go to her window and poke her head out so that we could yell, "Bye, Aunt Marie!"

Maria Gluck, 96 years old, using IBM's ViaVoice - March 3, 2013

www.ingramcontent.com/pod-product-compliance
Lightning Source LLC
Chambersburg PA
CBHW062108290426
44110CB00023B/2746